Networking for Home and Small Businesses
CCNA Discovery Learning Guide

Allan Reid
Jim Lorenz

W9-BGA-297

Cisco Press

800 East 96th Street

Indianapolis, Indiana 46240 USA

Networking for Home and Small Businesses
CCNA Discovery Learning Guide

Allan Reid ▪ Jim Lorenz

Copyright © 2008 Cisco Systems, Inc.

Cisco Press logo is a trademark of Cisco Systems, Inc.

Published by:
Cisco Press
800 East 96th Street
Indianapolis, IN 46240 USA

Printed in the United States of America

Seventh Printing September 2011

Library of Congress Cataloging-in-Publication data is on file.

ISBN-13: 978-1-58713-209-4

ISBN-10: 1-58713-209-5

Warning and Disclaimer

Publisher
Paul Boger

Associate Publisher
Dave Dusthimer

Cisco Representative
Anthony Wolfenden

Cisco Press Program Manager
Jeff Brady

Executive Editor
Mary Beth Ray

Managing Editor
Patrick Kanouse

Development Editors
Dayna Isley, Drew Cupp

Project Editor
Seth Kerney

Copy Editor
Paula Lowell

Technical Editors
Nolan Fretz, Charles Hannon,
Bill Shurbert, Matt Swinford,
Michael Duane Taylor

Editorial Assistant
Vanessa Evans

Book and Cover Designer
Louisa Adair

Composition
Bronkella Publishing

Indexer
Heather McNeill

Proofreader
Mike Henry

CISCO

Trademark Acknowledgments

All terms mentioned in this book that are known to be trademarks or service marks have been appropriately capitalized. Cisco Press or Cisco Systems, Inc., cannot attest to the accuracy of this information. Use of a term in this book should not be regarded as affecting the validity of any trademark or service mark.

Corporate and Government Sales

The publisher offers excellent discounts on this book when ordered in quantity for bulk purchases or special sales, which may include electronic versions and/or custom covers and content particular to your business, training goals, marketing focus, and branding interests. For more information, please contact: **U.S. Corporate and Government Sales** 1-800-382-3419 corpsales@pearsontechgroup.com

For sales outside the United States please contact: **International Sales** international@pearsoned.com

Feedback Information

At Cisco Press, our goal is to create in-depth technical books of the highest quality and value. Each book is crafted with care and precision, undergoing rigorous development that involves the unique expertise of members from the professional technical community.

Readers' feedback is a natural continuation of this process. If you have any comments regarding how we could improve the quality of this book, or otherwise alter it to better suit your needs, you can contact us through e-mail at feedback@ciscopress.com. Please make sure to include the book title and ISBN in your message.

We greatly appreciate your assistance.

Americas Headquarters	Asia Pacific Headquarters	Europe Headquarters
Cisco Systems, Inc.	Cisco Systems, Inc.	Cisco Systems International BV
170 West Tasman Drive	168 Robinson Road	Haarlerbergpark
San Jose, CA 95134-1706	#28-01 Capital Tower	Haarlerbergweg 13-19
USA	Singapore 068912	1101 CH Amsterdam
www.cisco.com	www.cisco.com	The Netherlands
Tel: 408 526-4000	Tel: +65 6317 7777	www-europe.cisco.com
800 553-NETS (6387)	Fax: +65 6317 7799	Tel: +31 0 800 020 0791
Fax: 408 527-0883		Fax: +31 0 20 357 1100

Cisco has more than 200 offices worldwide. Addresses, phone numbers, and fax numbers are listed on the Cisco Website at **www.cisco.com/go/offices.**

About the Authors

Allan Reid is the curriculum lead and a CCNA/CCNP instructor at the Centennial College CATC in Toronto, Canada. Allan is a professor in the Information and Communications Engineering Technology department and an instructor and program supervisor for the School of Continuing Education at Centennial College. He has developed and taught networking courses for both private and public organizations and has been instrumental in the development and implementation of numerous certificate, diploma, and degree programs in networking. Allan is also a curriculum developer for the Cisco Networking Academy. Outside of his academic responsibilities, he has been active in the computer and networking fields for more than 25 years and is currently a principal in a company specializing in the design, management, and security of network solutions for small and medium-sized companies. Allan authored the first edition of *WAN Technologies CCNA 4 Companion* Guide (Cisco Press, ISBN: 1-58713-172-2) and *Using a Networker's Journal*, which is a supplement to *A Networker's Journal* (Cisco Press, ISBN: 1-58713-158-7). Most recently, Allan co-authored the CCNA Discovery online academy courses "Networking for Home and Small Businesses" and "Introducing Routing and Switching in the Enterprise" with Jim Lorenz.

Jim Lorenz is an instructor and curriculum developer for the Cisco Networking Academy. Jim co-authored several Cisco Press titles including *Fundamentals of UNIX Companion Guide*, Second Edition (ISBN 1-58713-140-4), *Fundamentals of UNIX Lab Companion*, Second Edition (ISBN 1-58713-139-0), and the third editions of the CCNA Lab Companions. He has more than 20 years' experience in information systems ranging from programming and database administration to network design and project management. Jim has developed and taught computer and networking courses for both public and private institutions. As the Cisco Academy Manager at Chandler-Gilbert Community College in Arizona, he was instrumental in starting the Information Technology Institute (ITI) and developed a number of certificates and degree programs. Most recently, Jim co-authored the CCNA Discovery online academy courses "Networking for Home and Small Businesses" and "Introducing Routing and Switching in the Enterprise" with Allan Reid.

About the Technical Reviewers

Nolan Fretz is currently a college professor in network and telecommunications engineering technology at Okanagan College in Kelowna, British Columbia. He has almost 20 years of experience in implementing and maintaining IP networks and has been sharing his experiences by educating students in computer networking for the past nine years. He holds a master's degree in information technology.

Charles Hannon is an assistant professor of network design and administration at Southwestern Illinois College. He has been a Cisco Certified Academy Instructor (CCAI) since 1998. Charles has a master of arts in education from Maryville University, St. Louis, Missouri, currently holds a valid CCNA certification, and has eight years' experience in Management of Information Systems. Charles' priority is to empower students to become successful and compassionate lifelong learners.

Bill Shurbert is a professor of information technology at New Hampshire Technical Institute, in Concord, New Hampshire. Bill holds a bachelor's degree in technical management from Southern New Hampshire University. He enjoys teaching Cisco CCNA, Wireless, and IT Essentials classes. In his off time, you can find Bill and Joanne, his wife of 25+ years, sailing the waters of Lake Winnipesaukee.

Matt Swinford, associate professor of network design and administration at Southwestern Illinois College, has been an active Cisco Certified Academy Instructor (CCAI) since 1999. Matt is dedicated to fostering a learning environment that produces certified students and quality IT professionals. Matt has a masters of business administration from Southern Illinois University at Edwardsville, Edwardsville, Illinois and currently holds valid CCNP, A+, and Microsoft Certifications.

Michael Duane Taylor is department head of computer information sciences at the Raleigh Campus of ECPI College of Technology. He has more than seven years' experience teaching introductory networking and CCNA-level curriculum and was awarded the Instructor of the Year Award. Previously, Michael was a lab supervisor with Global Knowledge working with router hardware configuration and repair. He holds a bachelor's degree in business administration from the University of North Carolina at Chapel Hill and a masters of science in industrial technology/computer network management from East Carolina University. His certifications include CCNA, CCNP-router, and MCSE.

Acknowledgments

From Allan and Jim:

We want to thank Mary Beth Ray, Dayna Isley, and Drew Cupp with Cisco Press for their help and guidance in putting this book together. We also want to thank the technical editors, Mike Taylor, Bill Shurbert, Nolan Fretz, Charlie Hannon, and Matt Swinford. Their attention to detail and suggestions made a significant contribution to the accuracy and clarity of the content.

We would also like to acknowledge the entire CCNA Discovery development team from Cisco Systems, especially Carole Knieriem and Amy Gerrie for their input, support, and cooperation in the development of the book.

Dedications

This book is dedicated to my children: Andrew, Philip, Amanda, Christopher, and Shaun. You are my inspiration, and you make it all worthwhile. Thank you for your patience and support.

— Allan Reid

To the three most important people in my life: my wife Mary, and my daughters, Jessica and Natasha. Thanks for your patience and support.

— Jim Lorenz

Contents at a Glance

Contents

Icons Used in This Book

Command Syntax Conventions

The conventions used to present command syntax in this book are the same conventions used in the IOS Command Reference. The Command Reference describes these conventions as follows:

- **Boldface** indicates commands and keywords that are entered literally as shown. In actual configuration examples and output (not general command syntax), boldface indicates commands that are manually input by the user (such as a **show** command).

- *Italics* indicate arguments for which you supply actual values.

- Vertical bars (|) separate alternative, mutually exclusive elements.

- Square brackets [ ] indicate optional elements.

- Braces { } indicate a required choice.

- Braces within brackets [{ }] indicate a required choice within an optional element.

Introduction

Cisco Networking Academy is a comprehensive e-learning program that delivers information technology skills to students around the world. The Cisco CCNA Discovery curriculum consists of four courses that provide a comprehensive overview of networking, from fundamentals to advanced applications and services. The curriculum emphasizes real-world practical application, while providing opportunities for you to gain the skills and hands-on experience needed to design, install, operate, and maintain networks in small to medium-sized businesses, as well as enterprise and service provider environments. The Networking for Home and Small Businesses course is the first course in the curriculum.

Networking for Home and Small Businesses, CCNA Discovery Learning Guide is the official supplemental textbook for the first course in v4.x of the CCNA Discovery online curriculum of the Networking Academy. As a textbook, this book provides a ready reference to explain the same networking concepts, technologies, protocols, and devices as the online curriculum. In addition, it contains all the interactive activities, Packet Tracer activities, and hands-on labs from the online curriculum as well as bonus labs.

This book emphasizes key topics, terms, and activities and provides many alternative explanations and examples as compared with the course. You can use the online curriculum as directed by your instructor and then also use this *Learning Guide's* study tools to help solidify your understanding of all the topics. In addition, the book includes

- Expanded coverage of CCENT/CCNA exam material
- Additional key glossary terms
- Bonus labs
- Additional Check Your Understanding and Challenge questions
- Interactive activities and Packet Tracer activities on the CD-ROM

Goal of This Book

First and foremost, by providing a fresh, complementary perspective of the online content, this book helps you learn all the required materials of the first course in the Networking Academy CCNA Discovery curriculum. As a secondary goal, individuals who do not always have Internet access can use this text as a mobile replacement for the online curriculum. In those cases, you can read the appropriate sections of this book, as directed by your instructor, and learn the topics that appear in the online curriculum. Another secondary goal of this book is to serve as your offline study material to help prepare you for the CCENT and CCNA exams.

Audience for This Book

This book's main audience is anyone taking the first CCNA Discovery course of the Networking Academy curriculum. Many Networking Academies use this textbook as a required tool in the course, while other Networking Academies recommend the *Learning Guides* as an additional source of study and practice materials.

Book Features

The educational features of this book focus on supporting topic coverage, readability, and practice of the course material to facilitate your full understanding of the course material.

Topic Coverage

The following features give you a thorough overview of the topics covered in each chapter so that you can make constructive use of your study time:

- **Objectives**: Listed at the beginning of each chapter, the objectives reference the core concepts covered in the chapter. The objectives match the objectives stated in the corresponding chapters of the online curriculum; however, the question format in the *Learning Guide* encourages you to think about finding the answers as you read the chapter.

- **"How-to" feature**: When this book covers a set of steps that you need to perform for certain tasks, the text lists the steps as a how-to list. When you are studying, the icon helps you easily refer to this feature as you skim through the book.

- **Notes, tips, cautions, and warnings**: These are short sidebars that point out interesting facts, timesaving methods, and important safety issues.

- **Chapter summaries**: At the end of each chapter is a summary of the chapter's key concepts. It provides a synopsis of the chapter and serves as a study aid.

Readability

The authors have compiled, edited, and in some cases rewritten the material so that it has a more conversational tone that follows a consistent and accessible reading level. In addition, the following features have been updated to assist your understanding of the networking vocabulary:

- **Key terms**: Each chapter begins with a list of key terms, along with a page-number reference from inside the chapter. The terms are listed in the order in which they are explained in the chapter. This handy reference allows you to find a term, flip to the page where the term appears, and see the term used in context. The Glossary defines all the key terms.

- **Glossary**: This book contains an all-new Glossary with more than 350 computer and networking terms.

Practice

Practice makes perfect. This new *Learning Guide* offers you ample opportunities to put what you learn to practice. You will find the following features valuable and effective in reinforcing the instruction that you receive:

- **Check Your Understanding questions and answer key**: Updated review questions are presented at the end of each chapter as a self-assessment tool. These questions match the style of questions that you see in the online course. Appendix A, "Check Your Understanding and Challenge Questions Answer Key," provides an answer key to all the questions and includes an explanation of each answer.

- **(NEW) Challenge questions and activities**: Additional, and more challenging, review questions and activities are presented at the end of chapters. These questions are purposefully designed to be similar to the more complex styles of questions you might see on the CCNA exam. This section might also include activities to help prepare you for the exams. Appendix A provides the answers.

- **Packet Tracer activities**: Interspersed throughout the chapters you'll find many activities to work with the Cisco Packet Tracer tool. Packet Tracer allows you to create networks, visualize how packets flow in the network, and use basic testing tools to determine whether the network would work. When you see this icon, you can use Packet Tracer with the listed file to perform a task suggested in this book. The activity files are available on this book's CD-ROM; Packet Tracer software, however, is available through the Academy Connection website. Ask your instructor for access to Packet Tracer.

- **Interactive activities**: These activities provide an interactive learning experience to reinforce the material presented in the chapter.

- **Labs**: This book contains all the hands-on labs from the curriculum plus additional challenge labs for further practice. Part I includes references to the hands-on labs, as denoted by the lab icon, and Part II of the book contains each lab in full. You may perform each lab as you see each lab referenced in the chapter or wait until you have completed the chapter.

A Word About Packet Tracer Software and Activities

Packet Tracer is a self-paced, visual, interactive teaching and learning tool developed by Cisco. Lab activities are an important part of networking education. However, lab equipment can be a scarce resource. Packet Tracer provides a visual simulation of equipment and network processes to offset the challenge of limited equipment. Students can spend as much time as they like completing standard lab exercises through Packet Tracer, and have the option to work from home. Although Packet Tracer is not a substitute for real equipment, it allows students to practice using a command-line interface. This "e-doing" capability is a fundamental component of learning how to configure routers and switches from the command line.

Packet Tracer v4.x is available only to Cisco Networking Academies through the Academy Connection website. Ask your instructor for access to Packet Tracer.

A Word About the Discovery Server CD

The CCNA Discovery series of courses is designed to provide a hands-on learning approach to networking. Many of the CCNA Discovery labs are based on Internet services. Because it is not always possible to allow students access to these services on a live network, the Discovery Server has been developed to provide them.

The Discovery Server CD is a bootable CD developed by Cisco that transforms a regular PC into a Linux server running several preconfigured services for use with the CCNA Discovery labs. The Discovery Server is available from the Academy Connection website *only*. Your instructor can download the CD files from the Instructor Tools section of the Academy Connection website, burn a CD, and show you how to make use of the Server. Hands-on labs that make use of the Discovery Server are identified within the labs themselves.

Once booted, the server provides many services to clients including

- Domain Name Services

- Web Services

- FTP

- TFTP

- Telnet

- SSH

- DHCP

- Streaming Video

- VPN Termination

How This Book Is Organized

This book covers the major topics in the same sequence as the online curriculum for the CCNA Discovery Networking for Home and Small Businesses course. The online curriculum has 10 chapters for this course, so this book has 10 chapters with the same names and numbers as the online course chapters.

To make it easier to use this book as a companion to the course, the major topic headings in each chapter match, with just a few exceptions, the major sections of the online course chapters. However, the *Learning Guide* presents many topics in slightly different order inside each major heading. Additionally, the book occasionally uses different examples than the course. As a result, students get more detailed explanations, a second set of examples, and different sequences of individual topics, all to aid the learning process. This new design, based on research into the needs of the Networking Academies, helps typical students lock in their understanding of all the course topics.

Chapters and Topics

Part I of this book has 10 chapters, as follows:

- **Chapter 1, "Personal Computer Hardware,"** discusses different types of personal computers, how they are used, and the difference between local and network applications. This chapter describes how data is represented and manipulated in a computer system. Also covered is the role of the various computer components and peripherals and the proper way to install and test them.

- **Chapter 2, "Operating Systems,"** introduces the OS, its key components, and user interfaces as well as some of the more common operating systems. It provides an overview of the commercial and GPL software licensing schemes. This chapter presents different options for OS installation and describes the process for upgrading and maintaining the OS. It covers the common types of file systems used with PCs and hard disk partitioning. You will also learn the IP parameters that must be configured to prepare a computer to participate on the network.

- **Chapter 3, "Connecting to the Network,"** introduces communications protocols and describes how communication occurs on an Ethernet network. The main components of an information network are explored as are the roles clients and servers play. In this chapter you will build a peer-to-peer computer network and verify it is functioning. Logical and physical topologies are compared and the layered networking model is introduced. You will learn how hubs, switches, and routers function. Also covered are broadcast and collision domains, ARP, default gateways, and prototyping.

- **Chapter 4, "Connecting to the Internet Through an ISP,"** introduces ISP services, options for connecting to the Internet, and components of an ISP Network Operations Center (NOC). This chapter discusses the Internet Protocol (IP) and how information is sent across the Internet through an ISP. Other major areas covered by this chapter are the cabling and connectors used for connecting network devices, with focus on Ethernet UTP cables and how they are constructed. You will build Ethernet cables and test them.

- **Chapter 5, "Network Addressing,"** examines the IP address and subnet mask and how they are used on a network. Unicast, multicast, and broadcast IP addresses are introduced as well as the three classes of assignable IP addresses. This chapter covers how IP addresses are obtained, the differences between public and a private addresses, and how network address translation (NAT) functions.

- **Chapter 6, "Network Services,"** builds on the client/server model as it relates to common network services. This chapter describes the TCP and UDP transport protocols, the function of port numbers, and the protocols and applications that use them. Focus is on major Internet services, applications, and protocols including DNS, e-mail, WWW, FTP, and IM. The concept of a protocol stack and how protocols interact on a host when sending and receiving a message are introduced. The purpose of a layered networking model is discussed as are the two major models in use, the Open Systems Interconnect (OSI) and the TCP/IP model.

- **Chapter 7, "Wireless Technologies,"** explores the benefits and limitations of wireless technology and where it is used. This chapter compares the wireless personal-area network (WPAN), wireless local-area network (WLAN), and wireless wide-area network (WWAN). It describes components required to build a WLAN and their functions as well as the current standards for WLANs and how they compare. In this chapter, you will configure parameters on a wireless access point (AP) to allow a wireless client to access network resources. You will also explore techniques available to help secure the WLAN.

- **Chapter 8, "Basic Security,"** introduces networking threats, their characteristics, and different methods of attack. This chapter also describes security procedures and applications that can help prevent attacks and focuses on firewalls, their capabilities, and how a DMZ is structured. You will configure a DMZ and port forwarding with an integrated router device. You will also learn about vulnerability analysis software and how can it help to prevent attacks.

- **Chapter 9, "Troubleshooting Your Network,"** identifies the steps involved in the troubleshooting process and some of the common troubleshooting techniques. Utilities available for troubleshooting connectivity issues are explored. This chapter also covers some of the more common issues with wired and wireless LANs and suggests some possible sources of help when troubleshooting.

- **Chapter 10, "Putting It All Together."** In this summary activity, you use what you have learned about computer hardware and software, wired and wireless networking components, protocols and applications, and techniques for securing a network to plan and implement a technical solution for a small business.

Part II of this book includes the labs that correspond to each chapter.

This book also includes the following:

- An appendix, **"Check Your Understanding and Challenge Questions Answer Key,"** provides the answers to the Check Your Understanding questions that you find at the end of each chapter. It also includes answers for the Challenge questions and activities that conclude most chapters.

- The **Glossary** provides a compiled list of all the key terms that appear throughout this book plus additional computer and networking terms.

About the CD-ROM

The CD-ROM included with this book provides many useful tools and information to support your education:

- **Packet Tracer Activity files**: These are files to work through the Packet Tracer activities that are referenced throughout the book, as indicated by the Packet Tracer activity icon.

- **Interactive Activities**: The CD-ROM contains the interactive activities referenced throughout the book.

- **OSI Model Overview**: The CD-ROM also contains a brief overview of the OSI model for your reference.

- **Taking Notes**: This section includes a .txt file of the chapter objectives to serve as a general outline of the key topics of which you need to take note. The practice of taking clear, consistent notes is an important skill for not only learning and studying the material but for on-the-job success as well. Also included in this section is "A Guide to Using a Networker's Journal"; a PDF booklet providing important insight into the value of the practice of using a journal, how to organize a professional journal, and some best practices on what, and what not, to take note of in your journal.

- **IT Career Information**: This section includes a Student Guide to applying the toolkit approach to your career development. Learn more about entering the world of Information Technology as a career by reading two informational chapters excerpted from *The IT Career Builder's Toolkit:* "Information Technology: A Great Career" and "Breaking into IT."

- **Lifelong Learning in Networking**: As you embark on a technology career, you will notice that it is ever-changing and evolving. This career path provides new and exciting opportunities to learn new technologies and their applications. Cisco Press is one of the key resources to plug into on your quest for knowledge. This section of the CD-ROM provides an orientation to the information available to you and tips on how to tap into these resources for lifelong learning.

PART I

Concepts

CHAPTER 1

Personal Computer Hardware

Objectives

Upon completion of this chapter, you will be able to answer the following questions:

- Where are personal computers found and what use do they serve?

- What is the difference between a local application and a network application?

- What are some types of computing devices and what are their main applications?

- How is data represented and manipulated in a computer system?

- What is the role of the various computer components and peripherals?

- What is the proper way to install and test computer components and peripherals?

Key Terms

This chapter uses the following key terms. You can find the definitions in the Glossary.

hardware   page 5

application software   page 5

basic input output system (BIOS)   page 6

firmware   page 6

local application   page 6

network application   page 6

Internet   page 6

mainframe   page 8

server   page 8

services   page 8

client   page 8

personal computer (PC)   page 9

workstation   page 9

laptop   page 10

notebook   page 10

Tablet PC   page 11

Pocket PC   page 11

personal digital assistant (PDA)   page 11

cellular phone   page 12

binary   page 12

bit   page 12

American Standard Code for Information Interchange (ASCII)   page 12

byte   page 12

modem   page 14

pixel   page 15

hertz   page 16

motherboard   page 17

central processing unit (CPU)   page 18

random-access memory (RAM)   page 19

adapter cards   page 20

Accelerated Graphic Port (AGP)   page 21

hard disk drive (HDD)   page 22

floppy disk drive (FDD)   page 23

tape drive   page 23

Blu-ray   page 23

static memory   page 24

USB memory keys   page 24

Computers provide us with a gateway to a world of information. They allow us to connect from anywhere at any time to share information and collaborate with others in the human network. This chapter introduces the different types of computers and the applications that make them useful. Part II of this book includes the corresponding labs for this chapter.

Personal Computers and Applications

Computers have become an almost indispensable part of everyday life. They help control power grids, telecommunications and financial networks, and even traffic-flow patterns in most major cities. We interact with these systems every day without even considering the role that computers are playing. In addition to these major systems, we interact with many other types of computers on a regular basis, as described in this section.

How and Where Computers Are Used

Computers are used all over the world and in all types of environments. They are used in businesses, manufacturing environments, homes, government offices, and non-profit organizations. Schools use computers for instruction and for maintaining student records. Hospitals use computers to maintain patient records and to provide medical care.

In addition to these types of computers, there are also many customized computers designed for specific purposes. These computers can be integrated into devices such as televisions, cash registers, sound systems, and other electronic devices. They can even be found embedded in appliances such as stoves and refrigerators and used in automobiles and aircraft. Think about being able to call your home refrigerator to see whether you have the ingredients for your favorite dinner or being able to adjust the temperature in your house before you come home from a day at school or work.

Computers are used for many reasons and in many different places. They may be of different sizes and processing power, but all computers have some features in common that allow them to do their job. For most computers to perform useful functions, three components have to work together:

- Hardware
- Operating system
- Application software

Hardware consists of the physical components, both internal and external, that make up a computer. Some common examples of computer hardware include disk drives, memory, monitors, and motherboards.

The operating system is a set of computer programs that manages the hardware of a computer. An operating system controls the resources on a computer, including memory and disk storage, and provides a mechanism for the application software to make use of the underlying hardware. Examples of common operating systems include Windows XP, Windows Vista, and Linux.

Application software is any program loaded on the computer to perform a specific function. These programs work between the operating system and the user. The user interacts with the application software, which in turn communicates with the underlying operating system to gain access to the hardware resources. An example of application software is a word processor or a computer game.

Without software, the computer is merely a collection of hardware components. The software must direct the hardware in order for the computer to be of any use. Both operating system and application software programs are large in size and normally stored on a physical medium such as a hard disk.

Before the computer can make use of the software, the information must be moved from the physical storage medium into the machine's electronic memory. This requires that a basic set of instructions be available to perform hardware functionality tests and then find and load the operating system. These instructions are known as the *basic input output system (BIOS)* and are stored in a memory chip in the computer. BIOS instructions run automatically whenever the computer is started. Because these instructions (software) are permanently stored in a memory chip (hardware) they are often referred to as *firmware*.

Types of Computer Applications

The computer is only as useful as the program or application running on it. Applications can be divided into two general categories, as shown in Figure 1-1:

- **Business/industry software**: Software that is designed for use by a specific industry or market. Examples include medical practice management tools, educational tools, and programs designed for use by the law profession.

- **General-use software**: Software that has been designed for use by a wide range of organizations and home users for various purposes. These applications can be used by any business or individual.

Figure 1-1   Industry-Specific and General-Use Applications

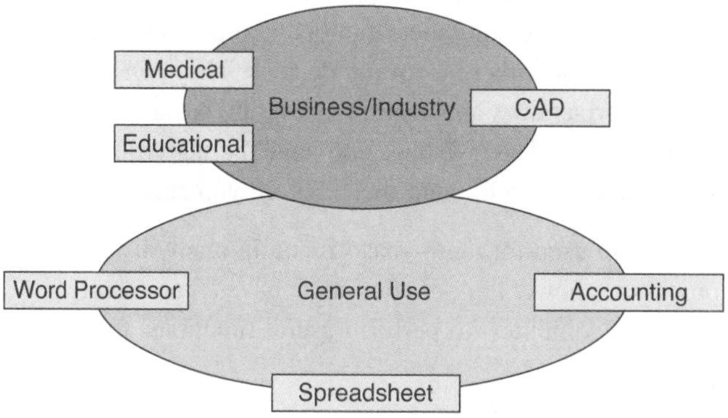

One of the most common general-use application software packages encountered is known as an *office suite*. This software includes such applications as word processing, spreadsheet, database, presentation, and contact management software all integrated into a single application package. All of these applications are designed to work together and allow information to be quickly moved from one application to another. For example, financial information from a spreadsheet program can be quickly converted into a graphical representation and then inserted into a word processing document.

Other popular applications include graphics editing software and multimedia authoring applications. These tools allow users to manipulate photos as well as create rich media presentations that use voice, video, and graphics.

In addition to business/industry and general-use software, an application can be classified as either local or network, as shown in Figure 1-2. A *local application* is a program, such as a word processor, that is stored on the hard disk of the computer. The application runs only on that computer. A *network application* is one that is designed to run over a network, such as the *Internet*. A network application has two components, one that runs on the local computer and one that runs on a remote computer. E-mail is a common example of a network application.

Figure 1-2   Local and Network-Based Applications

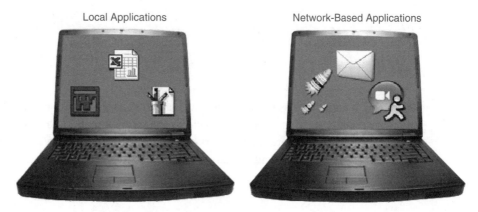

Most computers have a combination of local and network applications installed. For example, consider the use of a home computer system. It is commonly used for local applications such as word processing and maintaining spreadsheets but may also be used to surf the Internet and exchange e-mail, which are activities that use network applications.

Interactive Activity 1-1: Classification of Applications (1.1.2.3)

In this interactive activity you will classify applications as either business/industry or general use and also either local or network. Use file ia-1123 on the CD-ROM that accompanies this book to perform this interactive activity.

Types of Computers

With all the different tasks that computers are designed to do, it is understandable that no one type of computer can handle all applications and roles efficiently. Many different types of computers have been designed, each with a specific role or application in mind.

Classes of Computers

Some of the different classes of computers include the following:

- Mainframes
- Servers
- Desktops
- Workstations
- Laptops
- Handheld portable devices

The icons used to represent these types of computers are shown in Figure 1-3.

Figure 1-3   Icons for Various Types of Computers

Mainframe   Server   Desktop   Workstation   Laptop   Handheld

Each type of computer has been designed with a particular purpose in mind, such as portable access to information, processing of detailed graphics, and so on. The most common types of computers used in homes and businesses are servers, workstations, desktops, laptops, and other portable devices. *Mainframes*, on the other hand, are large centralized computers found in sizeable enterprises and purchased through specialized resellers.

Servers, Desktops, and Workstations

Servers, desktops, and workstations are all similar in size and appearance but each has specific features that make it more suited to a specific task or environment. For example, it is not uncommon for a desktop computer to be used as a server for less demanding applications. This practice is very dangerous because desktop computers lack many of the features built into servers that are designed to protect data from loss or corruption.

Servers

Servers are high-performance computers used in businesses and other organizations to provide *services* to many end users or *clients*. Server hardware is optimized for quick response time to multiple network requests. They often have multiple central processing units (CPU), large amounts of random-access memory (RAM), and multiple high-capacity disk drives that provide very fast information retrieval. More recently servers are being equipped with multi-core processors and are running advanced software that allows the resources to be shared efficiently between multiple applications.

Servers are designed to provide services to end users and devices. Common services found on a server include file and e-mail storage, web pages, and print sharing. In addition they normally provide services, such as name resolution and addressing, that are critical to the efficient operation of a network.

The services provided by a server are often important and might need to be available to users at all times. This type of service is referred to as *business critical* and depending on the business, the cost associated with the loss of these services can be enormous. Servers, therefore, often contain duplicate, or redundant, parts to prevent them from failing. They are often configured in such a way that if one hardware component fails, another will automatically take over, giving the technician time to make repairs without encountering any downtime. Servers are usually kept in secure areas where access is controlled and are administered by knowledgeable individuals. Because servers can often contain large amounts of user data, automatic and manual backups are usually done on a regular basis.

Servers can be one of three types, as shown in Figure 1-4:

- **Standalone**: Standalone servers offer great flexibility in selection of internal components but take up quite bit of floor space.

- **Rack-mounted**: Rack-mounted servers save floor space when racks are available.

- **Blade**: Blade servers provide the highest concentration of computing power in the smallest amount of space.

Figure 1-4   Types of Servers

Blade Server   Rack Mount Server   Standalone Server

Because a server is typically used as a storage point and not a day-to-day end-user device, it may not have a monitor or keyboard, or it may share a monitor and keyboard with other devices.

Desktops

Desktop computers, also commonly termed *personal computers (PC)* or simply PCs, are designed as end-user devices. They support many options and capabilities and can be customized depending on the requirements of the user. A wide variety of cases, power supplies, hard drives, video cards, monitors, and other components are available. Desktop computers can have many different connection types, video options, and a wide array of supported peripherals.

Desktop computers are commonly used to run applications such as word processors, spreadsheets, and network applications such as e-mail and web browsing. They do not normally have redundant components as are found in servers. They are housed in the normal work environment and normally support only a single individual at any one time. A desktop computer is shown in Figure 1-5.

Figure 1-5   Desktop Computers

Workstations

Another end-user computing device that is very similar to the desktop computer is the *workstation*. Although similar to a desktop computer in appearance, workstations are usually high-powered machines designed for specialized, high-end applications. Some of the application programs that normally run on workstations include various engineering programs such as CAD (Computer-Aided Design), 3-D modeling and graphics design, video animation, and virtual reality simulation.

Workstations can also be used as management stations for telecommunications or medical equipment. As with servers, workstations typically have multiple CPUs, large amounts of RAM, and multiple high-capacity disk drives that are very fast. Workstations usually have very powerful graphics capabilities and a large monitor or multiple monitors, as shown in Figure 1-6.

Figure 1-6   Computer Workstation with Multiple Monitors

Interactive Activity 1-2: Function of a Computer (1.2.2.4)

In this interactive activity you will determine whether a computer is acting as a server, workstation, or desktop in a given scenario. Use file ia-1224 on the CD-ROM that accompanies this book to perform this interactive activity.

Portable Devices

Servers, desktops, and workstations are all designed as stationary devices. In addition to these various types of stationary computers, many different portable electronic devices are available.

Portable computing devices allow an individual to have access to high-power computing wherever and whenever necessary. These devices vary in size, power, and graphics capability and include the following:

- Laptop or notebook PC

- Tablet PC

- Pocket PC

- Personal Digital Assistant (PDA)

- Gaming device

- Cell phones

Figure 1-7 shows examples of each device.

The key advantage of portable computers is that they allow information and services to be accessed immediately from almost anywhere. For example, most mobile phones have built-in address books for contact names and telephone numbers. PDAs are available with built-in telephone, web browser, e-mail, and other software. This section introduces the features of each type of portable device.

Laptops

Laptops, also called *notebooks*, are comparable to desktops in usage and processing capability; however, they are portable devices built to be lightweight and use less power. These computers often come with a built-in mouse, monitor, and keyboard. Laptops can also be attached to a docking station that allows the user to utilize a larger monitor, mouse, full-sized keyboard, and other external devices when at home or in the office. Laptop computers normally have a limited number of configurations available and are not as easily upgradeable as desktop computers.

Figure 1-7   Portable Devices

Tablet PC   Pocket PC   PDA

Laptop   Game Device   Cell Phone

Tablet PC

A specialized form of the notebook computer is known as a *Tablet PC*. It is typically a wireless device with an LCD touch screen that allows a user to write on it using a special stylus-type pen. The notes or handwritten text can be digitized using built-in handwriting recognition software. Tablet PCs can have comparable power and functionality to desktops and laptops. A Tablet PC can have a convertible screen that allows it to function like a laptop or the screen can be rotated and folded down over the integrated keyboard. The "slate" type of Tablet PC is a one-piece design that uses a stylus and on-screen keyboard. Tablet PCs run a special OS such as Microsoft's Windows XP Tablet Edition.

Other portable devices, such as Pocket PCs, Personal Digital Assistants (PDAs), game devices, and cell phones usually have less powerful CPUs and less RAM than a conventional notebook computer. They have small screens with limited display capabilities and may have either a small input keyboard or no keyboard at all.

Pocket PC

A *Pocket PC* is a scaled-down version of a laptop, with a less powerful CPU, less RAM, and no hard disk. Most Pocket PCs have small QWERTY-style keyboards and color display screens with fairly good resolution. They use memory cards to store user documents and photographs and run a special OS such as Microsoft Mobile. They are typically about the size of a candy bar and weigh less than 7 ounces. Features can include mini-applications such as PowerPoint viewer and Mobile Excel, cellular phone, wireless networking, non-volatile storage, memory card storage, touch screen, mega-pixel camera, camcorder, voice recorder, and high-speed Internet capability.

PDA

Personal digital assistants (PDAs) are also known as handhelds or palmtops. These generic terms are applied to any small portable device that provides storage for personal information, such as calendars and contacts. They use primarily touch screen technology although some also have a small keyboard. The distinction between these devices and the Pocket PC is blurred. PDAs are increasingly being combined with cell phones and PC-like functionality. Some PDAs use Microsoft Windows CE and others use a proprietary OS such as Palm OS or Blackberry OS.

Game Device

Portable gaming devices are small computers that are dedicated to playing various computer games. They have good quality displays and are increasing more powerful. Some include wireless capabilities to allow multiperson gaming. Examples include Sony PlayStation Portable (PSP) and Nintendo DS (dual screen). Gaming devices run a proprietary OS and games are written to run on a specific OS or device. Many of these gaming devices also allow the user to connect to the Internet to browse online content, read e-mail, and download files.

Cell Phone

Cellular phones (commonly called cell phones or mobile phones) are pervasive and are replacing regular land-line phones in some areas. Newer cell phones have many features of handheld PDAs and pocket PCs, including calendars, contact information, memory card storage, digital camera, camcorder, MP3 player, games, wireless networking capabilities, and Internet access.

Binary Representation of Data

Humans have the ability to interpret a wide variety of inputs by internally processing the input as electrical impulses in the nerves and brain. Similarly, computers process inputs as electrical signals; however, computers represent that information digitally. This section describes how computers represent information using binary format and also describes how to measure data capacity, speed, resolution, and frequency.

Representing Information Digitally

Within a computer, information is represented, stored, and processed in *binary* format. In the binary system only two values exist: a binary zero and a binary one. The term *bit* is an abbreviation of binary digit and represents the smallest piece of data that can be manipulated. Humans interpret words and pictures; computers interpret only patterns of bits.

Because a bit can have only two possible values, a one digit (1) or a zero digit (0), it can only be used to represent one of two states. For example, a light switch can be either on or off; in binary representation, these states would correspond to 1 and 0, respectively.

Computers use bit patterns to represent and interpret letters, numbers, and special characters. Bit patterns or codes can be used to represent almost any type of information digitally: computer data, graphics, photos, voice, video, and music. A commonly used code is the *American Standard Code for Information Interchange (ASCII)*. With ASCII, each character is represented by a string of seven bits. This allows for a total of 128 different characters to be represented. Extended ASCII uses eight bits per character allowing representation of 256 different characters. Each group of eight bits is referred to as a *byte* and each byte is used to represent a single character using extended ASCII. For example, the uppercase letter *A* is represented by the bit pattern 0100 0001, the number 9 is represented by the pattern 0011 1001, and the # symbol is represented by 0010 0011. These strings of bits can be stored and manipulated by the computer at great speeds.

Interactive Activity 1-3: ASCII Digital Translator (1.3.1.1)

In this interactive activity you will use a translator to convert ASCII characters into their digital representation. Use file ia-1311 on the CD-ROM that accompanies this book to perform this interactive activity.

Measuring Storage Capacity

Although a bit is the smallest representation of data, the most basic unit of digital storage is the byte. As previously stated, a byte is a collection of 8 bits and is the smallest unit of measure (UOM) used to represent digital data storage capacity.

Because a single byte can only be used to represent a single character, it is necessary to collect multiple bytes together to allow storage of large amounts of information. When referring to storage space, we use the terms byte (B), kilobyte (KB), megabyte (MB), gigabyte (GB), and terabyte (TB). Examples of components and devices that use byte storage include RAM, hard disk drive space, CDs, DVDs, and MP3 players.

One kilobyte is a little more than 1000 bytes, specifically 1024. A megabyte represents more than a million bytes, or 1,048,576 to be exact. A gigabyte is 1,073,741,824 bytes and a terabyte is 1,099,511,627,776 bytes. The exact number is calculated by taking 2^n power, for example, $KB = 2^{10}$; $MB = 2^{20}$; $GB = 2^{30}$; $TB = 2^{40}$. Note that these values are all multiples of 2 unlike in the International System of Units (SI) where the units are multiples of 10. This is because every bit can have only one of two values in the binary number system (base 2) whereas SI uses the decimal (base 10) numbering system.

> **TIP**
>
> The difference between the meaning of the prefixes in the binary and decimal numbering systems is often an area of confusion. The unit "kilo" if represented with a lowercase k refers to the base 10 system and means times 1000. The same term, if represented by an uppercase K implies the binary number system and means times 1024. For example, 64 kbytes implies 64 x 1000 or 64,000 bytes whereas 64 Kbytes implies 64 x 1024 or 65,536 bytes. For units of measure greater than kilo, usually no distinction is made between the binary and decimal prefixes. It is important to understand the context of the term to know which should be used.

In general, when information is represented digitally, the greater the detail, the greater the number of bits needed to represent it. A low-resolution picture from a digital camera might only use around 360 KB to store the image whereas a high-resolution picture of the same scene could use 2 MB or more, as shown in Figure 1-8.

Figure 1-8   High- and Low-Resolution Images

High Resolution   Low Resolution

 Lab 1-1: Determining Data Storage Capacity (1.3.2.2)

In this lab you will determine the amount of RAM available in a PC as well as the total size of the hard disk and how much space is remaining. You will also explore other storage devices on the PC.

 Interactive Activity 1-4: Byte Conversion Calculator (1.3.2.3)

In this interactive activity you will convert between common units of measure for digital storage capacity. Use file ia-1323 on the CD-ROM that accompanies this book to perform this interactive activity.

Measuring Speed, Resolution, and Frequency

One of the advantages of digital information is that it can be transmitted over long distances without its quality becoming degraded. A *modem* is commonly used to convert the binary information into a form suitable for transmitting through the medium. At the source, modems encode digital information onto an analog carrier signal for transfer across the media. They also decode the binary information from the analog carrier signal at the destination. Many different types of media are available to carry this digital information. A description of some of the more commonly employed media is given in Table 1-1.

Table 1-1   Commonly Employed Networking Media

Media	Description
Metallic cables	Usually made out of copper but aluminum cables are also used in some instances. Metallic cables carry digital information in the form of electromagnetic waves.
Fiber-optic cables	Can be made from either glass or plastic and carry the digital information in the form of light pulses.
Wireless	Uses pulses of low-power radio waves or infrared (IR) light to carry the information between source and destination.

Metallic cables carry information in the form of electromagnetic waves that travel through the wire. Fiber-optic cables carry the same information using pulses of light. Wireless communication normally relies on radio waves or infrared light to carry the information. Figure 1-9 illustrates how information can be transferred between source and destination.

Figure 1-9   Transmission of Digital Data

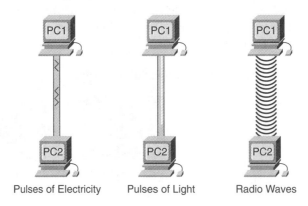

Pulses of Electricity   Pulses of Light   Radio Waves

There are two measures for the size of a file: bits (b) and bytes (B). Communication engineers think in terms of transferring bits, whereas computer users think in terms of file sizes, which are usually measured in bytes (such as kilobytes, megabytes, and so on). There are eight bits to one byte.

Computer systems are compared based on many different criteria. Among these are the length of time that it takes to transfer a file; the screen resolution; and the speed of various system components. Generally, the faster the files transfer, the higher the resolution, and the faster the component speed, the better the computer system.

File Transfer Time

The data rate determines how long it takes to transfer a file between source and destination. Large files contain more information than small files and therefore take longer to transfer. Data transfer rates are measured in thousands of bits per second (kbps) or millions of bits per second (Mbps). Notice that in the kbps acronym, a lowercase *k* is used instead of the uppercase *K*. This is because when talking about the transfer of data, most engineers round the number down. So a kbps actually refers to the transfer of 1000 bits of information in 1 second, whereas a Kbps refers to the transfer of 1024 bits of information in 1 second. A DSL or a cable modem can operate in ranges of 512 kbps, 2 Mbps, or higher depending on the technology being used.

TIP

Be careful about the units used to represent data transfer rate. A lowercase *b* represents a single bit of information but an uppercase *B* represents a byte or collection of 8 bits. When calculating download time it is important to work with the same unit.

Calculated download times are theoretical and depend on cable connection (see Figure 1-10), computer processor speed, and other overheads. To obtain an estimate of the length of time it takes to download a file, divide the file size by the data rate.

Figure 1-10   Download Times

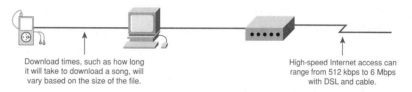

Download times, such as how long it will take to download a song, will vary based on the size of the file.

High-speed Internet access can range from 512 kbps to 6 Mbps with DSL and cable.

For example, to determine how long it will take to transfer a low-resolution digital photo of 256 KB via a 512 kbps cable connection, follow these steps:

Step 1.   Convert the file size into bits. Because the size of the file is represented in KB and the transfer speed is given in kbps, you must convert the size of the file to bits. In this case 256 KB equals 2,097,152 bits (256 KB x 1024 bytes/Kbyte x 8 bits/byte).

Step 2.   Convert the file size in bits to kilobits. To convert the file size in bits to kilobits, simply divide by 1000. In this example 2,097,152 bits would equal approximately 2097 kb (2,097,152 bits / 1000).

Step 3.   Divide the file size in kilobits by the transfer rate in kilobits per second. In this example 2097 kb divided by 512 kbps equates to approximately 4 seconds. It would take approximately 4 seconds to download a 256 KB file at a speed of 512 kbps.

In addition to storage capacity and data transfer speed, there are other units of measure when working with computers.

Computer Screen Resolution

Graphics resolution is measured in pixels. A *pixel* is a distinct point of light displayed on a monitor or captured by a digital camera. The quality of a computer screen is defined by the number of horizontal and vertical pixels that can be displayed. For example a widescreen monitor may be able to display 1280 x 1024 pixels with millions of colors, as shown in Figure 1-11. In digital cameras, image resolution is measured by the number of pixels that can be captured in a photograph. Because this number is usually very high it is represented as millions of pixels, or megapixels.

Figure 1-11   Computer Screen Resolution

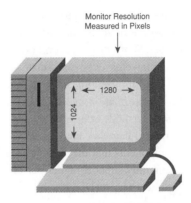

NOTE

The term *pixel* is derived from the words *pic*ture *el*ement. The more elements that make up a picture, the higher the resolution, and the better the image quality will be.

Lab 1-2: Determining the Screen Resolution of a Computer (1.3.3.4)

In this lab you will identify the graphics card and monitor installed on a PC. You will also determine both the current and maximum possible resolution supported by the card and monitor.

Analog Frequencies

Hertz is a measurement of how fast something cycles or refreshes. One *hertz* represents one cycle per second. In computers, the speed of the computer processor is measured by how fast it can cycle in order to execute instructions, measured in hertz. For example, a processor that runs at 1.8 GHz (gigahertz) executes 1800 million cycles per second. The radio frequencies used in wireless communications are also measured in hertz.

Computer Components and Peripherals

Many types of computers exist. What makes one computer better suited to play a new game or play a new audio file over another? The answer is the components and peripherals that make up the computer system. The requirements for a machine dedicated mainly to word processing are very different from one designed mainly for graphics applications or gaming. It is important to determine the intended uses for a computer system before deciding on the type of computer and components to purchase.

Computer Systems

Many manufacturers mass-produce computer systems and sell them either through direct marketing or retail chains. These computer systems are designed to function well for a variety of tasks but are not optimized for a single one.

In addition to mass-produced systems, a number of vendors can custom-assemble computer systems to the end user's specifications. The advantages and disadvantages for both are shown in Table 1–2.

Table 1-2   Advantages and Disadvantages of Computer Purchase Options

	Advantages	**Disadvantages**
Preassembled computer	Lower cost Adequate to perform most applications No waiting period for assembly	Typically used by less-knowledgeable consumers who do not require special needs Often lack the performance level that can be obtained from custom-built computers
Custom-built computer	The end user can specify exact components that meet user needs Generally support higher performance applications such as graphics, gaming, and server applications	Generally more costly than a preassembled device Longer waiting periods for assembly

Purchasing the individual parts and components of a computer and building it yourself is also possible. Regardless of the decision to buy a preassembled or custom-built system or build it yourself, the final product must match the requirements of the end user. When purchasing a computer system, you must consider the motherboard, processor, RAM, storage, adapter cards, and the case and power supply.

Motherboard, CPU, and RAM

Regardless of whether you decide to purchase a prebuilt system, have one built to match a specific application, or build your own, you must pay attention to the choice of the motherboard, CPU, and system RAM.

Motherboard

The *motherboard* is a large circuit board used to connect the electronics and circuitry required for the computer to function. Motherboards contain much of the electronics used to interconnect various components and also contain connectors that allow major system components such as the CPU and RAM to attach to the board. The motherboard moves data between the various connections and system components. A typical motherboard is shown in Figure 1-12.

A motherboard can also contain connector slots for network, video, and sound cards. However, many motherboards now come equipped with these features as integrated components. The difference between the two is how they are upgraded. When using connectors on the motherboard, system components are easily unplugged and changed or upgraded as technology advances. When upgrading or replacing an on-board feature, you cannot remove it from the motherboard. Therefore, disabling the on-board functionality and adding an additional dedicated card using a connector is often necessary.

Remember that the motherboard not only controls the flow of information between the various system components but also provides the connection point for these components. Not paying attention to the selection of the motherboard can have a serious negative impact on the performance of the final computer system. The motherboard must meet the following criteria:

- Support the selected CPU type and speed

- Support the amount and type of system RAM required by the applications

- Have sufficient slots of the correct type to accept all required interface cards

- Have sufficient interfaces of the correct type

Figure 1-12   A Typical Motherboard

Top View

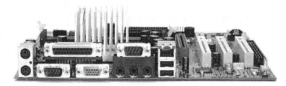

Side View

Central Processing Unit (CPU)

The *central processing unit (CPU)*, or processor, is the nerve center of the computer system. It is the component that processes all the data within the machine. The type of CPU should be the first decision made when building or updating a computer system. Important factors when selecting a CPU include the processor and bus speed as well as the number of cores. Many modern CPUs have multiple cores, or processing entities, on a single chip. This setup is similar to having multiple CPUs in the machine. Figure 1-13 shows a CPU attached to a motherboard.

Figure 1-13   CPU on a Motherboard

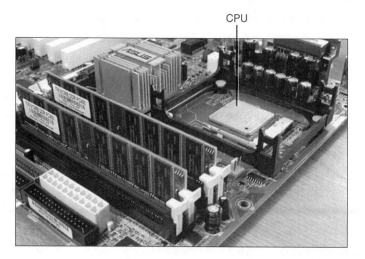

Processor speed measures how fast a CPU cycles information. It is normally measured in MHz or GHz. In general terms, the higher the CPU speed the better the performance. Faster processors consume more power and create more heat than their slower counterparts. For this reason, mobile devices, such as laptop computers, typically use processors that are slower and have been specifically designed to consume less power in order to extend the time they can operate using batteries.

A CPU must transfer data between various types of memory on the system board during its operation. The pathway for this movement of data is called the *bus*. In general, the faster the bus, the faster the computer will be. There are many different types of busses in a computer system. When selecting a CPU you may encounter the terms *front-side bus (FSB)* and *back-side bus (BSB)*. The FSB is also known as the system bus and is used to carry data between the CPU, the system RAM, and the various other secondary data busses. The BSB is used to move data between the CPU and high-speed cache memory.

A recent trend in CPUs is to include more than one processing core in a single processor. The terms *dual-core* and *quad-core* are now quite common. Essentially this setup is the same as running multiple CPUs in a single machine. Most modern operating systems support these newer CPUs and massive improvements in system performance can be obtained with very little additional cost.

NOTE

A multicore processor is different from a multiprocessor system. In a multiprocessor system, there are separate CPUs each with its own resources. In a multicore processor, resources are shared and the cores reside on the same chip. A multiprocessor system is generally faster than a system with a multicore processor, whereas a multicore system is normally faster than a single-core system.

When selecting a CPU, keep in mind that applications continue to evolve. Purchasing a CPU of moderate speed may satisfy current requirements. Future applications, however, may be more complicated and require more resources. If the purchased CPU is not sufficiently fast, the overall performance, measured in terms of response time, will be reduced. Thorough research must be conducted before purchasing a CPU to ensure that it will function reliably with the desired applications.

The CPU is mounted through a socket on the motherboard and is normally the largest component on the board. The motherboard must be equipped with a compatible socket to accept the selected CPU. In addition the chipset on the motherboard must be able to support the processor and all of its capabilities.

Random-Access Memory (RAM)

Random-access memory (RAM) is a type of data storage medium used in computers. It is used to store programs and data while they are being processed by the CPU. The information stored in RAM is accessed in any order, or at random, as needed. All computer programs run from RAM. Many different types of RAM are available and it must be matched to both the CPU and the capabilities of the motherboard. Besides the CPU, the amount and type of RAM is the most important factor in computer performance. Figure 1-14 shows RAM attached to a motherboard.

Every operating system requires a minimal amount of RAM in order for the OS to function. Most modern computers are often used to run multiple applications simultaneously, or to multitask. For example, many users run e-mail programs and Instant Messenger clients as well as anti-virus tools or firewall software. All of these applications require memory. The more applications that need to run simultaneously, the more RAM is required.

Figure 1-14   RAM on a Motherboard

More RAM is also recommended for computer systems with multiple processors or multicore processors. Additionally, as the speed of the CPU and the bus increase, so must the speed of the memory it accesses. The amount and type of RAM that can be installed on a system is dictated by the motherboard.

CAUTION

System RAM is connected to the FSB of the CPU. As CPU speeds continue to increase, so must the speed that the data can be written to and read from the connected memory. If the RAM is of the wrong type or speed, the CPU will not be able to use it and the computer will be rendered non-operational. Because of this, it is advisable to buy as much RAM as possible when purchasing or building the computer. Doing so helps ensure that the memory chips are compatible. Memory from different manufacturers or even different batches from the same manufacturer may not function together.

Adapter Cards

Adapter cards add enhanced functionality to a computer system. They are designed to be plugged into a connector or slot on the motherboard and, once this is done, become part of the system. Many modern motherboards are designed to incorporate the functionality of many of the basic adapter cards on the motherboard itself thus removing the necessity to purchase and install separate cards. Although this does provide basic functionality, the addition of dedicated adapter cards can often provide an enhanced level of performance.

Some of the more common adapter cards include the following:

- Video cards
- Sound cards
- Network interface cards
- Modems
- Controller cards

Video Cards

Video cards, also commonly referred to as graphics cards, accept information from the computer and translate it into a format that can be displayed on a monitor screen. Most current video cards contain large amounts of RAM and dedicated processor chips for manipulating video content. Figure 1-15 shows a video card.

Figure 1-15   Video Card

Most motherboards have a specialized, high-speed port that has been designed to allow the video card to exchange information with the system bus at extremely fast rates. This specialized bus is known as the *Accelerated Graphic Port (AGP)*. The choice of video card is made based on the video speed, resolution, and price. Graphic artists and gamers require faster speed and higher-resolution cards than those individuals concerned mainly with text. The video card output must match the capabilities of the connected monitor both in resolution and signal type. Some video cards output a digital signal but others output an analog one. Some video cards are capable of running multiple monitors for specialized applications.

Sound Cards

A sound card, as shown in Figure 1-16, accepts digital information from the system and converts it into a signal that is transmitted to a speaker to produce an audio output. Some sound cards also accept analog input and sample the sound to produce a file that can be stored and manipulated digitally. Current sound cards can produce an audio output that rivals some of the best stereo equipment available.

Figure 1-16   Sound Card

Network Interface Cards (NICs)

A network interface card (NIC), as shown in Figure 1-17, enables a computer system to exchange information with other systems on a local network. The speed of the network and the type of technology help determine what type of NIC is required. The most common networking technology is currently Ethernet. This type of NIC normally has an RJ-45 type connector to allow it to connect into the local network.

Figure 1-17   Network Interface Card

Modems

Modems enable computer systems to connect to remote networks such as the Internet. Figure 1-18 shows a modem. At the source, modems encode digital information onto an analog carrier signal that is carried across analog networks such as the public telephone network. At the receiving end, modems remove the encoded information from the carrier and pass the digital signal to the receiving device. Modems allow digital devices to communicate over analog networks such as the public telephone network, as well as DSL and cable networks. Each type of network requires a different type of modem.

Figure 1-18   Modem

Controller Cards

Controller cards are a large group of adapter cards that add additional interfaces or act as controllers for specialized hardware devices such as an external hard disk drive or tape drive. These cards are usually specific to a single device or group of devices and format the information in a manner specific to the end device. Specialized controller cards are less common now that most devices use standard interfaces. The most common controller card encountered is the small computer systems interface (SCSI) card used to connect a wide range of devices from printers to hard drives and other storage devices. Figure 1-19 shows an example of a controller card.

Figure 1-19   Controller Card

Storage Devices

When power is removed from the computer, any data stored in RAM is lost. Programs and user data must be stored in a form that will not disappear when the power is removed. This is known as *non-volatile storage*. Many types of non-volatile storage are available for computer systems including the following:

- Magnetic storage devices
- Optical storage devices
- Static memory (flash) drives

Magnetic Storage

Magnetic storage devices are the most common form found in computers. These devices store information in the form of magnetic fields. The following three main types of magnetic storage, shown in Figure 1-20, are found in many computer systems:

- *Hard disk drive (HDD)*: Also known simply as hard drives, HDDs are the main storage medium found in almost all computers including servers, desktops, and laptops. Hard drives are typically internal components attached to the motherboard, although external hard drives can be connected to the computer via a USB, FireWire, or hard disk controller card. The cost of hard disk drives is rapidly falling and the available capacity is increasing. Hard disks of 500 GB or more are now common in most home computers.

- *Floppy disk drive (FDD)*: FDDs, or simply floppy drives, can store 1.44 MB of data on a removable plastic disk. Floppy disks are becoming quite rare, and are being replaced by static memory devices, which offer higher storage capacities at lower prices. Most new computer systems do not include a FDD.

- *Tape drive*: Tape drives are used to back up information for archival or disaster recovery purposes. They are often found on file servers but are not normally found on home computers.

Figure 1-20   Common Magnetic Media Devices

Hard Disk Drive   Floppy Disks

Tape Drive

TIP

All magnetic media can be affected by storage conditions such as humidity and stray magnetic fields. Data stored on tapes or floppy disks should not be considered permanent. This information should be refreshed on a regular basis to ensure that it is still readable. For critical data it is wise to keep multiple copies in different locations or to consider optical storage devices.

Optical Storage

Optical storage devices use laser beams to record information by creating differences in optical density. These devices include both compact discs (CD) and digital versatile/video discs (DVD). Both CDs and DVDs come in three different formats:

- **Read only**: CD, DVD

- **Write once**: CD-Recordable (CD-R), DVD-Recordable (DVD-R)

- **Write many**: CD-Read/Write (CD-RW), DVD-Read/Write (DVD-RW)

The prices of these devices continue to fall and most computers now incorporate DVD-RW drives that can store approximately 4.7 GB of data on a single disc. Compact disc (CD) devices have a much lower storage capacity than DVDs and are therefore becoming less common. Another form of DVD drive, called *Blu-ray*, is also available. It uses a different type of laser to read and write data. The color of the laser used to store this information is blue-violet. For this reason, disks are called Blu-ray, to distinguish them from conventional DVDs, which use a red laser. Blu-ray disks have storage capacities of 25 GB and more. A typical optical drive and disc are shown in Figure 1-21.

Figure 1-21   A Typical Optical Drive and Disc

Static Memory and Memory Sticks

Static memory devices use memory chips to store information. This information is retained even after the power is turned off. They connect to a USB port on the computer and offer capacities of 8 GB or more. Due to their size and shape, these devices are known as *USB memory keys* or *flash drives* and have widely replaced floppy disks for transportation of files between systems.

The cost of these devices is rapidly decreasing as the maximum available capacity continues to increase. Larger capacity static memory storage units are available for use in portable devices where the weight and susceptibility to vibration of a conventional hard drive are limiting factors. Many portable and handheld devices rely entirely on static memory for storage. In addition, many networking devices rely on flash memory to store the operating system and retain user configurations.

TIP

When purchasing storage for a computer system, it is generally good practice to have a mix of magnetic storage, optical drives, and static memory available. When determining storage requirements, be sure to allow for growth. Anticipating just how much storage is enough is difficult but a good general rule is to purchase the largest storage devices that you can afford.

Peripheral Devices

A *peripheral* is a device that is added to the computer to expand its capabilities. These devices are optional in nature and are not required for the basic functioning of the computer. Instead they are used to increase the usefulness of the machine. Peripheral devices are connected externally to the computer using a specialized cable or wireless connection.

Peripheral devices can fit into one of four categories, as follows:

- **Input:** Trackball, joystick, scanner, digital camera, digitizer, barcode reader, microphone
- **Output:** Printer, plotter, speakers, headphones
- **Storage:** Secondary hard drive, external CD/DVD devices, flash drives
- **Network:** External modems, external NIC

Figure 1-22 shows examples of common peripherals, and Table 1–3 describes each device.

Figure 1-22   Common Peripheral Devices

Disk Drive   Scanner   Mouse

Flash Drive   Network Interface Card   Printer

Modem

Table 1-3   Common Peripherals

Device	Type	Description
Disk drive	Storage and input/output (I/O)	Allows a user to easily increase the available storage capacity of a computer and also move large amounts of data between different computers. A disk drive that is external to a computer and is not required for the computer to function is considered a peripheral device. Different types of disk drives exist including FDDs, HDDs, CD drives, and DVD drives.
Scanner	Input	Enables the user to convert printed pages, handwriting, diagrams, and pictures into digital format for storage on a computer.
Mouse	Input	Enables the user to select items displayed on the monitor.
Flash drive	Storage and I/O	Connects to the USB interface and allows files to be saved and moved between computers. Functions similarly to an external floppy disk drive.
Network Interface Card (NIC)	Network and I/O	Allows communications between computers. Not required for the individual computer to function; therefore, it is considered a peripheral device.
Printer	Output	Converts the digital information stored in a computer to a printed page. Many different types of printers exist and can have either monochrome or color output.
Monitor	Output	Used to visually display output from the computer.
Keyboard	Input	Enables the end user to enter information into the computer.
Modem	Network and I/O	Allows communication between digital devices over an analog medium. At the source, modems encode digital information onto an analog carrier signal for transfer across the media. At the destination, the digital information is removed from the analog carrier signal.

Cases and Power Supplies

Once all internal components and connections are determined, the case and power supply is the next consideration. The *case* holds and protects the internal computer components whereas the *power supply* converts the wall outlet power source to the low voltage required by the components.

Some cases are designed to sit on top of the user's desk whereas other cases sit below the desk. Computers designed to sit on the desk provide easy access to interfaces and drives but occupy valuable desk space. A tower or mini-tower type case can either be used on the desk or beneath the table. Whatever the case's style, select one that has enough space for all the components. Typical computer cases and power supply are shown in Figure 1-23.

Figure 1-23   Computer Cases and Power Supply

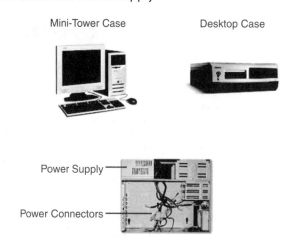

The case and power supply are usually sold together as a unit. The power supply must be sufficient to power the system. It is a good idea to always overestimate the requirement for a computer power supply to allow for the later addition of larger or additional hard disk drives, DVD and tape drives, and additional system RAM.

TIP

Many power supplies that come shipped with computer cases are severely under-rated for today's powerful computer systems. If the computer behaves erratically, locks up unexpectedly, or fails to start reliably, it may be due to faulty power.

Computer systems require a steady supply of continuous power. The power from many electricity supply companies is subject to voltage reductions and cuts. A poor supply can affect the performance of computer hardware and possibly damage it. These power issues can also corrupt software and data. In order to help protect the computer system from these power problems, devices such as surge suppressors and uninterruptible power supplies (UPS) have been developed.

Surge Suppressors

A *surge suppressor*, as shown in Figure 1-24, is designed to remove voltage spikes and surges from the power line and prevent them from damaging a computer system. They are relatively inexpensive and easy to install. Generally the surge suppressor is plugged into the power outlet and the computer system is plugged into the surge suppressor. Many surge suppressors also have connectors for phone lines to protect modems from damage due to voltage surges that may be carried through the telephone lines. It is important to purchase a surge suppressor with a sufficient rating to protect both the main computer system and any connected peripherals.

Figure 1-24   Surge Suppressor

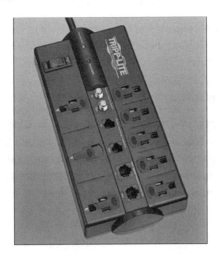

Uninterruptible Power Supplies

An *uninterruptible power supply (UPS),* as shown in Figure 1-25, is a device that continually monitors the power to a computer system and maintains the charge on an internal battery. If the power is interrupted, the UPS provides backup power to the system without interruption. The backup power comes from a battery inside the UPS and can power the computer system for only a short period of time. A UPS is designed to provide the end user with sufficient time to properly shut down a computer system should the main power fail. An in-line UPS can provide an even flow of power to the computer and prevent damage caused by voltage surges. Some low-end UPSs act only as a backup power supply. These do not adequately protect the computer system and should be avoided if possible.

Figure 1-25   Uninterruptible Power Supply (UPS)

UPSs suitable for home and small business use are relatively inexpensive and often incorporate surge suppressors and other functionality to stabilize the power supplied by the utility company. It is highly recommended that all computers be protected by a UPS regardless of their functionality or location.

Computer System Components

Computers are a collection of very complex components and peripherals, all working together to accomplish a task. Occasionally one of these components fails or needs to be upgraded to improve the functionality of the system. Sometimes a new peripheral must be added to enhance the machine's functionality. When adding, upgrading, or replacing system components and peripherals, it is important to follow proper safety precautions and procedures to help ensure success.

Adherence to best practices and proper safety precautions when working on computer systems is extremely important. These practices and procedures are designed to help protect both the components and devices being installed and the technician doing the installation. Computer systems pose threats from high voltage, sharp edges, and small components. Great care must be taken when upgrading or repairing computer systems to avoid these dangers.

Safety and Best Practices

Computer systems and monitors can be very heavy and should be lifted with caution. Before opening a computer system, be sure to have a proper work area. The work area should be a clean flat surface, strong enough to support the weight of heavy equipment. It should be well organized, free from clutter and distractions, and adequately lit to prevent eye strain. Proper eye protection must be worn to prevent accumulated dust, small screws, and components from causing damage to the eyes.

Caution

Most computer systems accumulate dust. A technician encountering a significant amount of dust when opening a computer case is not uncommon. Stirring up old, stale dust can be a health concern for people with asthma-like symptoms. Proper use of a small vacuum for removal of this dust is more appropriate than the use of compressed gas, which simply redistributes the dust into the surrounding air.

Before the computer case is opened, make sure the computer is switched off and the power cable is unplugged. Most components function at only a few volts, but power supplies and monitors operate at dangerously high voltages and should be opened only by individuals with special training.

When working inside a computer case, it is important to keep precautions in mind to prevent damage to the system components as well as harm to the technician. When opening a computer case, be aware that there are sharp edges usually on the inside of the case that should be avoided.

Some computer systems are specially designed to enable components to be hot-swapped, meaning that turning off the computer before adding or removing components is not necessary. This feature allows the system to remain operational during repairs or upgrades and is usually found in high-performance servers. Unless you are sure that the system is hot-swappable, turn it off before opening the case or removing components. Inserting or removing components with the power on, in a system that is not *hot-swappable*, can cause permanent and serious damage to the system and technician.

Internal system components are especially sensitive to static electricity. *Electrostatic discharge (ESD)* is static electricity that can be transferred from your body to electronic components in the computer. The static electricity doesn't have to be felt by you in order to occur. If the discharge is felt more than 3000 volts has moved from your body to the object.

ESD can cause *catastrophic failures* in components, making them nonfunctional. ESD can also cause intermittent faults that are very difficult to isolate. For this reason, proper grounding is essential. A special wrist *grounding strap*, shown in Figure 1-26, is used to connect the technician to the computer case. Grounding ensures that they both reach the same voltage potential and ESD is prevented.

Figure 1-26 Wrist Grounding Strap

Caution

ESD occurs when two objects at different voltages are connected together through a conductor. Electrons flow between the two objects in an attempt to balance out the difference in charge. Unfortunately computer components are easily damaged by this flow of electrons, and great care must be taken to prevent it from occurring. Never touch any internal computer components without first properly grounding yourself and the computer system.

Excessive force should never be used when installing components because it can damage both the motherboard and the component being installed and can prevent the system from functioning properly. Damage is not always visible. Force can also damage connectors which, in turn, can damage new system components.

To make certain that all safety precautions are followed, creating a safety checklist is a good idea. The following precautions should always be observed when working on a computer system:

❐ Use an antistatic mat and grounding wrist strap.

❐ Use antistatic bags to store and move computer components. Do not put more than one component in each bag because stacking them can cause some of the components to break or become loose.

❐ Do not remove or install components while the computer is on.

❐ Ground often to prevent static charges from building up by touching a piece of bare metal on the chassis or power supply.

❐ Work on a bare floor because carpets can build up static charges.

❐ Hold cards by the edges to avoid touching chips or the edge connectors on the expansion cards.

❐ Do not touch chips or expansion boards with a screwdriver.

❐ Turn off the computer before moving it. This is to protect the hard drive, which is always spinning when the computer is turned on.

❐ Keep installation/maintenance CDs and disks away from heat and cold.

❐ Do not place a circuit board of any kind onto a conductive surface, especially a metal foil. The Lithium and Nickel Cadmium (Ni-Cad) batteries used on boards may short out.

❐ Do not use a pencil or metal-tipped instrument to change the settings on the small internal switches or to touch components. The graphite in the pencil is conductive and could easily cause damage.

❐ Do not allow anyone who is not properly grounded to touch or hand off computer components. This is true even when working with another individual. When passing components, always touch hands first to neutralize any charges.

Installing Components and Verifying Operation

When installing or upgrading components be certain to follow all safety precautions. The following procedures apply to most system components.

How To

Step 1. Determine whether the computer component is hot-swappable. If not, or if in doubt, unplug the system unit before opening the case.

Step 2. Attach a grounding strap from your body to the system framework, or chassis, to prevent any damage that could be caused by ESD.

Step 3. If replacing a component, remove the old component. Components are often held into the system with small screws or clips. When removing screws, do not let them drop on the system motherboard. Also, be careful not to break any plastic clips.

Step 4. Check the connection type on the new component. Each card is designed to work only with a certain type of connector and should not be forced when inserting or removing the card.

Step 5. Place the new component in the correct connection slot, with the correct orientation, carefully following all installation instructions that may have accompanied the component.

Step 6. After the component has been added or upgraded, close the case and reconnect the power and other cables.

Step 7. Switch on the system and watch for any messages that may appear on the screen. If the system fails to start, disconnect all cables and verify that the component was properly installed.

If the system still will not start with the new component installed, remove it and try to start the system. If the system starts without the new component, the component may not be compatible with the current hardware and software and additional research into the problem is required. Figure 1-27 illustrates the process of installing a memory in a computer.

Figure 1-27   Installing Memory in a Computer System

Certain components require the addition of a specialized piece of software, or *driver*, to function. For commonly encountered components the drivers are usually contained in the operating system itself, but for more specialized components the driver must be added separately. Newer operating systems will usually prompt for the addition of any required drivers. Drivers are continually updated to improve efficiency and functionality. The most current driver can be obtained from the manufacturer's website and should normally be used. Always read any documentation that accompanies the driver software for potential problems and the proper installation procedure.

TIP

Always make certain that the driver installed is the correct one for the operating system. Using the wrong driver can cause unexpected results. The newest driver may not be the best. Problems with drivers often take some time to surface and using the newest release of a driver may cause unknown problems. If the component fails to function as expected after you upgrade the driver for a component, try rolling back the driver to a previous version.

After installation, the component should be tested for complete functionality. Components are designed to make use of specific sets of *system resources* as shown in Figure 1-28. If two components try to use the same resources, one, or both, will fail. The solution is to change the resources used by one of the devices. Newer components and operating systems are able to dynamically assign system resources but older devices must have the resources set manually or through software configuration.

Figure 1-28 System Resource Utilization

If the device fails to function properly, verify that the correct and most recent driver is installed. Also check that the operating system has correctly detected and identified the device. If this fails to correct the problem, power down the system, carefully reseat the component, and verify that all connections are correct. Check the component documentation for the correct settings. If the device continues to be nonfunctional, it is possible that the component is defective and it should be returned to the vendor.

Installing Peripherals and Verifying Operation

Peripheral devices, unlike internal components, do not require the computer case to be opened for installation. Peripherals connect to an interface on the outside of the case with a wired or wireless link. Historically, peripherals were designed to function when connected to a specific type of port. For example, PC printers were designed to connect to a parallel port, which transferred data from the computer to the printer in a specific format. Figure 1-29 shows some of the more common ports available on a computer system, and Table 1-4 provides a brief description of these ports.

Figure 1-29   Common Ports on a Personal Computer

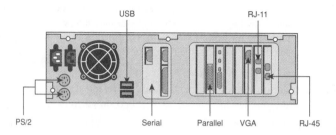

Table 1-4   Common Ports Found on a PC

Port	Description
PS/2	These connectors are commonly used for both the keyboard and the mouse. They have a very compact design and are keyed to allow the plugs to be inserted in the correct orientation only. The functionality of these ports is replaced by USB on many new computer systems.
USB	The Universal Serial Bus allows the connection of many different devices and supports hot-swapping and Plug-and-Play (PnP) technology. PnP allows the operating system to automatically detect and configure devices plugged into the USB port. An increasing number of USB devices are becoming available. These devices now include mice, keyboards, sound cards, speakers, NICs, modems, and external storage devices.
Serial	Serial ports were originally designed as a 25-pin male connector (DB25) but only nine wires were actually used. The original DB25 connector took up quite a bit of space and has been widely replaced by a more compact 9-pin connector (DB9). Both DB25 and DB9 connectors can be found on modern computers and are used to connect devices such as modems. They may also be used to connect a printer or mouse but this is becoming less common. This port can also be used to connect two computers to transfer data between them. The functionality of these ports is replaced by USB on many new computer systems.
Parallel	The parallel port was designed to connect a printer to the PC. It is a 25-pin connector but has a female gender. Parallel ports are also commonly used to connect printers, external tape drives, and CD or DVD drives to the host computer. This port can also be used to connect two computers to transfer data between them. The functionality of these ports is replaced by USB on many new computer systems.
VGA	The 15-pin video connector is standard on most personal computers. It is designed to connect to either VGA or super-VGA monitors. Most PCs use a DB15HD connector, which has three rows of five pins.
RJ-11	The RJ-11 connector is the connector used by telephone companies in many areas of the world. This connector is usually found on a modem and is used to connect the computer to the telephone network.

Port	Description
RJ-45	The RJ-45 connector is the standard connector used for Ethernet networks. This connector is used to connect the computer into a local-area network (LAN) or to connect it to an external modem such as those provided by cable and DSL companies for high-speed Internet access.
FireWire (not pictured)	The FireWire port provides a high-speed connection into the computer system. It can support up to 63 peripherals and allows them to communicate without the intervention of the CPU or system memory. FireWire supports PnP and hot-swapping. It is normally used to connect digital video devices to a computer.

More recently the development of the *Universal Serial Bus (USB)* interface has greatly simplified the connection of peripheral devices that use wires. USB devices require no complex configurations and can merely be plugged into an appropriate interface, assuming that the proper driver has been installed. There have also been an increasing number of peripheral devices that connect to the host computer through wireless technology.

The installation of a peripheral device requires several steps. The order and detail of these steps varies depending on the type of physical connection and whether or not the peripheral is a *Plug-and-Play (PnP)* device. The steps include the following:

Step 1.   Connect the peripheral to the host using the appropriate cable or wireless connection.

Step 2.   Connect the peripheral to a power source.

Step 3.   Install the appropriate driver.

Some old peripheral devices, called legacy devices, are not PnP enabled. For these, driver installation occurs after the device has been connected to the computer and powered up. For PnP-enabled USB devices, the driver is preinstalled on the system. In this case, when the PnP device is connected and powered on, the operating system recognizes the device and installs the appropriate driver. Installation of outdated or incorrect drivers can cause a peripheral device to behave unpredictably. For this reason, installing the most current drivers available is necessary.

If the peripheral device does not function after it is connected and installed, verify that all cables have been properly connected and that the device is powered up. Many devices, such as printers, offer a testing functionality on the device directly, and not through the computer. This is shown in Figure 1-30. Use this feature to verify that the device itself is functioning properly.

If the device is operational, but not connecting to the computer system, the problem could be with the cable connection. If the cable is suspected, swap it with a known good one. If this fails to solve the problem, the next step is to verify that the port the peripheral device is connected to is recognized by the operating system.

If everything appears to be functioning properly, the device may not be compatible with the current hardware or operating system and requires more research to solve the problem.

After installation, the full functionality of the peripheral device must be tested. If only partial functionality is available, the most likely cause is an outdated driver. This is easily remedied by downloading and installing the most current driver from the manufacturer's website.

Figure 1-30   Printer Test Function

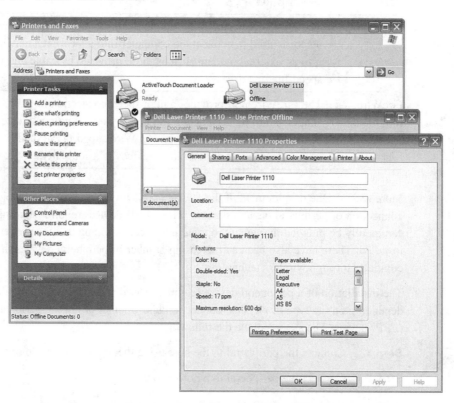

 Lab 1-3: Installing a Printer and Verifying Its Operation (1.5.3.4)

In this lab you will manually install a printer using the default Windows XP driver and verify printer functionality. You will then download and install the latest printer driver from the manufacturer's website and compare functionality.

Summary

This chapter has introduced computers and their applications. Highly specialized computers are integrated into many common items, including automobiles, refrigerators, televisions, and other electronic devices. The hardware, operating system, and application program all work together to accomplish specific tasks.

Application programs may either be business/industry-specific such as software used to manage a medical office, or may be more generalized and designed to be used across many different industries. A common example of a generalized application is the office suite.

Applications may also be designed to run only on a local machine or may be designed to work in a network environment. Network-based applications require that client software be installed on the local machine and that the remote machine is running server software. The client software communicates with the server software to carry out a task. A common network application is e-mail.

Many different types of computers exist, each designed for a specific task or application. Mainframes and servers are designed to service multiple clients at the same time and have built-in redundancy to ensure their continued operation. PCs and laptops are designed to be used by only a single person at any one time and often lack the redundant hardware found in servers. Some computers are designed to remain stationary whereas others, such as laptops and PDAs, are powered by batteries and designed to be portable.

Computers may be highly specialized and designed to run only one or two applications or may be very generic in nature. Workstations are computers that have been optimized to run engineering and graphics-intensive programs such as CAD and virtual reality software. Portable gaming devices are smaller computers but have been optimized to play games that have been specially designed to run on the device. Many devices, such as cellular phones, are now integrating multiple functions into a small portable device. These often incorporate a digital camera, PDA, and audio/video player in addition to the basic phone capabilities.

All information within a computer system is represented digitally by a series of 1s and 0s known as bits. While the computer is processing data, these bits are stored in RAM, moved through the various computer buses, and manipulated by the CPU. In addition, this digital information can be stored on optical, magnetic, or solid-state memory chips for archival and transportation purposes. All of these devices are usually located inside the computer case and are known as components. Most components connect directly to the motherboard, which houses most of the electronics required to make the computer function.

Peripherals are devices located outside of the case and are designed to enhance system functionality. Peripherals are not required for the normal operation of the computer system but provide additional services. Printers and scanners are common examples of a computer peripheral.

Activities and Labs

This summary outlines the activities and labs you can perform to help reinforce important concepts described in this chapter. You can find the activity files on the CD-ROM accompanying this book. The complete hands-on labs appear in Part II.

Interactive Activities on the CD-ROM:

Interactive Activity 1-1: Classification of Applications (1.1.2.3)

Interactive Activity 1-2: Function of a Computer (1.2.2.4)

Interactive Activity 1-3: ASCII Digital Translator (1.3.1.1)

Interactive Activity 1-4: Byte Conversion Calculator (1.3.2.3)

Hands-on Labs in Part II of This Book:

Lab 1-1: Determining Data Storage Capacity (1.3.2.2)

Lab 1-2: Determining the Screen Resolution of a Computer (1.3.3.4)

Lab 1-3: Installing a Printer and Verifying Its Operation (1.5.3.4)

Check Your Understanding

Complete all the review questions listed here to test your understanding of the topics and concepts in this chapter. The "Check Your Understanding and Challenge Questions Answer Key" appendix lists the answers.

1. Which of the following would be classified as an application program? (Choose all that apply.)

   A. Spreadsheet

   B. Windows Vista

   C. Linux

   D. Word Processor

   E. Windows XP

   F. Database

2. What allows a computer to locate and load an operating system when it is first powered on?

   A. Application program

   B. Operating system

   C. Hard disk drive

   D. BIOS

   E. Hardware

3. Which of the following is considered a network application?

   A. E-mail

   B. Spreadsheet

   C. Word processor

   D. Database

4. Which type of computer is normally a large centralized computer found in enterprise environments?

  A. Mainframe

  B. Server

  C. Desktop

  D. Workstation

  E. Laptop

5. Which type of computer is normally designed to run high-end graphics and engineering applications such as CAD?

  A. Mainframe

  B. Server

  C. Desktop

  D. Workstation

  E. Laptop

6. Which types of computers are designed to be used by a single end user? (Choose two.)

  A. Mainframe

  B. Server

  C. Desktop

  D. Workstation

7. How long would it take to download a 600 KB file from the Internet with a 256 kbps connection?

  A. 2 seconds

  B. 19 seconds

  C. 2343 seconds

  D. 2400 seconds

8. What is the unit used to measure the resolution of a computer monitor?

  A. gigahertz

  B. KB

  C. pixel

  D. kbps

9. What are some advantages of purchasing a prebuilt computer over having one custom built? (Choose two.)

  A. Ability to specify exactly which parts are used in the system

  B. Ability to optimize system performance for a specific application

  C. Less expensive than building your own computer with the same components

  D. No waiting period

  E. Better system performance

10. What should be the first step when upgrading a computer with an on-board NIC to one that plugs into an expansion slot?

    A. Install the correct driver for the new NIC.

    B. Disable the on-board NIC.

    C. Update the operating system.

    D. Upgrade the system BIOS.

11. When selecting a new motherboard, which of the following factors should you consider? (Choose all that apply.)

    A. Support for the selected CPU type and speed

    B. Support for the amount and type of system RAM required by the applications

    C. Sufficient slots of the correct type to accept all required interface cards

    D. Sufficient interfaces of the correct type

12. When building your own computer system, what is the first component that should be decided upon?

    A. CPU

    B. RAM

    C. HDD

    D. Motherboard

13. From where is an application program normally run?

    A. HDD

    B. FDD

    C. RAM

    D. BIOS

14. Which of the following peripherals are considered input devices? (Choose all that apply.)

    A. Scanner

    B. Digital camera

    C. Mouse

    D. Keyboard

    E. Microphone

15. What is the first step when upgrading an internal video card in a computer system?

    A. Reformat the hard disk drive.

    B. Upgrade the system BIOS.

    C. Unplug the computer.

    D. Remove the old video card.

16. Before passing a CPU or a piece of memory to another individual, what should you do?

    A. Touch hands first to equalize charges.

    B. Place the component on a plastic table and then allow the other person to pick it up.

    C. Touch the component to a grounding plate to remove any excess charge.

    D. No precautions are necessary.

17. What is the sequence of steps required to install and verify a USB printer under Windows XP?

    1. Physically connect the printer to the computer.

    2. Power up the printer.

    3. Install the driver.

    4. Power up the computer.

    5. Generate a test print.

    A. 1, 2, 4, 3, 5

    B. 4, 3, 1, 2, 5

    C. 1, 2, 4, 3, 5

    D. 4, 1, 2, 3, 5

    E. 4, 2, 3, 1, 5

    F. 4, 2, 1, 3, 5

Challenge Questions and Activities

These questions require a deeper application of the concepts covered in this chapter. You can find the answers in the appendix.

1. Charlene must upgrade the memory in her new laptop computer by installing a single 2 GB stick. She quickly unscrews the door on the bottom of the computer and snaps the new stick into an empty connector. She then powers up the machine only to see that the new memory is not recognized by the computer. Checking the manual for the computer, she verifies that the memory type and capacity should be recognized. What is the problem and how would you correct it?

2. Juri has just installed a new PnP printer on his home computer system using the drivers on the Windows XP CD. The advertisement stated that the printer could print high-resolution pictures on various types of paper. Unfortunately Juri cannot see how to set this information. What advice would you give to Juri?

CHAPTER 2

Operating Systems

Objectives

Upon completion of this chapter, you will be able to answer the following questions:

- What is the purpose of an OS?

- What role do the shell and kernel play?

- What is the difference between a CLI and GUI interface?

- What is a network redirector?

- What are some of the common operating systems available?

- What is the difference between commercial and GPL software licensing?

- What are the different options for OS installation?

- What is an OS upgrade and how is it performed?

- What is a file system and what types are used with PCs?

- What IP parameters must be configured to prepare a computer to participate on the network?

- How are operating systems maintained?

Key Terms

This chapter uses the following key terms. You can find the definitions in the Glossary.

How we interact with our computer, and what applications it can run, affects our ability to communicate with others. Computer operating systems enable us to use application software, store information, and join the network. The operating system is the most important program running on a computer. Without it the other programs and features will not operate. In this chapter you will learn about the most popular operating systems, and how to choose the one that will be right for your computer. Part II of this book includes the corresponding labs for this chapter.

Choosing the Operating System

There are a number of operating systems in use with modern computers. Most client computers purchased in a retail outlet come with the operating system preloaded. If a computer is ordered from an online retail output, the purchaser frequently has a choice of which OS is installed. Business environments often need to consider other options depending on the intended function of the computer. They may even build their own computers and install the desired OS.

Purpose of an Operating System

System components and peripherals, by themselves, are nothing more than a collection of electronics and mechanical parts. To get these parts to work together to perform a specific task, a special type of computer program, known as an *operating system (OS)*, is required.

Suppose that a user wants to write a report and print it out on an attached printer. A word processing application is required to accomplish this task. Information is entered from the keyboard, displayed on the monitor, saved on the disk drive, and then finally sent to the printer.

In order for the word processing program to accomplish all of this, it must work with the OS, which controls input and output functions. The OS uses specialized software programs known as drivers to interact with the various hardware components. Every major electronic component inside the computer or attached to it requires a driver. These drivers might be integrated into the OS or standalone software modules used by the OS. The OS and its drivers are what accepts the information entered from the keyboard, displays it on the monitor, saves it to disk, and sends the document to the printer. As shown in Figure 2-1, the keyboard, mouse, and disk drivers are typically integrated into the OS whereas video and printer drivers are typically external software modules. The entered data is manipulated inside of the computer, stored in RAM, and processed by the CPU. This internal manipulation and processing is also controlled by the OS. All computerized devices, such as servers, desktops, laptops, or handhelds, require an OS in order to function.

Figure 2-1   Computer Components and OS Drivers

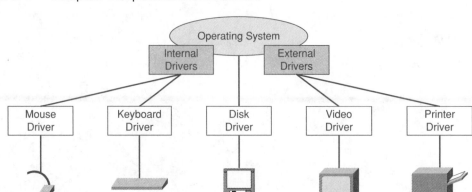

The OS acts like a translator between user applications and the hardware. A user interacts with the computer system through an application, such as a word processor, spreadsheet, or computer game. Application programs are designed for a specific purpose, such as word processing, and know nothing of the underlying electronics. For example, the application is not concerned with how information is entered into the application from the keyboard. The operating system is responsible for the communication between the application and the hardware.

When a computer is powered on, it loads the OS, normally from a permanent storage device, such as a hard disk drive, into RAM. The portion of the OS code that interacts directly with the computer hardware is known as the *kernel*. The portion that interfaces with the applications and user is known as the *shell*. The user can interact with the shell using either the *command line interface (CLI)* or *graphical user interface (GUI)*. Figure 2-2 shows the relationship between the OS shell, the kernel, and the computer hardware.

Figure 2-2   OS Shell, Kernel, and Hardware Relationship

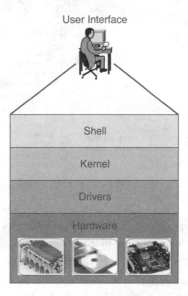

When using the CLI, the user interacts directly with the system in a text-based environment by entering commands on the keyboard at a command prompt. The system executes the command, often providing textual output on the monitor. Figure 2-3 shows the Windows CLI interface command prompt screen with a directory of drive C:\ displayed using the **dir** command.

Figure 2-3   Directory of Drive C:\ Using the Windows CLI Command Prompt Window

The GUI allows the user to interact with the system in an environment that uses graphical images, multimedia, and text. Actions are performed by interacting with the images onscreen. GUI is more user friendly than CLI and requires less knowledge of the command structure to utilize the system. For this reason, many individuals rely on the GUI environments. Most operating systems offer both GUI and CLI. Although the GUI is more user friendly, knowing how to work with the CLI is still useful. The GUI depends on the graphics subsystems of the computer to display the high-resolution, multicolor images. If a problem occurs with the graphics hardware or drivers, the CLI might be the only interface available to the user for troubleshooting. Figure 2-4 shows the Windows Explorer GUI interface screen with a directory of drive C:\ displayed by clicking with the mouse.

Figure 2-4   Directory of Drive C:\ Using the Windows Explorer GUI

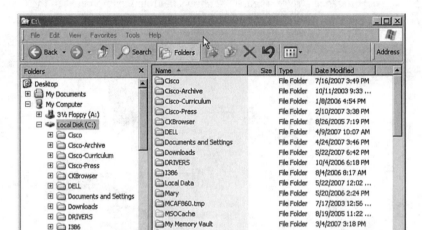

Figure 2-5 shows a Linux CLI terminal window for entering commands. The structure of the file system is displayed using the **ls –l** UNIX command, which is similar to the Windows **dir** command. The **ls –l** command lists directories (also called folders) and files, using the –l or "long" option. This option provides additional information for each file and directory. Without the –l option, only the directory and filenames would be displayed. With this listing, the name of the directory (or file) is the last entry in blue.

Figure 2-6 shows a Linux GUI window for displaying and managing directories and files. The structure of the file system is displayed using the *K Desktop Environment (KDE)* File Browser application. KDE File Browser is similar to the Windows Explorer application. Notice that directories are referred to as folders in the GUI screen.

Operating systems have complete control of local hardware resources. They are designed to work with one user at a time. They enable the user to do more than one thing at a time using multiple applications. This capability is known as *multitasking*. The operating system keeps track of which resources are used by which application. A single processor can only manipulate memory to give the impression of multitasking. The CPU is actually giving each application a portion or slice of its processing time. The more applications the system is running, the smaller the time slice for each application. Multiprocessor systems can have multiple independent CPU chips or multiple CPUs on one chip (for example, dual-core). These systems can actually perform multiple tasks simultaneously.

Figure 2-5   Display of File System Directories Using the Linux CLI Terminal Window

```
                              root@localhost:/                       _ □ ×

 File  Edit  View  Terminal  Tabs  Help

[root@localhost /]# ls -l
total 158
drwxr-xr-x   2 root root  4096 May 13 05:05 bin
drwxr-xr-x   4 root root  1024 May 12 21:37 boot
drwxr-xr-x  11 root root  3760 Jul 29 14:14 dev
drwxr-xr-x  99 root root 12288 Jul 29 14:10 etc
drwxr-xr-x   2 root root  4096 Oct 10  2006 home
drwxr-xr-x   2 root root  4096 May 11 18:31 Junk
drwxr-xr-x  14 root root  4096 May 12 21:30 lib
drwx------   2 root root 16384 Mar 16 16:51 lost+found
drwxr-xr-x   2 root root  4096 Jul 29 14:10 media
drwxr-xr-x   2 root root     0 Jul 29 14:10 misc
drwxr-xr-x  10 root root  4096 Apr 11 18:57 mnt
drwxr-xr-x   2 root root     0 Jul 29 14:10 net
drwxr-xr-x   2 root root  4096 Oct 10  2006 opt
dr-xr-xr-x 123 root root     0 Jul 29 14:08 proc
drwxr-x---  23 root root  4096 Jul 29 14:14 root
drwxr-xr-x   2 root root  4096 Apr 16 19:02 rpm
drwxr-xr-x   2 root root 12288 May 13 05:05 sbin
drwxr-xr-x   2 root root  4096 Mar 16 16:53 selinux
drwxr-xr-x   5 root root  4096 Apr  8 10:57 sqash
drwxr-xr-x   2 root root  4096 Oct 10  2006 srv
drwxr-xr-x  11 root root     0 Jul 29 14:08 sys
drwxrwxrwt  14 root root  4096 Jul 29 14:15 tmp
```

Figure 2-6   Display of File System Directories Using the Linux KDE File Browser GUI

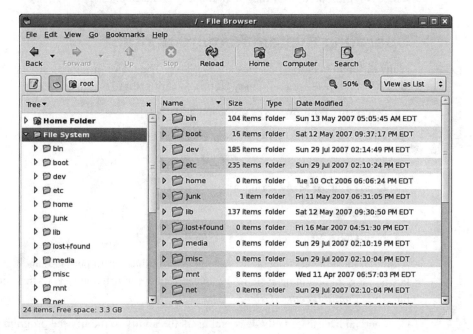

In order to work with resources that are not directly connected to the computer system, a special piece of software called a *redirector* must be added. Redirectors make it possible to reroute a data request from the OS out of the local machine onto the network to a remote resource. The redirector can either be an integral part of the OS or can be installed separately. With a redirector, the local PC can access remote resources as a ***network client***. With a redirector installed, the operating system acquires some of the characteristics of a network operating system (NOS). Figure 2-7 shows the use of the OS redirector when a host needs access to a remote resource on the network. The document being retrieved might appear to the user that it is on the local machine. However, the redirector must send the request out the network interface card (NIC) to contact the remote server and actually retrieve the document.

Figure 2-7   Accessing Remote Network Resources with the Redirector

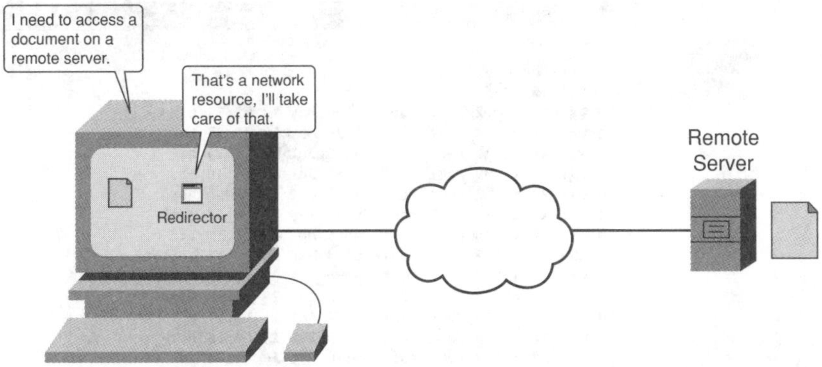

An operating system that is specifically designed for a network is referred to as a *network operating system (NOS)*. A NOS includes features that allow management of network resources like files, printers, LAN users, and security, and is typically installed on a server. Most network resources appear to the end users as if they were on their local machine, when in reality the NOS is providing the resource to the PC. A true NOS offers complex scheduling and user management software that allows a server to share resources between many users and resources. The client OS with a redirector can access the server NOS resources as if they were directly connected.

Operating System Requirements

Many different operating systems are available. The major groupings are listed here with some examples. Most of these are proprietary commercial offerings.

- **Microsoft Windows**: XP, Vista, and 2003 Server

- **UNIX-Based:** IBM AIX, Hewlett Packard HPUX, and Sun Solaris

- **BSD:** Free BSD

- **Linux-Based**: Many varieties

- **Macintosh OS X**

- **Non-UNIX Proprietary**: IBM OS/400, z/OS

Although most of these operating systems require the user to purchase and agree to a commercial license, several operating systems are released under a different type of licensing scheme known as the *GNU Public License (GPL)*.

Commercial licenses usually deny end users the ability to modify the program in any way. Windows XP, Mac OS X, and *UNIX* are all examples of commercial OS software.

In contrast, the GPL allows end users to modify and enhance the code, if they desire, to better suit their environment. Some common operating systems released under the GPL include *Linux* and BSD. Refer to Table 2-1 for a comparison of commercially licensed operating systems and those released under GPL.

Table 2-1   Commercial and GPL License Comparison

Criteria	Commercial License	GNU Public License (GPL)
Access	Restrictive in nature and limits what the user can do with the code.	Ensures everyone has full access to the source code and can participate in enhancement of the product.
Cost	Often very expensive depending on deployment (for example, a Windows XP license must normally be purchased for every client machine on a network).	Often released free-of-charge (for example, Linux can be freely installed on as many machines as desired). However, the cost of retraining for a GPL product might exceed the discounted cost of a commercial license.
Development Cycle	Very structured development cycle and changes not quickly available.	Development cycle is less structured and changes are more quickly implemented.
Support	Structured support available for a fee.	Less of a structured support arrangement, often relying on community (user-based) support. Some companies that distribute GPL products provide fee- based support.

Operating systems require a certain amount of hardware resources. These resources are specified by the manufacturer and include such things as

- Amount of RAM
- Hard disk space required
- Processor type and speed
- Video resolution

Manufacturers often specify both a minimum and recommended level of hardware resources. System performance at the minimum specified hardware configuration is usually poor and only sufficient to support the OS and little other functionality. The recommended configuration is usually the better option and is more likely to support standard additional applications and resources. Adding hardware over that recommended, such as another CPU and more RAM, can further improve system performance, but at a significant cost.

To take advantage of all the features provided by an operating system and installed applications, hardware resources such as sound cards, NICs, modems, microphones, and speakers are generally required. Many of the OS developers test various hardware devices and certify that they are compatible with the operating system. Always confirm that the hardware has been certified to work with the operating system before purchasing and installing it. Table 2-2 shows a sample comparison of the minimum amount of hardware needed and the recommended hardware necessary to get the most out of the OS and applications running on the computer.

Table 2-2   Minimum and Recommended OS Requirements

		Minimum	Recommended
CPU		512 Megahertz	1 Gigahertz
RAM		256 Megabytes	1 Gigabyte
Hard drive		40 Gigabytes	80 Gigabytes
Graphics card		800 x 600 pixels	1024 x 768 pixels
Optical drive		CD-ROM	DVD

Interactive Activity 2-1: Software Licensing Scenarios (2.1.2.3)

In this interactive activity, you determine the appropriate type of software licensing for a scenario. Use file ia-2123 on the CD-ROM that accompanies this book to perform this interactive activity.

Operating System Selection

You need to consider many factors before deciding on which OS to use in a given environment.

The first step in selecting an OS is to ensure that the OS being considered fully supports the requirements of the end user. Does the OS support the applications that will be run? Is the security and functionality sufficient for the needs of the users?

Next, conduct research to make sure that sufficient hardware resources are available to support the OS. This includes such basic items as memory, processors, and disk space, as well as peripheral devices such as scanners, sound cards, NICs, and removable storage.

Another consideration is the level of human resources needed to support the OS. In a business environment, a company might limit support to one or two operating systems and discourage, or even disallow, the installation of any other OS. In the home environment, the ready availability of technical support for an OS might be a determining factor. The following are some of the factors that should be considered when selecting an OS:

- Security
- Support
- Politics
- Cost
- Availability

- Resources

- Platform

- Use

When implementing an OS, you should consider *total cost of ownership (TCO)* of the OS in the decision-making process. This not only includes the costs of obtaining and installing the OS, but also all costs associated with supporting it.

Another factor that might come into play in the decision-making process is the availability of the operating system. Some countries and/or businesses have made decisions to support a specific type of OS or might have restrictions barring individuals from obtaining certain types of technologies. In this type of environment, considering a particular OS, regardless of its suitability to the task, might not be possible.

The process for selecting an operating system, as shown in Figure 2-8, must take all of these factors into account.

Figure 2-8   Considerations and Requirements for Selecting an Operating System Process

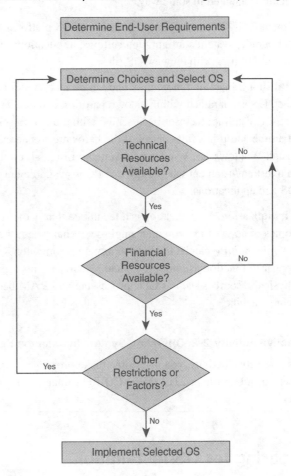

Installing the Operating System

Most operating systems are installed on a clean hard drive by the manufacturer of the computer system. However, several other options are available depending on the existing operating system installed and the circumstances and goals of the user.

OS Installation Methods

An OS is installed in a defined section of the hard disk, called a *disk partition*. Various methods exist for installing an OS. The method selected for installation is based on the system hardware, the OS being installed, and user requirements. Four basic options are available for the installation of a new OS:

- **Clean install**: A clean install is done on a new system or in cases where no *upgrade* path exists between the current OS and the one being installed. It deletes all data on the partition where the OS is installed and requires application software to be reinstalled. A new computer system requires a clean install. A clean install is also performed when the existing OS installation has become damaged in some way.

- **Upgrade**: If you are staying with the same OS platform, doing an upgrade is often possible. With an upgrade, system configuration settings, applications, and data are preserved. It simply replaces the old OS files with the new OS files.

- **Multiboot**: Installing more than one OS on a computer to create a multiboot system is possible. Each OS is contained within its own partition and can have its own files and configuration settings. On startup, the user is presented with a menu to select the desired OS. Only one OS can run at a time and it has full control of the hardware. As an example of multiboot, it is possible to install Windows XP, Windows Server, and Linux all on the same system. This setup can be useful in a test environment where only one PC is available but there is a need to test several different OS and applications.

- **Virtualization**: Virtualization is a technique that is often deployed on servers. It enables multiple copies of an OS to be run on a single set of hardware, thus creating many virtual machines. Each *virtual machine* can be treated as a separate computer. This enables a single physical resource to appear to function as multiple logical resources. This type of approach generally demands more physical resources such as CPU processing and RAM because multiple OSs are running on the same machine.

Interactive Activity 2-2: Operating System Installation Scenarios (2.2.1.2)

In this interactive activity, you determine the appropriate operating system installation technique for each scenario. Use file ia-2212 on the CD-ROM that accompanies this book to perform this interactive activity.

Preparing for OS Installation

A pre-installation checklist helps ensure that the installation process is successful:

Step 1.   Verify that all hardware is certified to work with the selected OS. Experienced users can monitor tech blogs to see what problems are being experienced on specific machines/motherboards and so on. This can save the installer time and potential problems.

Step 2.   Verify that the hardware resources meet or exceed the published minimum requirements.

Step 3.   Confirm that the appropriate installation medium is available. Due to the file size of current operating systems, they are usually available on both CD and DVD media.

Step 4.   If the OS is to be installed on a system that already contains data:

      a. Use system diagnostic tools and utilities to ensure that the current OS installation is in good condition, free of malicious or damaging files and codes.

      b. Complete a full backup of all important files.

Step 5.   If performing a clean install, verify that all application software is available for installation.

Step 6.   If connecting the computer to a network at this time, verify that the network configuration information is available.

Step 7.   If this is an end-user computer and a different OS is to be installed, verify that the user has adequate training in the use of the new OS.

Before starting the installation, determining the partition structure that best meets user requirements is necessary. Figure 2-9 depicts hard disk partitioning.

Figure 2-9   Hard Disk Partitioning

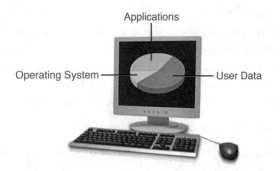

One of the techniques available to help protect data is to divide the hard drive into multiple partitions. With a clean install, many technicians prefer to create one partition for data and a separate partition for the OS. This technique enables an OS to be upgraded without the risk of losing data. It also simplifies backup and recovery of data files. Applications might be installed on yet another partition. With all data files on a single partition, backing up only that partition is necessary. The OS and applications can be reinstalled in the event of a system failure.

When installing an OS, determining the type of file system to use is also necessary. A *file system* is the method the OS uses to keep track of the files. Many different file system types exist. Each OS is designed to work with one or more of these file system types and each file system type offers specific advantages:

- *File Allocation Table (FAT) 16/32*: 16- and 32-bit file systems are common with the earlier home versions of Windows OS but do not provide file security. Proprietary.

- *New Technology File System (NTFS)*: Developed with Windows NT. A more robust and secure file system available with some newer home versions of Windows such as XP and Vista, and the professional and server version of other Windows OSs. Provide journaling of file system changes. Proprietary.

- *Ext2* and *ext3*: Second and third extended file systems. Used primarily with Linux distributions. The ext2 file system supports large files, long filenames, and file security and also provides high-performance lookups. Ext3 adds journaling capabilities to ext2. Both ext2 and ext3 are open source.

Careful consideration should be made to the type of file systems supported by the selected OS and the benefits of each.

Although tools exist to modify the partitioning structure and file system of a hard drive after installation, they should be avoided if possible. Modifying either the file system or partition structure on a hard drive might result in *data loss*. Careful planning can help preserve the integrity of the data.

Configuring a Computer for the Network

After an OS is installed, the computer can be configured to participate in a network. A network is a group of devices, such as computers, that are connected to each other for the purposes of sharing information and resources. Shared resources can include printers, documents, and Internet access connections.

To physically connect to a network, a computer must have a *network interface card (NIC)*. The NIC is a piece of hardware that allows a computer to connect to the network medium. It might be integrated into the computer motherboard or might be a separately installed card.

In addition to the physical connection, some configuration of the operating system is required for the computer to participate in the network. Most modern networks connect to the Internet and use it to exchange information. Each computer on these networks requires an *Internet Protocol (IP)* address, as well as other information, to identify it. The IP configuration contains three parts, which must be correct for the computer to send and receive information on the network. These three parts are

- *IP address*: Identifies the computer on the network.
- **Subnet mask**: Identifies the network on which the computer is connected.
- **Default gateway**: Identifies the device that the computer uses to access the Internet or another network.

In Figure 2-10, the PC must have a NIC installed, usually an Ethernet NIC on modern local networks. It is then configured with an IP address and a subnet mask for the local network it is on. The default gateway entered as part of this configuration is the IP address of the router interface on this local network. All packets that are not destined for local hosts will be sent to the default gateway.

Figure 2-10   Configuration Requirements for Connecting to the Network

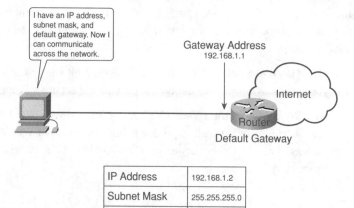

IP Address	192.168.1.2
Subnet Mask	255.255.255.0
Default Gateway	192.168.1.1

A computer IP address can be configured manually or assigned automatically by another device, as shown in Figure 2-11.

Figure 2-11   Manual and Dynamic IP Configuration

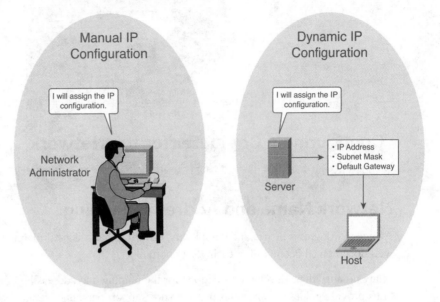

With manual configuration, the required values are entered into the computer via the keyboard, typically by a network administrator. The IP address entered is referred to as a static address and is permanently assigned to that computer.

Computers can be set up to receive their network configuration dynamically. This feature allows a computer to request an address from a pool of addresses assigned by another device within the network. When the computer is finished with the address it is returned to the pool for assignment to another computer.

Computer Naming

In addition to the IP address, some network operating systems make use of computer names. In this environment each individual system must have a unique name assigned to it.

A *computer name* provides a user-friendly way to identify a computer, making it easier for users to connect to shared resources such as folders and printers on other computers.

The network administrator should determine a logical naming scheme that helps to identify a device's type and/or its location. For example, the name PRT-CL-Eng-01 could represent the first network-attached color laser printer in the Engineering Department.

These names are manually assigned to each device, although some tools do exist to help automate the naming process. A computer description can also be entered when assigning a name to provide additional information on the location or function of the device. Figure 2-12 shows the use of Windows System Properties to enter a computer name.

Figure 2-12   Using Windows System Properties to Name a Computer

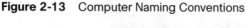

Network Name and Address Planning

As a network grows in size and complexity, ensuring that it is well planned, logically organized, and well documented becomes increasingly important.

Many organizations develop conventions for the naming and addressing of computers. These conventions provide guidelines and rules that network support personnel can use when performing these tasks. Computer names must be unique and should have a consistent format that conveys meaningful information. This method can help to determine device type, function, location, and sequence number based on the device name. IP addresses must also be unique to each device.

The use of logical device naming and addressing conventions that are well documented can greatly simplify the tasks of training and network management and can help with troubleshooting when problems arise. Figure 2-13 illustrates a logical naming scheme that can assist the network administration staff.

Figure 2-13   Computer Naming Conventions

Maintaining the Operating System

As operating systems and applications software continue to evolve, users need to keep their systems up to date to ensure they have the latest features and that their systems operate efficiently and are protected against attacks.

Why and When to Apply Patches

After an OS or application is installed, keeping it up to date with the latest patches is important.

A *patch* is a piece of program code that can correct a problem or enhance the functionality of an application program or OS. It is usually provided by the manufacturer to repair a known vulnerability or reported problem. In most cases a patched OS results in a healthier, more stable computer, as shown in Figure 2-14.

Figure 2-14   Operating System Patches

Computers should be continually updated with the latest patches unless a good reason exists not to do so. Sometimes patches negatively impact the operation of another system feature. The impact of the patch should be clearly understood before it is applied. The software manufacturer's website usually provides this information.

Applying OS Patches

Patches to operating systems can be installed in different ways, depending on the OS and the needs of the user. Options for downloading and installing updates include the following:

- **Automatic installation**: The OS can be configured to connect to the manufacturer's website and then download and install minor updates without any user intervention. Updates can be scheduled to occur during times when the computer is on, but not in use.

- **Prompt for permission**: Some users want to have control over which patches are applied. This choice is often the one for users who understand what impact a patch can have on system performance. The system can be configured to notify the end user when a patch is available. The user must then decide whether to download and install the patch.

- **Manual**: Updates that require major pieces of code to be replaced on a system should be run manually. These major updates are often called service packs and are designed to correct problems with an application or OS, and sometimes to add functionality. These service packs usually require the end user to manually connect to a website, download files, and install the update. They can also be installed from a CD available from the manufacturer.

Figure 2-15 shows the Automatic Updates options in Windows System Properties.

Figure 2-15   Windows Automatic Updates

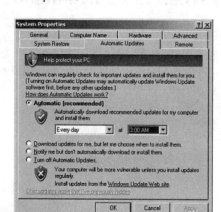

Interactive Activity 2-3: OS Update Options (2.3.2.2)

In this interactive activity, you determine what type of update the scenario is describing. Use file ia-2322 on the CD-ROM that accompanies this book to perform this interactive activity.

Application Patches and Updates

Applications also require patches and updates. Patches are usually released by the manufacturer to repair a detected vulnerability in the application that could lead to undesirable behavior.

Browsers and office software such as word processors and spreadsheet and database applications are common targets for network attacks. These applications require updates to correct the code that might allow the attack to succeed. The manufacturer might also develop updates that can improve product functionality, at no additional cost.

OS and application patches are generally found through the manufacturer's website. The installation process might request permission to install the update and to verify that any supporting software is present. The installation process might also install any programs that are required to support the update. Web updates can be downloaded to the system from the Internet and installed automatically. Figure 2-16 shows the Internet Explorer Security Warning that is displayed before an update is downloaded and installed.

Figure 2-16   Installing an Update from the Internet

Lab 2-1: Examining Operating System and Application Versions (2.3.3.2)

In this lab you will examine the current version of OS and installed applications and determine whether additional patches or updates are available. Refer to the Hands-on lab in Part II of this *Learning Guide*. You may perform this lab now or wait until the end of the chapter.

 Challenge Lab 2-2: Evaluating an OS Upgrade

In this lab you will evaluate the existing hardware of a Windows XP computer and determine whether it can support an upgrade to Windows Vista. Refer to the Hands-on lab in Part II of this *Learning Guide*. You may perform this lab now or wait until the end of the chapter.

Summary

An operating system (OS) is the most important software in a PC. It is responsible for making all the hardware components and software applications work together. An OS can be installed by the manufacturer, an end user, or a network administrator.

The OS is comprised of a kernel, a shell, and device drivers. The kernel is the main OS program and interacts directly with the hardware through the use of device drivers. The shell interacts with the applications and the user. The user interacts with the shell through the command-line interface (CLI) or a graphical user interface (GUI).

A network operating system (NOS) is a sophisticated OS that allows a computer to share resources among many users and to treat networked resources as if they are directly connected. A NOS includes features that allow management of network resources such as files, printers, LAN users, and security, and is typically installed on a server.

Performing a pre-installation checklist before installing any new OS is important. An OS is installed in a disk partition, which is a defined section of the hard disk. Decide on partition schemes before installing the OS.

Operating systems use various file systems. The most common file systems are Windows FAT 16/32 and NTFS. For Linux they are ext2 and ext3.

To participate in a network, a computer requires a network interface card (NIC) configured with an IP address, subnet mask, and default gateway. The network should be well planned, logically organized, and well documented using standard addressing and naming conventions.

Keeping OS and application software up to date with the latest revisions, upgrades, or patches is important. A patch is a piece of program code that corrects a problem or enhances the functionality of an OS. An OS can be configured to connect automatically to the manufacturer's website and download and install minor updates without any user intervention. Service packs are major updates to an OS or software application. Application software can also require patches and updates to repair a detected vulnerability in the application. Applications patches are generally found through the manufacturer's website.

Part II of this book includes the corresponding labs for this chapter.

Activities and Labs

This summary outlines the activities and labs you can perform to help reinforce important concepts described in this chapter. You can find the activity and Packet Tracer files on the CD-ROM accompanying this book. The complete hands-on labs appear in Part II.

Interactive Activities on the CD-ROM:

Interactive Activity 2-1: Software Licensing Scenarios (2.1.2.3)

Interactive Activity 2-2: Operating System Installation Scenarios (2.2.1.2)

Interactive Activity 2-3: OS Update Options (2.3.2.2)

Labs in Part II of This Book:

Lab 2-1: Examining Operating System and Application Versions (2.3.3.2)

Challenge Lab 2-2: Evaluating an OS Upgrade

Check Your Understanding

Complete all the review questions listed here to test your understanding of the topics and concepts in this chapter. The "Check Your Understanding and Challenge Questions Answer Key" appendix lists the answers.

1. A network technician is installing the Linux OS on a computer. What are the most likely file systems she will select from?

2. A network technician needs to install a new operating system on a computer. In order to preserve the data, application, and configuration settings as well as the partitioning already present, which installation method should be used?

   A. Clean install

   B. Upgrade

   C. Multiboot

   D. Virtualization

3. Allan just purchased a new PC for attachment to an Ethernet local network. What three basic static IP configuration parameters will he need to enter to allow this PC to participate on the network?

4. When developing a naming scheme for a network, which two pieces of information are most beneficial when determining a computer name? (Choose two.)

   A. Device type

   B. Location

   C. Year purchased

   D. Operating system

   E. Software installed

5. What is the term used to describe the software added to an OS that allows a user to access remote network resources as if they were local?

6. What portion of operating system code interacts directly with computer hardware?

7. Which two operating systems issued under the GPL allow end users to modify and enhance code? (Choose two.)

   A. Windows XP

   B. Mac OS X

   C. Linux

   D. BSD

   E. UNIX

8. What three factors need to be considered when choosing an operating system? (Choose three.)

   A. The operating system has limited availability.

   B. The operating system supports end-user requirements.

   C. Sufficient hardware resources are available.

   D. Users can provide training on the new software without help.

   E. Human resources exist to support the product.

   F. The operating system is backward compatible with MS-DOS.

9. Jessica's home computer is currently running Windows 98. She wants to convert to Windows Vista but wants to keep her data and applications. She checks the Microsoft website and finds that there is no upgrade path from Windows 98 to Vista. What steps should she take to convert to Vista? (Choose all that apply.)

   A. Back up her data

   B. Verify her hardware has enough resources to support Vista

   C. Reinstall her applications

   D. Perform a clean install of Vista

10. A network administrator wants to set up the OS update options on the Windows PCs in his network so that he is made aware of updates when they are available but has the opportunity to check what changes the updates contain before downloading and installing them. Which update option does he need to use?

    A. Prompt for permission

    B. Automatic installation

    C. Manual installation

CHAPTER 3

Connecting to the Network

Objectives

Upon completion of this chapter, you will be able to answer the following questions:

- What is meant by the term *network* and what are some of the more common networks we use in everyday life?

- What are communication protocols?

- How does communication occur across a local Ethernet network?

- What are the main high-level components of an information network?

- When does a computer play the role of a client, server, or both on a network?

- How do you build a computer peer-to-peer network and verify it is functioning?

- How are networks graphically represented and what is the difference between logical and physical network topologies?

- What is the purpose of the access and distribution layers and what devices does each normally contain?

- How do hubs, switches, and routers function?

- What are a broadcast domain and a collision domain and why are they important?

- What is ARP and how does it function?

- What is the importance of a default gateway?

- What is prototyping?

Key Terms

This chapter uses the following key terms. You can find the definitions in the Glossary.

physical address   page 91

logical address   page 91

access layer   page 94

hub   page 95

collision domain   page 95

MAC address table   page 96

flooding   page 97

local network   page 99

hexadecimal   page 99

broadcast domain   page 99

*Address Resolution Protocol (ARP) table
page 101*

Address Resolution Protocol (ARP)   page 101

distribution layer   page 103

router   page 105

routing   page 105

default gateway   page 108

routing table   page 108

default route   page 109

local-area network (LAN)   page 112

prototype   page 116

multi-function device   page 117

integrated services router (ISR)   page 119

light-emitting diode (LED)   page 119

baseline   page 120

More and more often, networks connect us. People communicate online from everywhere. Conversations in coffeehouses carry over into chat rooms. Online debates continue at school. Efficient, reliable technology enables networks to be available whenever and wherever we need them. In this chapter, you learn how communication occurs over a network. You also learn about the many different components that need to operate together to make it work.

Part II of this book includes the corresponding labs for this chapter.

Introduction to Networking

An awareness of the components that make up a network and their roles is critical to understanding how networks function. This section provides an overview of different types of networks, including modern converged information networks. It describes the benefits of networking and the different roles computers can play. Basic network components, such as hosts, network devices, and media are discussed. This chapter compares peer-to-peer networks to server-based networks and introduces network topology maps.

What Is a Network?

Many types of networks provide different kinds of services. In the course of a day, a person might make a phone call, watch a television show, listen to the radio, look up something on the Internet, or even play a video game with someone in another country. All of these activities depend on robust, reliable. Networks provide the ability to connect people and equipment no matter where they are in the world. People use networks without thinking about how they work or what it would be like if the networks did not exist.

Figure 3-1 is a picture of an airport and people using various types of networks to share information, use resources, and communicate with others. This scene shows multiple types of networks. Can you identify some of the networks in the picture?

Figure 3-1   Common Types of Networks

A close examination of Figure 3-1 reveals several different types of networks, many of which we use every day:

- **Power network**: Distributes electrical power to homes and businesses via the power grid.

- **Mobile phone network**: Connects mobile callers to voice, text, and Internet via the mobile phone system.

- **Telephone network**: Connects callers and allows modem connections via traditional land lines.

- **Television network**: Provides regular and high-definition broadcasts over the air, via cable and satellite networks.

- **Computer network**: Provides communications between computer users via copper, fiber-optic, and wireless connections.

Other types of networks can include a network of personal or business contacts, water distribution networks, and radio networks.

Communication technology in the 1990s and before required separate, dedicated networks for voice, video, and computer data communications. Each of these networks required a different type of device in order to access the network. Telephones, televisions, and computers used specific technologies and different dedicated network structures to communicate. Accessing all of these network services at the same time, possibly using a single device, required a new type of network.

Unlike dedicated networks, these new networks are capable of delivering voice, video, and data services over the same communication channel or network structure. They are frequently referred to as *converged networks*, meaning that networks that were previously independent have come together or converged and become one.

New products are coming to market that take advantage of the capabilities of converged information networks. People can now watch live video broadcasts on their computers, make a telephone call over the Internet, or search the Internet using a television.

In this book, the term *network* refers to these new multipurpose, converged information networks, shown in Figure 3-2. Many of today's service providers now offer telephone service, high-speed Internet access, and television broadcasts over the same network.

Figure 3-2   Converged Information Networks

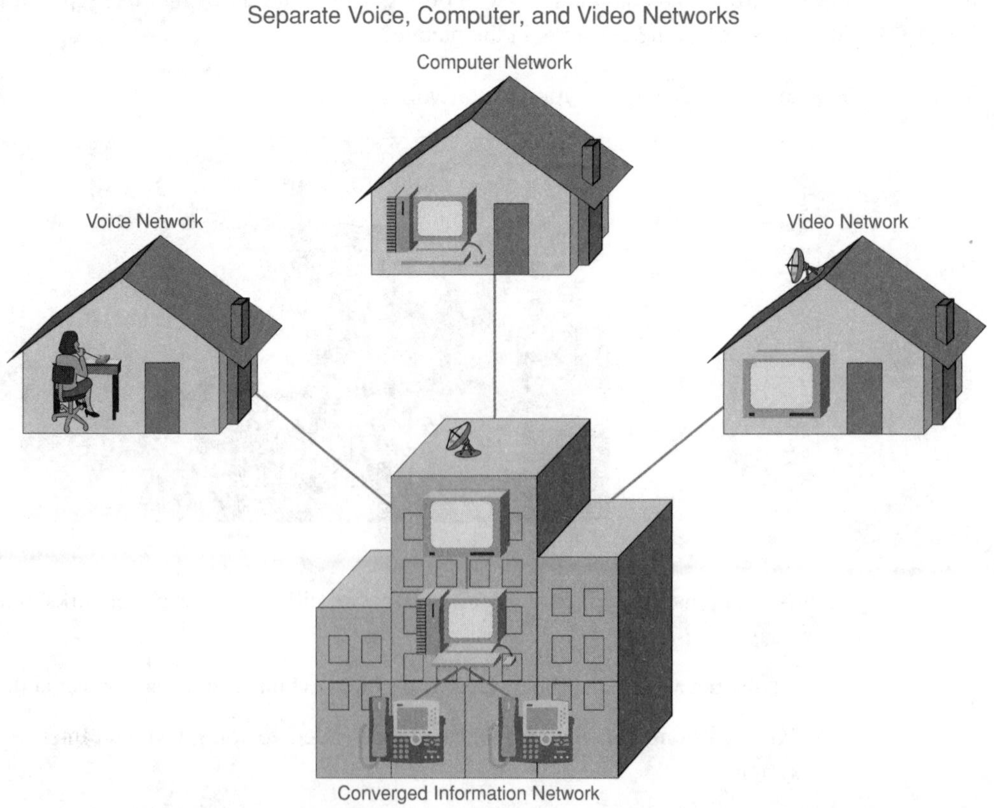

Benefits of Networking

Networks come in all sizes. The simplest possible network consists of just two computers, but large complex networks can connect millions of devices. Networks installed in small offices, homes, and home offices are referred to as *small office/home office (SOHO) networks*. SOHO networks enable sharing of resources, such as printers, documents, pictures, and music, among a few local computers.

In business, large networks can be used to advertise and sell products, order supplies, and communicate with customers. Communication over a network is usually more efficient and less expensive than traditional forms of communication, such as regular mail or long distance phone calls. Networks allow for rapid communication such as e-mail and instant messaging, and provide consolidation of, storage of, and access to information on network servers.

Business and SOHO networks usually provide a shared connection to the Internet. The Internet is considered a "network of networks" because it is literally made up of thousands of networks that are connected to each other.

Here are some other uses of a network and the Internet:

- Sharing music and video files
- Research and online learning
- Chatting with friends
- Planning vacations
- Purchasing gifts and supplies
- Keeping track of your favorite sports teams
- Investing and banking

Figure 3-3 shows how networks can be defined by their size and area they serve. Small home networks connect a few computers to each other and the Internet. Small business networks enable computers within a home office or a remote office to connect to a corporate network for access to centralized, shared resources. Medium to large networks, such as those used by major corporations and schools, can have many locations with hundreds or thousands of interconnected computers. The Internet is a network of networks that connects hundreds of millions of computers worldwide.

Basic Network Components

Many components can be part of a network, such as personal computers, servers, networking devices, and cabling. These components can be grouped into four main categories:

- *Hosts*: Hosts send and receive user information traffic. A host is a generic name for most end-user devices. A host has an Internet Protocol (IP) network address. Examples of hosts are personal computers, servers, and network-attached printers.

- *Peripherals*: Peripheral devices do not communicate directly on the network. Instead, peripherals rely on their connected host to perform all network operations. Examples of shared peripherals are scanners, locally attached printers, and fax machines.

- *Networking devices*: Networking devices connect other devices, mainly hosts. These devices move and control network traffic. Examples of network devices include hubs, switches, and routers.

- *Media*: Media provide connections between hosts and network devices. Media can be wired, such as copper and fiber optic, or use wireless technologies.

Figure 3-3 Networks Vary in Size

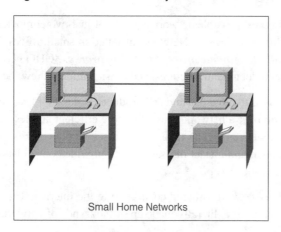

Small Home Networks

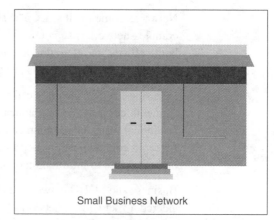

Small Business Network

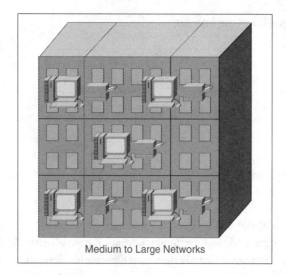

Medium to Large Networks

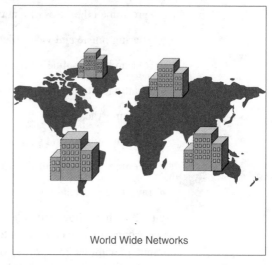

World Wide Networks

The network components that people are most familiar with are hosts and shared peripherals. Hosts are devices that send and receive messages directly across the network. Shared peripherals are not directly connected to the network, but instead are connected to hosts. The host is then responsible for sharing the peripheral across the network. The user of a computer can choose whether to share a peripheral attached to his or her computer. When a peripheral is shared, other users have access to it. Hosts have computer software configured to enable people on the network to use the attached peripheral devices.

The network devices, as well as networking media (cabling), are used to interconnect hosts. With the simplest possible network, where two computers are directly connected, only a single cable or wireless connection is required. All other networks require cabling as well as some sort of interconnecting device.

Some types of devices can play more than one role, depending on how they are connected. For example, a printer directly connected to a host (local printer) is a peripheral. A printer directly connected to a network device and participating directly in network communications is a host.

Figure 3-4 shows a small network with various typical components. All four categories are represented including hosts, peripherals, networking devices, and media.

Figure 3-4   Basic Network Components

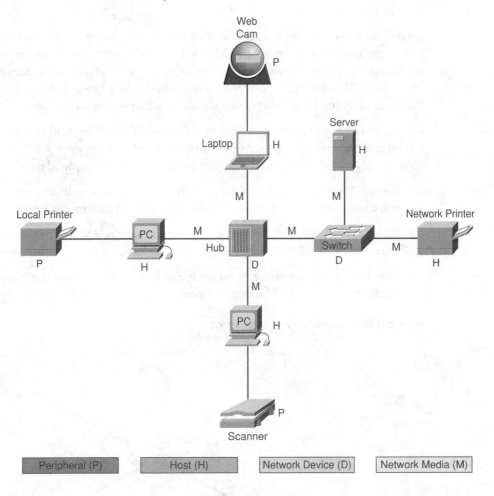

In Figure 3-4, the desktop PCs, laptop, server, and network printer are all considered hosts and will normally be assigned IP addresses. Notice that hosts are connected directly to a networking device such as a hub or switch and can communicate directly with other hosts. The local printer, scanner, and web cam are peripherals. The printer and scanner could be shared for use by other hosts if desired. The hub and switch are networking devices and the cabling between hosts and networking devices is the media. Note that the cabling from a host to a peripheral is not considered part of the network media.

Look around the classroom or your home network and identify various network components. The main factor that determines the category for a device (peripheral, host, or network) is how the component is connected and how it is used.

Interactive Activity 3-1: Identifying Network Components (3.1.3.2)

In this interactive activity, you identify network components. Use file ia-3132 on the CD-ROM that accompanies this book to perform this interactive activity.

Computer Roles in a Network

All computers connected to a network that participate directly in network communication are classified as hosts. Hosts can send and receive messages on the network. In modern networks, a computer host can act as a client, a server, or both. The software installed on the computer determines which role the computer plays.

Servers are hosts that have software installed that enable them to provide information, like e-mail or web pages, to other hosts on the network. Each service requires separate server software. For example, a host requires web server software in order to provide web services to the network. Server software running on UNIX and Linux hosts is usually referred to as a *daemon*. A service or daemon is software that is normally loaded on a server and running, waiting for clients to request its services.

Clients are computer hosts that have software installed that enable them to request and display the information obtained from the server. An example of client software is a web browser, such as Internet Explorer. Figure 3-5 shows some examples of the client/server relationship:

- **E-mail**: The e-mail server runs server software such as Microsoft Exchange, and clients use mail client software, such as Microsoft Outlook, to access e-mail on the server.

- **Web pages**: The web server runs server software such as Apache, and clients use browser software, such as Windows Internet Explorer or Firefox, to access web pages on the server.

- **File sharing**: The file server stores the file or folder, and the client device accesses the file with client software such as Windows Explorer.

Figure 3-5   Client/Server Relationships

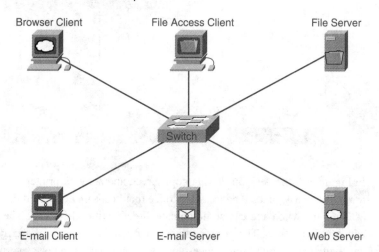

A computer with server software can provide services simultaneously to one or many clients. Additionally, a single computer can run multiple types of server software. In a home or small business, one computer might need to act as a file server, a web server, and an e-mail server.

A single computer can also run multiple types of client software. Client software must exist for every service required. With multiple clients installed, a host can connect to multiple servers at the same time. For example, a user can check e-mail and view a web page while instant messaging a friend and downloading a file. Figure 3-6 shows a single computer performing multiple server roles and clients with multiple types of client software accessing the server.

Figure 3-6   Supporting Multiple Clients Simultaneously

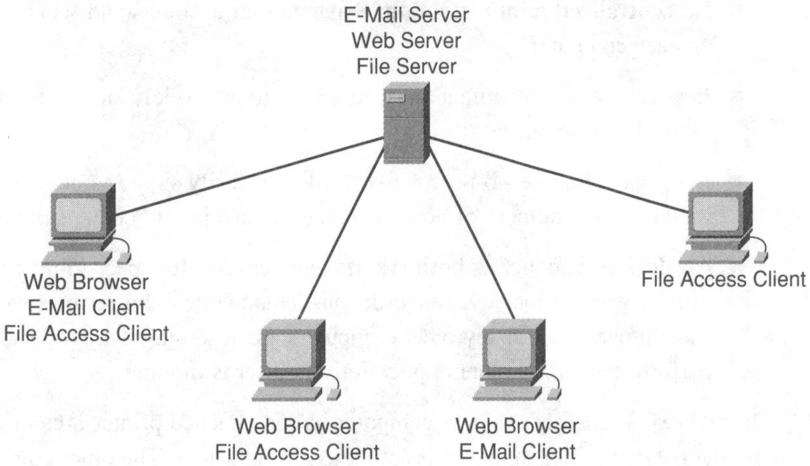

E-Mail Server
Web Server
File Server

Web Browser
E-Mail Client
File Access Client

File Access Client

Web Browser
File Access Client

Web Browser
E-Mail Client

Interactive Activity 3-2: Matching Client and Server Capabilities (3.1.4.3)

In this interactive activity, you match the client capabilities to the appropriate server. Use file ia-3143 on the CD-ROM that accompanies this book to perform this interactive activity.

Peer-to-Peer Networks

Client and server software usually run on separate computers, but having one computer carry out both roles at the same time is also possible. In small businesses and homes, many computers function as the servers and clients on the network. This type of network is called a *peer-to-peer network*.

The simplest peer-to-peer network consists of two directly connected computers using a wired or wireless connection. Multiple PCs can also be connected to create a larger peer-to-peer network but it requires a network device, such as a hub, to interconnect the computers. The main disadvantage of a peer-to-peer environment is that the performance of a host can be slowed down if it is acting as both a client and a server at the same time.

In larger businesses, due to the potential for high amounts of network traffic, having dedicated servers to support the number of service requests is often necessary. They are referred to as *server-based networks*.

Peer-to-peer networking has the following characteristics and advantages:

- **Easy to set up**: In most cases peer computers can be connected to a hub or switch and resources can be shared quickly and easily.

- **Used for simple tasks**: The most common tasks include transferring files and sharing printers. If the networking needs are basic, a simple peer-to-peer network can be a good choice.

- **Lower cost**: Network devices and dedicated servers might not be required. In general, when network devices are required they are simpler and less expensive than those required for server-based networks.

- **Less complexity**: There are generally fewer components than with server-based networks and no server setup is required.

The disadvantages of peer-to-peer networking include the following:

- **No centralized administration**: Separate user accounts and security must be set up and managed on each computer.

- **Less secure**: Gaining unauthorized access to network resources is easier than with centralized server-based security.

- **Less scalable**: Peer-to-peer networks do not easily support network expansion. As the network grows and the number of hosts increases, managing it becomes more difficult.

- **All devices may act as both clients and servers**: In a peer-to-peer network all computers are usually workstations where a user runs local applications such as word processing and spread-sheet programs. If many other computers are accessing that workstation's resources, it can slow performance of the other applications the user is running.

In Figure 3-7, one peer-to-peer computer has an attached printer it can share with the other computer on the network. This computer is acting as a print server. The other computer is acting as a file server and provides access to its files. These two computers are directly connected without a networking device.

Figure 3-7   Peer-to-Peer Networks

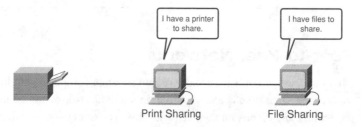

NOTE

Microsoft operating systems have built-in server software that allows any computer to share stored files with other computers on the network. When you share a file, your computer acts as a server. Also, Microsoft comput-er operating systems have built-in client software that allows any computer to access shared files on another computer. When you access a shared file, your computer acts as a client.

Interactive Activity 3-3: Determining Client and Server Roles (3.1.5.2)

In this interactive activity you determine whether the computer is acting as a server, a client, or both for each scenario. Use file ia-3152 on the CD-ROM that accompanies this book to perform this inter-active activity.

Lab 3-1: Building a Peer-to-Peer Network (3.1.5.3)

In this lab you build a simple peer-to-peer network using two PCs and an Ethernet crossover cable. You also verify connectivity. Refer to the hands-on lab in Part II of this *Learning Guide*. You may perform this lab now or wait until the end of the chapter.

Network Topologies

In a simple network consisting of a few computers, visualizing how all the various components connect is easy. As networks grow, keeping track of the location of each component, and how each is connected to the network becomes more difficult. Large wired networks can require considerable cabling and many network devices to provide connectivity for all network hosts.

When networks are installed, a *physical topology* map is created to record where each host is located and how it is connected to the network. The physical *topology* map also shows where the wiring is installed, the location of wiring closets, and the locations of the networking devices that connect the hosts. The physical topology map is usually based on a building floorplan diagram, as shown in Figure 3-8. Icons represent the actual physical devices within the topology map. Maintaining and updating physical topology maps is very important to aid future installation and troubleshooting efforts.

Figure 3-8   Physical Topology

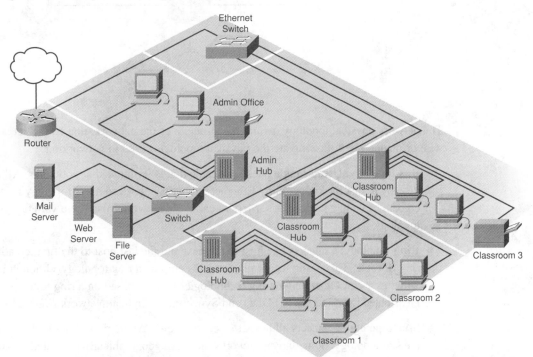

In addition to the physical topology map, having a logical view of the network topology is also sometimes necessary. A *logical topology* map groups hosts by how they use the network, no matter where they are physically located. Host names, addresses, group information, and applications can be recorded on the logical topology map, as shown in Figure 3-9. Logical topology maps usually hide the details of the cabling and networking devices that actually interconnect host computers. In the logical topology map, a group of host computers might be represented by a single icon.

The number and types of devices that you must go through to get to a server can vary from just one or two for local servers to hundreds for remote servers on the other side of the world, which can create very large and complex topologies. Imagine the connections and devices involved in getting to a server in the classroom, across the campus, or around the world.

Figure 3-9   Logical Topology

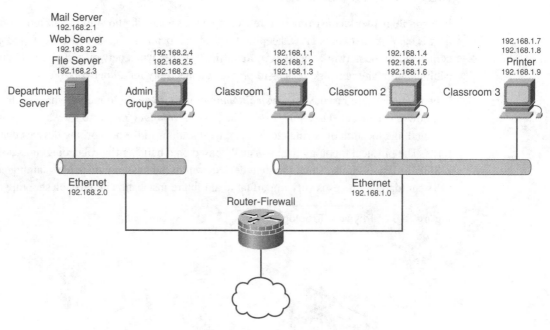

The network physical topology defines the structure of the network; that is, the actual layout of the wire or media. The following are the physical topologies used in networking:

- **Bus topology**: Uses a single backbone cable that is terminated at both ends. All the hosts connect directly to this backbone. Early Ethernet networks employed a bus topology using a common coaxial cable to connect hosts. Modern cable TV networks also use a variation of the bus topology.

- **Ring topology**: Connects one host to the next and the last host to the first, creating a physical ring of cable. Token ring local-area networks employ a ring topology, although it is physically wired as a star. Other networking technologies that are based on a ring topology include Fiber Distributed Data Interface (FDDI) and Synchronous Optical Network (SONET).

- **Star topology**: Connects all hosts to a central point. All modern Ethernet local area networks use the star topology. Some larger networks that have geographically separated locations might also employ the star design, also known as a *hub-and-spoke* network. With these networks, all the remote sites are connected to a single central site.

- **Extended star topology**: Links individual stars together by connecting the hubs or switches. Networks that use the star topology can usually be expanded using extended star topology.

- **Hierarchical topology**: Similar to an extended star. However, with a LAN, instead of linking the hubs or switches together, they are linked to a networking device. This device is usually a router that controls the traffic on the topology.

- **Mesh topology**: Provides redundant connections between network devices and/or locations. A full mesh is implemented to provide as much protection as possible from interruption of service. For example, a nuclear power plant might use a mesh topology in the networked control systems.

A variation of the full mesh is known as a partial mesh, where not all sites have multiple connections to all others, providing some redundancy. With a full mesh, each site location has its own connections to all sites. Although the Internet has multiple paths to any one location, it does not adopt the full mesh topology.

Refer to Figure 3-10 to see how these physical topologies are connected.

Figure 3-10   Network Topologies

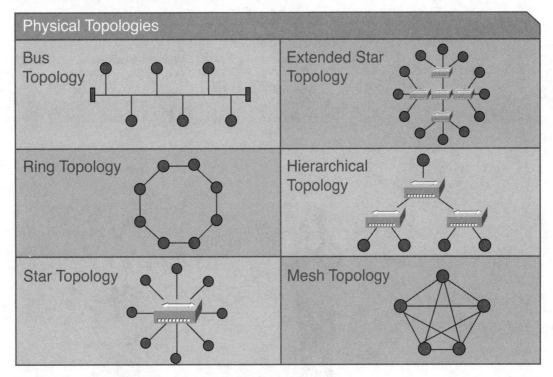

Principles of Communication

Computer communications on a network are similar in many ways to human communication. An appreciation of these similarities will help develop a good foundation on which to build further studies. This section provides an overview of the components, message types, and rules necessary for human and computer communication.

Source, Channel, and Destination

The primary purpose of any network is to provide a method to communicate information. From the very earliest primitive humans to the most advanced scientists of today, sharing information with others is crucial for human advancement.

All communication begins with a message, or information, that must be sent from one individual or device to another. The methods used to send, receive, and interpret messages change over time as technology advances.

All communication methods have three elements in common. The first of these elements is the message *source*, or sender. Message sources are people, or electronic devices, that need to communicate a message to other individuals or devices. The second element of communication is the *destination*, or receiver, of the message. The destination receives the message and interprets it. A third element, called a *channel*, provides the pathway over which the message can travel from source to destination.

Figure 3-11 shows human communication with a message source, a transmission medium (channel), and a receiver. These same basic components are required with computer communications, as shown in Figure 3-12.

Figure 3-11   Human Communication

Rules of Communication

In any conversation between two people, they must follow many rules, or protocols, in order for the message to be successfully delivered and understood. Among the protocols for successful human communication are

- Identification of sender and receiver
- Agreed-upon medium or channel (face-to-face, telephone, letter, or photograph)
- Appropriate communication mode (spoken, written, illustrated, interactive, or one-way)
- Common language
- Grammar and sentence structure
- Speed and timing of delivery

Figure 3-12   Computer Communication

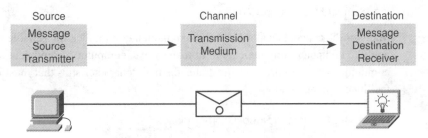

Imagine what would happen if no protocols or rules existed to govern how people communicate with each other. Would you be able to understand them? In Figure 3-13, compare the top paragraph to the bottom paragraph. Are you able to read the top paragraph? Notice that it seems to follow no rules or structure. It does not follow commonly accepted protocols.

Figure 3-13   Communication With and Without Protocols

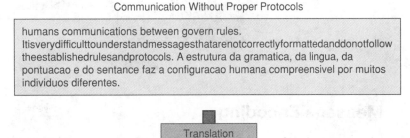

Protocols are specific to the characteristics of the source, channel, and destination of the message. The rules used to communicate over one medium, like a telephone call, are not necessarily the same as communication using another medium, such as a letter.

Protocols define the details of how the message is transmitted and delivered. This includes issues of

- Message format
- Message size
- Timing
- Encapsulation

- Encoding

- Standard message pattern

Many of the concepts and rules that make human communication reliable and understandable also apply to computer communication. In many ways, computer communications are similar to human communications. Figure 3-14 illustrates the main characteristics that must be defined for protocols to facilitate communication.

Figure 3-14   Main Protocol Characteristics

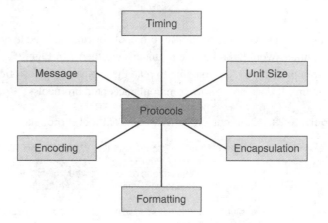

Message Encoding

One of the first steps to sending a message is encoding it. Written words, pictures, and spoken languages each use a unique set of codes, sounds, gestures, and symbols to represent the thoughts being shared. Encoding is the process of converting thoughts into the language, symbols, or sounds for transmission. Decoding reverses this process in order to interpret the thought.

Imagine a person watching a sunset and then calling someone else to talk about how beautiful the sunset looks. To communicate the message, the sender must first convert, or encode, her thoughts and perceptions about the sunset into words. The words are spoken into the telephone using the sounds and inflections of spoken language that convey the message. On the other end, the person listening to the description receives and decodes the sounds in order to visualize the image of the sunset described by the sender. This concept is illustrated in Figure 3-15, where the human communication is depicted by a person who encodes a concept using words spoken over airwaves.

Encoding also occurs in computer communication. Encoding between hosts must be in an appropriate form for the medium. Messages sent across the network are first converted into bits by the source. Each bit is encoded into a pattern using light waves, electrical impulses, or electromagnetic waves, depending on the network media over which the bits are transmitted. The destination receives and decodes the signals in order to interpret the message. In Figure 3-15, the source host computer captures an image of a sunset and then encodes it using electrical bit patterns. These signals are then sent to the destination host through a physical cable. The destination host receives the encoded bits and decodes them in order to display the image on its monitor.

Figure 3-15   Human and Computer Message Encoding and Decoding

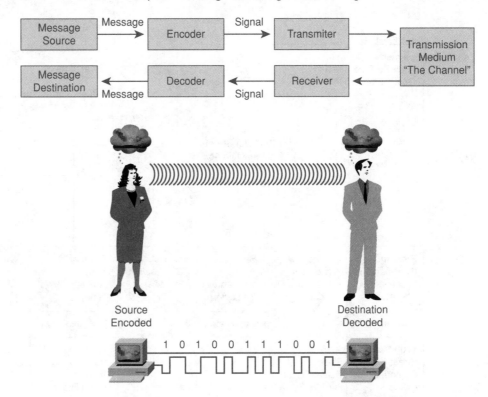

Message Formatting

When a message is sent from source to destination, it must use a specific format or structure. Message formats depend on the type of message and the channel that is used to deliver the message.

Letter writing is one of the most common forms of written human communication. For centuries, the agreed format for personal letters has not changed. In many cultures, a personal letter contains the following elements:

- An identifier of the recipient
- A salutation or greeting
- The message content
- A closing phrase
- An identifier of the sender

In addition to having the correct format, most personal letters must also be enclosed, or encapsulated, in an envelope for delivery. The envelope has the address of the sender and receiver on it, each located at the proper place on the envelope. If the destination address and formatting are not correct, the letter is not delivered.

The process of placing one message format (the letter) inside another message format (the envelope) is called *encapsulation*. De-encapsulation occurs when the process is reversed by the recipient and the letter is removed from the envelope. In Figure 3-16, the envelope has a commonly accepted addressing format as does the letter it encapsulates. Most letters conform to a format similar to this.

Figure 3-16 Message Formatting: Human Letter Encapsulation

Recipient (Destination) Location Address	Sender (Source) Location Address	Salutation (Start of Message Indicator)	Recipient (Destination) Identifier	Content of Letter (Encapsulated Data)	Sender (Source) Identifier	End of Frame (End of Message Indicator)
Envelope Addressing		Encapsulated Letter				
1400 Main Street Canton, Ohio 44203	4085 SE Pine Street Ocala, Florida 34471	Dear	Jane	I just returned from my trip. I thought you might like to see my pictures.	John	

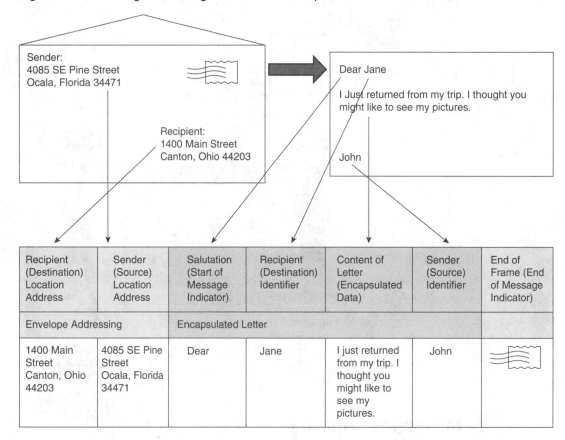

A letter writer uses an accepted format to ensure that the letter is delivered and understood by the recipient. In the same way, a message that is sent over a computer network follows specific format rules for it to be delivered and processed. Just as a letter is encapsulated in an envelope for delivery, so computer messages are encapsulated. Each computer message is encapsulated in a specific format, called a *frame*, before it is sent over the network. A frame acts like an envelope; it provides the address of the intended destination and the address of the source host.

The format and contents of a frame are determined by the type of message being sent and the channel over which it is communicated. Messages that are not correctly formatted are not successfully delivered to or processed by the destination host. Figure 3-17 shows a computer message with the frame addressing performing a function similar to the addresses on an envelope. The message encapsulated inside the frame contains information similar to that of a written letter.

Figure 3-17 Message Formatting: Computer Frame Encapsulation

Destination (Physical/ Hardware Address)	Source (Physical/ Hardware Address)	Start Flag (Start of Message Indicator)	Recipient (Destination Identifier)	Sender (Source Identifier)	Encapsulated Data (Bits)	End of Frame (End of Message Indicator)
Frame Addressing		Encapsulated Message				

Interactive Activity 3-4: Placing Communications Components (3.2.4.3)

In this interactive activity you place the components of a voice message into the proper location within a frame. Use file ia-3243 on the CD-ROM that accompanies this book to perform this interactive activity.

Message Size

Imagine what it would be like to read this book if all the text appeared as one long sentence; it would not be easy to read and comprehend. When people communicate with each other, the messages that they send are usually broken into smaller parts or sentences. These sentences are limited in size to what the receiving person can process at one time. An individual conversation is made up of many smaller sentences to ensure that each part of the message is received and understood. Figure 3-18 shows what can happen when a person speaks in run-on sentences and does not pause to break up the message into understandable pieces.

Figure 3-18 Message Size: Human Communication

Likewise, when a long message is sent from one host to another over a network, breaking the message into smaller pieces is necessary. The rules that govern the size of the pieces, or frames, communicated across the network are very strict. They can also be different, depending on the channel used. Frames that are too long or too short are not delivered.

The size restrictions of frames require the source host to break a long message into individual pieces that meet both the minimum and maximum size requirements. Each piece is encapsulated in a separate frame with the address information and is sent over the network. At the receiving host, the messages are de-encapsulated and put back together to be processed and interpreted. The host computer in the top portion of Figure 3-19 is sending frames that are too short or too long and the receiving computer cannot interpret them. This situation can happen when frames collide and also when the network interface card (NIC) is malfunctioning. The computer in the lower portion of Figure 3-19 is breaking up the message into appropriate-sized pieces so that the receiving computer can understand them.

Figure 3-19   Message Size: Computer Communication

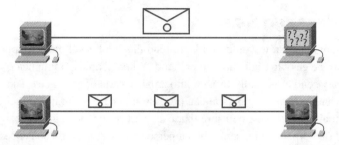

Message Timing

Another major factor that affects how well a message is received and understood is timing. People use timing to determine when to speak (access method), how fast or slow to talk (flow control), and how long to wait for a response (response timeout). These rules of engagement apply to both human and computer communications.

Access Method

An access method determines when someone is able to send a message. These timing rules are based on the environment. For example, if a person has something to say, he normally waits until no one else is talking before speaking. If two people talk at the same time, a collision of information occurs, and the two people need to back off and start again. These rules ensure that communication is successful.

In Figure 3-20, both people started talking at the same time and their messages interfered with each other, resulting in neither person understanding the other. Computers must also deal with this same type of communication issue. Computers need to have an *access method* in order to know when to begin sending messages and how to respond when errors occur.

Flow Control

Timing also affects how much information can be sent and the speed that it can be delivered. If one person speaks too quickly, it is difficult for the other person to hear and understand the message. The receiving person must ask the sender to slow down.

In network communication, a sending host can transmit messages at a faster rate than the destination host can receive and process. Source and destination hosts use flow control to negotiate correct timing for successful communication.

Figure 3-20   Message Timing

Response Timeout

If a person asks a question and does not hear a response within an acceptable amount of time, the person assumes that no answer is coming and reacts accordingly. The person might repeat the question, or might go on with the conversation. Hosts on the network also have rules that specify how long to wait for responses and what action to take if a response timeout occurs.

Message Patterns

Sometimes, a person wants to communicate information to a single individual. At other times, the person might need to send information to a group of people at the same time, or even to all people in the same area. A conversation between two people is an example of a one-to-one pattern of communication. When a group of recipients needs to receive the same message simultaneously, a one-to-many or one-to-all message pattern is necessary.

Times also occur when the sender of a message needs to be sure that the message is delivered successfully to the destination. In these cases, the recipient needs to return an acknowledgement to the sender. If no acknowledgement is required, the message pattern is referred to as *unacknowledged*. Hosts on a network use similar message patterns to communicate. Humans and computers use the concepts of unicast, multicast, and broadcast to accomplish various types of communications.

Unicast

A one-to-one message pattern is referred to as a *unicast*, meaning that only a single destination exists for the message. Figure 3-21 illustrates a human unicast where one individual is communicating directly with another individual. The computer equivalent is one host communicating directly with another, to transfer a file, for example. This type of communication is usually acknowledged.

Figure 3-21   Unicast (Human and Computer)

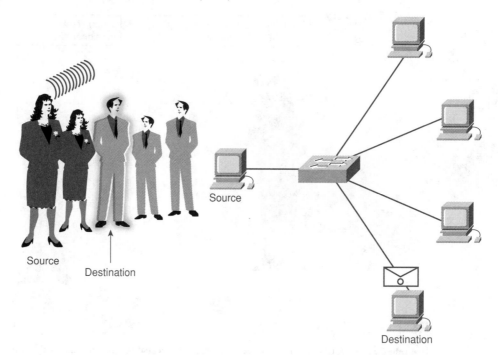

Multicast

When a host needs to send messages using a one-to-many pattern, it is referred to as a *multicast*. Multicasting is the delivery of the same message to a specific group of host destinations simultaneously. Figure 3-22 illustrates a human multicast where one individual communicates directly with several other individuals simultaneously. An example of this is when a teacher needs to communicate with the members of the math club in a classroom at school. Only the students in the math club need to listen to the communication. The computer equivalent is one host communicating with several other hosts. For example, a video server might send a video training session to only those computers whose users want to see it. This type of communication is usually unacknowledged because the sender does not need to be told specifically that everyone on the multicast group heard the message.

Broadcast

If all hosts on the network need to receive the message at the same time, a *broadcast* is used. Broadcasting represents a one-to-all message pattern. Additionally, hosts have requirements for acknowledged versus unacknowledged messages. Figure 3-23 illustrates a human broadcast where one individual communicates with all individuals in the classroom at the same time. An example of this is when a teacher introduces herself and tells the entire class her name. All students need to listen to the communication.

Figure 3-22   Multicast (Human and Computer)

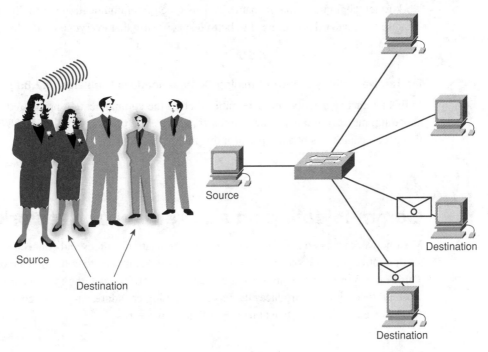

Figure 3-23   Broadcast (Human and Computer)

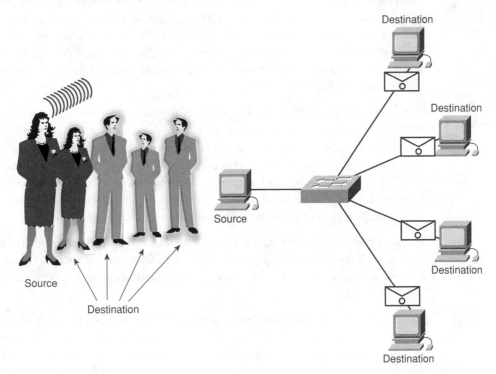

The computer equivalent of a broadcast is one host communicating with all other hosts on a local network to let them know what its name is. This type of communication is usually unacknowledged because the sender does not need to be told specifically that everyone on the local network heard the message.

Interactive Activity 3-5: Determining Communications Problems (3.2.8.2)

In this interactive activity you determine whether the communication problem described deals with encoding, message format, timing, unit size, or message pattern. Use file ia-3282 on the CD-ROM that accompanies this book to perform this interactive activity.

Communicating on a Wired Local Network

Most network users connect to a local network to share resources and connect to the Internet. This section introduces the concept of protocols to allow computers to communicate on a local network. This section covers the evolution and characteristics of Ethernet, the most widely used local-area network protocol. It also introduces the physical and logical addressing required to deliver messages on a LAN as well as the hierarchical nature of today's networks.

Importance of Protocols

Computers, just like humans, use rules, or protocols, in order to communicate. Protocols are especially important on a local network. In a wired environment, a local network is defined as an area where all hosts must "speak the same language" or in computer terms "share a common protocol." The most common set of protocols used on local wired networks is Ethernet. The Ethernet protocol defines many aspects of communication over the local network, including message format, message size, timing, encoding, and message patterns.

If everyone in the same room spoke a different language, they would not be able to communicate. Likewise, if devices in a local network did not use the same protocols, they would not be able to communicate. For example, consider a group of people speaking the same language, in this case Japanese. If a person comes into the room who does not speak Japanese, that person would not be able to talk with the others. Similarly, consider a group of computers on a local network communicating with Ethernet. If a computer is attached to the local network that is not using the Ethernet protocol, it would not be able to communicate with the other computers.

In the early days of networking, each vendor used its own, proprietary methods of interconnecting network devices and networking protocols. Equipment from one vendor could not communicate with equipment from another. Examples of proprietary protocols include those from IBM, NCR, DEC, and others.

As networks became more widespread, standards were developed that defined rules by which network equipment from different vendors operated. Several standard protocols evolved in more recent years, including Ethernet, ARCnet, and Token Ring. Standards are beneficial to networking in many ways:

- Facilitate design
- Simplify product development
- Promote competition
- Provide consistent interconnections

- Facilitate training

- Provide more vendor choices for customers

There is no official local networking standard protocol, but over time, one technology, Ethernet, has become more common than the others. It has become a *de facto standard*. This means that although other local network protocols exist, most local networks use Ethernet. Figure 3-24 shows how standards have evolved over time from proprietary ones to the primary one used today, which is Ethernet.

Figure 3-24   Network Protocol Standards Evolution

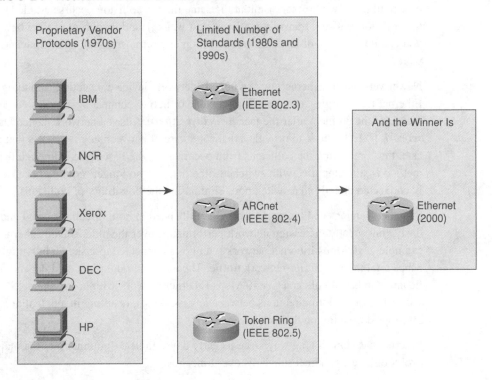

Standardization of Protocols

The *Institute of Electrical and Electronic Engineers (IEEE)*, pronounced eye-triple-e, maintains a number of local networking standards, including Ethernet and wireless standards. IEEE committees are responsible for approving and maintaining the standards for connections, media requirements, and communications protocols. Each technology standard is assigned a number that refers to the committee that is responsible for approving and maintaining the standard. The committee responsible for the Ethernet standards is 802.3. IEEE is headquartered in the United States although much of the committee work is done by volunteers from all over the world.

Since the creation of Ethernet in 1973, standards have evolved for specifying faster and more flexible versions of the Ethernet technology. This ability for Ethernet to improve over time is one of the main reasons that it has become so popular. Each version of Ethernet has an associated standard. For example, 802.3 100BaseT represents 100 Megabit per second (Mbps) Ethernet using the twisted-pair cable standard. The standard notation translates as follows:

- *100* is the speed in Mbps

- *Base* stands for *baseband* transmission

- *T* stands for the type of cable; in this case, it refers to twisted pair. The letter *F* would indicate fiber-optic cable.

Early versions of Ethernet were relatively slow at only 10 Mbps. The latest versions of Ethernet operate at 10 Gigabits per second and faster. This is a 1,000 times increase in speed.

Earlier versions of Ethernet used a shared medium where all hosts were connected to a common cable or a hub. With *shared Ethernet* networks, any host could begin transmitting at any time and collisions often occurred. The more hosts and traffic on the network, the greater the number of collisions. These versions of the Ethernet protocol depended on an access method known as *Carrier Sense, Multiple Access with Collision Detection (CSMA-CD)*. This means that multiple hosts are sensing (listening) to the carrier (cable) for a *transmission* from another host and if none is detected, they can begin transmitting. If two hosts transmit at the same time, a collision occurs and the hosts are able to detect the collision and stop transmitting. Each host waits a random period of time before retransmitting. As you can imagine, all of this collision detection and retransmission takes time and slows down the network.

Newer versions of Ethernet use "switched" network device connection technologies. The older shared Ethernet technologies, using a common cable or hub to connect hosts, allowed collisions to occur and corrected the problem after the fact. *Switched Ethernet* uses a network device known as a *local-area network (LAN) switch* to provide a dedicated circuit between any two hosts that need to communicate, thus preventing the collisions from occurring in the first place. Although the CSMA-CD access method is still supported with switched Ethernet, it is no longer required because each host is normally connected directly to a switch port, eliminating the possibility of collisions.

Switched versions of Ethernet can provide full speed in both directions (send and receive) simultaneously, thus greatly increasing network performance over the older shared Ethernet versions. As an example, a 10 Mbps Ethernet network with hosts connected to a shared hub might provide only 5 Mbps total throughput for network traffic. The actual throughput would depend on the amount of traffic and number of collisions. A 10 Mbps Ethernet network with hosts connected to a *switch* can provide 10 Mbps in both directions between any two hosts, resulting in a potential increase in speed up to 20 Mbps depending on the technology used.

Ethernet has come a long way since its early days. Table 3-1 summarizes the major improvements and evolution in the Ethernet standards over time.

Table 3-1   Ethernet Evolution and Standards Development

Year	Standard	Description
1973	Ethernet invented	Ethernet invented by Dr. Robert Metcalf of Xerox Corp.
1980	DIX standard	Digital Equipment Corp, Intel, and Xerox (DIX) release a standard for 10 Mbps Ethernet over coaxial cable.
1983	IEEE 802.3 10Base5	10 Mbps Ethernet over thick coaxial cable.
1985	IEEE 802.3a 10Base2	10 Mbps Ethernet over thin coaxial cable.
1990	IEEE 802.3i 10BaseT	10 Mbps Ethernet over unshielded twisted pair (UTP).
1993	IEEE 802.3j 10BaseF	10 Mbps Ethernet over fiber optic.
1995	IEEE 802.3u 100Base-xx	Fast Ethernet – 100 Mbps Ethernet over UTP and fiber (various standards).

Year	Standard	Description
1998	IEEE 802.3z 1000BaseX	Gigabit Ethernet over fiber optic.
1999	IEEE 802.3ab 1000BaseT	Gigabit Ethernet over twisted pair.
2002	IEEE 802.3ae 10GBase-xx	10 Gigabit Ethernet over fiber (various standards).
2006	IEEE 802.3an 10GBaseT	10 Gigabit Ethernet over UTP.

Physical Addressing

All communication requires a way to identify the source and destination. The source and destination in human communication are represented by names. When a name is called, the person with that name listens to the message and responds. Other people in the room might hear the message, but they ignore it because it is not addressed to them.

On Ethernet networks, a similar method exists for identifying source and destination hosts. Each host connected to an Ethernet network is assigned a physical address that serves to identify the host on the network.

Every Ethernet network interface has a physical address assigned to it when it is manufactured. This address is known as the *Media Access Control (MAC) address*. The MAC address identifies each source and destination host on the local network. The MAC address is a 48-bit address that is normally represented as 12 hexadecimal (hex) characters of 4 bits each. An example of a MAC address is 00-1B-53-8A-4E-01. The first six hex characters (24 bits) represent the manufacturer of the Ethernet interface and are known as the Organizational Unique Identifier (OUI). The last 24 bits identify a particular interface or NIC from that manufacturer. The OUI is assigned to an organization by the IEEE to ensure that MAC addresses are not duplicated. In the example 00-1B-53-8A-4E-01, 00-1B-53 indicates that this Ethernet interface was manufactured by Cisco. In this case the interface is on a Cisco router. Cisco devices display the MAC address using the format 001B.538A.4E01. The MAC address is the same in either case, just a different display format.

Ethernet networks are cable based, meaning that a copper or fiber-optic cable connects hosts and networking devices. This is the channel used for communications between the hosts.

When a host on an Ethernet network communicates, it sends frames containing its own MAC address as the source and the MAC address of the intended recipient. Any hosts that receive the frame will decode the frame and read the destination MAC address. If the destination MAC address matches the address configured on the NIC, it will process the message and store it for the host application to use. If the destination MAC address does not match the host MAC address, the NIC will ignore the message. Figure 3-25 shows a host sending a frame out on an Ethernet network. Although other hosts might see the frame, only the host to which it is addressed will accept it.

The newer Windows operating systems provide a method of displaying the host's MAC address using a GUI Network Connection application. You may also use the command line **ipconfig** command. The UNIX and Linux operating systems can also use GUI applications to view computer addresses but use the **ifconfig** command, instead, from the command line.

Figure 3-25   Computer Communication Using Physical Addresses

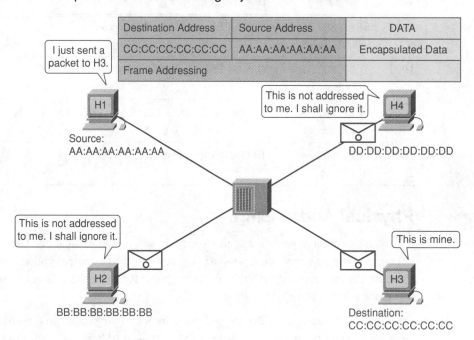

 Lab 3-2: Determine the MAC Address of a Host (3.3.3.2)

In this lab you use the **ipconfig /all** command to determine the MAC address of your computer. Refer to the hands-on lab in Part II of this *Learning Guide*. You may perform this lab now or wait until the end of the chapter.

Ethernet Communication

Ethernet protocol standards define many aspects of network communication including frame format, frame size, timing, and encoding.

When messages are sent between hosts on an Ethernet network, the hosts format the messages into the frame layout that is specified by the standards. Frames are one type of data grouping in a family referred to as *protocol data units (PDU)*.

The format for Ethernet frames specifies the location of the destination and source MAC addresses, and additional information including

- Preamble for sequencing and timing
- Start of frame delimiter
- Length and type of frame
- Frame check sequence to detect transmission errors

Figure 3-26 shows the structure of a standard IEEE 802.3 frame. Note that the maximum amount of data that the frame can contain is 1500 bytes.

Figure 3-26 Structure of the Ethernet Frame

Preamble	SFD	Destination MAC Address	Source MAC Address	Length/ Type	Encapsulated Data	FCS
7	1	6	6	2	46 to 1500	4

Table 3-2 lists the main components of the Ethernet frame and provides a brief description of their purpose or function.

Table 3-2   Fields in an Ethernet Frame

Frame Field	Bytes	Description / Contents
Preamble	7	Used to announce data transmission.
Start of Frame Delimiter (SFD)	1	Marks the end of the timing information and start of the frame.
Destination MAC Address	6	Contains the destination MAC address (receiver). The destination MAC address can be unicast (a specific host), multicast (a group of hosts), or broadcast (all hosts on the local network).
Source MAC Address	6	Contains the source MAC address (sender). This is the unicast address of the Ethernet node that transmitted the frame.
Length/Type	2	Supports two different uses. A type value indicates which protocol will receive the data. The length indicates the number of bytes of data that follows this field.
Encapsulated Data	46 to 1500	Contains the packet of information being sent. Ethernet requires each frame to be between 64 and 1518 bytes.
Frame Check Sequence (FCS)	4	Contains a 4-byte value that is created by the device that sends data and is recalculated by the destination device to check for damaged frames.

The size of Ethernet frames is limited to a maximum of 1518 bytes and a minimum size of 64 bytes. Frames that do not fall within these limits are not processed by the receiving hosts. By adding the number of bytes for the data (1500 bytes), destination MAC address (6 bytes), source MAC address (6 bytes), length/type (2 bytes), and the FCS (4 bytes) we arrive at the maximum Ethernet frame size of 1518 bytes. The preamble and the SFD are not counted in the total frame size because they are only there for timing and to indicate where the frame begins.

In addition to the frame format, size, and timing, Ethernet standards define how the bits making up the frames are encoded onto the channel. Bits are transmitted as either electrical impulses over copper cable or as light impulses over fiber-optic cable.

Interactive Activity 3-6: Building an Ethernet Frame (3.3.4.2)

In this interactive activity you build a standard IEEE 802.3 Ethernet frame based on the source and the destination device. Use file ia-3342 on the CD-ROM that accompanies this book to perform this interactive activity.

Hierarchical Design of Ethernet Networks

Imagine how difficult communication would be if the only way to send a message to someone was to use the person's name. If there were no street addresses, cities, towns, or country boundaries, delivering a message to a specific person across the world would be nearly impossible. Figure 3-27 shows the hierarchy of land boundaries that allow the delivery of mail to a person living in a particular city based on knowing where that city is located in the world.

Figure 3-27   Continent, Country, Province, and City Boundary Hierarchy

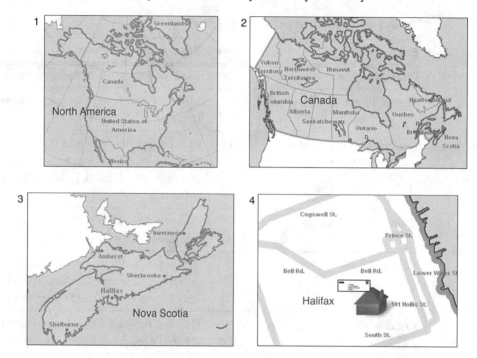

On an Ethernet network, the host MAC address is similar to a person's name. A MAC address indicates the individual identity of a specific host, but it does not indicate where on the network the host is located. If all hosts on the Internet (more than 400 million of them) were each identified by only their unique MAC address, imagine how difficult locating a single one would be.

Additionally, Ethernet technology generates a large amount of broadcast traffic in order for hosts to communicate. Broadcasts are sent to all hosts within a single network. Broadcasts consume bandwidth and slow network performance. Imagine what would happen if the millions of hosts attached to the Internet were all in one Ethernet network and were using broadcasts. Communication would be nearly impossible.

Another way to understand the concept of Ethernet broadcasts is with a phone analogy. What if the process of answering the phone involved having everyone's phone ring every time anyone wanted to make a call to anyone else? Everyone has to answer the phone but unless they hear their name being called from the other end, they hang up. Even in a small town this broadcast behavior would be overwhelming, not just to the system, but to everyone on the system trying to answer all those rings.

For these reasons, large Ethernet networks consisting of many hosts are not efficient. Dividing larger networks into smaller, more manageable pieces is better. One way to divide larger networks is to use a hierarchical design model.

In networking, hierarchical design is used to group devices into multiple networks that are organized in a layered approach. It consists of smaller, more manageable groups that allow local traffic to remain local. Only traffic that is destined for other networks is moved to a higher layer.

A hierarchical, layered design provides increased efficiency, optimization of function, and increased speed. It allows the network to scale or grow as required because additional local networks can be added without impacting the performance of the existing ones.

The hierarchical design has three basic layers:

- **Access layer**: To provide connections to hosts in a local Ethernet network

- **Distribution layer**: To interconnect the smaller local networks

- **Core layer**: High-speed connections between distribution layer devices

With this new hierarchical design comes a need for a logical addressing scheme that can identify the location of a host. This is the Internet Protocol (IP) addressing scheme. Figure 3-28 shows how networks can also be hierarchical in nature.

To expand the telephone analogy, the telephone network is an extremely large physical network but it is divided logically using a phone number addressing scheme. To properly route a call, a phone number consists of a hierarchy structured using prefixes (local access networks), area codes (distribution networks), and country codes (core networks). If you make a long-distance call, you must include the area code in the number you dial. Doing so ensures that the telephone system knows to route your call to the right area. This analogy illustrates a logical division of a physical network.

Logical Addressing

A person's given name usually does not change. A person's address, on the other hand, relates to where they live and can change. On a host, the MAC address, also known as the physical or hardware address, does not change; it is physically assigned to the host NIC. The *physical address* remains the same regardless of where the host is placed on the network.

The IP address is similar to the mailing address of a person. It is known as a *logical address* because it is assigned logically based on where the host is located. A network administrator assigns the IP address to each host based on the local network where it resides. Both the physical MAC and logical IP addresses are required for a computer to communicate on a hierarchical network, just as both the name and address of a person are required to deliver a letter.

IP addresses contain two parts: the local network and the host. The network portion of the IP address will be the same for all hosts connected to the same local network. The second part of the IP address identifies the individual host. Within the same local network, the host portion of the IP address is unique to each host.

In Figure 3-29, host H3 is on network 192.168.200 and the individual host portion of the address on that network is .3. Hosts H1, H2, and H4 are also on the 192.168.200 network. Host H8 is on the 192.168.1 network and its host address is .4. Note that the host portion of the address for host H4 (.4) is the same as for host H8 (.4). This is not a problem because they live on different networks using a hierarchical network design where a two-part address is employed. When a packet is sent to H4's IP address, it is sent to 192.168.200.4. When a packet is sent to H8's IP address, it is sent to 192.168.1.4.

Figure 3-28 Core, Distribution, and Access Layer Network Hierarchy

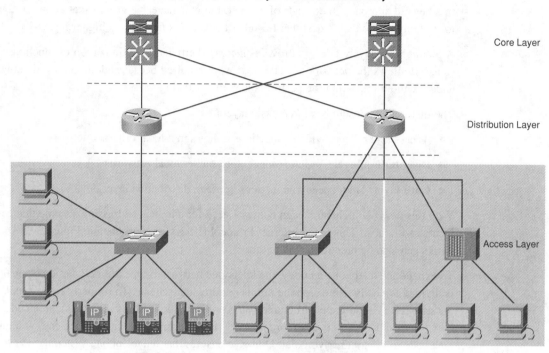

 Lab 3-3: Determine the IP Address of a Computer (3.3.6.2)

In this lab you use the **ipconfig /all** command to display the IP address of your computer. Refer to the hands-on lab in Part II of this *Learning Guide*. You may perform this lab now or wait until the end of the chapter.

Access, Distribution, and Core Layers and Devices

IP traffic is managed based on the characteristics and devices associated with each of the three layers: access, distribution, and core. The IP address is used to determine whether traffic should remain local or be moved up through the layers of the hierarchical network.

The access layer provides a connection point to the network for end-user devices and allows multiple hosts to connect to other hosts through a network device. Typically, all devices within a single access layer area will have the same network portion of the IP address.

If a message is destined for a local host, based on the network portion of the IP address, the message remains local. If it is destined for a different network, it is passed up to the distribution layer. Hubs and switches provide the connection to the distribution layer devices, usually a router.

The distribution layer provides a connection point for separate local networks and controls the flow of information between the networks. It typically contains more powerful switches than the access layer as well as routers for routing between networks. In a three-layer design, distribution layer devices also control the type and amount of traffic that flows from the access layer to the core layer.

Figure 3-29 Network Address and Host Address

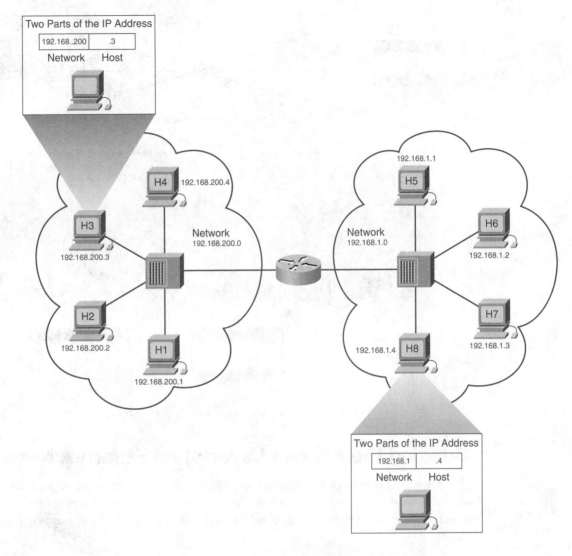

The core layer is a high-speed backbone layer with redundant (backup) connections. It is responsible for transporting large amounts of data between multiple end networks. Core layer devices typically include very powerful, high-speed switches and routers. The main goal of the core layer is to transport data quickly. Hubs, switches, and routers are discussed in more detail in the next two sections "Building the Access Layer of an Ethernet Network" and "Building the Distribution Layer of a Network."

Figure 3-30 shows a conceptual diagram of the three-layer network design and also provides photographs of the type of devices that represent the icons shown.

Interactive Activity 3-7: Working with Addresses, Network Components, and Layers (3.3.7.2)

In this interactive activity you determine which addresses, network components, and layers are necessary to accomplish each task. Use file ia-3372 on the CD-ROM that accompanies this book to perform this interactive activity.

Figure 3-30   Access, Distribution, and Core Layers and Devices

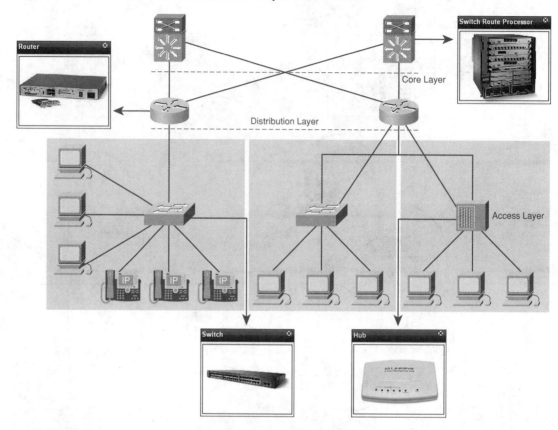

Building the Access Layer of an Ethernet Network

The portion of the network that the end user typically associates with is the access layer. This section describes the network devices at this layer, such as hubs and switches, and their functions. It also discusses the interaction between logical and physical addressing to deliver messages and introduces ARP.

Access Layer

The *access layer* is the most basic level of the network. It is the part of the network in which people gain access to other hosts and to shared files and printers. The access layer is composed of host devices, as well as the first line of networking devices to which they are attached.

Networking devices enable us to connect many hosts with each other and also provide these hosts access to services offered over the network. Unlike the simple network consisting of two hosts connected by a single cable, in the access layer, each host is connected to a networking device.

Within an Ethernet network, each host is able to connect directly to an access layer networking device using a point-to-point cable. These cables are manufactured to meet specific Ethernet standards and are used to connect the host NIC to a port on the networking device. Several types of networking devices can be used to connect hosts at the access layer, including Ethernet hubs and switches. Some devices, such as IP phones, should be attached only to switches in order to function properly.

An increasing number of business and home users are installing wireless access to allow users to connect without the requirement for cumbersome wires. This wireless connectivity functions at the access layer, and the access points used to allow the end users to connect are access layer devices.

Function of Hubs

A *hub* is one type of networking device that is installed at the access layer of an Ethernet network. Hubs contain multiple ports that are used to connect hosts to the network. They are simple networking devices that do not have the necessary electronics to decode the messages sent between hosts and therefore cannot determine which host should get any particular message. A hub simply accepts electronic signals from one port and regenerates (or repeats) the same message out of all the other ports.

Recall that the NIC on a host accepts messages only addressed to the correct MAC address. Hosts ignore messages that are not addressed to them. Only the host specified in the destination MAC address of the frame processes the message and responds to the sender. Although all hosts receive the message, only the one that it is destined for accepts and processes it, as shown in Figure 3-31.

Figure 3-31   Message Delivery in a Hub-Based Network

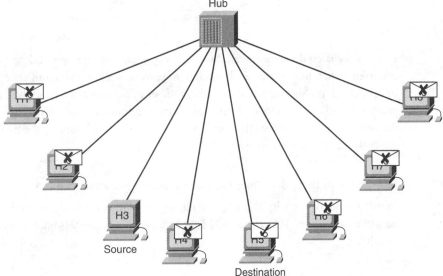

All the ports on the Ethernet hub connect to the same channel to send and receive messages. Because all hosts must share the bandwidth available on that channel, a hub is referred to as a *shared-bandwidth* device.

Because an Ethernet hub consists of a single channel, only one message can be sent through the hub at a time. If two or more hosts connected to a hub attempt to send a message at the same time, the electronic signals that make up the messages collide with each other on the channel.

A collision causes the messages to become garbled and unreadable by the hosts. A hub does not decode the messages; therefore it does not detect that the message is garbled and repeats it out all the ports, wasting valuable bandwidth. The area of the network where a host can receive a garbled message resulting from a collision is known as a *collision domain*. Figure 3-32 illustrates such a collision domain.

Figure 3-32   Collision Domain

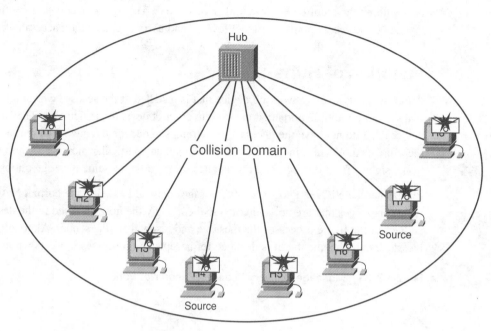

Inside a collision domain, when a host receives a garbled message, it detects that a collision has occurred. When this occurs, each sending host waits a short amount of time and then attempts to send, or retransmit, the message again. As the number of hosts connected to the hub increases, so does the chance of collisions. More collisions cause more retransmissions. Excessive retransmissions can clog the network and slow down network traffic. For this reason, limiting the number of hosts within a single collision domain is necessary.

Interactive Activity 3-8: Data Flow in a Hubbed Network (3.4.2.3)

In this interactive activity you practice identifying which hosts will receive a message on a hub-based network. Use file ia-3423 on the CD-ROM that accompanies this book to perform this interactive activity.

Function of Switches

Because of the problems associated with being a shared bandwidth device, hubs are no longer commonly deployed at the access layer. Most modern Ethernet networks employ a device known as an Ethernet switch to connect hosts into the network. Like a hub, a switch connects multiple hosts to the network. Unlike a hub, a switch can make decisions based on the information contained within the Ethernet frame and can forward a message to a specific host. When a host sends a message to another host on the switch, the switch accepts and decodes the frames to read the physical (MAC) address portion of the message.

A table on the switch, called a *MAC address table*, contains a list of all the active ports and the host MAC addresses that are attached to them. When a message is sent between hosts, the switch checks to see whether the destination MAC address is in this table. If it is, the switch builds a temporary connection, called a circuit, between the source and destination ports. This new circuit provides a dedicated channel over which the two hosts can communicate. Other hosts attached to the switch do not share the bandwidth on this channel and do not receive messages that are not addressed to them. A new circuit is built for every new conversation between hosts. These separate circuits allow many conversations to take place at the same time, without collisions occurring.

In Figure 3-33 host H3 is connected to fast Ethernet port fa0/3. H3, with a MAC address of 00E0:FE00:3333, and is sending a frame to host H7 that is connected to port fa0/7 at MAC address 00E0:FE00:7777. The MAC address table for the switch is shown in Table 3-3. Please note that the MAC addresses shown are for illustration only. The MAC addresses in the table are the MAC addresses of the connected device and are not related to the switch port number. Because the destination MAC address is already in the MAC address table, the switch forwards the message to the correct destination.

Table 3-3   A MAC Address Table

Switch Port	Device MAC Address
fa 0/1	00E0:FE00:1111
fa 0/2	00E0:FE00:2222
fa 0/3	00E0:FE00:3333
fa 0/4	00E0:FE00:4444
fa 0/5	00E0:FE00:5555
fa 0/6	00E0:FE00:6666
fa 0/7	00E0:FE00:7777
fa 0/8	00E0:FE00:8888

If the destination MAC address is not in the table, the switch does not have the necessary information to create an individual circuit. When the switch cannot determine where the destination host is located, it uses a process called *flooding* to forward the message out to all attached hosts. Each host compares the destination MAC address in the message to its own MAC address, but only the host with the correct destination address processes the message and responds to the sender.

Figure 3-33   Message Delivery in a Switched Network

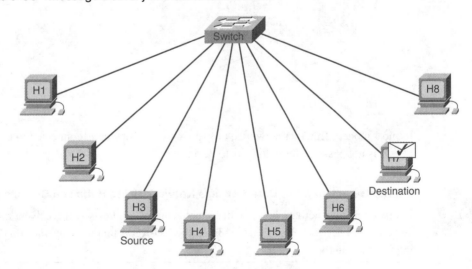

A switch builds the MAC address table by examining the source MAC address of each frame that is sent between hosts. When a new host sends a message or responds to a flooded message, the switch immediately learns its MAC address and the port to which it is connected. The table is dynamically updated each time a new source MAC address is read by the switch. In this way, a switch quickly learns the MAC addresses of all attached hosts.

In this case the destination MAC address is not in the MAC address table and the message must be flooded out all ports except the one that the message was received on. When H7 responds to the original message, the switch updates its MAC address table with the MAC address of H7 and associates it with the inbound port, fa0/7. These entries are not normally permanent and expire after a certain period of time. This reduces the chance that the switch will have a stale entry in the MAC address table, which could cause it to send frames out the wrong port.

Sometimes, connecting another networking device, such as a hub, to a switch port is necessary. Doing so increases the number of hosts that can be connected to the network. When a hub is connected to a switch port, the switch associates the MAC addresses of all hosts connected to that hub with the single port on the switch. Occasionally, one host on the attached hub sends a message to another host attached to the same hub. In this case, the switch receives the frame and checks the table to see where the destination host is located. If both the source and destination hosts are located on the same port, the switch does not forward or flood the message out any other port.

When a hub is connected to a switch port, collisions can occur. If this happens, the hub forwards the damaged message, resulting from the collision, to all ports. The switch receives the garbled message, but, unlike a hub, a switch does not forward the damaged messages. As a result, every switch port creates a separate collision domain. This is shown in Figure 3-34. The creation of multiple collision domains is good because it limits the number of hosts contained in each. The fewer hosts contained in a collision domain, the less likely it is that a collision will occur.

Figure 3-34   Collision Domains in a Switched Network

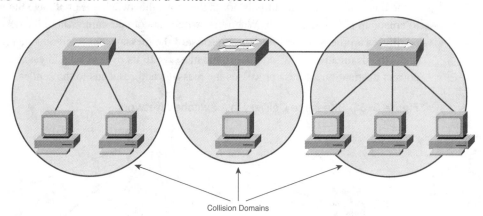

Collision Domains

In most modern Ethernet networks, only a single host device is connected to each switch port. In this case it is not possible for collisions to occur.

Interactive Activity 3-9: Data Flow in a Network Using Hubs and Switches (3.4.3.4)

In this interactive activity you practice identifying which hosts will receive a message on a hub and switch-based network. Use file ia-3434 on the CD-ROM that accompanies this book to perform this interactive activity.

Broadcast Messaging

When hosts are connected using a hub or a switch, a single *local network* is created. Within the local network often one host needs to be able to send messages to all the other hosts at the same time. It can perform this task using a broadcast message. Broadcasts are useful when a host needs to find information without knowing exactly which other host can supply the information. Broadcasts are also used to send information to all hosts on a network.

A message can contain only one destination MAC address. So, how is it possible for a host to contact every other host on the local network without sending out a separate message to each individual MAC? To solve this problem, broadcast messages are sent to a unique MAC address that is recognized by all hosts. The broadcast MAC address is a 48-bit address made up of all 1s. Because of their length, MAC addresses are usually represented in *hexadecimal* notation. The broadcast MAC address in hexadecimal notation is FFFF.FFFF.FFFF. Each F in the hexadecimal notation represents four ones (1111) in the binary address. Figure 3-35 shows a new host using broadcast messaging to announce its presence on the network.

Figure 3-35   Sending a Broadcast Message

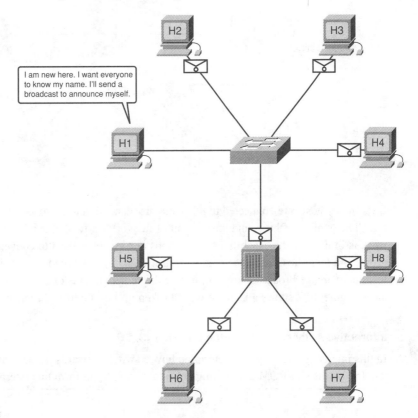

When a host receives a message addressed to the broadcast address, it accepts and processes the message as if the message were addressed directly to it, as shown in Figure 3-36.

When a host sends a broadcast message, hubs and switches forward the message to every connected host within the same local network. For this reason, a local network is also referred to as a *broadcast domain*.

Figure 3-36 Replying to a Broadcast Message

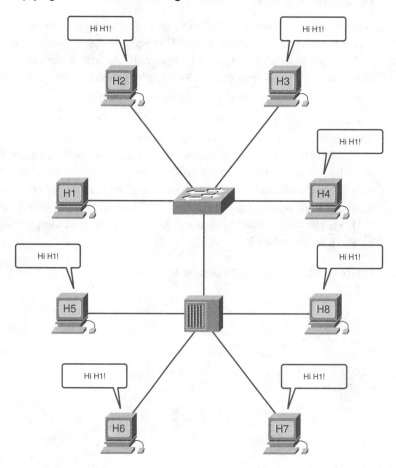

If too many hosts are connected to the same broadcast domain, broadcast traffic can become excessive. The number of hosts and the amount of network traffic that can be supported on the local network is limited by the capabilities of the hubs and switches used to connect them. As a local network grows and more hosts are added, network traffic, including broadcast traffic, increases. Dividing one local network, or broadcast domain, into multiple networks is often necessary to improve performance. Figure 3-37 shows a large network broken up into multiple broadcast domains.

Interactive Activity 3-10: Switch Behavior (3.4.5.1)

In this interactive activity you determine how a switch forwards frames based on a scenario. Use file ia-3451 on the CD-ROM that accompanies this book to perform this interactive activity.

Figure 3-37   Broadcast Domains

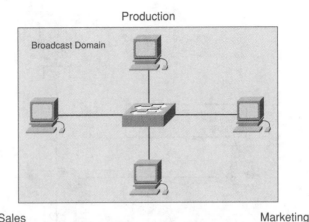

Production

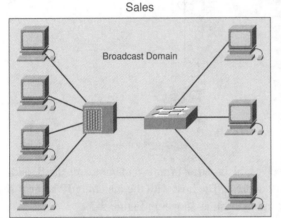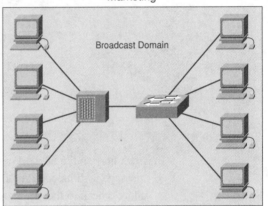

Sales   Marketing

MAC and IP Addresses

On a local Ethernet network, a NIC accepts a frame only if the destination address is either the broadcast MAC address or corresponds to the MAC address of the NIC itself. Most network applications, however, rely on the logical destination IP address to identify the location of the servers and clients.

Each Ethernet interface builds a table that contains the IP address and corresponding MAC address of all hosts that are active on the same local network. This table is known as the *Address Resolution Protocol (ARP) table*. The information in this table is used to encapsulate data before sending it out onto the network. This table is stored in RAM and the information it contains has a limited lifetime.

If the sending host knows the logical IP address of the destination host but not the MAC address, it must determine the MAC address before any communication between the source and destination host can occur. The sending host can use an IP protocol called Address Resolution Protocol (ARP) to discover the MAC address of any host on the same local network.

Address Resolution Protocol (ARP)

Address Resolution Protocol (ARP) uses a three-step process to discover and store the MAC address of a host on the local network when only the IP address of the host is known.

1. The sending host creates and sends a frame addressed to a broadcast MAC address. Contained in the frame is a message with the IP address of the intended destination host, as shown in Figure 3-38.

Figure 3-38   ARP Request

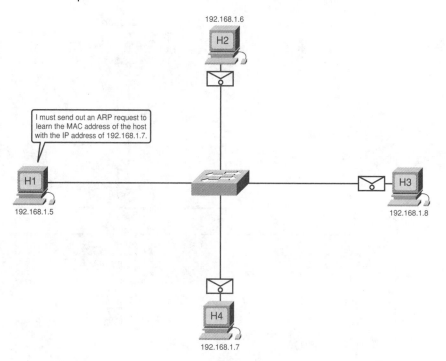

2. Each host on the network receives the broadcast frame and compares the IP address inside the message with its configured IP address. The host with the matching IP address sends its MAC address back to the original sending host, as shown in Figure 3-39.

Figure 3-39   ARP Reply

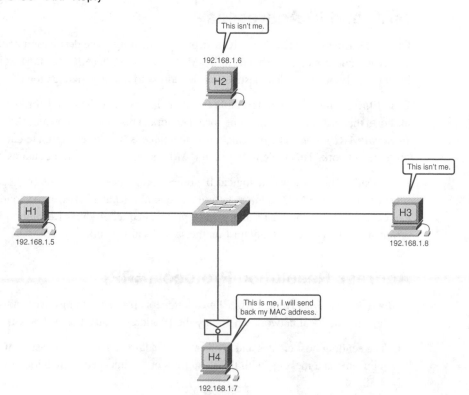

3. The sending host receives the message and stores the MAC address and IP address information in a table called an ARP table. After the sending host has the MAC address of the destination host in its ARP table, it can send frames directly to the destination without first having to send an ARP request, as shown in Figure 3-40.

Figure 3-40   Updated ARP Information

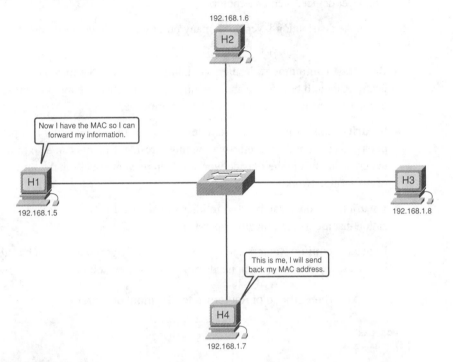

All hosts that hear the broadcast ARP request use this information to update their ARP tables with the sender's information.

Building the Distribution Layer of a Network

To interconnect multiple local networks, a distribution layer is required. This section describes the purpose of the distribution layer and the network devices that operate there. It also describes the process of sending packets outside the local network using the router as a default gateway.

Distribution Layer

As networks grow, dividing one local network into multiple access layer networks is often necessary. Many ways exist for dividing networks based on different criteria, including the following:

- Physical location

- Logical function

- Security requirements

- Application requirements

The *distribution layer* connects these independent local networks and controls the traffic flowing between them. It is responsible for ensuring that traffic between hosts on the local network stays local.

Only traffic that is destined for other networks is passed on. The distribution layer can also filter incoming and outgoing traffic for security and traffic management.

Networking devices that make up the distribution layer are designed to interconnect networks, not individual hosts. Individual hosts are connected to the network via access layer devices, such as hubs and switches. The access layer devices in each network are in turn connected to each other via a distribution layer device, such as a router.

Routers in the distribution layer serve many purposes, as shown in Figure 3-41. These include the following:

- **Broadcast containment**: Routers contain broadcasts in the local network where they must be heard. Although broadcasts are a required part of network communication, too many broadcasts can have a serious impact on network performance.

- **Security**: Routers provide a certain level of security by separating and protecting groups of computers where confidential information might reside. Routers can also hide the addresses of internal computers from the outside world to help prevent attacks and control who can get into or out of the local network.

- **Locations**: Routers can be used to interconnect local networks at various locations of an organization that are geographically separated.

- **Logical grouping**: Routers can be used to logically group users, such as departments within a company, who have common needs or for access to resources.

Figure 3-41   The Purpose of Routers in the Distribution Layer

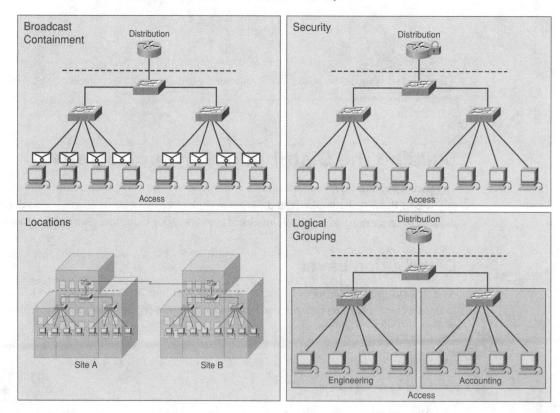

Function of Routers

A *router* is a networking device that connects a local network to other local networks. At the distribution layer of the network, routers direct traffic and perform other functions critical to efficient network operation. Routers, like switches, are able to decode and read the messages that are sent to them. Unlike switches, which only decode (unencapsulate) the frame containing the MAC address information, routers decode the packet that is encapsulated within the frame.

The packet contains the IP addresses of the destination and source hosts, as well as the actual message data being sent between them. Figure 3-42 shows the structure of a frame and the IP packet that it contains. The router reads the network portion of the destination IP address and uses it to find which one of the attached networks is the best way to forward the message to the destination.

Figure 3-42   IP Datagram

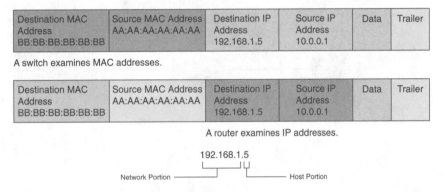

Anytime the network portion of the IP addresses of the source and destination hosts do not match, a router must be used to forward the message. For example, if a host located on network 1.1.1.0 needs to send a message to a host on network 5.5.5.0, the host will forward the message to the router. The router receives the message and unencapsulates it to read the destination IP address to determine which network it needs to be sent to. The router then determines how to forward the message to that network through one of its network interfaces. It re-encapsulates the packet back into a frame and forwards the frame on to its destination.

Each port, or interface, on a router connects to a different network. Every router contains a table of all locally connected networks and the interfaces that connect to them. These routing tables can also contain information about the routes, or paths, that the router can use to reach other remote networks that are not locally attached.

When a host sends a message to another host on the same local network, the destination host receives the message because it is connected to the same medium. If a message is sent to a host on a different network, as shown in Figure 3-43, the message must be sent to a router for processing.

When a router receives a frame, it decodes the frame to get to the packet containing the destination IP address. It matches the network portion of the destination address to all the networks that are contained in the routing table as shown in Figure 3-44. If the destination network address is in the table, the router encapsulates the packet in a new frame in order to send it out. It forwards the new frame out of the interface associated with the path and to the destination network, as shown in Figure 3-45. The process of forwarding the packets toward their final destination network is called *routing*.

Figure 3-43 Sending a Message to a Host on a Different Network

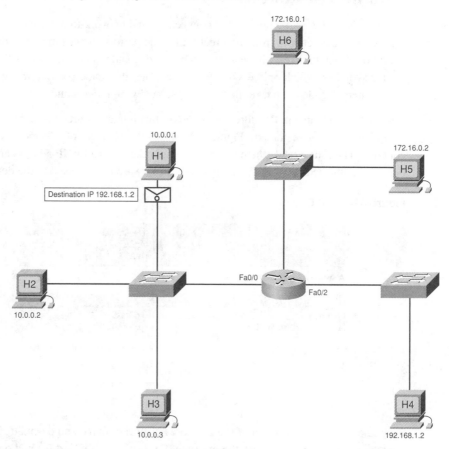

Figure 3-44 Consulting the Routing Table

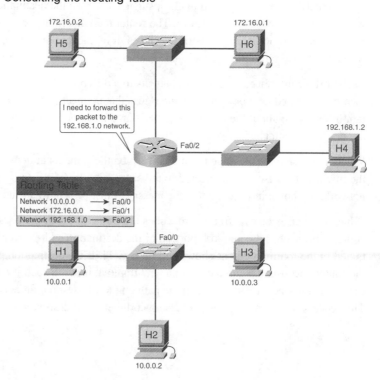

Figure 3-45   Routing the Packet

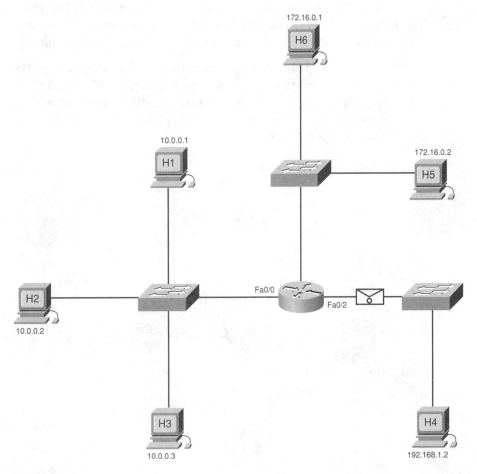

Router interfaces do not forward messages that are addressed to the broadcast MAC address. As a result, local network broadcasts are not sent across routers to other local networks.

 Lab 3-4: IP Addresses and Network Communication (3.5.2.2)

In this lab you build a simple network and work with host IP addresses to see the effect on network communication. Refer to the hands-on lab in Part II of this *Learning Guide*. You may perform this lab now or wait until the end of the chapter.

Default Gateway

The method that a host uses to send messages to a destination on a remote network differs from the way a host sends a message to another host on the same local network. When a host needs to send a message to another host located on the same network, it will forward the message directly. A host uses ARP to discover the MAC address of the destination host. Once the MAC address of the destination host is known, the sending host includes the destination IP address within the packet and encapsulates the packet into a frame containing the MAC address of the destination. This frame is then forwarded out onto the network.

When a host needs to send a message to a remote network, it must use the router. The host includes the IP address of the destination host within the packet just like before. However, when it encapsulates the packet into a frame, it uses the MAC address of the router as the destination for the frame. In this way, the router will receive and accept the frame based on the MAC address.

A host is given the IP address of the router through the *default gateway* address configured in its TCP/IP settings. The default gateway address is the address of the router interface connected to the same local network as the source host. All hosts on the local network use the default gateway address to send messages to the router. For example, in Figure 3-46, the IP address of H2 is 192.168.1.2 and the default gateway is 192.168.1.254.

Figure 3-46   Default Gateway

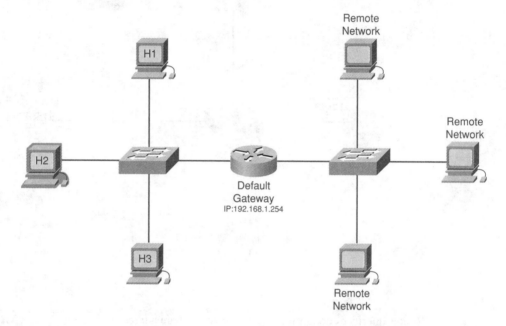

After the host knows the default gateway IP address, it can use ARP to determine the MAC address. The MAC address of the router interface is then placed in any frames that are destined for another network.

Ensuring that the correct default gateway is configured on each host on the local network is important. If no default gateway is configured in the host TCP/IP settings, or if the wrong default gateway is specified, messages addressed to hosts on remote networks cannot be delivered.

Interactive Activity 3-11: Configuring a Default Gateway Address (3.5.3.2)

In this interactive activity you configure the proper default gateway address for multiple hosts. Use file ia-3532 on the CD-ROM that accompanies this book to perform this interactive activity.

Tables Maintained by Routers

Routers move information between local and remote networks. To do this, routers must use both ARP and routing tables to store information, as shown in Figure 3-47. ARP tables map the IP addresses of the remote host to their MAC addresses as shown in Table 3-4. *Routing tables* are not concerned with the addresses of individual hosts. Routing tables contain the addresses of networks and the best path to reach those networks as shown in Table 3-5.

Figure 3-47 ARP and Routing Tables

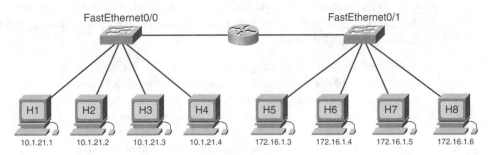

Table 3-4 ARP Table Information

IP Address	MAC Address	Interface
10.1.21.1	0072.5e34.6bd2	FastEthernet 0/0
10.1.21.2	0b76.ac13.a132	FastEthernet 0/0
10.1.21.3	00c0.dee5.7ec3	FastEthernet 0/0
10.1.21.4	Oaac.de43.0013	FastEthernet 0/0
172.16.1.3	00c3.cd45.00c3	FastEthernet 0/1
172.16.1.4	0d01.cde2.456e	FastEthernet 0/1
172.16.1.5	000e.456d.435c	FastEthernet 0/1
172.16.1.6	0124.54cd.ae56	FastEthernet 0/1

Table 3-5 Routing Table Information

Type	Network	Port
C	10.0.0.0/8	FastEthernet 0/0
C	172.16.0.0/16	FastEthernet 0/1

Entries can be made to the routing table in two ways:

- Dynamically updated by information received from other routers in the network

- Manually entered by a network administrator

Routers use the routing tables to determine which interface to use to forward a message to its intended destination. If the router cannot determine where to forward a message, it will drop it. To prevent this from occurring, network administrators usually configure a default route in the routing table. A *default route* is the interface through which the router forwards a packet containing an unknown destination IP network address. This default route usually connects to another router that can forward the packet toward its final destination network.

A router forwards a frame to one of two places:

- A directly connected network containing the actual destination host

- Another router on the path to reach the destination host

When a router encapsulates the frame to forward it onto a directly connected Ethernet network, it must include a destination MAC address. This is the MAC address of the actual destination host, if the destination host is part of a network locally connected to the router. Routers obtain these MAC addresses from ARP tables.

In Figure 3-48, host 1 is sending a message to a host that is not on the same network. Because the MAC address of the remote host is not known, the sending host sends the message to the default gateway, as shown in Figure 3-49, for delivery by the router. The default gateway is part of the same local network, so the sending host consults its ARP table for the correct information.

Figure 3-48   Message Destined for a Host on Another Network

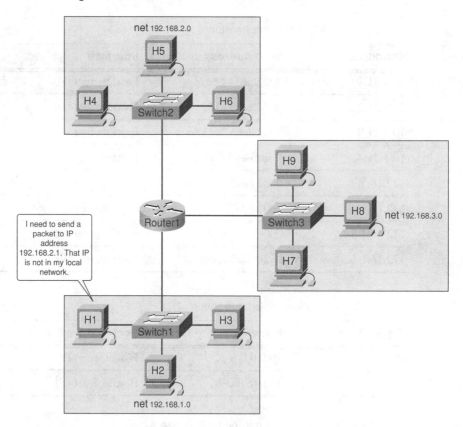

After the router has the packet, it must decide what to do with it. The router examines the packet header to gather the IP information. When the router determines the network that the remote host is on, it checks to see whether it has information on how to deliver the message. In Figure 3-50, the remote host is part of a network that is directly connected to the router. Because the host is directly connected, the router consults its ARP table and encapsulates the data with the destination IP and MAC address then forwards the message to the remote host.

Figure 3-49   Sending the Message to the Default Gateway for Delivery

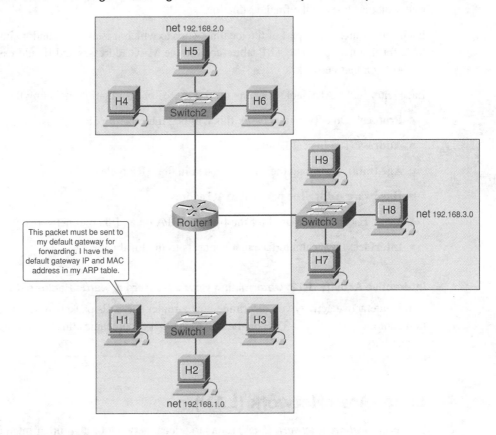

Figure 3-50   Forwarding the Message to the Remote Host

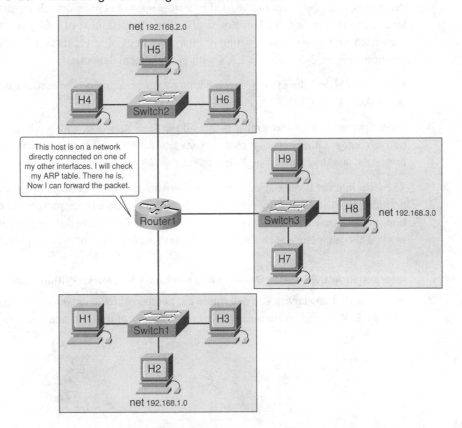

If the remote host is not on a directly connected network, the router will pass the message to another router that is closer to the final destination.

Each router interface is part of the local network to which it is attached and maintains its own ARP table for that network. The ARP tables contain the MAC addresses and IP addresses of all the individual hosts on that network.

Each entry in the ARP table contains several pieces of information including the following:

- **Protocol**: On a TCP/IP network this will be "Internet" for IP
- **Address**: The logical IP address
- **Age (min)**: How long the entry has been in the ARP table
- **Hardware Addr**: The physical MAC address
- **Type**: Encapsulation used for the frame (ARPA on an Ethernet network)
- **Interface**: Physical interface that connects to the local network

Interactive Activity 3-12: Determining How a Router Forwards Packets (3.5.4.3)

In this interactive activity you determine how a router forwards packets based on source and destination addresses. Use file ia-3543 on the CD-ROM that accompanies this book to perform this interactive activity.

Local-Area Network (LAN)

The term *local-area network (LAN)* refers to a local network or a group of interconnected local networks that are under the same administrative control. In the early days of networking, LANs were defined as small networks that existed in a single physical location. Although LANs can be a single local network installed in a home or small office, the definition of LAN has evolved to include interconnected local networks consisting of many hundreds of hosts, installed in multiple buildings and locations. Figure 3-51 shows a LAN with a single local network.

Figure 3-52 shows the same network with a router breaking up the network into three separate local networks.

The important point to remember is that all the local networks within a LAN are under one administrative control. Other common characteristics of LANs are that they typically use Ethernet or wireless protocols, and they support high data rates.

The term intranet is often used to refer to a private LAN that belongs to an organization and is designed to be accessible by only the organization's members, employees, or others with authorization. Intranets use technology normally found on the Internet to deliver information on a private network. This can include such things as web servers accessible only to employees.

Interactive Activity 3-13: Determining the Local Networks Within a LAN (3.5.5.2)

In this interactive activity you determine the number of local networks within a LAN. Use file ia-3552 on the CD-ROM that accompanies this book to perform this interactive activity.

Figure 3-51   LAN with a Single Local Network

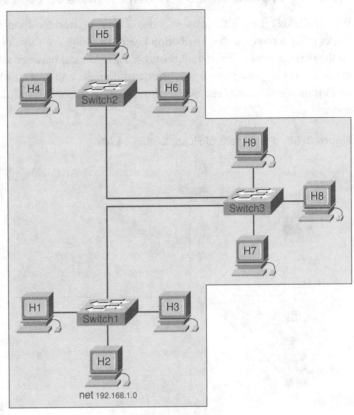

Figure 3-52   LAN with Multiple Local Networks

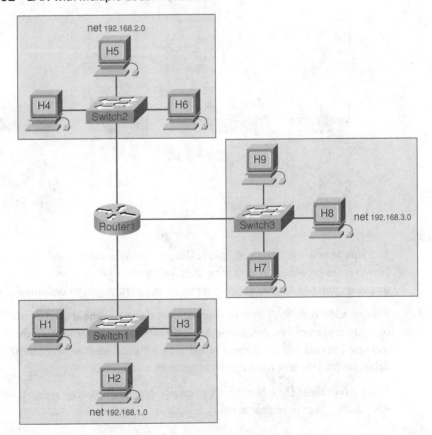

Adding Hosts to Local and Remote Networks

Within a LAN, placing all hosts on a single local network or dividing them up between multiple networks using a router at the distribution layer is possible, as shown in Figure 3-53. The choice depends on the desired results. Placing all hosts on a single local network allows them to be seen by all other hosts. This is because there is one broadcast domain, and hosts use ARP to find each other. Unfortunately, this setup can also lead to excessive broadcast traffic and degraded network performance.

Figure 3-53 Placement of Hosts Within a LAN

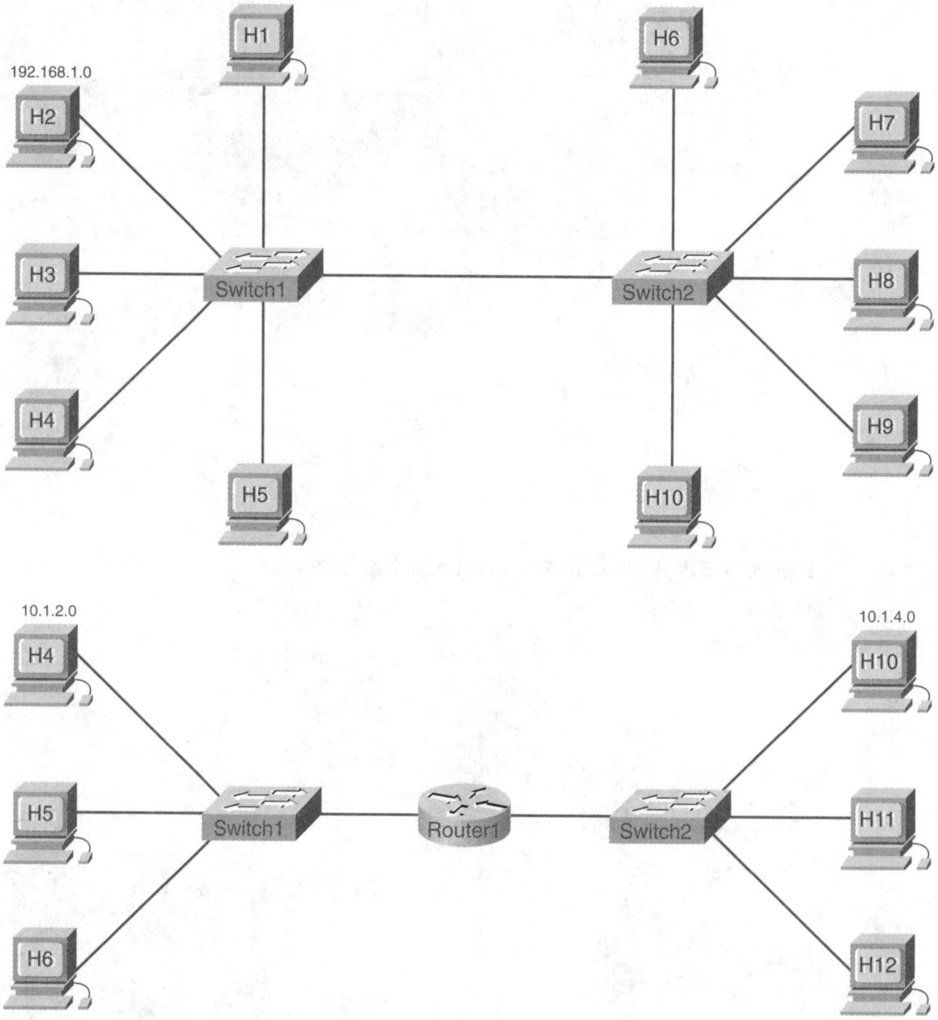

In a simple network design, keeping all hosts within a single local network might be beneficial. However, as networks grow in size, increased traffic will decrease network performance and speed. In this case, moving some hosts onto a remote network might be beneficial.

Placing additional hosts on a remote network decreases the impact of traffic demands. However, hosts on one network cannot communicate with hosts on the other without the use of routing. Routers increase the cost and complexity of the network configuration and can introduce latency, or time delay, on packets sent from one local network to the other.

Table 3-6 outlines the advantages and disadvantages of placing all hosts on a single local network versus placing them in remote network segments.

Table 3-6   Placing Hosts on the Network

	Placing All Hosts on One Local Network	Placing Hosts in Remote Network Segments
Advantages	Appropriate for simpler networks.	More appropriate for larger, more complex networks.
	Less complexity and lower network cost.	Splits up broadcast domains and decreases traffic.
	Allows devices to be "seen" by other devices.	Can improve performance on each segment.
	Faster data transfer; more direct communication.	Makes the machines invisible to those on other local network segments.
	Ease of device access.	Can provide increased security.
		Can improve network organization.
Disadvantages	All hosts are in one broadcast domain, which causes more traffic on the segment and might slow network performance.	Requires the use of routing (distribution layer). Router can slow traffic between segments. More complexity and expense (requires router).

Plan and Connect a Local Network

You have seen the components of a local network and how they function together; now you learn how to plan, design, and build a simple Ethernet network using a multifunction device, which can include a router, a multiport switch, and wireless capability.

Plan and Document an Ethernet Network

Most local networks are based on Ethernet technology. This technology is both fast and efficient when used in a properly designed and constructed network. The key to installing a good network is proper planning before the network is actually built.

A network plan starts with the gathering of information about how the network will be used. This information includes

- **The number and type of hosts to be connected to the network**: Where are the end users located? What type of hardware are they using? Where are the servers, printers, and other network devices located?

- **The applications to be used**: What type of applications are running on the network?

- **Sharing requirements**: Who requires access to which files and network resources such as printers?

- **Internet connectivity requirements**: What is acceptable bandwidth (speed) for the end users? Do all users require the same throughput? What affect will the applications have on the throughput? Is a lower upload speed than download speed acceptable?

- **Security and privacy considerations**: Is the data being moved on the network of a personal or sensitive nature? Could unauthorized access to this information cause harm to anyone?

- **Reliability and uptime expectations**: How important is the network? Does it need to be available 100% of the time (this is known as uptime)? How much downtime can be tolerated?

- **Connectivity requirements including, wired and wireless**: Do any or all of the end users require wireless connectivity?

When planning for a network installation, you also need to design and document the logical and physical topology of the network before you purchase networking equipment and connect hosts.

When planning the physical and logical topologies, consider the following points:

- Physical environment where the network will be installed, including the following:

  - Temperature control (because all devices have specific ranges of temperature and humidity requirements for proper operation)

  - Need for power protection on network devices

  - Availability and placement of power outlets

- Physical configuration of the network, including the following:

  - Physical location of devices such as routers, switches, and hosts

  - How all devices are interconnected

  - Location and length of all cable runs

  - Hardware configuration of end devices such as hosts and servers

- Logical configuration of the network:

  - Location and size of broadcast and collision domains

  - IP addressing scheme

  - Naming scheme

  - Sharing configuration

  - Permissions

Prototypes

After you document the network requirements and create the physical and logical topology maps, the next step in the implementation process is to test the network design. One of the ways to test a network design is to create a working model, or *prototype*, of the network.

Prototyping is essential as networks grow in size and complexity. A prototype allows a network administrator to test whether the planned network will operate as expected, before money is spent on equipment and installation. You should maintain documentation on all aspects of the prototyping process.

Various tools and techniques are available for network prototyping, including real equipment set up in a lab environment as well as modeling and simulation tools. Cisco's Packet Tracer is one example of a simulation and modeling tool that you can use for prototyping. Figure 3-54 shows a sample prototype using Cisco Packet Tracer.

Figure 3-54 Prototyping Using Cisco Packet Tracer

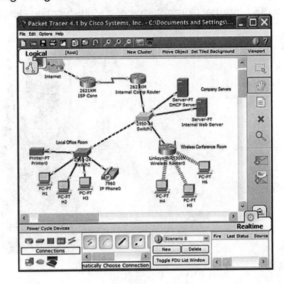

Learn to Use Packet Tracer (3.5.7.2)

In this Packet Tracer activity you familiarize yourself with the user interface of the Packet Tracer graphical network simulation tool. Use file d1-3572.pka on the CD-ROM that accompanies this book to perform this activity using Packet Tracer.

Interactive Activity 3-14: Prototyping with Packet Tracer (Demonstration) (3.6.2.2)

In this interactive activity you see a demonstration of how to prototype a network using Packet Tracer. Use file ia-3622 on the CD-ROM that accompanies this book to perform this interactive activity.

Prototyping a Network (3.6.2.3)

In this Packet Tracer activity you use Packet Tracer to prototype a simple network. Use file d1-3623.pka on the CD-ROM that accompanies this book to perform this activity using Packet Tracer.

Multi-function Device

Most home and small business networks do not require the high-volume devices used in large business environments; smaller scale devices might well be suitable. However, the same functionality of routing and switching is required. This need has led to the development of products that have the functionality of multiple network devices, such as a router with switching functionality and a wireless access point. These devices go by many different names but can be referred to generically as *multi-function devices* or integrated routers. Integrated routers can range from small devices, designed for home and small business applications, to more powerful devices that can support enterprise branch offices.

An integrated router is like having several different devices connected together. For example, the connection between the switch and the router still occurs, but it occurs internally, as shown in Figure 3-55. When a broadcast is received on a switch port, the integrated switch forwards the broadcast to all ports including the internal router connection. The router portion of the integrated router stops the broadcasts from going any further.

Figure 3-55   Internal Components of a Multi-function Device

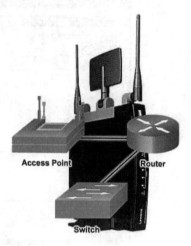

Many low-cost multi-function devices are available for home and small business networks that offer integrated routing, switching, wireless, and security capabilities. An example of this type of integrated device is a Linksys wireless router as shown in Figure 3-56. These devices are simple in design and do not typically have separate components. In the event of a failure, replacing any single failed component is not possible. As such, they create a single point of failure, and are not optimized for any one function.

Figure 3-56   Linksys WRT300N Wireless Router

Another example of an integrated router is the Cisco *integrated services router (ISR)*. The Cisco ISR product family offers a wide range of products, including those designed for small office and home office environments as well as those designed for larger networks. Many of the ISRs offer modularity and have separate components for each function. For example, adding a switching module to the Cisco 1841 ISR can eliminate the requirements for a separate standalone switch for smaller companies. This enables individual components to be added, replaced, and upgraded as necessary.

Connecting the Linksys Router

Linksys multi-function devices have two kinds of ports: switch ports and network ports. Ensuring that local devices are connected only to the switch ports is important. The connection to the Internet or another network must be made via the Internet port. The Internet port represents the router portion of the device. Figure 3-57 shows the ports on the Linksys WRT300N.

Figure 3-57   Linksys WRT300N Ports

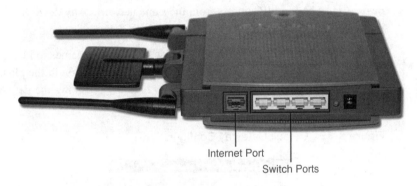

Internet Port

Switch Ports

Multiple switch ports are connected to the internal switch portion of the multi-function device. These ports are often labeled "Ethernet" and all devices connected to these Ethernet ports are on the same local network. The switch portion of the multi-function device is connected internally to the router portion.

These multi-function devices usually contain a single port for connecting the device to an external network or Internet. This port is often labeled "Internet." The router portion of the multi-function device maintains routing tables and has an internal connection to the switch portion of the local network.

The condition of the multi-function device and the connection status of each port are shown by *light-emitting diodes (LED)* as shown in Figure 3-58. These LEDs can either change color or flash to indicate operational or connection status. Although their meaning can differ between devices manufactured by different vendors, some commonality usually exists. The following LED status states and meanings are fairly universal:

- A solid green LED indicates a connection is made with an end device.

- A blinking LED indicates activity on the port.

- A red or yellow LED usually indicates a problem with the connection.

- An illuminated power LED indicates the presence of power to the device.

Figure 3-58 Linksys WRT300N Indicator LEDs

Indicator LEDs

All devices connected to the switch ports should be in the same broadcast domain. This means that all devices must have an IP address from the same network. Any devices that have a different network portion within their IP address will not be able to communicate.

Additionally, Microsoft Windows makes use of computer names to identify other devices on the network. Using these names as well as all IP address information in the planning and documentation is important to assist in future troubleshooting. Figure 3-59 shows the default gateway configuration on Windows hosts.

Figure 3-59 Default Gateway Configuration

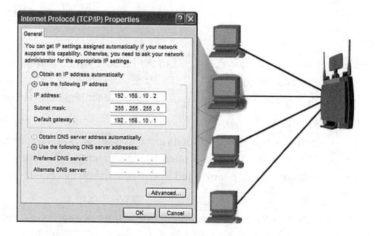

To display the current IP configuration in Microsoft Windows, use the command **ipconfig**. More detailed information, including host name, is available with the **ipconfig / all** command. Be certain to document all information from the connection and configuration process.

After hosts are communicating across the network, documenting network performance is important. This task is known as determining the *baseline* for the network and is used as an indication of normal operations. Comparing future network performance against this baseline can indicate whether possible issues exist.

Lab 3-5: Connect and Configure Hosts (3.6.4.3)

In this lab you connect hosts to the multi-function device and configure IP addressing. You also configure NetBIOS names and verify connectivity. Refer to the hands-on lab in Part II of this *Learning Guide*. You may perform this lab now or wait until the end of the chapter.

Sharing Resources

One of the most common purposes of networking is to share resources such as files and printers. Windows XP enables remote users to access a local machine and its resources through sharing. When planning a network, considering security issues and assigning specific permissions to shared resources is important.

By default, Windows XP uses a process known as Simple File Sharing. With Simple File Sharing, specific users and groups cannot be prevented from accessing shared files.

You can disable Simple File Sharing to assign more specific security access levels. When this is done, the following permissions are available to assign to resources:

- Full Control
- Modify
- Read and Execute
- List Folder Contents
- Read
- Write

When a user accesses a file on a remote device, Windows Explorer allows the user to map a drive to a remote folder or resource. This maps a specific drive letter, for example, M:, to the remote resource and allows the user to treat the resource as if it were locally connected.

Interactive Activity 3-15: Sharing Resources (Demonstration) (3.6.5.2)

In this interactive activity you see a demonstration of how to share resources on a network. Use file ia-3652 on the CD-ROM that accompanies this book to perform this interactive activity.

Lab 3-6: Sharing Resources (3.6.5.3)

In this lab you map a network drive and share files across the network. Refer to the hands-on lab in Part II of this *Learning Guide*. You may perform this lab now or wait until the end of the chapter.

Summary

This chapter introduced many of the basic networking concepts that will be built upon in this and future studies. In general, networks have many characteristics.

Information networks carry many different types of traffic, including voice, video, and data. They consist of hosts, peripherals, network devices, and media and have both a physical and a logical topology. Hosts on a network can take on the role of a client, a server, or both.

The role of any network is to allow the sharing of information and resources. Providing a mechanism for communication to occur, consisting of a source, a destination, and a channel, accomplishes this goal. Computer communication operates under a set of special rules called protocols that define the characteristics of a message, including encoding, formatting, encapsulation, size, timing, and patterns. Ethernet has become the most common protocol in use on local networks.

As networks grow in size and complexity, breaking them up into smaller, more manageable ones through a hierarchical network design is common. The most common hierarchical network design model is the three-layer design, consisting of the access, distribution, and core layers.

The access layer has the following traits:

- First point of entry into the network for all hosts.

- Hosts are normally connected to an access layer device such as a hub or switch, through the use of Ethernet technology.

- Both MAC and IP addresses are used to identify individual hosts.

The distribution layer has the following traits:

- Connects independent local networks and controls the flow of data between them.

- Uses routers and IP addresses to move information between networks.

- Does not concern itself with individual hosts.

The core layer has the following traits:

- Concerned with the high-speed delivery of information between locations.

- Built using high-speed switches and routers.

- Does not have any knowledge of individual hosts.

Local networks normally use Ethernet technology. To communicate between hosts on the same local network, both the IP address and the MAC address must be known. A process known as ARP is used to resolve an IP address to a MAC address for local delivery.

Moving information from one host to a host on a remote network requires routing. Routers move information between local networks. Routers know only about networks and do not concern themselves with individual hosts. An exception to this is that routers do build up ARP tables of any directly connected hosts and will use this information for final delivery.

Proper planning is the first step in any network development, beginning with determining the end use of the network. The types of information to gather include the following:

- Number and types of hosts to be connected to the network

- Applications to be used

- Sharing and Internet connectivity options

- Security and privacy considerations

- Reliability and uptime expectations

- Connectivity requirements including wired and wireless

The current trend for both home and small business networks is the use of multi-function devices that incorporate the functionality of switches, routers, wireless access points, and security appliances into a single unit. These multi-function devices can either be units designed for small, low-volume networks or devices with the capability of handling many more hosts and providing more advanced capabilities and reliability. The Linksys WRT300N integrated router is an example of a device designed for the small business and home markets whereas the Cisco Integrated Services Router (ISR) family of products are designed for larger, more demanding environments.

Activities and Labs

This summary outlines the activities and labs you can perform to help reinforce important concepts described in this chapter. You can find the activity and Packet Tracer files on the CD-ROM accompanying this book. The complete hands-on labs appear in Part II.

Interactive Activities on the CD:

Interactive Activity 3-1: Identifying Network Components (3.1.3.2)

Interactive Activity 3-2: Matching Client and Server Capabilities (3.1.4.3)

Interactive Activity 3–3: Determining Client and Server Roles (3.1.5.2)

Interactive Activity 3–4: Placing Voice Message Components in a Frame (3.2.4.3)

Interactive Activity 3–5: Classifying Communication Problems (3.2.8.2)

Interactive Activity 3-6: Building a Standard IEEE 802.3 Ethernet Frame (3.3.4.2)

Interactive Activity 3–7: Using Addresses, Network Components, and Layers (3.3.7.2)

Interactive Activity 3-8: Data Flow on a Hubbed Network (3.4.2.3)

Interactive Activity 3-9: Data Flow in a Network Using Hubs and Switches (3.4.3.4)

Interactive Activity 3–10: Switch Behavior (3.4.5.1)

Interactive Activity 3–11: Configuring a Default Gateway Address (3.5.3.2)

Interactive Activity 3–12: Determining How a Router Forwards Packets (3.5.4.3)

Interactive Activity 3–13: Determining the Local Networks Within a LAN (3.5.5.2)

Interactive Activity 3–14: Prototyping with Packet Tracer (Demonstration) (3.6.2.2)

Interactive Activity 3–15: Sharing Resources (Demonstration) (3.6.5.2)

Packet Tracer
☐ Activity

Packet Tracer Activities on the CD:

Learn to Use Packet Tracer GUI (3.5.7.2)

Prototyping a Network (3.6.2.3)

Labs in Part II of This Book:

Lab 3-1: Building a Peer-to-Peer Network (3.1.5.3)

Lab 3-2: Determine the MAC Address of a Host (3.3.3.2)

Lab 3-3: Determine the IP address of a Computer (3.3.6.2)

Lab 3-4: IP Addresses and Network Communication (3.5.2.2)

Lab 3-5: Connect and Configure Hosts (3.6.4.3)

Lab 3-6: Sharing Resources (3.6.5.3)

Check Your Understanding

Complete all the review questions listed here to test your understanding of the topics and concepts in this chapter. The "Check Your Understanding and Challenge Questions Answer Key" appendix lists the answers.

1. Of the following types of networking components, which are considered peripherals? (Choose two.)

   A. A printer attached to a network device

   B. A web camera attached to a PC

   C. A printer attached to a PC for personal use

   D. A PC attached to a network device

   E. An IP phone attached to a network device

2. Of the following networking components, which are considered hosts? (Choose three.)

   A. A flat-screen monitor attached to a PC

   B. A printer attached to a hub

   C. A printer attached to a PC for personal use

   D. A server attached to a switch

   E. An IP phone attached to a switch

3. What are the major advantages of a peer-to-peer network? (Choose two.)

   A. Simple to set up

   B. Scale easily

   C. Sophisticated security capabilities

   D. Less expensive

   E. Centralized administration

4. Which statements apply to a logical network topology map? (Choose two.)

   A. Usually shows details of cabling runs

   B. Can provide IP addressing and computer naming information

   C. Normally includes the location of all wiring closets

   D. Shows all servers, switches, and routers

   E. Groups hosts by how they use the network

5. What is it called when a computer needs to send a message to a selected group of computers?

   A. Unicast

   B. Broadcast

   C. Simulcast

   D. Multicast

6. Jim is browsing the Internet with his computer and reading his e-mail. What role is his computer currently playing?

   A. Server

   B. Client

   C. Master

   D. Both client and server

7. Allan is sharing a folder for other users to access on his home network and reading his e-mail. What role is his computer currently playing?

   A. Server

   B. Client

   C. Master

   D. Both client and server

8. What is the process of a placing a message inside a frame so it can be transmitted on the medium?

   A. Encoding

   B. Access insertion

   C. Unicasting

   D. Encapsulation

   E. Injection

9. What Windows command can you use to display the IP address and MAC address of a computer?

   A. **maconfig /a**

   B. **ipconfig /all**

   C. **tcpconfig /all**

   D. **pcconfig /a**

10. How many collision domains are associated with a 24-port switch?

    A. 0

    B. 1

    C. 24

    D. Depends on which devices are connected to the switch

11. Which devices can you use to limit the size of a collision domain?

    A. NIC

    B. Hub

    C. Switch

    D. Router

12. What does a switch do with a frame addressed to a MAC address that is not in its MAC address table?

    A. Drops the frame

    B. Forwards the frame

    C. Floods the frame

    D. Issues a MAC request message

13. Which hosts will hear an ARP request? Choose the best answer.

    A. All devices connected to the LAN

    B. All devices in the broadcast domain

    C. All devices in the collision domain

    D. Only the device to which the request is addressed

14. Which hosts will hear an ARP reply?

    A. All devices connected to the LAN

    B. All devices in the broadcast domain

    C. All devices in the collision domain

    D. Only the device to which the reply is addressed

15. Which are good criteria to break a large network into multiple access layer networks?

    A. Logical grouping

    B. Physical location

    C. Application usage

    D. Security

16. Which device is normally found in the distribution layer?

    A. NIC

    B. Hub

    C. Switch

    D. Router

17. What does a router normally do when it receives a broadcast?

    A. Drops the frame

    B. Forwards the frame

    C. Floods the frame

18. Which definition best defines LAN?

    A. A LAN is a single local network under the control of a single administrative entity.

    B. A LAN is one or more connected local networks under the control of a single administrative entity.

    C. A LAN is a collection of local and remote networks under the control of a single administrative entity.

    D. A LAN is a collection of remote networks that might be under the control of multiple administrators.

19. Which of the following would be recorded as part of the physical topology of a network?

    A. Permissions

    B. Addressing scheme

    C. Naming scheme

    D. Location of cable runs

20. What are the two types of addresses required to deliver a message to a host in an Ethernet local network?

    A. MAC address and NIC address

    B. MAC address and IP address

    C. Protocol address and physical device name

    D. Logical devices name and IP address

21. When is a default gateway required?   •

22. What problem might you encounter when adding hosts to a single switched local network?

Challenge Questions and Activities

These questions require a deeper application of the concepts covered in this chapter. You can find the answers in the appendix.

1. Tebuc has brought a new laptop computer home from school to complete an overdue assignment. He plugs the computer into his home multi-function device but is unable to connect to the Internet. His desktop computer is connected to the same multi-function device and can connect without problem. At school, the laptop functioned properly. What is the most probable cause, and how should Tebuc correct the problem?

2. A small graphics design company has just acquired a contract with the local government. In order to handle the increased work, the company increased the number of employees from 11 to 46. All employees are now complaining that the network is slow. What is the most probable cause of this problem, and how would you correct it? All computers are directly connected to a single large switch.

CHAPTER 4

Connecting to the Internet Through an ISP

Objectives

Upon completion of this chapter, you will able to answer the following questions:

- What is the Internet?

- What is an Internet service provider (ISP) and what services can it provide?

- What are the options for connecting to the Internet using an ISP?

- How is the Internet Protocol (IP) used in sending messages across the Internet?

- How is information sent across the Internet through an ISP?

- What are the primary components of an ISP Network Operations Center (NOC)?

- What are the environmental requirements of a home/small business network as compared to those of an ISP NOC?

- What different types of cables and connectors are used for connecting the devices in a NOC?

- What are the two main Ethernet unshielded twisted-pair (UTP) cable wiring standards?

- What is the difference between a straight-through and crossover cable and where are they used in an Ethernet local network?

- How are UTP cables constructed and terminated to provide a reliable connection?

- What are UTP cabling best practices?

Key Terms

This chapter uses the following key terms. You can find the definitions in the Glossary.

Every day new people come online and join the human network. From the most remote areas in Africa to metropolitan London, we need to be able to connect and communicate. Internet service providers (ISP) are the links to the Internet. The web of interconnected ISPs makes the Internet accessible to everyone. In this chapter you will learn why ISPs are necessary and about the Network Operations Centers that are crucial to the function of the Internet. Part II of this book includes the corresponding labs for this chapter.

The Internet and How We Connect To It

The Internet has become an integral part of our lives. An understanding of what the Internet is, how it is constructed, and how we connect to it helps us appreciate the capabilities of the world's largest network.

Explain What the Internet Is

Every day millions of people exchange information through the Internet, but what exactly is the Internet? The Internet is a worldwide collection of computer networks, cooperating with each other to exchange information using common standards. Through telephone wires, fiber-optic cables, wireless transmissions, and satellite links, Internet users can exchange information in a variety of forms.

The Internet is a network of networks that connects users in every country in the world. There are currently more than one billion Internet users worldwide. Figure 4-1 depicts the use of the Internet to connect users on every continent.

Figure 4-1   The Internet Connects People Around the Globe

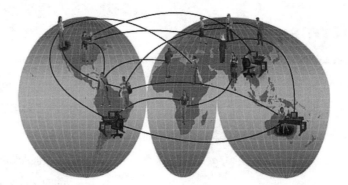

Previously, the networks we have discussed have been controlled by one individual or organization. The Internet is a conglomerate of networks and is owned by no one individual or group. However, several major international organizations exist that help manage the Internet so that everyone uses the same rules.

The Internet Society (ISOC) provides leadership in addressing issues that confront the future of the Internet. It is the home for the groups responsible for Internet infrastructure standards, including the Internet Engineering Task Force (IETF) and the Internet Architecture Board (IAB).

Some of the main organizations that help manage and develop the Internet are

- **Internet Society (ISOC)**: http://www.isoc.org/isoc/

- **Internet Architecture Board (IAB)**: http://www.iab.org/

- **Internet Engineering Task Force (IETF)**: http://www.ietf.org/

- **Internet Research Task Force (IRTF)**: http://www.irtf.org/

- **Internet Assigned Numbers Authority (IANA)**: http://www.iana.org/

NOTE

The Infoplease website is a good source of Internet usage statistics and resources: http://www.infoplease.com/ipa/A0873826.html

Internet Service Providers (ISP)

Any home, business, or organization that connects to the Internet must use an *Internet service provider (ISP)*, as shown in Figure 4-2. An ISP is a company that provides the connections and support to access the Internet. It can also provide additional services such as e-mail and *web hosting*.

Figure 4-2   All Home Users and Organizations Connect to the Internet Through an ISP

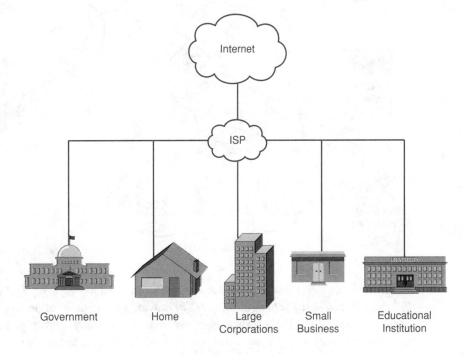

ISPs are essential to gaining access to the Internet. No one gets on the Internet without a host computer, and no one gets on the Internet without going through an ISP.

ISPs range in size from small to very large and differ in terms of the area they service. ISPs might provide limited services to a small geographical area or can have a wide variety of services and support entire countries with millions of customers. ISPs also differ in the types of connection technologies and speeds they offer. Examples of well-known ISPs include AOL, EarthLink, and Roadrunner. Do you have Internet access? Who is your ISP?

The ISP's Relationship with the Internet

Individual computers and local networks connect to the ISP at a *point of presence (POP)*. A POP is a building or facility that provides a connection point between the ISP's network and the particular geographical region that the POP is servicing.

An ISP might have many POPs depending on its size and the area it services. Within an ISP, a network of high-speed routers and switches move data between the various POPs. Multiple links interconnect the POPs to provide alternative routes for the data should one link fail or become overloaded with traffic and congested.

ISPs connect to other ISPs in order to send information beyond the boundaries of their own network. The Internet is made up of very high-speed data links that interconnect ISP POPs and ISPs to each other. Figure 4-3 shows two ISPs connected so that their users can communicate.

Figure 4-3   Multiple ISPs Link Users Through POPs

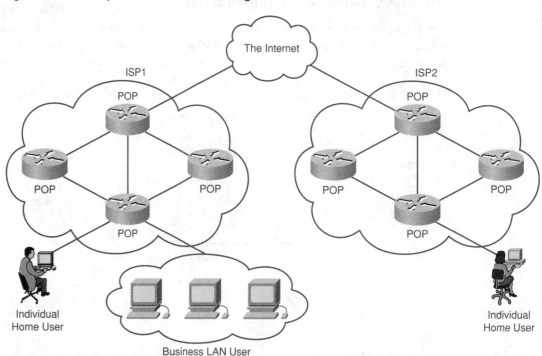

The Internet has thousands of interconnected ISPs. To avoid having every ISP connect to every other ISP directly, *Internet Exchange Points (IXP)* provide a common location where multiple ISPs can connect to other ISPs. These interconnections are part of the very large, high-capacity network known as the Internet backbone. Figure 4-4 shows some of the Internet backbone connections between major cities worldwide.

Connecting to the ISP at the POP provides users with access to the ISP's services and the Internet.

Figure 4-4   Major Internet Backbone Connections

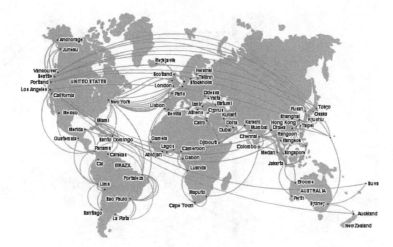

Options for Connecting to the ISP

ISPs provide a variety of ways to connect to the Internet, depending on location and desired connection speed.

Major cities typically have more choices for ISPs and more connection options than rural areas. For example, cable Internet access is available only in certain metropolitan areas where cable TV service is available. Remote areas might have access only via *dial-up* or *satellite*.

Each Internet access technology uses a network access device, such as a modem, in order to connect to the ISP. It can be built-in to a computer or can be provided by the ISP.

The simplest arrangement is a modem that provides a direct connection between a computer and the ISP. However, if multiple computers connect through a single ISP connection, additional networking devices are needed. This includes a hub or switch to connect multiple hosts on a local network, and a router to move packets from your local network to the ISP network. A home networking device, such as an integrated router, can provide these functions, as well as wireless capability, in a single package.

Figure 4-5 shows a single PC directly connected through a modem to the ISP. Also shown is a group of PCs in a small network that can all share a single Internet connection using an integrated router device. The individual PCs connect to a switch contained in the device and the router portion of the device connects to the ISP through the modem. The modem is required in either case and can be purchased from the ISP or leased.

The choice of Internet access technologies depends on availability, cost, access device used, media used, and the speed of the connection.

Most of the technologies shown in Figure 4-6 are used for both home and small business. Leased lines are typically used for business and large organizations, but can be used to provide high-speed connectivity in areas where cable or DSL are not available. With the exception of dial-up and cell modem, the other connection technologies listed are generally referred to as *broadband* and *always-on* connections. There are various definitions of broadband, but it generally refers to technologies with download speeds of 500 Kbps or greater. A dial-up connection can provide actual download speeds of about 30 Kbps.

Figure 4-5   Single PC and LAN Connections to ISP

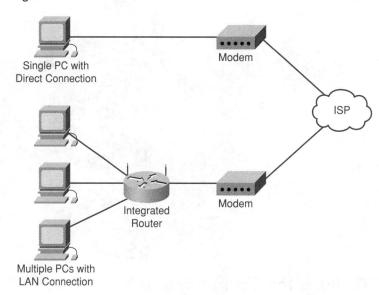

Figure 4-6   ISP Connection Options

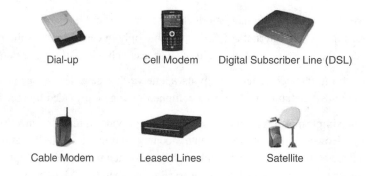

The ISP connections options include the following:

- **Dial-up**: The slowest and most widely available service. Dial-up uses regular voice-grade telephone lines. It is the least expensive connection technology. Dial-up takes time to establish the connection to the ISP. It can also present problems if someone needs to make a call. Requires an analog modem, either one built-in to the computer or standalone.

- **Cell modem**: Cellular service is available through cellular telephone providers. It provides relatively slow access speeds but is becoming more popular and speeds are increasing as the technology evolves. It allows Internet access when mobile, such as driving a car. Access speeds might be higher in metropolitan areas. Requires a special cell modem or the modem might be built in to the cell phone.

- **Digital subscriber line (DSL)**: A relatively high-speed service available from most telephone companies (*telco*). DSL provides a high-speed digital connection over regular telephone lines. DSL availability and speeds are based on the distance from a telco office that has a DSL switch. Users that are close might receive very high speeds; users beyond a certain distance might not be able to get the service at all. Requires a special DSL modem.

- **Cable modem**: A service available from most cable companies. Provides high-speed connection over the cable TV network. If cable TV service is available, cable Internet access is also likely to be available. Requires a special cable modem.

- **Leased lines**: Service available from most telephone companies. Provides high-speed connection over dedicated digital data lines. The most common example of a leased line is a T1. Leased lines are primarily for business-class service. Requires a special type of modem known as a CSU/DSU.

- **Satellite**: Two-way satellite service is available from Internet dish satellite companies. Provides medium speeds via satellite. Satellite might be the only choice faster than dial-up in some rural areas. Requires a special modem similar to cable.

ISP Levels of Service

Depending on the ISP and the connection technology, various services are available such as virus scanning, video on demand, and file storage. The contract with the ISP determines the type and level of services that are available. Most ISPs offer two different contract levels: home service or business-class service.

Home service is normally less expensive than business services, and generally provides scaled-down services such as slower connection speed, reduced web space storage, and fewer e-mail accounts. A typical home account might include a minimum of five e-mail addresses with additional addresses being available for a fee.

Business-class service is more expensive but provides faster connection speeds and additional web space and e-mail accounts. A business-class service might include 20, 50, or more e-mail addresses. Business service also includes agreements between the ISP and the customer specifying items such as network availability and service response time. These are known as *service-level agreements (SLA)*. Services available vary from one ISP to the next. Figure 4-7 shows some of the main services available from a major ISP, and they are described here.

The following list describes these services in more detail:

- **Connection speed**: Download speeds can vary from 56 Kbps for dial-up to 1.5 Mbps or higher for technologies such as DSL and cable modem. A high-speed connection is recommended for individuals who download a lot of large programs or video, perform gaming, or run their own servers.

- **E-mail accounts**: ISPs generally provide multiple user e-mail addresses on one account. These e-mail addresses can be distributed among individuals or used to separate business mail from personal mail. Web mail allows users to access their e-mail accounts from any computer connected to the Internet.

- **Personal home pages**: Personal web page space is frequently provided with service. Usually both the size of the web space and the traffic generated are limited. Design and maintenance of the website is maintained by the individual author.

- **Web hosting services**: Organizations that do not have web servers can use the ISP's servers for their website. This often comes with design and maintenance services. Web hosting services are usually purchased based on the size of the website and the anticipated monthly volume.

- **File storage**: Organizations can use the ISP's online storage and file management systems to provide 24/7 access to important files. File storage can range from a few megabytes (millions) to terabytes (trillions) of online storage. Online file storage is usually password protected.

Figure 4-7   ISP Services

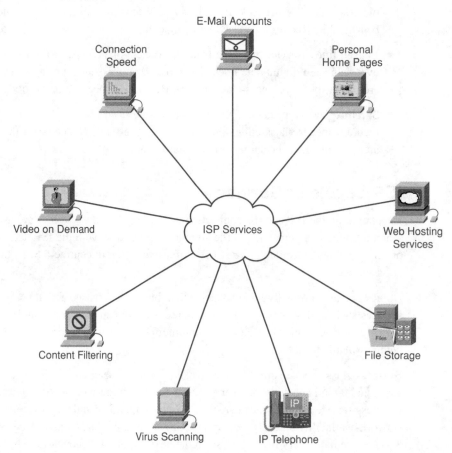

- **IP telephone**: ISPs might provide IP telephone services that allow users to make and receive voice calls over the Internet. When using the Internet, regular long-distance tolls do not normally apply.

- **Virus scanning**: ISPs often include virus scanning and anti-spam services as part of their connection package. Most ISPs scan for malicious code both on files that have been uploaded from the end user and those arriving for delivery to the end user.

- **Content filtering**: ISPs can provide software that prevents specific material from being downloaded, based on user specifications. This software is often used to block objectionable and/or offensive websites.

- **Video on demand**: Real-time downloading of movies allows users to watch movies over the Internet. This is known as streaming video.

When data is transferred, it is either uploaded or downloaded. Downloading refers to information coming from the Internet to your computer, whereas uploading indicates the reverse path, from your computer to the Internet. When the download transfer rate is different from the upload transfer rate, it is called asymmetric. When the transfer rate is the same in both directions, it is called symmetric. ISPs can offer both asymmetric and symmetric services, as shown in Figure 4-8.

Figure 4-8   Asymmetric and Symmetric Service

The following is a summary of asymmetric service:

- Most commonly used for the home.

- Download speeds are faster than upload speeds.

- Necessary for users who download significantly more than they upload.

- Most Internet users, especially those who use graphics or multimedia-intensive web data, need lots of download bandwidth.

- DSL and cable modem are typically considered asymmetric services, although they can be symmetric.

The following is a summary of symmetric service:

- Most commonly used for business or individuals hosting servers on the Internet.

- Used when necessary to upload large amounts of traffic such as intensive graphics, multimedia, or video.

- Can carry large amounts of data in both directions at equal rates.

- ISP leased lines, such as T1, are symmetric services.

Interactive Activity 4-1: Analyze ISP and End User Requirements (4.1.5.3)

In this interactive activity, you analyze the information provided for three ISPs and match the requirements of an end user to the ISP. Use file ia-4153 on the CD-ROM that accompanies this book to perform this interactive activity.

Sending Information Across the Internet

The Internet uses several important protocols that are critical to our ability to connect and communicate. ISPs make use of these and routing technologies to transmit data from one host to another, regardless of their location in the world.

Importance of the Internet Protocol (IP)

For hosts to communicate on the Internet, they must be running Internet Protocol (IP) software and have an ISP connection, as shown in Figure 4-9. IP is one of a group of protocols that are collectively referred to as Transmission Control Protocol/Internet Protocol (TCP/IP). The Internet Protocol uses packets to carry data. Whether you are playing an Internet video game, chatting with a friend, sending e-mail or searching the Web, the information you are sending or receiving is carried in the form of IP packets.

Figure 4-9   Basic Requirements for Internet Connectivity

Each IP packet must contain a valid source and destination IP address. Without valid address information, packets sent will not reach the destination host. Return packets will not make it back to the original source.

IP defines the structure of the source and destination IP addresses. It specifies how these addresses are used in routing of packets from one host or network to another.

All protocols that operate on the Internet, including IP, are defined in numbered standards documents called Request For Comments (RFC).

RFCs

RFCs are numbered documents that define protocols and other standards that determine how the Internet functions. The higher the number, the newer the RFC. RFCs are submitted to the IETF and go through a review process. As they are reviewed, they go through the following stages:

1. Proposed (entry level)
2. Draft (initial testing)
3. Standard (fully adopted)

You can view the IETF RFC website at http://www.ietf.org/rfc.html.

An IP packet has a *header* at the beginning that contains the source and destination IP addresses, as shown in Figure 4-10. The header also contains control information that describes the packet to network devices, such as routers, it passes through and also helps to control its behavior on the network. The IP packet is sometimes referred to as a *datagram*. The packet actually contains 0s and 1s in the form of bits in the proper sequence. The sending and receiving hosts and the network devices in between interpret these bits to direct traffic and deliver messages.

Figure 4-10   Sending an IP Packet from Source to Destination

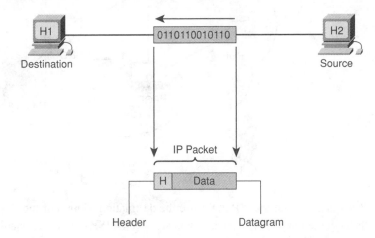

IP addresses must be unique on the Internet. Organizations exist that are responsible for controlling the distribution of IP addresses so that no duplication occurs. ISPs obtain blocks of IP addresses from a local, national, or *regional Internet registry (RIR)*. It is the responsibility of the ISPs to manage these addresses and assign them to organizations and end users.

Computers in homes, small businesses, and other organizations obtain their IP configuration from their ISP. Typically, this configuration is obtained automatically when the user connects to the ISP for Internet access.

How ISPs Handle Packets

Before being sent on the Internet, messages are divided into packets. IP packet size is between 64 to 1500 bytes for Ethernet networks and contains mostly user data. Downloading a single 1 MB song requires more than 600 packets of 1500 bytes. Each individual packet must have a source and destination IP address.

When a packet is sent across the Internet, the ISP determines whether the packet is destined for a local service located on the ISP network or a remote service located on a different network.

Every ISP has a control facility for its network, known as the *Network Operations Center (NOC)*. The NOC usually controls traffic flow and houses services such as e-mail and web hosting. The NOC might be located at one of the POPs or at a completely separate facility within the ISP network. Packets looking for local services are usually forwarded to the NOC and never need to go to another ISP network on the way to the server that provides the local service, as shown in Figure 4-11.

Figure 4-11   Packets Destined for Local Server in the ISP1 NOC

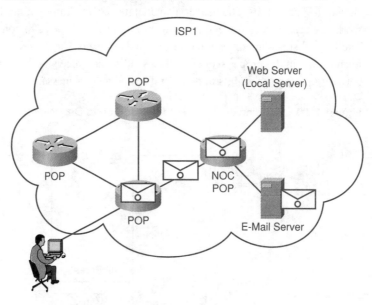

Routers in each of the ISP POPs use the destination address of the IP packets to choose the best path through the Internet. The packets you send to the ISP POP are forwarded by routers through the ISP's network and then through the networks of other ISPs. They pass from router to router until they reach their final destination. Figure 4-12 shows packets from an ISP1 user destined for the web server in the remote ISP2 network.

Figure 4-12   Packets from an ISP1 User Destined for the Web Server in the ISP2 Network

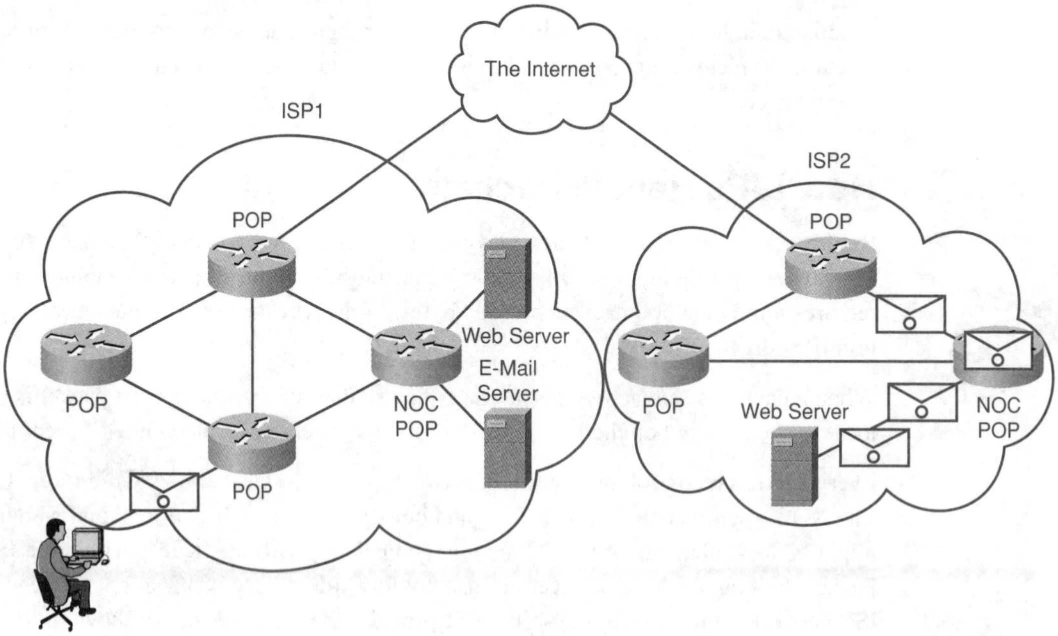

Forwarding Packets Across the Internet

Network utilities are available that test connectivity to the destination device. The **ping** utility tests end-to-end connectivity between source and destination. It measures the time that it takes for test packets to make a round trip from the source to the destination and whether the transmission is successful. However, if the packet does not reach the destination, or if delays are encountered along the way, no way exists for determining where the problem is located.

The **traceroute** utility traces the route from source to destination. Unlike **ping**, it can determine which routers the packets have passed through and detect the problem areas in the path. Each router through which the packets travel is referred to as a *hop*. Look at the network in Figure 4-13 as an example. The **traceroute** output from Example 4-1 displays each hop along the way and the time it takes for each one. If a problem occurs, the display of the time and the route that the packet traveled can help to determine where the packet was lost or delayed. When working with the UNIX or Linux OS and Cisco routers and switches, the command you issue at the command line is **traceroute**. The **traceroute** utility is called **tracert** in the Windows environment.

Figure 4-13   Tracing a Packet Through the Internet

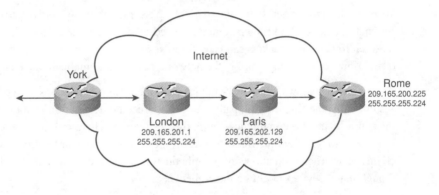

```
Example 4-1 Sample traceroute Output
York# traceroute Rome
Type escape to abort.
Tracing the route to Rome (209.165.200.225)
1. London (209.165.201.1) 8 msec   8 msec   4 msec
2. Paris (209.165.202.129) 9 msec   9 msec   7 msec
3. Rome (209.165.200.225) 7 msec   8 msec   5 msec
```

A number of GUI-based **traceroute** programs are also available that can provide a graphical display of the route that a packet takes. These programs can also provide other useful information such as ownership of Internet nodes. Examples include VisualRoute, PingPlotter, and 3d Traceroute.

Packet Tracer
☐ Activity

Observing Packets Across the Network (4.2.3.2)

In this Packet Tracer activity you use **ping** and **traceroute** to check connectivity and learn more about how packets travel through the Internet. Use file d1-4232.pka on the CD-ROM that accompanies this book to perform this activity using Packet Tracer.

Lab 4-1: Tracing Internet Connectivity (4.2.3.3)

In this lab you use **ping** and **traceroute** to check connectivity and learn more about how packets travel through the Internet. Refer to the hands-on lab in Part II of this *Learning Guide*. You may perform this lab now or wait until the end of the chapter.

Networking Devices in a NOC

The device requirements for home and small businesses often differ from the device requirements of larger enterprise networks. This section begins by explaining the representation of network devices and interconnections in diagrams. This section then contrasts the networking equipment necessary in large networks as compared to home and small businesses. You then learn about the different physical and environmental requirements for home and enterprise networks.

Internet Cloud

When packets travel across the Internet, they pass through many network devices. You can think of the Internet as a network of routers, interconnected with one another. Very often, alternative routes exist between routers, and packets can take different paths between source and destination. If a problem with traffic flow occurs at any point in the network, packets automatically take an alternative route.

A diagram that shows all network devices and their interconnections would be very complex. Additionally, the final routing path between source and destination is not usually important, only that the source is able to communicate with the destination. Therefore, in network diagrams a *cloud* is often used to represent the Internet or any other complex network, without showing the details of the connections. The cloud allows for simple diagrams that focus on source and destination only, even though many devices might be linked between.

Figure 4-14 shows a map of the United States with two possible routes a packet may take, depending on network conditions. In the figure, Internet backbone routes connect major cities. Part 1 shows one route a packet might take from a user PC in Los Angeles destined for a server in New York City. In this case a **traceroute** would show the packet going through Rialto, Austell, Washington D.C., and West Orange. Part 2 of the figure shows an alternative route from Los Angeles to New York City. If a problem occurs with the link between Los Angeles and Rialto, the next series of packets from the same host in Los Angeles might travel through San Francisco, Denver, and West Orange to reach the New York City server.

Devices in Internet Cloud

Routers are neither the only devices found in the Internet cloud nor are they the only devices found at an ISP. The ISP must be able to accept and deliver information to the end user as well as participate in the Internet.

Devices that provide connectivity to end users must match the technology used by the end user to connect to the ISP. For example, if the end user is using DSL modem technology to connect, the ISP must have a *DSL Access Multiplexer (DSLAM)* to accept these connections. For cable modems to connect, the ISP must have a *Cable Modem Termination System (CMTS)*. Figure 4-15 shows a home and business customer for both a DSL and cable ISP. Note that, with the cable ISP, both customers connect to a common cable bus network that goes back to the CMTS. With the DSL ISP each customer has a separate telephone line to the DSLAM. Some ISPs still accept analog calls through voice modems and have banks of corresponding modems to support these users. ISPs that provide wireless access have wireless bridging equipment.

Figure 4-14   Packets from Source to Destination Can Take Multiple Paths Through the Internet

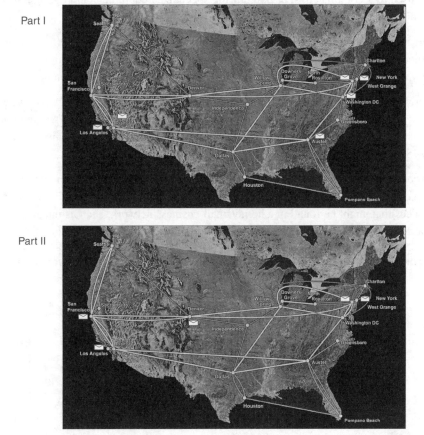

Figure 4-15   CMTS and DSLAM ISP Equipment in the Cloud

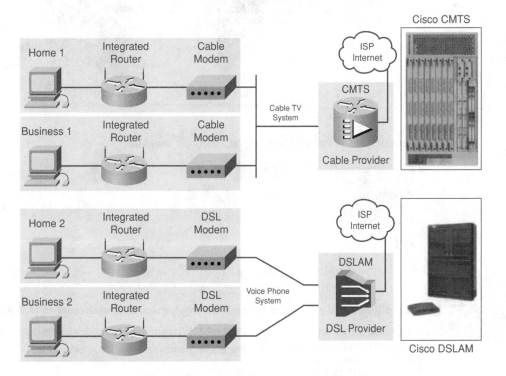

The ISP must also be able to connect to and transfer data with other ISPs. A variety of technologies are used to accomplish this, each requiring specialized equipment and configurations in order to function.

The type of equipment found in an ISP equipment room depends on the technology of the networks in which it is participating. Routers and switches make up most of this equipment. But these devices are very different from the ones found in the home or small business environment.

Networking devices used by the ISP handle extremely large volumes of traffic very quickly. They must function at near 100% uptime because the failure of a key piece of equipment at an ISP can have disastrous effects on network traffic and affect thousands of users. For this reason, the equipment used by ISPs is high-end, high-speed devices with redundancy.

In contrast, network devices used in the home or small business environment are lower-end, lower-speed devices that are not capable of handling large volumes of traffic. Figure 4-16 shows examples of devices that might be found in a home/small business network, such as integrated routers, as well as that found in an enterprise network.

Figure 4-16 Types of Equipment for the Home/Small Business Network and for the Enterprise Network

Equipment for the Home/Small Business Network

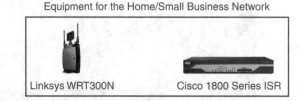

Linksys WRT300N   Cisco 1800 Series ISR

Equipment for the Enterprise Network

Cisco 6513 Chassis Bundle   Cisco 7204 - VXR Router

Integrated routers can perform several functions, including

- Wireless LAN access point
- Switching
- Routing
- Security firewall
- Automated addressing

Interactive Activity 4-2: Match the NOC Equipment to Requirements (4.3.2.3)

In this interactive activity, you match the NOC equipment room device to the requirements indicated. Use file ia-4323 on the CD-ROM that accompanies this book to perform this interactive activity.

Physical and Environmental Requirements

The network installation located at an ISP versus that of a home or small business is very different.

The home or small business network provides a limited number of services for relatively few users. Internet connectivity is purchased from an ISP. The volume of traffic is small, and no transport services are provided.

The ISP provides transport and other services to a large number of users. A number of different devices are required to accept input from end users. To participate in a transport network, it must be able to connect to other ISPs. It handles large volumes of traffic and requires very reliable equipment in order to handle the load.

Even though these two networks appear very different, they both require an environment where the equipment can function reliably and without interruption. The requirements are the same, but the scale of operation is different: At home, a single power outlet will suffice, whereas at an ISP the power requirements need to be planned out ahead of time and installed. Figure 4-17 shows a simple home networking integrated router compared to an aisle of servers and other networking devices that might be found at an ISP.

Figure 4-17   Home versus Enterprise Networking Equipment Environmental Requirements

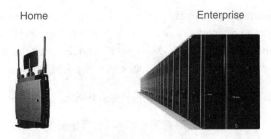

One major difference between an ISP and a home or small business network is the inclusion of servers. Most home users do not run servers, and small businesses usually have a few. They rely on the services offered by the ISP for such things as e-mail, address assignment, and web space. An ISP must consider the physical requirements of not only the networking equipment, but also the servers it houses.

One of the main considerations for electronic equipment is a reliable supply of stable power. Unfortunately the supply of power is not always reliable, which can lead to problems for network devices. ISPs install power conditioning equipment with substantial battery backup to maintain continuity of supply should the main power grid fail. For the home or small business, inexpensive uninterruptible power supplies (UPS) and battery backup units are usually sufficient for the relatively small amount of equipment they use. Figure 4-18 shows several small home or small business UPSs compared to larger ones that might be found in an enterprise or ISP.

Environmental factors, such as heat and humidity, must also be considered when planning a network installation. However, because of the volume of equipment and the amount of power consumed in an ISP, high-end air conditioning units are necessary to maintain controlled temperatures. For the home or small business, ordinary air conditioning, heating, and humidity controls are usually sufficient. In addition, the enterprise and ISP will require sophisticated fire suppression systems.

Cable management is another area of concern for both the home or small business network and the ISP. Cables must be protected from physical damage and organized in a manner that will aid in the troubleshooting process. Small networks have only a few cables, but in ISP networks, thousands of cables must be managed. This can include not only copper data cables but also fiber-optic and power cables.

Figure 4-18 Enterprise UPS and Home or Small Business UPS

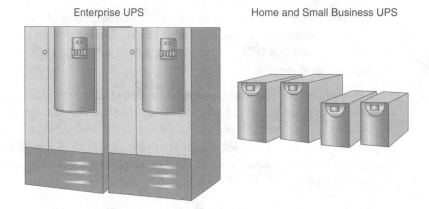

All of these factors, namely power supply, environment, and cable management, must be considered when setting up a network of any size. There is a big variation in size and therefore requirements for an ISP and a home network. Most networks fall somewhere between these two extremes. Figure 4-19 shows the cabling complexity of an enterprise-level network.

Figure 4-19 Enterprise Network Patch Panels and Cable Management

Cables and Connectors

The physical cabling of a network is the most critical component and the most common source of problems. The use of quality cabling and connectors wired to industry standards helps to ensure a stable network and minimize link failures.

Common Network Cables

In order for communication to occur, a source, destination, and some sort of channel must be present. A channel, or medium, provides a path over which the information is sent, as shown in Figure 4-20. In the networked world, the medium is usually some sort of physical cable. It might also be electromagnetic radiation, in the case of wireless networking. The connection between the source and destination can either be direct or indirect, and can span multiple media types.

Figure 4-20   Channel from Source to Destination

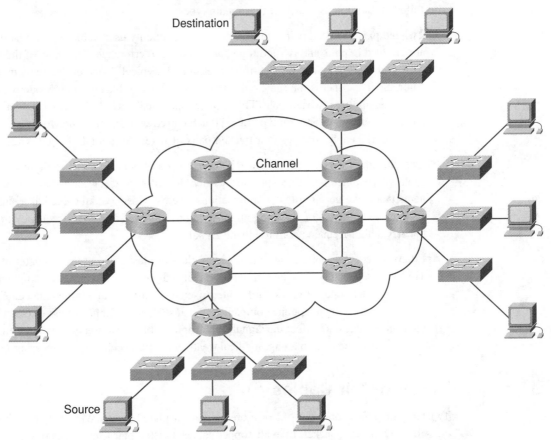

Different types of cables exist to interconnect the various devices in a NOC or local network.

There are two general categories of physical cable, metal and fiber-optic. Metal cables, usually copper, have electrical impulses applied to them to convey information. Twisted-pair and coaxial cable are in this category. Fiber-optic cables, made of glass or plastic, use flashes of light to convey information.

Figure 4-21 shows the primary types of cabling used in today's networks: twisted pair, coaxial, and fiber-optic.

Figure 4-21   Major Types of Network Cables

Twisted Pair   Coaxial Cable   Fiber Optic

The following summarizes each of these main types:

■ **Twisted pair**: Twisted pair is one of the most commonly used cable types in networking. Wires are grouped in pairs and twisted together to reduce interference. The pairs of the wires are colored so that the wire can be identified at each end. Typically, one of the wires in a pair is a solid color and its partner is the same color striped into a white background. Modern Ethernet technology generally uses twisted-pair (TP), or more specifically, unshielded twisted-pair (UTP) to interconnect devices. A common type of UTP cable used with Ethernet networks is Category 5, or CAT5. CAT5 cable contains four twisted pairs of wires, for a total of eight wires.

■ **Coaxial cable**: Coaxial cable is usually constructed of either copper or aluminum and is used by cable television companies to provide service. It is also used for connecting the various components that make up satellite communication systems. Most coaxial cable has a single copper core surrounded by layers of shielding and insulation. It is used as a high-frequency transmission line to carry a high-frequency or broadband signals.

■ **Fiber-optic**: Fiber-optic cables are made of glass or plastic, about the diameter of a human hair. They have a very high bandwidth, which enables them to carry very large amounts of data. Fiber is used in backbone networks, large enterprise environments, and large data centers. It is also used extensively by telephone companies. Because they use light instead of electricity, electrical interference does not affect the signal. Fiber-optic cables have many uses other than communications, such as medical imaging, medical treatment, and mechanical engineering inspection.

Twisted-Pair Cables

Twisted-pair cables consist of one or more pairs of insulated copper wire that are twisted together and housed in a protective jacket. Like all copper cables, twisted pair uses pulses of electricity to transmit data.

Data transmission is sensitive to interference or noise, which can reduce the data rate that a cable can provide. A twisted-pair cable is susceptible to *electromagnetic interference (EMI)*, a type of electrical noise, and *radio frequency interference (RFI)*.

A source of interference, known as crosstalk, occurs when cables are bundled together for long lengths. The signal from one cable can leak out and enter adjacent cables.

When data transmission is corrupted due to interference such as crosstalk, the data must be retransmitted. This can degrade the data-carrying capacity of the medium.

In twisted-pair cabling, the number of twists per unit length affects the amount of resistance that the cable has to interference. Twisted-pair cable suitable for carrying telephone traffic, referred to as CAT3, has three to four turns per foot making it less resistant. Cable suitable for data transmission, known as CAT5, has three to four turns per inch, making it more resistant to interference. Figure 4-22 shows how interference or noise can affect data transmission. In the figure, an original pure data signal represents a specific bit pattern. Nearby electrical noise creates an interface signal on the same wire. The noise combines with the original signal and results in a corrupted or changed signal being received by the destination computer.

Figure 4-22   How Data Transmission Is Affected by Interference

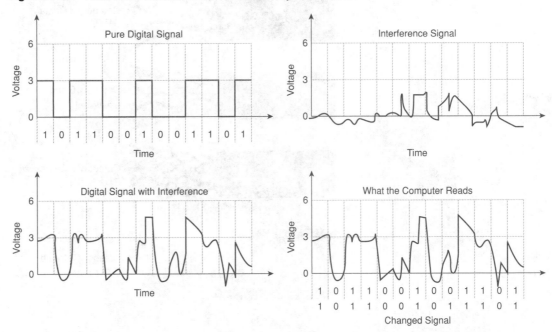

The three types of twisted-pair cable are unshielded twisted-pair, shielded twisted-pair, and screened twisted-pair.

Unshielded twisted-pair (UTP) is the most commonly encountered type of network cable in North America and many other areas. Shielded cables (ScTP and F-UTP) are used almost exclusively in European countries.

UTP cable is inexpensive, offers a high bandwidth, and is easy to install. This type of cable is used to connect workstations, hosts, and network devices. It can come with many different numbers of pairs inside the jacket, but the most common number of pairs is four. Each pair is identified by a specific color code.

Many different categories of UTP cables have been developed over time. Each category of cable was developed to support a specific technology and most are no longer encountered in homes or offices. The cable types that are still commonly found include Categories 3, 5, 5e, and 6. Some electrical environments exist in which EMI and RFI are so strong that shielding is a requirement to make communication possible, such as in a noisy factory. In this instance, using a cable that contains shielding, such as shielded twisted-pair (STP) and screened twisted-pair (ScTP) might be necessary. Unfortunately both STP and ScTP are very expensive, not as flexible, and have additional requirements due to the shielding that make them difficult to work with.

All categories of data-grade UTP cable are traditionally terminated into an RJ-45 connector. Figure 4-23 shows various types of twisted-pair cabling.

Figure 4-23   Categories of UTP

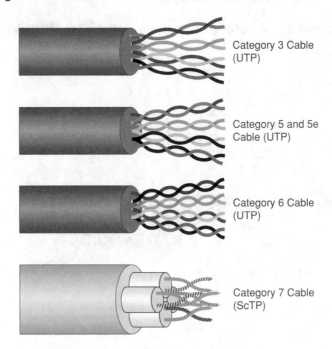

Category 3 Cable (UTP)

Category 5 and 5e Cable (UTP)

Category 6 Cable (UTP)

Category 7 Cable (ScTP)

The following are characteristics of Category 3 cable:

- Used for voice communication

- Most often used for phone lines

The following are characteristics of Category 5 and 5e cable:

- Used for data transmission.

- Cat 5 supports 100 Mbps and can support 1000 Mbps (Gigabit) but it is not recommended.

- Cat 5e supports 1000 Mbps (Gigabit).

- Defined in 568 standard.

The following are characteristics of Category 6 cable:

- Used for data transmission.

- An added separator is between each pair of wires allowing it to function at higher speeds.

- Supports 1000 Mbps (Gigabit) to 10 Gbps although 10 Gbps is not recommended.

- Defined in 568 standard.

The following are characteristics of Category 7 cable (ScTP):

- Used for data transmission.

- Individual pairs are wrapped in a shield and then the entire four pairs wrapped in another shield.

- Supports 1000 Mbps to 10 Gbps, although 10 Gbps is not recommended.

- Not currently defined in 568 standard.

Coaxial Cable

Like twisted pair, coaxial cable (or coax) also carries data in the form of electrical signals. It provides improved shielding compared to UTP, so has a lower signal-to-noise ratio and can therefore carry more data. It is most often used to connect a TV set to the signal source, be it a cable TV outlet, satellite TV, or conventional antenna. It is also used at NOCs to connect to the cable modem termination system (CMTS) and to connect to some high-speed device interfaces.

Although it employs the same basic construction as that used by early shared Ethernet networks, the coaxial cable used in cable TV networks is a different type. The modern communications technologies used with it support high-speed Internet, phone service, and television over the same coax cable.

Although coax has improved data-carrying characteristics, most local area networking uses twisted pair because coax is physically harder to install and is more expensive. As a result, current Ethernet standards no longer support the use of coax as a cabling medium. In addition, manufacturers of NICs and other networking devices no longer include coax connectors on their equipment.

Coax consists of a single center conductor, most often made of copper, although aluminum can be used as well. The center conductor is then surrounded by an insulator, such as polythene, which in turn is surrounded by a metallic braid made of aluminum or foil. The foil shields against EMI. The entire cable is then enclosed by a jacket for protection. Figure 4-24 shows the components of a typical coaxial cable.

Figure 4-24   Coaxial Cable Components

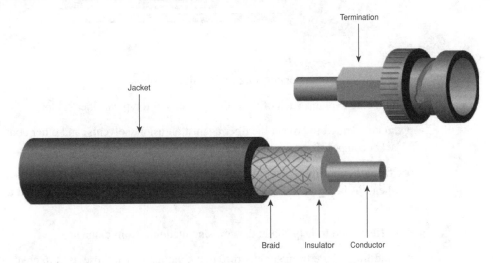

The following explains each of these components of a typical coaxial cable:

- **Termination**: Coax is normally terminated with a BNC or F-series connector. BNC is a crimped-down connector and is typically considered a stronger connection. An F-series connector is a screw-on connector.

- **Braid**: A metallic braid made of aluminum or foil helps to shield against EMI.

- **Insulator**: An insulator usually made of polythene, which provides strength to the cable, allows it to be more pliable.

- **Conductor**: A single center conductor, most often made of copper, although aluminum can be used as well.

Fiber-Optic Cables

Unlike TP and coax, fiber-optic cables transmit data using pulses of light. Although not normally found in home or small business environments, fiber-optic cabling is widely used in enterprise environments and large data centers.

Fiber-optic cable is constructed of either glass or plastic, neither of which conducts electricity. This means that it is immune to EMI and is suitable for installation in environments where interference is a problem.

In addition to its resistance to EMI, fiber-optic cables support a large amount of bandwidth making them ideally suited for high-speed data backbones. Fiber-optic backbones are found in many corporations and are also used to connect ISPs on the Internet.

Each fiber-optic circuit is actually two fiber cables. One is used to transmit data; the other is used to receive data. Figure 4-25 shows a fiber-optic cable with transmit (Tx) on one end and receive (Rx) on the other of each fiber.

Figure 4-25 Fiber-Optic Cable with Separate Transmit (Tx) and Receive (Rx) Fibers

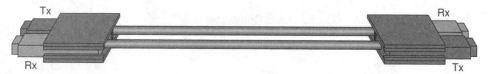

Figure 4-26 shows components of a typical fiber cable.

The following explains each of these components of a typical fiber cable:

- **Jacket**: Added to protect the fiber against abrasion, solvents, and other contaminants. This outer jacket composition can vary depending on the cable usage.

- **Strengthening material**: Surrounds the buffer and prevents the fiber cable from being stretched when it is being pulled. The material used is often the same material used to produce bulletproof vests.

- **Buffer**: Used to help shield the core and cladding from damage.

- **Cladding**: Made from slightly different chemicals than those used to create the core. It tends to act like a mirror by reflecting light back into the core of the fiber. This keeps light in the core as it travels down the fiber.

- **Core**: The core is actually the light transmission element at the center of the optical fiber. This core is typically silica, or glass. Light pulses from LEDs or lasers travel through the fiber core.

Figure 4-26   Fiber Cable Construction

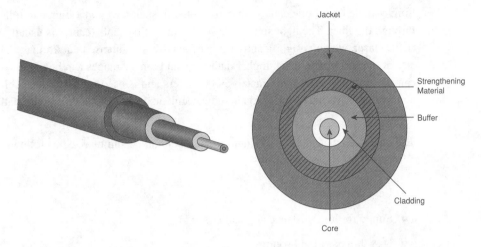

There are two forms of fiber-optic cable: multimode and single mode. Figure 4-27 shows a comparison of their construction.

Figure 4-27   Multimode and Single-Mode Fiber Cable Construction

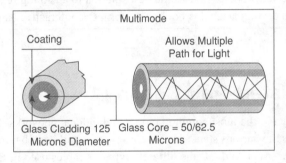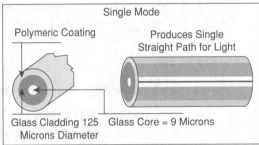

Multimode Fiber

Of the two forms of fiber optic, multimode is the less expensive and more widely used. The light source that produces the pulses of light is usually a light-emitting diode (LED). It is referred to as multimode because multiple rays of light, each carrying data, are transmitted through the cable simultaneously. Each ray of light takes a separate path through the multimode core. Multimode fiber-optic cables are generally suitable for links of up to 2000 meters. However, improvements in technology are continually improving this distance.

The characteristics and use of multimode fiber can be summarized as follows:

- Larger core than single-mode cable

- Permits greater dispersion and, therefore, loss of signal

- Suited for longer distances than UTP but shorter than single mode

- Uses LEDs as the light source

- Commonly used with LANs or distances of a couple hundred meters within a campus network

Single-Mode Fiber

Single-mode fiber-optic cables are constructed in such a way that light can follow only a single path through the fiber. The light source for single-mode fiber-optic cables is usually a light-emitting diode (LED) laser, which is significantly more expensive and intense than ordinary LEDs. Due to the intensity of the LED laser, much higher data rates and longer ranges can be obtained. Single-mode fibers can transmit data for approximately 3000 meters and is used for backbone cabling, including the interconnection of various NOCs. Again, advancements in technology are continually improving this distance.

The characteristics and use of single-mode fiber can be summarized as follows:

- Small core

- Less dispersion

- Suited for long-distance applications

- Uses lasers as light source

- Commonly used with campus backbones and distances of several thousand meters

Interactive Activity 4-3: Determine Whether Fiber Is the Best Solution (4.4.4.3)

In this interactive activity, you decide whether fiber is the best solution to a cabling requirement. Use file ia-4443 on the CD-ROM that accompanies this book to perform this interactive activity.

Working with Twisted-Pair Cabling

Twisted-pair (UTP) cabling is, by far, the most common type found in local networks. It is critical that a network technician understands the various standards for construction and installation of UTP. He or she must be able to recognize, construct, and test the different types of cables used in Ethernet networks.

Cabling Standards

Cabling is an integral part of building any network. When installing cabling, it is important to follow cabling standards, which have been developed to ensure that data networks operate to agreed levels of performance.

Cabling standards are a set of specifications for the installation and testing of cables. Standards specify types of cables to use in specific environments, conductor materials, pinouts, wire sizes, shielding, maximum cable lengths, connector types, and performance limits. As an example, standards specify that the maximum distance for Category 5e cable, from a host (workstation or server) to a switch is 100 meters (approximately 328 feet).

Many different organizations are involved in the creation of cabling standards. Although some of these organizations have only local jurisdiction, many offer standards that are adopted around the world.

Figure 4-28 shows some of the global organizations and the areas that they manage.

Figure 4-28   Global Cabling Standards Organizations

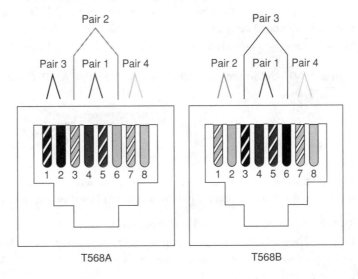

Power over Ethernet (PoE)

In 1999, IEEE began developing the standard for delivering power over Ethernet using structured cabling. Today that standard is known as IEEE 802.3af-2003. It is used to provide 48 volts DC along with Ethernet data on UTP or STP cable.

PoE allows network engineers to have flexibility in the placement of endpoint devices, such as wireless access points, video cameras, and IP telephones, because an electrical power outlet does not need to be near the device.

UTP Cables

Twisted-pair cable is most commonly used in network installations. The TIA/EIA organization defines two different patterns, or wiring schemes, called T568A and T568B. Each wiring scheme defines the pinout, or order of wire connections, on the end of the cable.

The two schemes are similar except two of the four pairs are reversed in the termination order. Figure 4-29 shows how the two pairs are reversed.

Figure 4-29   T568A and T568B UTP Termination Standards

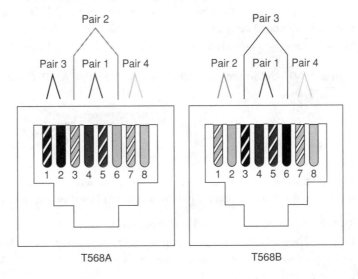

The actual cables have a different color coding than is shown in Table 4-1. When either standard is used with 10 Mbps or 100 Mbps Ethernet, data is carried on pairs 2 and 3. Notice that with both standards the wires for either pair 2 or pair 3 are separated. This helps reduce crosstalk between the wire pairs.

Table 4-1   T568 UTP Wiring Standards

Wire Pair	Wire Colors	T568A Standard	T568B Standard
Pair 1	Solid blue and blue with white stripe	Pins 4 and 5	Pins 4 and 5
Pair 2	Solid orange and orange with white stripe	Pins 3 and 6	Pins 1 and 2
Pair 3	Green with white stripe and solid green	Pins 1 and 2	Pins 3 and 6
Pair 4	Brown with white stripe and solid brown	Pins 7 and 8	Pins 7 and 8

On a network installation, one of the two wiring schemes (T568A or T568B) should be chosen and followed. Ensuring that the same wiring scheme is used for every termination in that project is important. If working on an existing network, use the wiring scheme already employed.

Using the T568A and T568B wiring standards, two types of cables can be created: a straight-through cable and a crossover cable. These two types of cable are found in data installations.

A *straight-through cable* is the most common cable type. It maps a wire to the same pins on both ends of the cable. In other words, if T568A is on one end of the cable, T568A is also on the other. If T568B is on one end of the cable, T568B is on the other. This means that the order of connections (the pinout) for each color is the same on both ends.

It is the type of straight-through cable (T568A or T568B) used on the network that defines the wiring scheme for the network.

A *crossover cable* uses both wiring schemes. T568A is on one end of the cable and T568B is on the other end of the same cable. This means that the order of connection on one end of the cable does not match the order of connections on the other.

The straight-through and crossover cables each have a specific use on the network. The type of cable needed to connect two devices depends on which wire pairs the devices use to transmit and receive data. Figure 4-30 shows the wire pairs of an unterminated UTP cable. The way in which the cable ends are terminated determine whether the cable will be T568A straight-through, a T568B straight-through cable, or a crossover cable with T568A on one end and T568B on the other.

Figure 4-30   Unterminated Unshielded Twisted-Pair (UTP) Cable

Specific pins on the connector are associated with a transmit function and a receive function. The transmit pin versus the receive pin is determined based on the device.

Two devices directly connected and using different pins for transmit and receive are known as unlike devices. They require a straight-through cable to exchange data. Devices that are directly connected and use the same pins for transmit and receive are known as like devices. They require the use of a crossover cable to exchange data.

Unlike Devices

The pins on the RJ-45 data connector of a PC have pins 1 and 2 as transmit and pins 3 and 6 as receive, as shown in Figure 4-31. The pins on the data connector of a switch have pins 1 and 2 as receive and pins 3 and 6 as transmit. The pins used for transmit on the PC correspond to those used for receive on the switch. Therefore, a straight-through cable is necessary.

Figure 4-31   TIA/EIA Straight-Through UTP Wiring—Unlike Devices

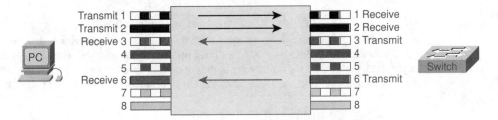

The wire connected to pin 1 (transmit pin) on the PC on one end of the cable is connected to pin 1 (receive pin) on the switch on the other end of the cable.

Other examples of unlike devices that require a straight-through cable include switch port to router port and hub port to PC.

Like Devices

If a PC is directly connected to another PC, pins 1 and 2 on both devices are transmit pins and pins 3 and 6 are receive pins. A crossover cable would ensure that the green wire connected to pins 1 and 2 (transmit pins) on one PC connect to pins 3 and 6 (receive pins) on the other PC, as shown in Figure 4-32.

Figure 4-32   TIA/EIA Crossover UTP Wiring—Like Devices

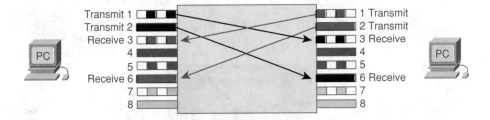

If a straight-through cable were used, the wire connected to pin 1, the transmit pin, on PC1 would be connected to pin 1, the transmit pin, on PC2. Receiving data on a transmit pin is not possible. It is easy to see why two PCs or two switches would be considered like devices, but why are a PC and a router like devices? The reason is that both the PC and the router have an Ethernet NIC (interface) and either one would normally be connected to a hub or switch so that they could communicate. When connecting a PC directly to a router, you must use a crossover cable.

Other examples of like devices that require a crossover cable include

- Switch port to switch port

- Switch port to hub port

- Hub port to hub port

- Router interface to router interface
- PC to router interface
- PC to PC

If the incorrect cable type is used, the connection between network devices will not function.

Some devices can automatically sense which pins are used for transmit and receive and will adjust their internal connections accordingly.

TIP

A 10BASE-T straight-through or crossover cable only uses the wires on pins 1, 2, 3, and 6. If constructing a cable to function at speeds above 10 Mbps it is important to terminate all wires. Failure to connect all the wires might result in the cable not functioning or the connection speed dropping back to 10 Mbps depending on the network interface cards in use. Cat 6 cable and Gigabit Ethernet require all eight wires to be terminated.

UTP Cable Termination

UTP and STP cable is usually terminated into an RJ-45 connector. The RJ-45 connector is considered a male component, which is crimped to the end of the cable. When a male connector is viewed from the front with the metal contacts facing up, the pin locations are numbered from 8 on the left to 1 on the right.

The jack is considered the female component and is located in networking devices, wall outlets, or patch panels. The RJ-45 connector on the wire plugs into the jack.

You can purchase cables that are pre-terminated with RJ-45 connectors. You can also manually terminate them, onsite, using a crimping tool. When manually terminating UTP cable into an RJ-45 connector, untwist only a small amount of wire to minimize crosstalk. Also be sure that the wires are pushed all the way into the end of the connector and that the RJ-45 connector is crimped onto the wire jacket. This ensures good electrical contact and provides strength to the wire connection. Figure 4-33 shows an RJ-45 wall jack and a UTP cable with an RJ-45 connector.

Figure 4-33 RJ-45 Jack and RJ-45 Cable Connector

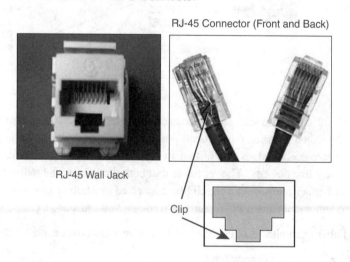

RJ-45 Connector (Front and Back)

RJ-45 Wall Jack

Clip

Lab 4-2: Building Straight-Through and Crossover UTP Cables (4.5.3.2)

In this lab you construct both straight-through and crossover UTP cables. Refer to the hands-on lab in Part II of this *Learning Guide*. You may perform this lab now or wait until the end of the chapter.

Terminating UTP at Patch Panels and Wall Jacks

In a NOC, network devices are usually connected to patch panels. Patch panels act like switchboards that connect workstations cables to other devices. The use of patch panels enables the physical cabling of the network to be quickly rearranged as equipment is added or replaced. These patch panels use RJ-45 jacks for quick connection on the front, but require the cables to be punched down on the reverse side of the RJ-45 jack.

Patch panels are no longer confined to enterprise network installations. They can be found in many small businesses and even homes where they provide a central connection point for data, telephone, and even audio systems. Figure 4-34 shows a patch panel and a *punchdown tool* for attaching wires to it.

Figure 4-34 Front and Rear of RJ-45 Patch Panel and Punchdown Tool

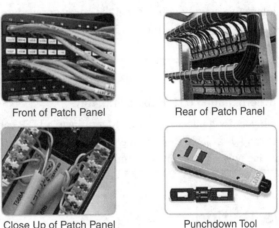

Front of Patch Panel Rear of Patch Panel

Close Up of Patch Panel Punchdown Tool

The RJ-45 jack has eight conductors and is wired according to either T568A or T568B. At the patch panel a device known as a punchdown tool is required to push the wires into the connector. The wires should be matched up to the appropriate *insulation displacement connector (IDC)* by color before punching them down. The punchdown tool also cuts off any excess wire.

A punchdown tool is not required to terminate most wall jacks. To terminate these connectors, the cables are untwisted and placed into the appropriate IDC. Placing the cap on the jack pushes the cables into the IDC and cuts through the insulation on the wires. Most of these connectors then require the installer to manually trim away excess cable.

In all cases, untwisting more cable than is necessary increases the amount of crosstalk and degrades overall network performance. Figure 4-35 shows a wall jack and the surface-mount wall enclosure in which it is to be inserted. Wall enclosures can contain two, four, or more RJ-45 jacks. The wall enclosure can also be of the flush-mounted design, which is inserted into a wall.

Figure 4-35 RJ-45 Wall Jacks and Multireceptacle Enclosure

Modular RJ-45 Jacks

Surface Mount Box with 4 RJ-45 Jacks Installed

Interactive Activity 4-4: Observe UTP Cable and Wall Jack Termination (4.5.4.3)

In this interactive activity you observe the correct procedure for punching down UTP cable and terminating RJ-45 wall jacks. Use file ia-4543 on the CD-ROM that accompanies this book to perform this interactive activity.

Lab 4-3: Terminating UTP Cables (4.5.4.4)

In this lab you use a punchdown tool to terminate a UTP cable into an IDC and terminate a UTP cable into an RJ-45 jack. Refer to the hands-on lab in Part II of this *Learning Guide*. You may perform this lab now or wait until the end of the chapter.

Cable Testing

When a new or repaired cable run is terminated, verifying that the cable operates correctly and meets connectivity standards is important. This can be done through a series of tests.

The first test is a visual inspection, which verifies that all wires are connected according to T568A or B.

In addition to visual examination, check the cable electrically in order to determine problems or flaws in a network cabling installation. The following are tools that you can use for cable diagnostics (see Figure 4-36):

- **Cable testers**: Cable testers test cables for various wiring faults such as a wires accidentally mapping to the wrong pin, or shorts or opens. They are frequently used to check patch cables and entire cable runs. Testing a newly constructed cable before putting it into service is a good idea. The cost of a sophisticated cable tester with an LCD screen can be relatively high. Simple cable testers with LED indicators can be very inexpensive.

- **Cable certifiers**: A cable certification tester determines the precise performance of a cable, and then records it in graphical form for the customer records. Cable certifiers are frequently used to confirm that new UTP and fiber cable installations will perform up to standards. If a particular cable run does not meet standards, the installer must troubleshoot the problem and correct it. Cable certifier is the most sophisticated cable testing device and can be very expensive.

■ **Multimeters**: Multimeters are a type of general-use electrical test equipment. They can measure AC/DC voltage, current, and resistance. For example, a multimeter could be used to verify the AC voltage coming from an electrical outlet or to test the resistance of a wire. Multimeter cost can vary from expensive to relatively inexpensive depending on accuracy, capabilities, and type of screen. Their use in cable testing is limited.

Figure 4-36   Cable Tester, Cable Certifier, and Multimeter

Cable Tester   Cable Certifier   Multimeter

The cable tester is used to perform initial diagnostics. The first test usually is called a *continuity* test and it verifies that there is end-to-end connectivity. It can also detect common cabling faults such as opens and shorts.

An *open* is an error in wiring that is caused by a break in the continuity of a circuit. An open circuit occurs when the wire is not properly pushed into the connector and there is no electrical contact. An open can also occur if there is a break in the wire.

A *short* occurs when the copper conductors touch each other. As the electric pulse travels down the wire, it will cross onto the touching wire. This creates an unintended path in the flow of the signal to its destination.

A cable tester can also create wire maps that will verify that the cable is terminated correctly. A wire map shows which wire pairs connect to which pins on the connectors and jacks. The wire map test verifies that all eight wires are connected to the correct pins and indicates whether cabling faults such as split pairs or reversals are present.

If any of these faults are detected, the easiest way to correct them is to reterminate the cable.

The reversed-pair fault occurs when a wire pair is correctly installed on one connector, but reversed on the other connector. If the white/orange wire is terminated on pin 1 and the orange wire is termi-nated on pin 2 at one end of a cable, but reversed at the other end, then the cable has a reversed-pair fault.

A split-pair fault occurs when one wire from one pair is switched with one wire from a different pair at both ends. Look carefully at the pin numbers in Figure 4-37 to detect the wiring fault. A split pair creates two transmit or receive pairs each with two wires that are not twisted together. This mixing hampers the cross-cancellation process and makes the cable more susceptible to crosstalk and interfer-ence.

Specialized cable testers provide additional information, such as the level of attenuation and crosstalk.

Attenuation

Attenuation, also commonly referred to as insertion loss, is a general term that refers to the reduction in the strength of a signal. Attenuation is a natural consequence of signal transmission over any medi-um. Electrical resistance in copper and impurities in fiber-optic cable contribute to attenuation. Attenuation limits the length of network cabling over which a message can be sent. A cable certifier measures attenuation by injecting a signal in one end and then measuring its strength at the other end.

Figure 4-38 shows the use of a repeater (in this case a hub) in a local network to increase the strength of a signal that has attenuated. Without the repeater the signal would be unreadable when it reached its destination. Copper and fiber-optic repeaters are also used in all long-distance data transmission to boost signal strength in order to overcome the problem of attenuation.

Figure 4-37   Reversed Pair, Split Pair, Open, and Short

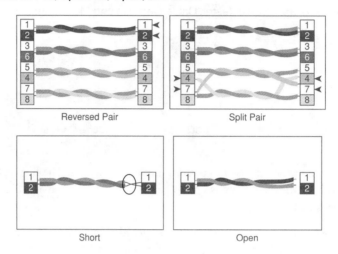

Figure 4-38   Attenuation—Loss of Signal Strength

Crosstalk

Crosstalk is the leakage of signals between pairs. If this is measured near the transmitting end, it is termed *near-end crosstalk (NEXT)*. If measured at the receiving end of the cable it is termed *far-end crosstalk (FEXT)*. Both forms of crosstalk degrade network performance and are often caused by untwisting too much cable when terminating. If high crosstalk values are detected, the best thing to do is check the cable terminations and reterminate as necessary.

Lab 4-4: Testing UTP Cables (4.5.5.4)

In this lab you test the cable created in a previous lab session. Refer to the hands-on lab in Part II of this *Learning Guide*. You may perform this lab now or wait until the end of the chapter.

Cabling Best Practices

The following best practices help to ensure that cable termination is successful:

- Ensuring that the type of cables and components used on a network adhere to the standards required for that network is important. Modern converged networks carry voice, video, and data traffic on the same wires; therefore, the cables used on converged networks must be able to support all these applications.

- Cable standards specify maximum lengths for different types of cables. Always adhere to the length restrictions for the type of cable being installed.

- UTP, like all copper cable, is susceptible to EMI and RFI. Installing cable away from sources of interference, such as high-voltage cables and fluorescent lighting, is important. Televisions, computer monitors, and microwaves are other possible sources of interference. In some environments installing data cables in conduit to protect them from EMI and RFI might be necessary.

- Improper termination and the use of low-quality cables and connectors can degrade the signal-carrying capacity of the cable. Always follow the rules for cable termination and test to verify that the termination has been done properly.

- Test all cable installations to ensure proper connectivity and operation. Figure 4-39 shows a network technician checking a cabling installation.

Figure 4-39 Checking Cabling

- Label all cables as they are installed, and record the location of cables in network documentation.

- In homes and small offices one might be tempted to cut corners. Avoid installing cables externally where they might become a lightning rod because this could both damage equipment as well as become a safety hazard to users.

Structured cabling is a method for creating an organized cabling system that can be easily understood by installers, network administrators, and any other technicians who deal with cables. One component of structured cabling is cable management. With the quantity of cabling shown previously in Figure 4-19, one can easily see why structured cabling and cable management is important.

Cable management serves multiple purposes. First, it presents a neat and organized system, which aids in the isolation of cabling problems. Second, by following cable management best practices, the cables are protected from physical damage, which greatly reduces the number of problems experienced.

Cables should be considered a long-term investment. What is sufficient now might not be in the near future. Always plan for the future by complying with all current standards. Remember that standards help to ensure that the cables will be able to deliver acceptable performance as the technology evolves.

Observing cabling best practices in all environments is important. Strict adherence to these practices, in home and business environments, helps reduce the number of potential problems. It will save a great amount of time, money, and frustration.

Interactive Activity 4-5: Determine Cabling Best Practices (4.5.6.3)

In this interactive activity, decide whether an operation is a cabling best practice or not. Use file ia-4563 on the CD-ROM that accompanies this book to perform this interactive activity.

Summary

This chapter described the Internet as a worldwide collection of computer networks, cooperating with each other to exchange information using common standards. In order to access the Internet you must connect through an ISP.

An ISP is a company that provides the connections and support to access the Internet. ISPs support small to large geographic areas and provide services such as e-mail, web pages, IP telephony, and DNS.

Individual computers and local networks connect to the ISP at a point of presence (POP) using technologies such as dial-up, DSL, cable, wireless, or satellite.

The most important protocol of the Internet is IP. The Internet Protocol formats data into packets that are from 64 to 1518 bytes in length and that must contain a valid source and destination IP address that must be unique on the Internet.

Every ISP has a control facility for its network, known as the Network Operations Center (NOC), which usually controls traffic flow and houses services such as e-mail and web hosting.

On network diagrams, a cloud is often used to represent the Internet without showing the details of the devices and connections. In the Internet cloud, routers are used to interconnect ISPs and can provide alternative paths from source to destination. **ping** and **tracert** are utilities that test connectivity to a destination device such as a router.

ISPs must be able to accept and deliver information to end users and other ISPs using a variety of technologies. Networking devices used in ISPs are high-end, high-speed devices with redundancy. An ISP must consider the physical requirements, such as power and air conditioning, of the networking equipment and the servers it houses.

For communication to occur, a channel must be present to carry the signals. In the networked world, the medium is usually a physical cable. Network cables are grouped into two categories: copper cables that carry electrical signals and fiber cables that carry light waves.

Copper wire, such as UTP and coaxial cable, is extremely vulnerable to both electromagnetic (EMI) and radio frequency interference (RFI). Fiber-optic cable is made of glass or plastic and is immune to EMI and RFI.

Unshielded twisted-pair (UTP) cable is used on most Ethernet networks whereas coaxial cable is used frequently for cable TV and Internet and has an extremely large bandwidth capacity that allows many signals to be combined or multiplexed together. Fiber-optic cable can provide a tremendous amount of bandwidth and is suitable for use as backbone cables.

Cabling standards are guidelines for the installation and testing of cables to ensure acceptable performance as technology evolves. TIA/EIA twisted pair termination standards are 568A and 568B. Different types of cables have different wiring schemes. Common UTP cable types are straight-through and crossover.

Activities and Labs

This summary outlines the activities and labs you can perform to help reinforce important concepts described in this chapter. You can find the activity and Packet Tracer files on the CD-ROM accompanying this book. The complete hands-on labs appear in Part II.

Interactive Activities on the CD:

Interactive Activity 4-1: Analyze ISP and End User Requirements (4.1.5.3)

Interactive Activity 4-2: Match the NOC Equipment to Requirements (4.3.2.3)

Interactive Activity 4-3: Determine Whether Fiber Is the Best Solution (4.4.4.3)

Interactive Activity 4-4: Observe UTP Cable and Wall Jack Termination (4.5.4.3)

Interactive Activity 4-5: Determine Cabling Best Practices (4.5.6.3)

Packet Tracer Activities on the CD:

Observing Packets Across the Network (4.2.3.2)

Labs in Part II of This Book:

Lab 4-1: Tracing Internet Connectivity (4.2.3.3)

Lab 4-2: Building Straight-Through and Crossover UTP Cables (4.5.3.2)

Lab 4-3: Terminating UTP Cables (4.5.4.4)

Lab 4-4: Testing UTP Cables (4.5.5.4)

Check Your Understanding

Complete all the review questions listed here to test your understanding of the topics and concepts in this chapter. The "Check Your Understanding and Challenge Questions Answer Key" appendix lists the answers.

1. Which two statements are true regarding IP packets?

   A. They are also called frames.

   B. They are also called segments.

   C. They are also called datagrams.

   D. They have a header that contains IP addresses.

   E. They are addressed using a source and destination MAC address.

2. Select the true statement regarding the **ping** and **tracert** commands.

   A. **tracert** shows each hop, whereas **ping** shows a destination reply only.

   B. **tracert** uses IP addresses; **ping** does not.

   C. Both **ping** and **tracert** can show results in a graphical display.

   D. **ping** shows whether the transmission is successful; **tracert** does not.

3. Connect the cabling term on the left to the correct definition on the right.

EMI	Uses a BNC or F-series connector
Coax cable	Used inside fiber-optic cabling to reflect light
ScTP	Uses two fibers: one to transmit, one to receive
Fiber-optic circuit	Signal from one cable interferes with another
Cladding	Noise created by an electrical environment
Crosstalk	Signal weakening over distance after it is transmitted
Attenuation	Expensive type of twisted-pair cabling

4. Where do ISPs get the public addresses that they assign to end users?

   A. ISPs create the addresses themselves.

   B. ISPs are assigned addresses through the RFC.

   C. ISPs obtain their addresses automatically.

   D. ISPs obtain address blocks from registry organizations.

5. Which of these statements regarding fiber-optic network cabling are true? (Choose 3.)

   A. Uses light to transmit data

   B. Uses eight wires

   C. Used by cable TV providers to connect to the customer's modem

   D. Used for long distances at high speeds

   E. Commonly used between buildings

6. Which of these statements regarding UTP network cabling are true? (Choose three.)

    A. Uses light to transmit data.

    B. Susceptible to EMI and RFI.

    C. Commonly used between buildings.

    D. Most difficult type of networking cable to install.

    E. Most commonly used type of networking cable.

    F. It provides four pairs of wire.

7. Which of the following statements apply to an ISP? (Choose 3.)

    A. Provides transport services to a large number of users

    B. Provides minimal services to a couple of users

    C. Contains many different networking devices

    D. Contains few devices

    E. Requires robust equipment

    F. Purchases access connectivity from end users

8. Which of the following statements regarding cabling are false? (Choose 2.)

    A. Coax is easier to install than UTP.

    B. Category 5 is commonly used for UTP data connectivity.

    C. Multimode is a type of fiber network cable.

    D. Fiber connectivity is common in home networking.

    E. Category 6 can support Gigabit speeds with Ethernet.

9. What are the two most common high-speed Internet access technologies for home users?

10. An integrated home networking device that connects to local computers and to the ISP modem can include which of the following functions? (Choose one or more answers.)

    A. Switching.

    B. Routing.

    C. Wireless communication.

    D. Automated addressing.

    E. Firewall service.

    F. All of these options are correct.

11. Home and small business networks frequently employ what type of Internet service: symmetric or asymmetric?

12. Which of the following is *not* an appropriate use of a crossover cable when connecting devices in an Ethernet network?

    A. Switch to switch

    B. PC to PC

    C. Switch to hub

    D. PC to router

    E. PC to switch

13. What is the purpose of a CMTS in an ISP's POP?

    A. To support DSL customers

    B. To support dial-up customers

    C. To support cellular customers

    D. To support cable modem customers

    E. To support T1 customers

14. Which of the following is *not* an example of a wiring problem that can occur with UTP?

    A. Open

    B. Short

    C. Close

    D. Reversed pair

    E. Split pair

15. When terminating an Ethernet UTP cable, which type of connector is normally used?

    A. BNC

    B. RJ-11

    C. RJ-45

    D. F-Series

    E. ST-45

16. What are two of the main problems that can occur with a UTP cable when transmitting data?

    A. Crossfire

    B. Crosstalk

    C. Overload

    D. Attenuation

    E. Aggregation

17. A user is sending a message from a PC on her home network that uses a Linksys integrated router, to a server at the ISP's POP. She has DSL service with the ISP. Based on the devices listed here, what is the proper sequence of devices the message will go through?

    A. PC → Linksys → cable modem → ISP CMTS at POP → server

    B. PC → DSL modem → ISP DSLAM at POP → Linksys → server

    C. PC → Linksys → DSL modem → ISP DSLAM at POP → server

    D. PC → ISP CMTS at POP → cable modem → Linksys → server

18. When tracing the route a packet takes through the Internet, what term refers to each router a packet goes through from source to destination?

    A. Port

    B. Interface

    C. NOC

    D. IXP

    E. Hop

19. The header of an Internet protocol datagram contains (choose 3)

    A. Control information

    B. Source IP address

    C. Destination IP address

    D. All intermediate router IP addresses

    E. The street address of the ISPs headquarters

Challenge Questions and Activities

These questions require a deeper application of the concepts covered in this chapter. You can find the answers in the appendix.

1. You have purchased a new home and desire to have high-speed Internet access as well as phone service and television service. Assuming that you live in a metropolitan area where most services are available, what are some options that you might consider to obtain these services? Would you obtain them from independent providers or from a single provider and why?

CHAPTER 5

Network Addressing

Objectives

Upon completion of this chapter, you will be able to answer the following questions:

- What is the purpose of an IP address and subnet mask and how are they used on the Internet?

- What is the difference between a unicast, multicast, and broadcast IP address?

- What are the three classes of assignable IP addresses and what are their ranges?

- How are IP addresses obtained?

- What is the difference between a public and a private IP address and when is each used?

- What is RFC 1918 address space?

- How does NAT function?

Key Terms

This chapter uses the following key terms. You can find the definitions in the Glossary.

In order to establish reliable communications channels, a global addressing scheme is required. This addressing scheme must be both flexible and dynamic. IP addresses have become the standard for network communications around the world. This chapter examines IP addresses and how unique IP addresses can be provided to host devices. It also explains the concept of private address space and the role of NAT. Part II of this book includes the corresponding labs for this chapter.

IP Addresses and Subnet Masks

The requirement for a simple, yet effective, global addressing system has been fulfilled by the IP addressing scheme. This system allows each host to be provided with a unique address but also allows these addresses to be grouped together into logical networks.

Purpose of an IP Address

In order to participate in communication on an IP network such as the Internet, a host needs an IP address. The IP address is a *logical network address* that identifies a particular host. It must be properly configured and unique in order to allow a device to communicate with other devices on the Internet.

An IP address is assigned to the network interface connection for a host. This connection is usually a network interface card (NIC) installed in the device. These NICs can be designed to participate in either a wired or a wireless network. Examples of end-user devices with network interfaces include workstations, servers, network printers, and IP phones. Some servers can have more than one NIC and each of these has its own IP address. Router interfaces that provide connections to an IP network also have an IP address because they behave as a host on the network.

Every packet sent across the Internet has both a *source* and destination IP address. This information is required by networking devices to ensure that the information gets to the destination and any replies can be returned to the source. Figure 5-1 shows this process.

Packet Tracer
☐ **Activity**

Connecting to a Web Server Using IP (5.1.1.2)

In this Packet Tracer activity you observe how packets are sent across the Internet using IP addresses. Use file d1-5112.pka on the CD-ROM that accompanies this book to perform this activity using Packet Tracer.

IP Address Structure

An IP address is simply a series of 32 *binary digits*. Although machines have no difficulty accurately reading these longs strings of ones and zeros, reading an IP address in binary IP form is very difficult for humans. For this reason, the 32 bits are grouped into four 8-bit bytes called *octets*. Even with this grouping, it is still hard for humans to read, write, and remember these addresses. To make the addresses easier to understand, each octet is presented as its decimal value, separated by a decimal point or period. This is referred to as *dotted-decimal notation* and is the usual way that humans work with IP addresses.

Figure 5-1   Purpose of a Host IP Address

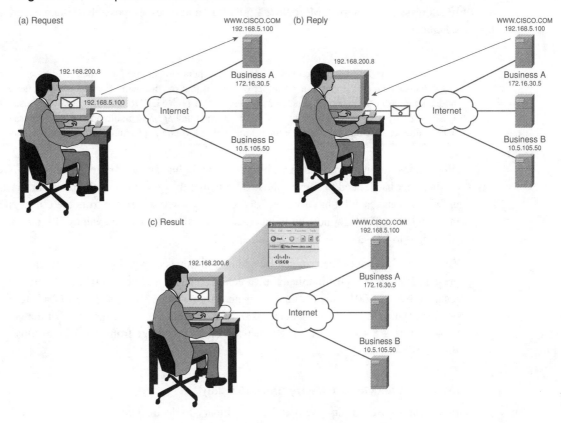

When a host is configured with an IP address, as shown in Figure 5-2, it is entered as a dotted-decimal number such as 192.168.1.5. Imagine if you had to enter the 32-bit binary equivalent of this: 11000000101010000000000100000101. If you mistyped just one bit, the address would be different and the host would not be able to communicate on the network.

Figure 5-2   Configuring an IP Address on a Host

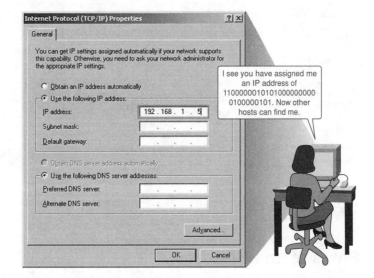

The 32-bit IP address is defined with *IP version 4 (IPv4)* and is currently the most common form of IP address on the Internet. More than 4 billion IP addresses are possible using a 32-bit addressing scheme.

> **TIP**
>
> Although IPv4 is still the most common addressing scheme in common use, these addresses are quickly becoming exhausted due to the increasing number of devices that require them. For this reason a newer version of IP addressing has been developed, known as *IP version 6 (IPv6)*. IPv6 uses 128 bits to represent hosts instead of the 32 used by IPv4. This feature greatly increases the number of available hosts (2^{128} addresses or roughly 5×10^{28} addresses for every person alive today) and will alleviate the problem of scarce addresses.

When a host receives an IP address, it looks at all 32 bits as they are received by the NIC. Humans, on the other hand, need to convert those 32 bits into the dotted-decimal equivalent. Each octet is made up of 8 bits and each bit has a value. Each octet is treated separately from the others and is converted independently. The rightmost bit in an octet has a value of 1 and the values of the remaining bits, from right to left, are 2, 4, 8, 16, 32, 64, and 128.

The value of an octet is determined by adding the values of positions wherever there is a binary 1 present. If a 0 is in a position then the value is not added in. For example, if the binary octet was represented by 1001 0011, the decimal equivalent would be 128 + 16 + 2 + 1 or 147. If all 8 bits in an octet are 0 then the value of that octet is 0. If all the bits are 1 then the value of the octet is 255 (128 + 64 + 32 + 16 + 8 + 4 + 2 + 1). The values for each octet range from 0 to 255, as illustrated in Figure 5-3.

Interactive Activity 5-1: Binary Game (5.1.2.3)

In this interactive activity you practice your binary-to-decimal conversion skills. Use file ia-5123 on the CD-ROM that accompanies this book to perform this interactive activity.

Figure 5-3   Decimal Equivalent of a Binary IP Address

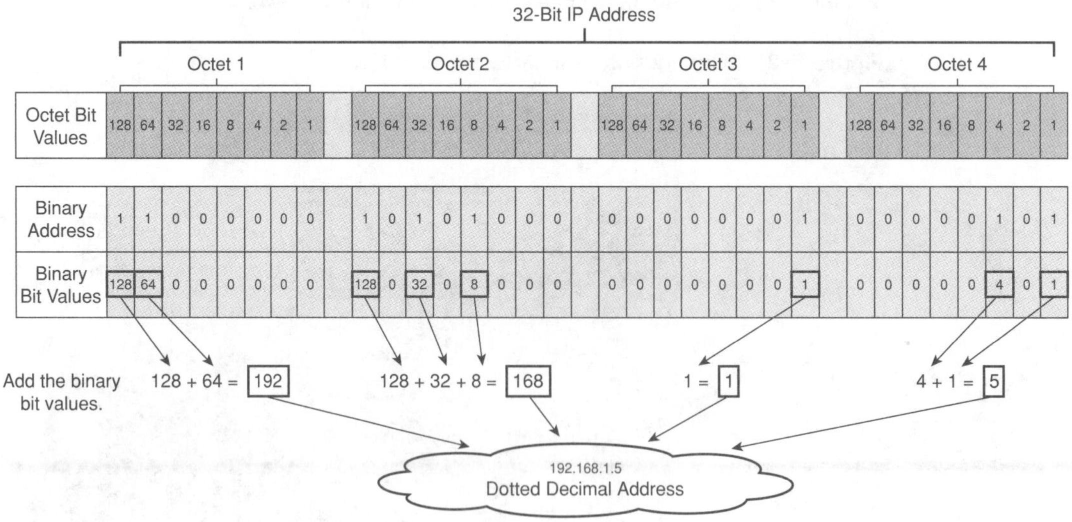

Parts of an IP Address

The logical 32-bit IP address is *hierarchical* and is made up of two parts, as shown in Figure 5-4. The first part identifies the network and the second part identifies a host on that network. Both parts are required in an IP address.

As an example, if a host has IP address 192.168.18.57, the first three octets, 192.168.18, identify the network portion of the address, and the last octet, 57 identifies the host. This is known as hierarchical addressing because the network portion indicates the network on which each unique host address is located. Routers only need to know how to reach each network, rather than needing to know the location of each individual host.

Figure 5-4   Parts of an IP Address

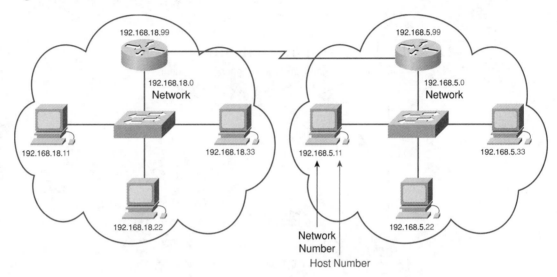

Another example of a hierarchical network is the telephone system. In a telephone number, the country code, area code, and exchange or prefix represent the network address, and the remaining digits represent a local phone number.

Interactive Activity 5-2: Identifying the Network Portion of an IP Address (5.1.3.2)

In this interactive activity you sort specific host IP addresses into the correct network containers. Use file ia-5132 on the CD-ROM that accompanies this book to perform this interactive activity.

How IP Addresses and Subnet Masks Interact

Every IP address is made up of two parts. How do hosts know which portion is the network and which is the host? This is the job of the subnet mask. When an IP host is configured, a *subnet mask* is assigned along with an IP address. Like the IP address, the subnet mask is 32 bits long. The subnet mask signifies which part of the IP address is network and which part is host. It acts like a filter to block out the host portion of the IP address to reveal the network portion.

The subnet mask is compared to the IP address from left to right, bit for bit. The 1s in the subnet mask represent the network portion; the 0s represent the host portion. In the example shown in Figure 5-5, the first three octets are the network, and the last octet represents the host.

When a host sends a packet, it compares its subnet mask to its own IP address and the destination IP address. If the network bits match, both the source and destination host are on the same network and the packet can be delivered locally. If they do not match, the sending host forwards the packet to the local router interface to be sent on to the other network. The local router interface is known as the default gateway to the host machine.

The subnet masks we see most often with home and small business networking are 255.0.0.0 (8 bits), 255.255.0.0 (16 bits), and 255.255.255.0 (24 bits). A subnet mask of 255.255.255.0 (decimal) or 11111111.11111111.1111111.00000000 (binary) uses 24 bits to identify the network number, which leaves 8 bits to number the hosts on that network, as shown in Figure 5-6.

Figure 5-5   Determining Whether Hosts Are on the Same Network

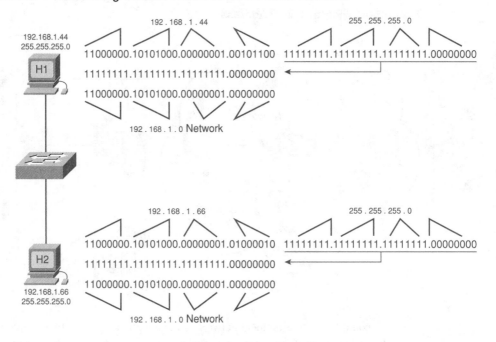

Figure 5-6   Number of Possible Hosts with Eight Host Bits

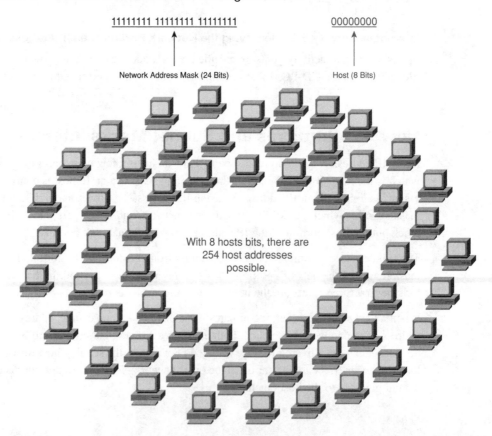

To calculate the number of hosts that can be on that network, take the number 2 to the power of the number of host bits ($2^8 = 256$). We do this because each bit can have one of two values, either a zero or a one. From this number, we must subtract 2 ($256 - 2 = 254$). The reason we subtract 2 is because we cannot assign an IP address that has either all 0s or all 1s in the host portion. An IP address with all 1s within the host portion is a broadcast address for that network and an address with all 0s within the host portion indicates the *network number*. Powers of 2 can be calculated easily with the calculator that comes with any Windows operating system.

Another way to determine the number of hosts available is to add up the values of the available host bits ($128 + 64 + 32 + 16 + 8 + 4 + 2 + 1 = 255$). From this number, subtract 1 ($255 - 1 = 254$), because the host bits cannot be all 1s. Subtracting 2 is not necessary because the value of all 0s is 0 and is not included in the addition.

With a 16-bit mask, there are 16 bits (two octets) for host addresses, and a host address could have all 1s (255) in one of the octets. This address might appear to be a broadcast but as long as the other octet is not all 1s, it is a valid host address. Remember that the host looks at all host bits together, not at octet values.

Lab 5-1: Using the Windows Calculator with Network Addresses (5.1.4.3)

In this lab you use the Windows calculator to work with binary and decimal representations of the IP address and binary and hexadecimal representations of the MAC address. Refer to the lab in Part II of this *Learning Guide*. You may perform this lab now or wait until the end of the chapter.

Types of IP Addresses

Many different types of IP addresses are available. Some addresses indicate a special form of communication should occur whereas others are designed to provide adequate address space for use inside a company or organization. Some are routable on the Internet whereas others are not. The pattern of bits within the IP address tells the network devices how the packet should be treated.

IP Address Classes and Default Subnet Masks

The IP address and subnet mask work together to determine which portion of the IP address represents the network address and which portion represents the host address. IP addresses are grouped into five classes. *Class A*, *Class B*, and *Class C* are commercial addresses and are assigned to hosts. *Class D* is reserved for multicast use and *Class E* is for experimental use. These last two classes of addresses are not normally assigned to any one organization.

> **NOTE**
>
> The *classful* system of IP addressing breaks up the available address space into five distinct classes. Another system that exists, the *classless* system, does not rely on class boundaries but instead treats all address space as being equal. Any number of bits can be assigned to represent the network portion of an address leaving the rest to represent hosts. This also introduces a new nomenclature for specifying the subnet mask. Subnet masks in the classless system are represented by a slash followed by the number of bits used by the network portion. For example, the network address 192.168.1.2 with a subnet mask of 255.255.255.0 would be written as 192.168.1.2/24. This notation is referred to as *classless interdomain routing (CIDR)*.

Class C address:

- Addresses have three octets for the network portion and one for the hosts

- Default subnet mask is 24 bits (255.255.255.0)

- Usually assigned to small networks

Class B address:

- Addresses have two octets to represent the network portion and two for the hosts

- Default subnet mask is 16 bits (255.255.0.0)

- Typically used for medium-sized networks

Class A address:

- Addresses have only one octet to represent the network portion and three to represent the hosts

- Default subnet mask is 8 bits (255.0.0.0)

- Typically assigned to large organizations

The class of an address can be determined by the value of the first octet. For example, if the first octet of an IP address has a value in the range 192 to 223, it is classified as a Class C address. As an example, 200.14.193.67 is a Class C address. Table 5-1 shows the ranges for the three assignable classes.

Table 5-1   IP Address Classes

Address Class	First Octet Range (Decimal)	First Octet Bits (Highlighted Bits Do Not Change)	Network (N) and Host (H) Portions of an Address	Default Subnet Mask (Decimal and Binary)	Number of Possible Networks and Hosts Per Network
A	1 – 127	00000000 – 01111111	N.H.H.H	11111111.00000000. 00000000.00000000 255.0.0.0	254 nets ($2^8 - 2$) 16.777.214 hosts per net ($2^{24} - 2$)
B	128 – 191	10000000 – 10111111	N.N.H.H	11111111.11111111. 00000000.00000000 255.255.0.0	65,534 nets ($2^{16} - 2$) 65,534 hosts per net ($2^{16} - 2$)
C	192 – 223	11000000 – 11011111	N.N.N.H	11111111.11111111. 11111111.00000000 255.255.255.0	16,777,214 nets ($2^{24} - 2$) 254 hosts per net ($2^8 - 2$)
D	224 – 239	11100000 – 11101111	Not for commercial use as a host		
E	240 – 255	11110000 – 11111111	Not for commercial use as a host		

TIP

The router reads the bits from the most significant bit (leftmost) to the least significant (rightmost). The values of the first several bits can tell the router what class address it is dealing with. For a Class A address the bit pattern starts as "0," for a class B it is "10," for a class C it is "110," and for a class D the pattern is "1110." Class E addresses are the remainder of the available values.

Interactive Activity 5-3: Subnet Mask Game (5.2.1.2)

In this interactive activity you must select the proper default subnet mask for an IP address. Use file ia-5212 on the CD-ROM that accompanies this book to perform this interactive activity.

Public and Private IP Addresses

All hosts that connect directly to the Internet require a unique *public IP address*. Because of the finite number of 32-bit addresses available, there is a risk of running out of IP addresses. One solution to this problem was to reserve some private addresses for use exclusively inside an organization. This allows hosts within an organization to communicate with one another without the need of a unique public IP address.

RFC 1918 is a standard that reserves several ranges of *private IP addresses* within each of the classes A, B, and C. As shown in Table 5-2, these private address ranges consist of a single Class A network, 16 Class B networks, and 256 Class C networks, which gives a network administrator considerable flexibility in assigning internal addresses.

Table 5-2   RFC 1918 Private Address Space

Address Class	Number of Network Numbers Reserved	Network Addresses
A	1	10.0.0.0
B	16	172.16.0.0 – 172.31.0.0
C	256	192.168.0.0 – 192.168.255.0

A very large network can use the Class A private network, which allows for more than 16 million private addresses. On medium-size networks, a Class B private network could be used, which provides more than 65,000 addresses. Home and small business networks typically use a single Class C private address, which allows up to 254 hosts.

The Class A network, the 16 Class B networks, or the 256 Class C networks, as defined by RFC 1918, can be used within any size organization. Typically many organizations use the Class A private network because it provides enough addresses to allow for easy organization of the internal hosts.

Hosts can use private addresses internally in an organization as long as they do not connect directly to the Internet. Therefore, the same set of private addresses can be used by multiple organizations. Private addresses are not routed on the Internet and will be quickly blocked by an ISP router, as shown in Figure 5-7.

Figure 5-7   Using Private Address Space on a Network

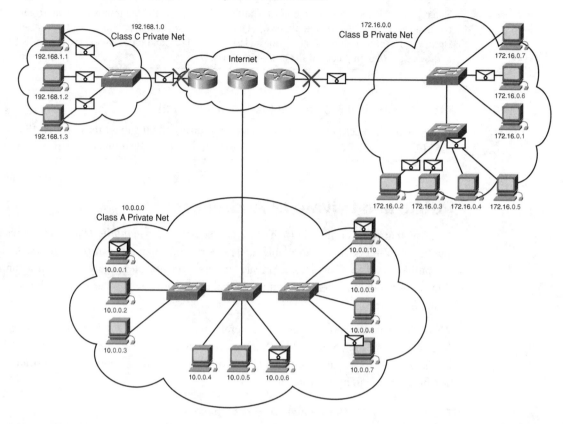

The use of private addresses can provide a measure of security because they are only visible on the local network, and outsiders cannot gain direct access to the private IP addresses.

There are also private addresses that can be used for the diagnostic testing of devices. One such private address is known as a *loopback address*. The Class A 127.0.0.0 network is reserved for loopback addresses. Another address range has been reserved by Microsoft for use with *Automatic Private IP Addressing (APIPA)*. With APIPA, a DHCP client automatically self-configures an IP address and subnet mask when a DHCP server is not available. The IP address range used for APIPA is 169.254.0.1 through 169.254.255.254. The client configures itself with an address from this range and a default Class B subnet mask of 255.255.0.0. A client uses the self-configured IP address until a DHCP server becomes available.

Interactive Activity 5-4: Address Blocker Game (5.2.2.3)

In this interactive activity you must decide to permit or deny an IP packet access to the Internet based on whether it is a private or public source IP address. Use file ia-5223 on the CD-ROM that accompanies this book to perform this interactive activity.

Unicast, Broadcast, and Multicast Addresses

In addition to address classes, we also categorize IP addresses as unicast, broadcast, or multicast depending on the nature of the message they carry. Hosts can use IP addresses to communicate one-to-one (unicast), one-to-many (multicast), or one-to-all (broadcast).

Unicast

A unicast address is the most common type on an IP network. A packet with a unicast destination address is intended for a specific host. An example is a host with IP address 192.168.1.5 (source) requesting a web page from a server at IP address 192.168.1.200 (destination), as shown in Figure 5-8.

Figure 5-8   Unicast IP Packet

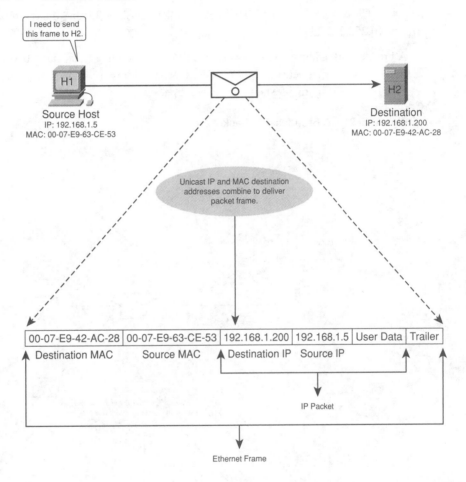

For a unicast packet to be sent and received, a destination IP address must be in the IP packet header. A corresponding destination MAC address must also be present in the Ethernet frame header. The IP address and MAC address combine to deliver data to one specific destination host.

> **TIP**
>
> If the destination IP address is on another network, the initial destination MAC address used in the frame is that of the router interface on the same network as the source IP.

Broadcast

With a broadcast, the packet contains a destination IP address with all ones (1s) in the host portion. This means that all hosts on that local network (broadcast domain) will receive and look at the packet. Many network protocols, such as ARP and DHCP, use broadcasts.

For example

- A Class C network 192.168.1.0 with a default subnet mask of 255.255.255.0 has a broadcast address of 192.168.1.255. The host portion is decimal 255 or binary 11111111 (all 1s).

- A Class B network of 172.16.0.0 with a default mask of 255.255.0.0 has a broadcast of 172.16.255.255.

- A Class A network of 10.0.0.0 with a default mask of 255.0.0.0 has a broadcast of 10.255.255.255.

A broadcast IP address for a network needs a corresponding broadcast MAC address in the Ethernet frame. On Ethernet networks, the broadcast MAC address is 48 ones displayed as hexadecimal FF-FF-FF-FF-FF-FF. Figure 5-9 shows a broadcast packet.

Figure 5-9   A Broadcast IP Packet

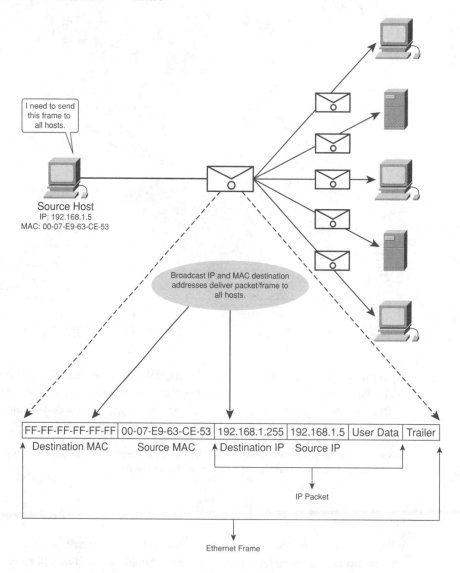

Multicast

Multicast addresses allow a source device to send a packet to a group of devices. Devices that belong to a multicast group are assigned a multicast group IP address. The range of multicast addresses is from 224.0.0.0 to 239.255.255.255. Because multicast addresses represent a group of addresses (sometimes called a host group), they can only be used as the destination of a packet. The source will always have a unicast address.

One example of where multicast addresses are used is in remote gaming, where many players are connected remotely but playing the same game. Another example is distance learning through video conferencing, where many students are connected to the same class. A third is in hard drive imaging applications used to restore the contents of many hard drives at the same time.

As with a unicast or broadcast address, multicast IP addresses need a corresponding multicast MAC address to actually deliver frames on a local network. The multicast MAC address is a special value that begins with 01-00-5E in hexadecimal. The value ends by converting the lower 23 bits of the IP multicast group address into the remaining 6 hexadecimal characters of the Ethernet address. An example, as shown in Figure 5-10, is hexadecimal 01-00-5E-0F-64-C5. Each hexadecimal character is four binary bits.

Figure 5-10   A Multicast IP Packet

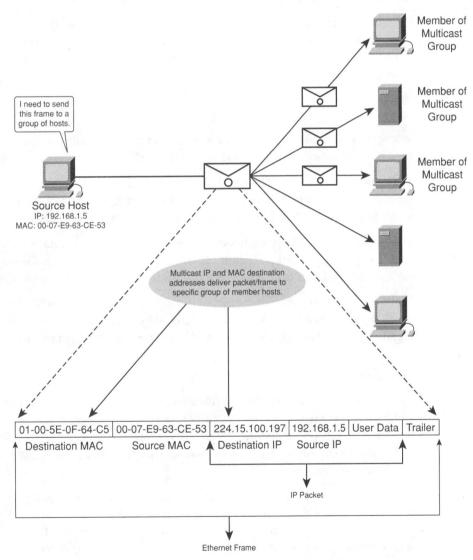

Interactive Activity 5-5: Who Will Receive the Message? Game (5.2.3.4)

In this interactive activity you determine which hosts will receive a message based on the destination IP address. Use file ia-5234 on the CD-ROM that accompanies this book to perform this interactive activity.

How IP Addresses Are Obtained

Because each host must be assigned a unique IP address, the management of IP addresses on a large network can be quite time-consuming if done manually. Luckily more automated methods of assigning IP addresses to hosts are available that relieve the network administrator from some of the burden.

Static and Dynamic Address Assignment

IP addresses can be assigned either statically or dynamically. Dynamic allocation allows the reuse of IP addresses and allows hosts to be configured without administrator intervention. Static assignment of host IP addresses is more labor intensive but also provides the network administrator with much more control over the flow of information on the network.

Static

With a static assignment, the network administrator must manually configure the network information for a host. At a minimum, this includes the host IP address, subnet mask, and default gateway.

Static addresses have some advantages. For example, they are useful for printers, servers, and other networking devices that need to be accessible to clients on the network. If hosts normally access a server at a particular IP address, it would not be good if that address changed.

Static assignment of addressing information can provide increased control of network resources, but entering the information on each host can be time-consuming. When you enter IP addresses statically, the host only performs basic error checks on the IP address. Therefore, errors are more likely to occur.

When using static IP addressing, maintaining an accurate list of which IP addresses are assigned to which devices is important. Additionally, these addresses are permanent and are not normally reused. Figure 5-11 shows the static assignment of IP information to a Windows machine.

Dynamic

On local networks it is often the case that the user population changes frequently. New users arrive with laptops and need a connection. Others have new workstations that need to be connected. Rather than have the network administrator assign IP addresses for each workstation, having IP addresses assigned automatically is easier. This is done using a protocol known as *Dynamic Host Configuration Protocol (DHCP)*.

DHCP provides a mechanism for the automatic assignment of addressing information such as IP address, subnet mask, default gateway, and other configuration information. DHCP is generally the preferred method of assigning IP addresses to hosts on large networks because it reduces the burden on network support staff and virtually eliminates entry errors. It is also the preferred method for many home and small business users who may lack the knowledge necessary to properly configure the IP settings manually. Figure 5-12 shows how to configure a Windows machine to obtain an address automatically from a DHCP server.

Figure 5-11   Static Assignment of IP Address Information

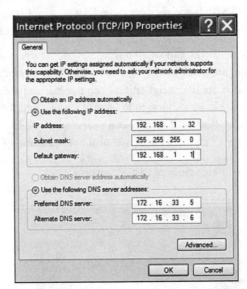

Figure 5-12   Dynamic Assignment of IP Address Information

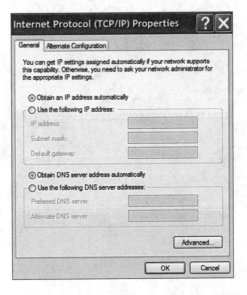

Another benefit of DHCP is that an address is not permanently assigned to a host but is only leased for a period of time. If the host is powered down or taken off the network, the address is returned to the pool for reuse. This feature is especially helpful with mobile users that come and go on a network.

DHCP Servers

If you enter a wireless hotspot at an airport or coffee shop, DHCP makes accessing the Internet possible for you. As you enter the area, your laptop *DHCP client* contacts the local *DHCP server* via a wireless connection. The DHCP server assigns an IP address to your laptop.

If hosts are going to obtain IP addresses dynamically, a DHCP server needs to be configured on the network. Various types of devices can be DHCP servers as long as they are running DHCP service software. With most medium to large networks, the DHCP server is usually a local dedicated PC-based server. With home networks, the DHCP server is usually located at the ISP, and a host on the home network receives its IP configuration directly from the ISP.

Many home networks and small businesses use an integrated router to connect to the ISP modem. In this case, the integrated router is both a DHCP client and a server. The integrated router acts as a client to receive its IP configuration from the ISP and then acts as a DHCP server for internal hosts on the local network. In addition to PC-based servers and integrated routers, other types of networking devices such as dedicated routers can provide DHCP services to clients, although this is not as common. Figure 5-13 shows an example of the distribution of DHCP servers.

Figure 5-13   Placement of DHCP Servers

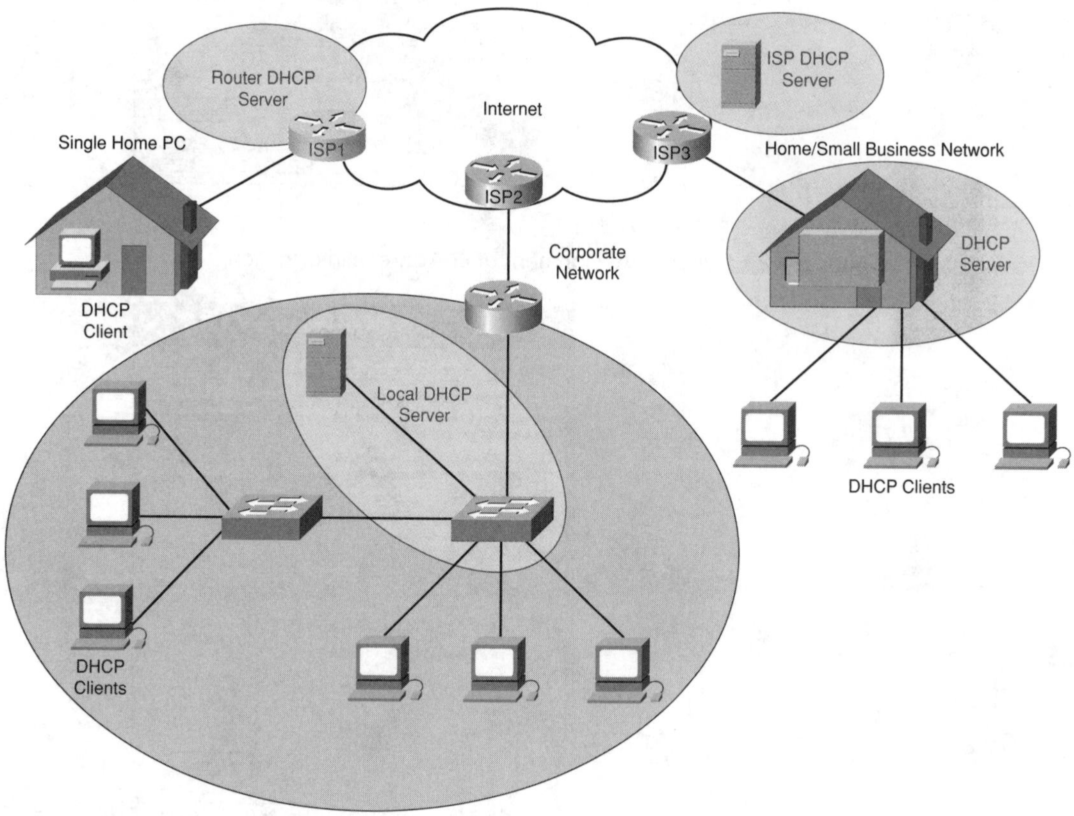

Configuring DHCP

When a host is first configured as a DHCP client, it does not have an IP address, subnet mask, or default gateway. It obtains this information from a DHCP server, either on the local network or one located at the ISP. The DHCP server is configured with a range, or pool, of IP addresses that can be assigned to DHCP clients.

A client that needs an IP address will send a DHCP Discover message to try and locate a DHCP server that is capable of providing it with the required information. The *DHCP Discover* is a broadcast message with a destination IP address of 255.255.255.255 (32 ones) and a destination MAC address of FF-FF-FF-FF-FF-FF (48 ones). All hosts on the network will receive this broadcast DHCP frame, but only a DHCP server will reply. These DHCP messages are sent to port 67. Only DHCP servers are configured to listen on port 67. The server will respond with a *DHCP Offer*, suggesting an IP address for the client. The host then sends a *DHCP Request* to that server asking to use the suggested IP address. The server responds with a *DHCP Acknowledgment* that informs the client that it has permission to start using the offered IP configuration information. Figure 5-14 shows this process.

Figure 5-14   DHCP Process

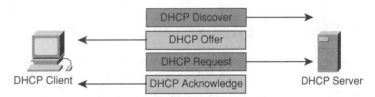

For most home and small business networks, a multi-function device provides DHCP services to the local network clients. Most of these home devices are configured through a graphical interface that is accessed using a web browser. For example, to connect to the Linksys multi-function device, open a web browser and enter the default IP address of 192.168.1.1 in the Address area. After you are connected, you can navigate to the screen that shows the DHCP server configuration.

The IP address of 192.168.1.1 and subnet mask of 255.255.255.0 are the defaults for the internal router interface on the Linksys device. This is the default gateway for all hosts on the local network and also the internal DHCP server IP address. Most Linksys wireless routers and other home integrated routers have DHCP Server enabled by default.

On the DHCP configuration screen, a default *DHCP range* is available or you can specify a starting address for the DHCP range and the number of addresses to be assigned. You can also modify the *lease time* (default is 24 hours). The DHCP configuration feature on most multi-function devices gives information about connected hosts and IP addresses, their associated MAC address, and lease times, as shown in Figure 5-15.

Figure 5-15   DHCP Server Configuration on a Multi-Function Device

Automatic Configuration - DHCP

Host Name:

Domain Name:

MTU: Auto   Size: 1500

IP Address: 192 . 168 . 1 . 1

Subnet Mask: 255.255.255.0

DHCP Server: Enabled   Disabled   DHCP Reservation

Start IP Address: 192 . 168 . 1 . 100

Maximum Number of Users: 50

IP Address Range: 192.168.1.100 ~ 149

Client Lease Time: 0   minutes (0 means one day)

Static DNS 1:   0 . 0 . 0 . 0

Static DNS 2:   0 . 0 . 0 . 0

Static DNS 3:   0 . 0 . 0 . 0

WINS: 0 . 0 . 0 . 0

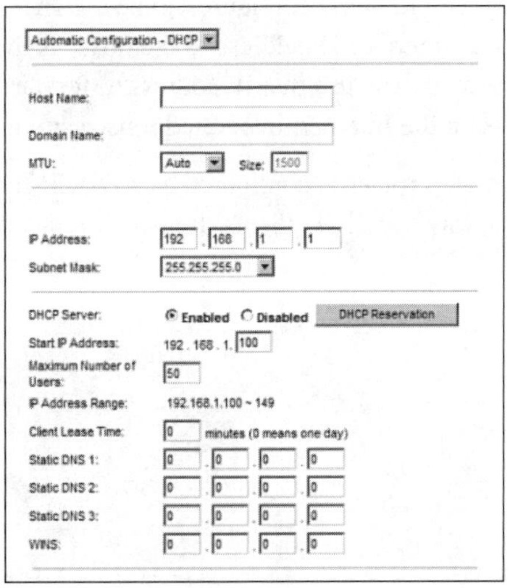

TIP

When configuring the starting address for the DHCP pool, be sure not to include the default gateway address.

The DHCP service maintains a list of all connected clients. The DHCP Client Table shows the client name and whether it is connected via the Ethernet or wireless Interface.

Packet Tracer
☐ Activity

Configuring DHCP on a Multi-Function Device (5.3.3.3)

In this Packet Tracer activity you configure both a DHCP server and a DHCP client. Use file d1-5333.pka on the CD-ROM that accompanies this book to perform this activity using Packet Tracer.

Address Management

IP addresses on a network must be carefully managed. Care must be taken to allow only DHCP servers to provide address information to local hosts. Private addresses must not be allowed to exit the internal network but the traffic carried in these packets must often be passed to the external network. Even though this task might seem difficult to accomplish, it is, in reality, quite simple.

Network Boundaries and Address Space

The router provides a gateway through which hosts on one network can communicate with hosts on different networks. Each interface on a router is connected to a separate network. The IP address assigned to the interface identifies which local network is connected directly to it.

Every host on a network must use the router as a gateway to other networks. Therefore, each host must know the IP address of the router interface connected to the network where the host is attached. This address is known as the default gateway address and can be either statically configured on the host or received dynamically by DHCP. This clearly establishes the edge of the network for addressing purposes. Figure 5-16 shows the network boundary.

TIP

Even though allowing the default gateway to receive its address via DHCP is possible, management is much easier if all network devices are assigned static addresses based on predefined criteria. For example, best practice often dictates that the default gateway be assigned either the first or last available host address on a network.

When an integrated router is configured to be a DHCP server for the local network, it automatically sends the correct interface IP address to the hosts as the default gateway address. In this manner, all hosts on the network can use that IP address to forward messages to hosts located at the ISP and gain access to hosts on the Internet. Integrated routers are usually set to be DHCP servers by default.

When an integrated router is configured as a DHCP server, it provides its own internal IP address as the default gateway to DHCP clients. It also provides them with their respective IP address and subnet mask.

Figure 5-16 Network Boundaries

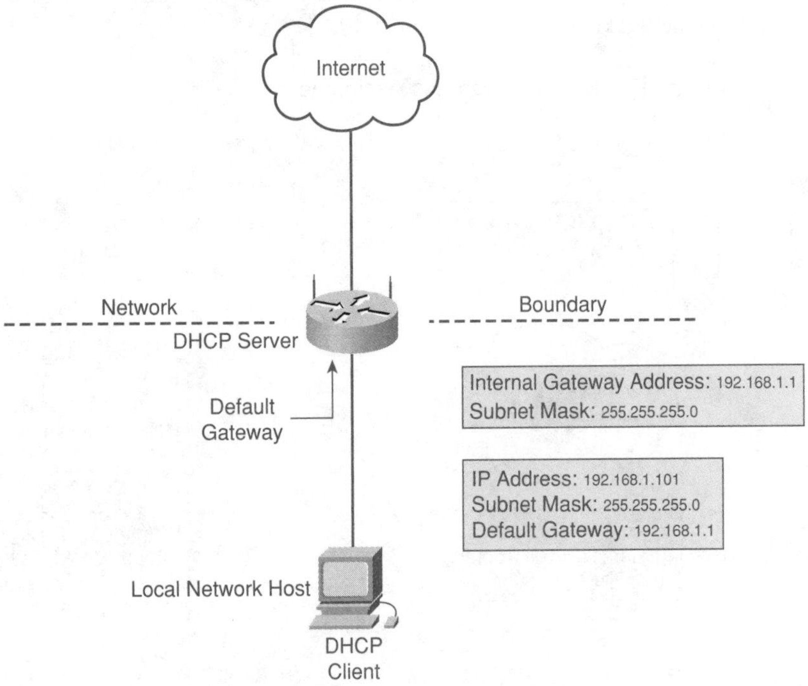

Address Assignment

The integrated router acts as a DHCP server for all local hosts attached to it, either by Ethernet cable or wirelessly. These local hosts are referred to as being located on an internal, or inside, network. Most DHCP servers are configured to assign private addresses to the hosts on the internal network, rather than Internet routable public addresses. This ensures that, by default, the internal network is not directly accessible from the Internet.

> **TIP**
>
> By default routers do not pass broadcast traffic. Because the first step in the DHCP process is a broadcast DHCP Discover, this message cannot normally pass through the router; therefore, only DHCP servers on the local network are able to respond to requests for IP address information. You can configure routers to pass this information to allow DHCP servers on other network segments to respond.

The default IP address configured on the local integrated router interface is usually a private Class C address. Internal hosts must be assigned addresses within the same network as the integrated router, either statically configured, or through DHCP. When configured as a DHCP server, the integrated router provides addresses in this range. It also provides the subnet mask information and its own interface IP address as the default gateway.

Many ISPs also use DHCP servers to provide IP addresses to the Internet side of the integrated router installed at their customer sites. The network assigned to the Internet side of the integrated router is referred to as the external, or outside, network.

When an integrated router is connected to the ISP, it acts like a DHCP client to receive the correct external network IP address for the Internet interface. ISPs usually provide an Internet-routable address, which enables hosts connected to the integrated router to have access to the Internet. The integrated router serves as the boundary between the local internal network and the external Internet. It acts as a DHCP client on the external or outside network and a DHCP server on the internal or inside network, as shown in Figure 5-17.

Figure 5-17   Network Address Assignment

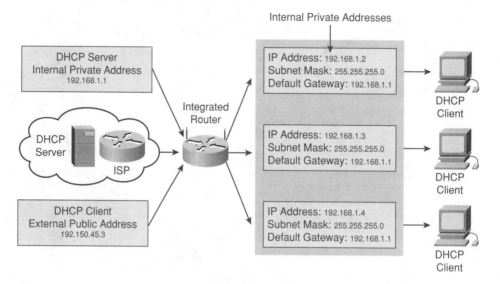

Hosts can be connected to an ISP and the Internet in several ways, as shown in Figure 5-18. Whether an individual host is assigned a public or private address depends on how it is connected.

The three main ways for a host to connect to an ISP are as follows:

■ **Direct connection**: Some customers have just a single computer with a direct connection from the ISP through a modem. In this case, the public address from the ISP DHCP server is assigned to the single host.

■ **Connection through an integrated router**: When more than one host needs access to the Internet, the ISP modem can be attached directly to an integrated router instead of directly to a single computer. Doing so enables the creation of a home or small business network. The integrated router receives the public address from the ISP. Internal hosts receive private addresses from the integrated router.

■ **Connection through a gateway device**: Gateway devices combine an integrated router and a modem in one unit and connect directly to the ISP service. As with integrated routers, the gateway device receives a public address from the ISP, and internal PCs receive private addresses from the gateway device.

Network Address Translation

On most networks the integrated router acts as a boundary. On the inside network it normally provides RFC 1918 private addresses, whereas on the outside interface it receives a public IP address from the ISP. Internally most network administrators deploy the Class A address space on the internal network because it provides a large number of addresses and is easy to logically divide to keep the internal network organized.

Figure 5-18   Host Connection to an ISP

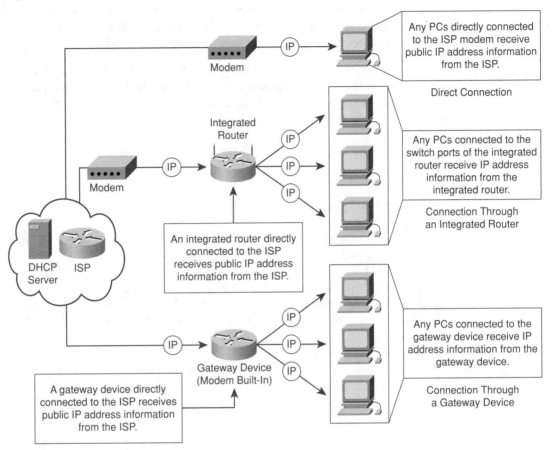

Because private addresses are not allowed on the Internet, a process is needed for translating private addresses into unique public addresses to allow local clients to communicate on the Internet. The process used to convert private addresses to Internet-routable addresses is called *Network Address Translation (NAT)*. With NAT, a private source IP address (*local address*) is translated to a public address (*global address*). The process is reversed for incoming packets. The integrated router is able to translate many internal IP addresses to the same public address by using NAT.

TIP

The process of many internal IP addresses being converted to a single external IP address is known as *Overloaded NAT* or *Port Address Translation (PAT)*. This specialized form of NAT is the most commonly deployed and is the form that is used on most home networking devices, which only obtain a single, routable IP address from the ISP.

Only packets destined for other networks need to be translated. These packets must pass through the gateway, where the integrated router replaces the source host's private IP address with its own public IP address. This process is reversed when replies are sent back to the source. The NAT process is illustrated in Figures 5-19 through 5-23. As the packet moves through the NAT device, the source IP address in the header is rewritten with a routable one before the packet is placed on the external network. When a reply is sent back to the NAT device, the routable IP address is replaced with the original private IP address before being placed on the internal network. The device that is responsible for carrying out the NAT function is responsible for maintaining a list of the active translations.

The packet is formed and placed on the internal network as shown in Figure 5-19. The source address is the address of the device that generated the packet and the destination address is the final destination for the packet. Because the destination address is not on the same local network, the packet travels to the default gateway, which is configured for NAT.

Figure 5-19 Network Address Translation Process—Packet Generation

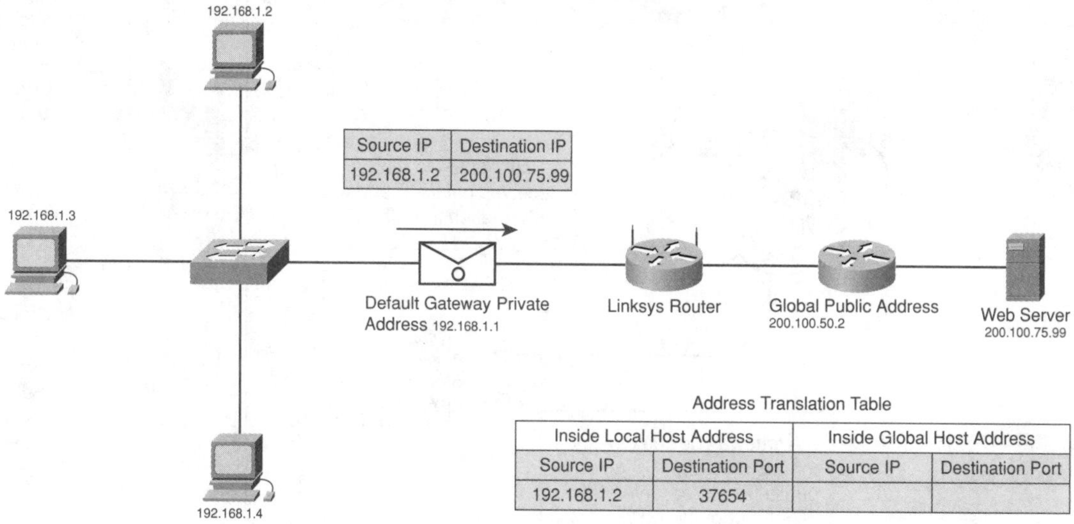

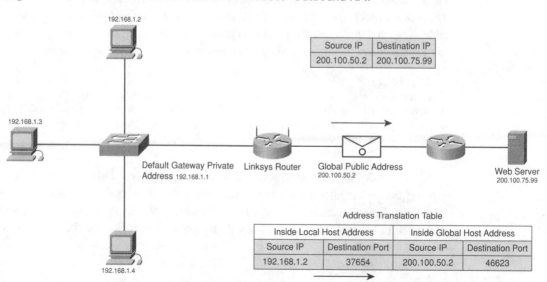

As the packet passes through the NAT device, the header is rewritten. The inside source address is replaced with a new address that is routable on the external network. The inside address as seen by another host on the inside network is known as the *inside local address*. The translated address is how a host on the outside network sees the inside host. This translated address is referred to as the *inside global address*. The NAT device builds a table to keep track of the NAT translations, as shown in Figure 5-20.

Figure 5-20 Network Address Translation Process–Outbound NAT

The packet now travels across the external network to the destination device. The destination device accepts the packet and replies to the inside global address as shown in Figure 5-21. The reply packet is placed back on the external network and finds its way back to the device that did the original NAT translation.

Figure 5-21   Network Address Translation Process–Destination Reply

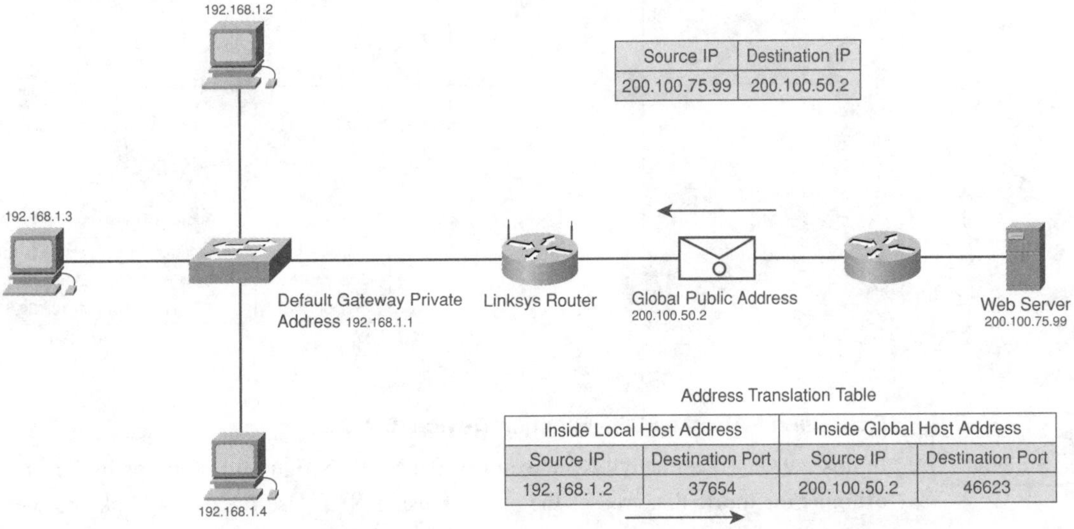

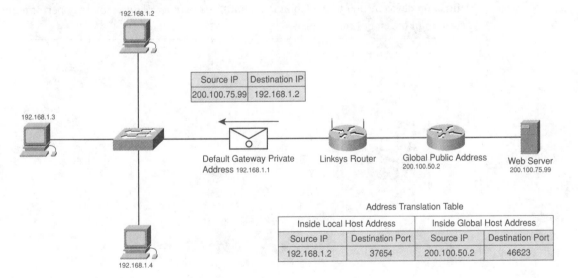

When the packet reaches the device that did the outbound NAT translation, it checks the translation table and replaces the inside global address with the inside local address, as shown in Figure 5-22.

Figure 5-22   Network Address Translation Process—Inbound NAT

This packet is then placed on the inside network where it finds its way to the device that generated the original packet, as shown in Figure 5-23.

Although each host on the internal network has a unique private IP address assigned to it, the hosts must usually share the single Internet-routable address assigned to the integrated router's Internet interface. This is accomplished by adding an extra piece of information into the header. This extra information is a port number that is used to identify the individual conversation.

Figure 5-23 Network Address Translation Process–Back at Source

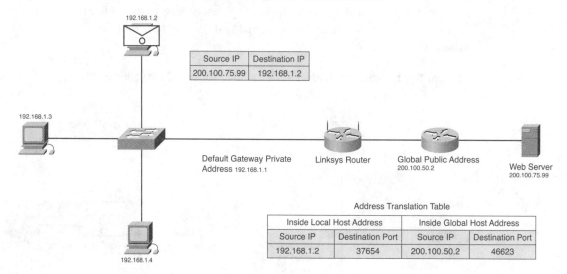

  Examining NAT on a Multi-Function Device (5.4.3.2)

In this Packet Tracer activity you examine the NAT configuration settings in the Linksys GUI and examine the traffic that crosses the network using NAT. Use file d1-5432.pka on the CD-ROM that accompanies this book to perform this activity using Packet Tracer.

Challenge Lab 5-2: Exploring IP Address Functions on a Multi-Function Device

In this lab you create and test a simple DHCP server/client network using four PCs and a multi-function device. Refer to the lab in Part II of this *Learning Guide*. You may perform this lab now or wait until the end of the chapter.

Summary

This chapter discussed the fact that a unique IP address is required in order to allow a network host to communicate with other hosts. The common IPv4 address is a 32-bit-long logical address that is divided into two parts: the network ID and the unique host ID. The subnet mask dictates which portion of the IP address represents the network and which portion represents the host. For easier readability the IP address is divided into four groups of 8 bits, each called an octet, and then each octet is converted to decimal and separated by periods. This human-readable form is known as dotted-decimal notation.

IP addresses are divided into five classes. The first three (A, B, and C) are normally assigned to companies and organizations whereas Class D is reserved for multicast use and Class E is for experimental use. Each class of addresses has its own default subnet mask.

Addresses can be classified as either private or public. Private address space is defined by RFC 1918 and is normally used on internal networks. Private addresses are not routable on the Internet and will quickly be removed by network routers. Public addresses are routable on the Internet.

Three types of messages are possible with IP addresses. A unicast is one-to-one communication, multicast is one-to-many, and a broadcast is one-to-all. Each type of IP address has a corresponding MAC address.

IP addresses can either be assigned statically by the network administrator or obtained dynamically through DHCP. Dynamic allocation of IP addresses is the preferred method. The multi-function device found in home and small business networks can act as both a DHCP server and a DHCP client. It obtains an external routable address from the ISP and then provides private addresses for internal hosts.

Routers provide a boundary between the internal and external networks. As traffic moves across this boundary the source IP must be rewritten. This process is known as Network Address Translation (NAT). When traffic moves from the internal network to the external network, the private source IP address is replaced with a public-routable one. When replies are received to the message, the routable address is replaced by the original private address before being placed on the internal network. The device responsible for the NAT process maintains a table of address translations to allow this to happen.

Activities and Labs

This summary outlines the activities and labs you can perform to help reinforce important concepts described in this chapter. You can find the activity and Packet Tracer files on the CD-ROM accompanying this book. The complete hands-on labs appear in Part II.

Interactive Activities on the CD:

Interactive Activity 5-1: Binary Game (5.1.2.3)

Interactive Activity 5-2: Identifying the Network Portion of an IP Address (5.1.3.2)

Interactive Activity 5-3: Subnet Mask Game (5.2.1.2)

Interactive Activity 5-4: Address Blocker Game (5.2.2.3)

Interactive Activity 5-5: Who Will Receive the Message? Game (5.2.3.4)

Packet Tracer Activities on the CD:

Connecting to a Web Server Using IP (5.1.1.2)

Configuring DHCP on a Multi-Function Device (5.3.3.3)

Examining NAT on a Multi-Function Device (5.4.3.2)

Labs in Part II of This Book:

Lab 5-1: Using the Windows Calculator with Network Addresses (5.1.4.3)

Challenge Lab 5-2: Exploring IP Addressing Functions on a Multi-Function Device

Check Your Understanding

Complete all the review questions listed here to test your understanding of the topics and concepts in this chapter. The "Check Your Understanding and Challenge Questions Answer Key" appendix lists the answers.

1. What is the decimal number 37 in binary?

   A. 0001 1001

   B. 0010 0101

   C. 0011 0001

   D. 0101 0001

   E. 0011 0011

2. What is the binary number 0011 0010 in decimal?

   A. 26

   B. 27

   C. 50

   D. 98

3. What is the network number for the host with an IP address of 172.16.25.14 and a subnet mast of 255.255.0.0?

   A. 172.0.0.0

   B. 172.16.0.0

   C. 172.16.25.0

   D. 0.16.25.14

   E. 0.0.25.14

   F. 0.0.0.14

4. What is the host number for the IP address 129.17.63.4 assuming a default subnet mask?

   A. 129

   B. 129.17

   C. 129.17.63

   D. 17.63.4

   E. 63.4

   F. 4

5. What is the maximum number of usable hosts that can be created if six host bits are available?

   A. 6

   B. 14

   C. 30

   D. 62

   E. 126

6. Which of the following hosts have the same network number?

   A. IP 137.17.3.4   SM 255.255.255.0

   B. IP 137.16.3.4   SM 255.255.0.0

   C. IP 137.16.7.1   SM 255.255.0.0

   D. IP 137.17.3.4   SM 255.255.0.0

   E. IP 137.17.3.4   SM 255.0.0.0

7. Which of the following are valid Class B host IP addresses?

   A. 177.16.0.0

   B. 177.16.255.255

   C. 123.14.2.1

   D. 193.16.4.0

   E. 163.15.17.2

8. Which of the following addresses are considered private IP addresses?

   A. 10.18.22.3

   B. 10.0.0.1

   C. 172.27.20.10

   D. 192.168.1.1

   E. 23.14.72.6

9. What is the default subnet mask for a public Class B network?

   A. 255.0.0.0

   B. 255.255.0.0

   C. 255.255.255.0

   D. 255.255.255.255

10. What is the MAC broadcast address?

    A. 0.0.0.0

    B. 255.255.255.255

    C. 00:00:00:00:00:00

    D. FF:FF:FF:FF:FF:FF

11. Which type of IP address allows a host to send a message to a group of hosts?

    A. Unicast

    B. Multicast

    C. Broadcast

12. Which of the following would be considered multicast MAC addresses?

    A. 00:00:00:2E:3F:6D

    B. 01:00:5E:AA:23:6D

    C. 01:5E:00:CA:2F:3C

    D. FF:FF:FF:00:3C:2F

13. What are some advantages of using DHCP to assign addresses within an organization?

    A. Lower administrative costs

    B. Works only with private address space

    C. Allows addresses to be shared between machines

    D. Ability to reuse addresses

14. What is the correct sequence of steps in the DHCP process?

    A. Discover, offer, request, acknowledge

    B. Discover, request, offer, acknowledge

    C. Request, discover, offer, acknowledge

    D. Request, offer, discover, acknowledge

15. When a host is looking for a DHCP server it issues a DHCP Discover. What type of message is the DHCP Discover?

    A. Unicast

    B. Multicast

    C. Broadcast

16. Which feature on the multi-function device can be used to display the client name and whether the host is connected via the wired or wireless interface?

    A. DHCP Client Table

    B. DHCP Connections Table

    C. Interface Connections Table

    D. Device Hosts Table

17. An integrated router is connected to an ISP and then internal hosts are connected to the integrated router. What role in the DHCP process is the integrated router taking?

    A. DHCP client only

    B. DHCP server only

    C. Both a DHCP client and a DHCP server

    D. Neither a DHCP client nor a DHCP server

18. What is the purpose of NAT in the home network?

    A. It is not used in the home network environment.

    B. It is used to allow traffic from a host with a private IP address to send information to the Internet.

    C. It allows one internal host to send information to another internal host.

    D. It converts private IP addresses to public address as information moves from the Internet to a private network.

19. How is DHCP used in most small home networks?

20. What is the purpose of APIPA?

Challenge Questions and Activities

These questions require a deeper application of the concepts covered in this chapter. You can find the answers in the appendix.

1. You have just set up a new server and assigned it the address 172.27.16.3 with a subnet mask of 255.255.255.0. The DHCP server is used to provide host addresses on the same network. The DHCP server has been configured to provide addresses in the range 172.27.17.50 to 172.27.17.100 with a subnet mask of 255.255.255.0. Unfortunately, none of the hosts on the network can connect to the server. Why is this happening and what would you do to fix the problem?

2. You have a small home network established with three hosts plugged into a multi-function device that is in turn connected to the Internet. You are experiencing a problem where you can connect to other hosts on your internal network but are unable to connect to any hosts on the Internet. A colleague tells you that the problem is that you must configure NAT. Explain how NAT would help solve this problem.

CHAPTER 6

Network Services

Objectives

After completing this chapter, you will be able to answer the following questions:

- What are the roles of a client and server and how do they interact over the network?

- What are some common network services available that operate in a client/server relationship?

- How do TCP and UDP transport protocols compare?

- What is the function of a port?

- What are well-known port numbers and the protocols/applications that use them?

- What is Domain Name System (DNS) and its purpose?

- How do various types of Internet applications, such as e-mail, World Wide Web, FTP (File Transfer Protocol), IM (instant messaging), and voice interact?

- How does a protocol stack interact on a host when sending and receiving a message?

- What is the purpose of a layered networking model?

- What is the Open Systems Interconnect (OSI) layered network model?

Key Terms

This chapter uses the following key terms. You can find the definitions in the Glossary.

Networks are facing new challenges and must offer more services than ever before. Video, music, and pictures are shared from large servers all over the world. Television, movies, and voice conversations can be streamed over the network, connecting to remote locations in ways never imagined. Even small businesses can reach customers at any time, in any place. In this chapter you learn how these popular services are delivered. Part II of this book includes the corresponding labs for this chapter.

Clients/Servers and Their Interaction

The Internet and most modern network applications utilize a client/server relationship. This distributed architecture is the basis for nearly all user interaction with the Internet. This section describes the client/server relationship and the roles that computers can play.

Client/Server Relationship

Every day, people use the services available over networks and the Internet to communicate with others and to perform routine tasks. We rarely think of the servers, clients, and networking devices that are necessary in order for us to receive an e-mail, enter information into a blog, or shop for the best bargains in an online store. Most of the commonly used Internet applications rely on complicated interactions between various different servers and clients.

The term *server* refers to a computer or other networking device running a software application that provides information or services to other hosts connected to the network. A well-known example of an application is a web server, shown in Figure 6-1. Millions of servers are connected to the Internet, providing services such as websites, e-mail, financial transactions, music downloads, and so on. A factor that is crucial to enabling these complex interactions to function is that they all use agreed standards and protocols.

Figure 6-1   Accessing a Web Server

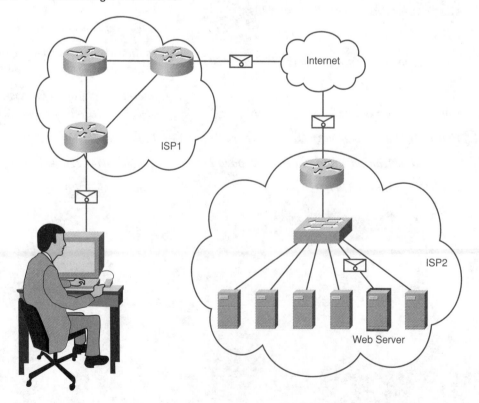

To request and view a web page, a person uses a device that is running web client software. *Client* is the name given to a computer application that someone uses to access information held on a server. A web browser is a good example of a client. Figure 6-2 shows a client displaying a page from a web server. This process has three steps:

1. The client first requests the page using the server IP address.

2. The server responds by sending the page to the client IP address.

3. The web client software formats and displays the page for the user.

Figure 6-2   Web Client Displaying a Web Page from a Server Request

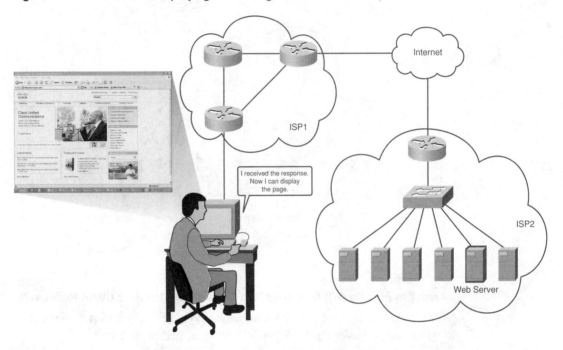

The key characteristic of a client/server system is that the client sends a request to a server, and the server responds by carrying out a function, such as sending information back to the client. The combination of a web browser and a web server is perhaps the most commonly used instance of a client/server system. The servers shown in Figure 6-3 are providing the most common services found in private networks and on the Internet. The following is a brief description of the services each provides:

- **Domain Name System (DNS) server**: Service that provides the IP address of a website or domain name so that a host can connect to it.

- *Telnet* **server**: Service that provides access to remote hosts as if they were connected locally.

- **E-mail server**: E-mail uses several services including Simple Mail Transfer Protocol (SMTP), Post Office Protocol (POP3), and Internet Message Access Protocol (IMAP4). SMTP is used to send e-mail messages from clients to servers over the Internet. Recipients are specified using the username@domainname.domain format. POP3 and IMAP are used to store and forward e-mail between servers and clients.

■ **Dynamic Host Configuration Protocol (DHCP) server**: Service that assigns IP address, subnet mask, default gateway, and other information to clients.

■ **Web server**: Web services use Hypertext Transfer Protocol (HTTP) to transfer information between web clients and web servers. Most web pages are accessed using HTTP.

■ *File Transfer Protocol (FTP)* **server**: Service that allows for the download and upload of files between a client and server.

Figure 6-3   Server Farm with Various Servers

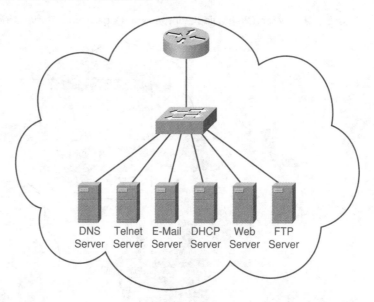

 Interactive Activity 6-1: Determine the Correct Service for a Client Request (6.1.1.4)

In this interactive activity, you match the service to the client's request. Use file ia-6114 on the CD-ROM that accompanies this book to perform this interactive activity.

Role of Protocols in Client/Server Communication

A web server and a web client use specific protocols and standards in the process of exchanging information to ensure that the messages are received and understood. These protocols include those that operate at the application, transport, internetwork, and network access layers.

Application Protocol

Hypertext Transfer Protocol (HTTP) is the application protocol that governs the way that a web server and a web client interact. HTTP defines the format of the requests and responses exchanged between the client and server. HTTP relies on other protocols to govern how the messages are transported between client and server.

Transport Protocol

Transmission Control Protocol (TCP) is the transport protocol that manages the individual conversations between web servers and web clients. TCP formats the HTTP messages into segments to be sent to the destination host. It also provides flow control and acknowledgement of packets exchanged between hosts.

Internetwork Protocol

The most common internetwork protocol is Internet Protocol (IP). IP is responsible for taking the formatted segments from TCP, assigning the logical addressing, and encapsulating them into packets for routing to the destination host.

HTTP, TCP, and IP are the key protocols required to download a web page from an Internet server, as shown in Figure 6-4.

Figure 6-4   HTTP, TCP, and IP Used to Access a Web Server

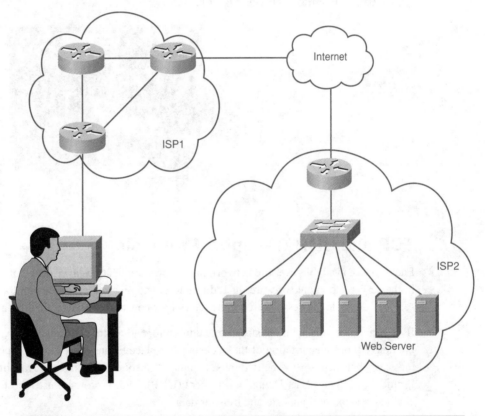

HTTP:	Specifies the format of the web page request (from client) and response (from server).
TCP:	Determines the flow control and acknowledgements of packet exchange.
IP:	Identifies the source and destination as packets are sent across the network.

Network Access Protocols

Ethernet is the most commonly used protocol for local networks. Network access protocols perform two primary functions:

- Data link management
- Physical network transmissions

Data link management protocols take the packets from IP and encapsulate them into the appropriate frame format for the local network. These protocols assign the physical addresses to the frames and prepare them to be transmitted over the network.

The standards and protocols for the physical media govern how the bits are represented on the media, how the signals are sent over the media, and how they are interpreted by the receiving hosts. Network interface cards (NIC) implement the appropriate protocols for the media that is being used. Figure 6-5 shows an Ethernet cable plugged into a built-in NIC on the back of a computer.

Figure 6-5   Ethernet Cable and Built-in NIC

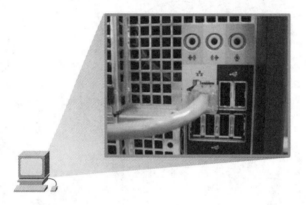

TCP and UDP Transport Protocols

Each service available over the network has its own application layer protocols that are implemented in the server and client software. In addition to the application protocols, all the common Internet services use IP to address and route messages between source and destination hosts.

IP is concerned only with the structure, addressing, and routing of packets. IP does not specify how the delivery or transportation of the packets takes place. Transport protocols specify how to transfer messages between hosts. The two most common transport protocols are Transmission Control Protocol (TCP) and User Datagram Protocol (UDP). The IP protocol uses these transport protocols to enable hosts to communicate and transfer data.

Figure 6-6 shows IP as the basic foundation protocol of the Internet, with all other protocols depending on it. The TCP and UDP transport protocols ride on top of IP, and the application protocols, such as HTTP and FTP, ride on top of either TCP or UDP. IP is the native network protocol of the Internet.

Using TCP

When an application requires acknowledgment that a message is delivered, it uses TCP. This process is similar to sending a registered letter through the postal system, where the recipient must sign for the letter to acknowledge its receipt.

Figure 6-6   Application Layer Protocols Depend on IP and Either TCP or UDP

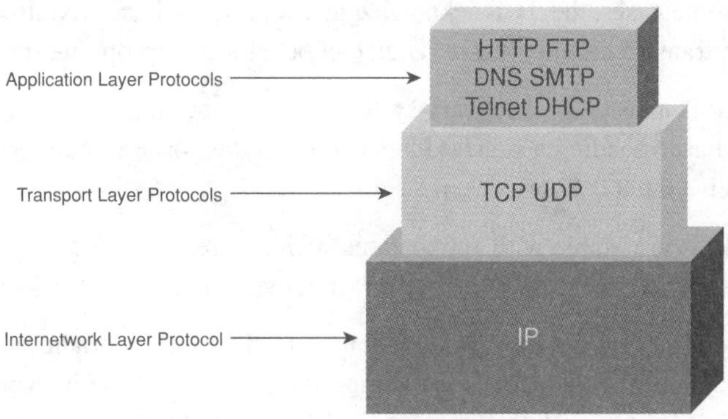

Application Layer Protocols ⟶ HTTP FTP DNS SMTP Telnet DHCP

Transport Layer Protocols ⟶ TCP UDP

Internetwork Layer Protocol ⟶ IP

TCP breaks up a message into small pieces known as segments. Each *segment* is numbered in sequence and passed to the IP process for assembly into packets. TCP keeps track of the number of segments that have been sent to a specific host from a specific application. TCP is also responsible for sending acknowledgments to ensure that packets are received. If the sender does not receive an acknowledgement within a certain period of time, it assumes that the segments were lost and retransmits them. Only the portion of the message that is lost is resent, not the entire message.

On the receiving host, TCP is responsible for reassembling the message segments and passing them to the application.

FTP and HTTP are examples of protocols that use TCP to ensure delivery of data. In Figure 6-7, the user is sending a file to the FTP server using an FTP client application, which makes use of TCP to help guarantee delivery.

Figure 6-7   FTP Depends on TCP to Provide Reliable Delivery

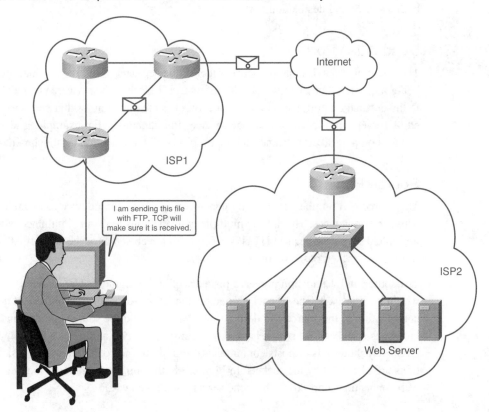

Using UDP

In some cases, the TCP acknowledgment protocol is not required and actually slows down information transfer. In those cases, UDP can be a more appropriate transport protocol.

UDP is a best-effort delivery system that does not require acknowledgment of receipt. This process is similar to sending a standard letter through the postal system. The letter is not guaranteed to be received, but delivery is expected.

UDP is preferable with applications such as streaming audio, video, and Voice over IP (VoIP). Acknowledgments would slow down delivery and retransmissions are undesirable.

An example of an application that uses UDP is Internet radio, which uses streaming audio technology. If some of the message is lost during its journey over the network, it is not retransmitted. If a few packets are missed, the listener might hear a slight break in the sound. If TCP were used and the lost packets were resent, the transmission would pause to receive them and the disruption would be more noticeable.

Interactive Activity 6-2: Match the Correct Transport Protocol to the Characteristics Described (6.1.3.4)

In this interactive activity, you match the correct transport protocol to the characteristic described. Use file ia-6134 on the CD-ROM that accompanies this book to perform this interactive activity.

TCP/IP Port Numbers

When a message is delivered using either TCP or UDP, the protocols and services requested are identified by a port number. A port is a numeric identifier within each segment that is used to keep track of specific conversations and destination services requested. Every message that a host sends contains both a source and destination port.

Destination Port

The client places a destination port number in the segment to tell the destination server what service is being requested. For example, port 80 refers to HTTP or web service. When a client specifies port 80 in the destination port, the server that receives the message knows that web services are being requested. A server can offer more than one service simultaneously. For example, a server can offer web services on port 80 at the same time that it offers FTP connection establishment on port 21.

Source Port

The source port number is randomly generated by the sending device to identify a conversation between two devices. This allows multiple conversations to occur simultaneously. In other words, multiple devices can request HTTP service from a web server at the same time. The separate conversations are tracked based on the source ports.

The source and destination ports are placed within the segment. The segments are then encapsulated within an IP packet. The IP packet contains the IP addresses of the source and destination hosts. The combination of the source and destination IP address and the source and destination port number is known as a socket. The socket is used to identify the server and service being requested by the client. Every day thousands of hosts communicate with thousands of different servers. Those communications are identified by the sockets. In Figure 6-8, the source computer is making an FTP (port 21) and web connection (port 80) to the same server simultaneously.

Figure 6-8   FTP Connection and Web Connection Using Port Numbers

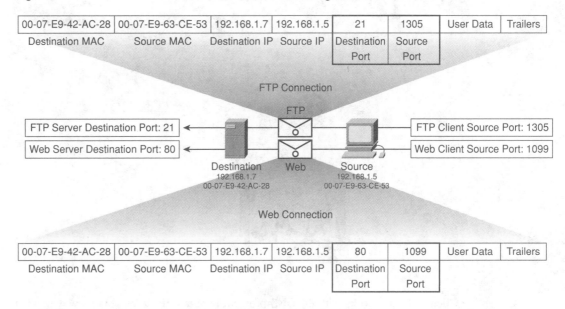

Application Protocols and Services

This section describes various client/server applications and the protocols used by those applications. This section concludes by describing the role of port numbers in client requests.

Domain Name Service

Thousands of servers, installed in many different locations, provide the services we use daily over the Internet. Each of these servers is assigned a unique IP address that identifies it on the local network where it is connected.

Remembering all the IP addresses for all the servers hosting services on the Internet would be impossible. Instead, an easier way exists to locate servers: by associating a name with an IP address.

The *Domain Name System (DNS)* provides a way for hosts to use a name to request the IP address of a specific server. Domain names are registered and organized on the Internet within specific high-level groups, or domains. Some of the most common high-level domains on the Internet are .com, .edu, .org, and .net. In Figure 6-9, the user enters the domain name of www.cisco.com into a browser. He does not need to know the IP address of the web servers. DNS will take care of that.

A DNS server running the DNS service contains a table that associates host names in a domain with corresponding IP addresses. When a client has the name of a server, such as a web server, but needs to find the IP address, it sends a request to the DNS server on port 53. The client uses the IP address of the DNS server configured in the DNS settings of the host's IP configuration.

When the DNS server receives the request, it checks its table to determine the IP address associated with that web server. If the local DNS server does not have an entry for the requested name, it queries another DNS server within the domain. When the DNS server learns the IP address, that information is sent back to the client. If the DNS server cannot determine the IP address, the request will time out and the client will not be able to communicate with the web server. The user will normally receive a message that the server cannot be found.

Figure 6-9   Using a Domain Name with a Browser

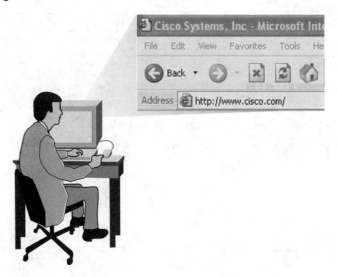

Client software works with the DNS protocol to obtain IP addresses in a way that is transparent to the user. In Figure 6-10, the user enters the **http://www.cisco.com** website in the web client browser and the server responds with the IP address.

Figure 6-10   Using DNS to Resolve a Domain to an IP Address

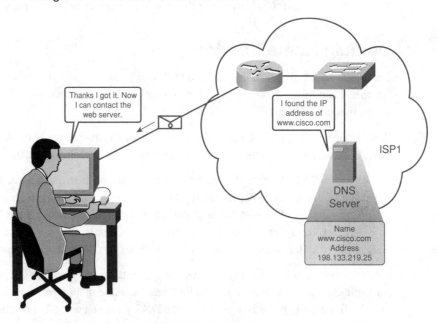

 Lab 6-1: Observing DNS Name Resolution (6.2.1.3)

In this lab you use the **ping** command, a browser, and **nslookup** to observe the relationship between domain names and IP addresses. Refer to the hands-on lab in Part II of this *Learning Guide*. You may perform this lab now or wait until the end of the chapter.

Web Clients and Servers

When a web client receives the IP address of a web server, the client browser uses that IP address and port 80 to request web services. This request is sent to the server using HTTP.

When the server receives a port 80 request, the server responds to the client request and sends the web page to the client. The information content of a web page is encoded using specialized "markup" languages. *Hypertext Markup Language (HTML)* is the most commonly used markup language, but others, such as Extensible Markup Language (XML) and Extensible HTML (XHTML), are gaining popularity.

HTTP is not a secure protocol; information could easily be intercepted by other users as it is sent over the network. In order to provide security for the data, a secure version of HTTP known as HTTPS can be used for data transmission. Requests for HTTPS are sent to port 443. These requests require the use of https: rather than http: in the site address in the browser.

Many different web services and web clients are available on the market. HTTP and HTML make it possible for these servers and clients from many different manufacturers to work together seamlessly.

When a web client requests the IP address of http://www.cisco.com from the ISP1 DNS server, the server responds to the client with the IP address of the website. It is not until the client computer has the web server's IP address that it can actually contact the http://www.cisco.com web server to request a web page. Figure 6-11 shows the client computer sending an HTTP request to port 80 on the destination web server in the cisco.com domain. The client knows how to contact the ISP1 DNS server because the IP address of the DNS server is part of the IP configuration of the client. The client's IP address, subnet mask, and default gateway, as well as the IP addresses of a primary and secondary DNS server, are provided to the client by ISP1 using DHCP.

Figure 6-11   Sending an HTTP Request to Port 80 on the Web Server

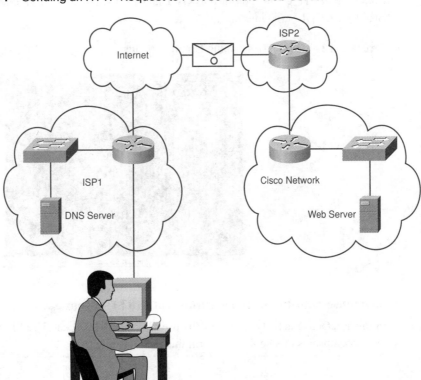

Observing Web Requests (6.2.2.2)

In this Packet Tracer activity, you observe traffic requests when a client browser requests web pages from a server. Use file d1-6222.pka on the CD-ROM that accompanies this book to perform this interactive activity.

FTP Clients and Servers

In addition to web services, another common service used across the Internet is one that allows users to transfer files. FTP provides an easy method for transferring files from one computer to another. A host running FTP client software can access an FTP server to perform various file management functions including file uploads and downloads.

An e-mail client can be used to send files as attachments, but ISPs and mail server administrators might limit attachment file size. FTP can be used to send and receive multiple files that are much larger than those allowed by e-mail. The FTP server can also act as a centralized file storage location for access by different people working on the same project.

The FTP server enables a user running FTP client software to exchange files between devices. It also enables the user to manage files remotely by sending file management commands such as delete or rename. To accomplish these tasks, the FTP service uses two different ports to communicate between client and server. Requests to begin an FTP session are sent to the server using destination port 21. After the session is opened, the server will change to port 20 to transfer the data files.

FTP client software is built into computer operating systems and into most web browsers. Figure 6-12 shows the Windows command prompt window as the CLI (command-line interface) FTP client is started. When the FTP client is started, the Windows command prompt changes to an FTP prompt that can interpret FTP commands such as **GET** and **PUT**. Standalone FTP clients offer many options in an easy-to-use GUI-based interface.

Figure 6-12   Using FTP from the Command Line

Interactive Activity 6-3: Demonstration of GUI FTP Client Use (6.2.3.2)

In this interactive activity, you view the use of a GUI FTP client. Use file ia-6232 on the CD-ROM that accompanies this book to perform this interactive activity.

Lab 6-2: Exploring FTP (6.2.3.3)

In this lab you use an FTP client to transfer files from an FTP server. Refer to the hands-on lab in Part II of this *Learning Guide*. You may perform this lab now or wait until the end of the chapter.

E-mail Clients and Servers

E-mail is one of the most popular client/server applications on the Internet. E-mail servers run server software that enables them to interact with e-mail clients and with other e-mail servers over the network. In addition to using e-mail client software such as Microsoft Outlook to access e-mail, some ISPs also offer web-based e-mail.

Each mail server receives and stores mail for users who have mailboxes configured on the mail server. Each user with a mailbox must then use an e-mail client to access the mail server and read these messages.

Mail servers are also used to send mail addressed to local mailboxes or mailboxes located on other e-mail servers.

Mailboxes are identified by the following format:

username@domainname.domain

Figure 6-13 shows an e-mail message being composing using the Windows Outlook e-mail client.

Figure 6-13   E-mail Client: Composing an E-mail Message

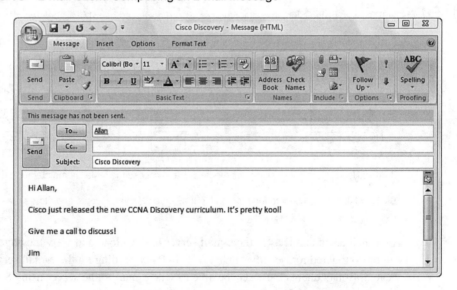

Various application protocols used in processing e-mail include the following:

- *Simple Mail Transfer Protocol (SMTP)*: SMTP is used by an e-mail client to send messages to its local e-mail server. The local server then decides whether the message is destined for a local mailbox or whether the message is addressed to a mailbox on another server.

   If the server has to send the message to a different server, SMTP is used between the two servers as well. SMTP requests are sent to port 25.

■ *Post Office Protocol (POP3)*: A server that supports POP3 clients receives and stores messages addressed to its users. When the client connects to the e-mail server, the messages are downloaded to the client. By default, messages are not kept on the server after they have been accessed by the client. With most POP3 clients, the user can choose to keep mail on the server if desired. Clients contact POP3 servers on port 110.

■ *Internet Message Access Protocol (IMAP4)*: A server that supports IMAP clients also receives and stores messages addressed to its users. However, it keeps the messages in the mailboxes on the server unless they are deleted by the user. The most current version of IMAP is IMAP4, which listens for client requests on port 143.

Many different e-mail servers exist for the various network operating system platforms. The top portion of Figure 6-14 shows a POP3 client downloading e-mail from the POP3 server. The bottom portion of the figure shows an IMAP4 client reading e-mail while it is still on the IMAP4 server. Both clients use SMTP to send mail to the POP3 and the IMAP4 servers. In addition to POP3 and IMAP4, each of the servers might have an SMTP server running to accept the e-mail being sent.

Figure 6-14 POP3 and IMAP4 Charts

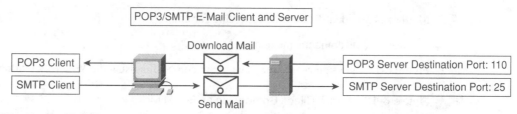

POP3: Used by the client to contact the server and download mail. Mail is deleted off the server.

SMTP: Used by the client to forward mail to the server. Server accepts and stores the mail in the proper queue.

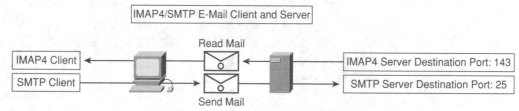

IMAP4: Used by the client to contact the server and access mail. Mail is maintained on the server.

SMTP: Used by the client to forward mail to the server. Server accepts and stores the mail in the proper queue.

An e-mail client connects to the e-mail server to download and view messages. Most e-mail clients can be configured to use either POP3 or IMAP4 depending on the e-mail server where the mailbox is located. E-mail clients must also be able to send e-mail to the server using SMTP.

Different e-mail servers can be configured for incoming and outgoing mail.

The following are typical entries when configuring an e-mail client:

■ POP3 or IMAP4 server name

■ SMTP server name

■ Username

■ User password

■ Spam and virus filters

Figure 6-15 shows the basic setup of a POP3 and SMTP e-mail account using Microsoft Outlook. Note that the incoming server is POP3 and the outgoing server is SMTP. Downloaded e-mail is received from the POP3 server and newly created or forwarded e-mail is sent to the SMTP server.

Figure 6-15   Microsoft Outlook E-mail Account Setup

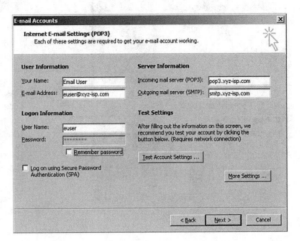

Lab 6-3: Configuring an E-mail Client (6.2.4.4)

In this lab you configure an e-mail client to access an e-mail server and send and receive e-mail. Refer to the hands-on lab in Part II of this *Learning Guide*. You may perform this lab now or wait until the end of the chapter.

IM Clients and Servers

Instant messaging (IM) is one of the most popular communication tools in use today. IM software is run locally on each computer and allows users to communicate or chat over the Internet in real time. Many different IM applications are available from various companies. Each instant messaging service can use a different protocol and destination port, so two hosts must have compatible IM software installed for them to communicate.

IM applications require minimal configuration to operate. After the client is downloaded, all that is required is to enter username and password information. This allows the IM client to authenticate to the IM network. Once logged into the server, clients can send messages to other clients in real-time in a peer-to-peer fashion. In addition to text messages, IM supports the transfer of video, music, and speech files. IM clients might have a telephony feature, which allows users to make phone calls over the Internet. Additional configuration can be done to customize the IM client with "buddy lists" and a personal look and feel.

IM client software can be downloaded and used on all types of hosts, including computers, PDAs, and cell phones. In Figure 6-16, John and Sarah are using an IM server to communicate in real time.

Figure 6-16   IM Conversation

Voice Clients and Servers

Making phone calls over the Internet is becoming increasingly popular. An Internet telephony client uses peer-to-peer technology similar to that used by instant messaging. IP telephony makes use of *Voice over IP (VoIP)* technology, which uses IP packets to carry digitized voice as data.

To start using an Internet telephone, download the client software from one of the companies that provides the service. Rates for Internet telephone services can vary greatly between regions and providers.

When the software has been installed, the user selects a unique name. This is so that calls can be received from other users. Speakers and a microphone, built-in or separate, are required. A headset is frequently plugged into the computer to serve as a phone.

Calls are made to other users of the same service on the Internet, by selecting the username from a list. A call to a regular telephone (land line or cell phone) requires the use of a gateway to access the *public switched telephone network (PSTN)*. Although it has evolved over the years, the PSTN is the traditional phone system originally developed by the Bell companies.

The protocols and destination ports used by Internet telephony applications vary based on the software. Figure 6-17 shows one voice client that uses a headset and another that uses a regular telephone connected to a PC.

Figure 6-17 Voice Clients and Voice Server

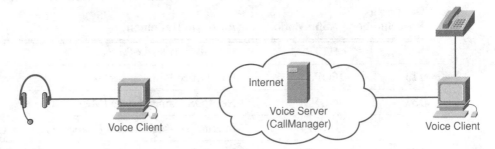

Port Numbers

DNS, web, e-mail, FTP, IM, and VoIP are just some of the many services provided by client/server systems over the Internet. These services might be provided by a single server or by several servers. In either case, it is necessary for a server to know which service is being requested by a client. Client requests can be identified because the request is made to a specific destination port. Clients are preconfigured to use a destination port that is registered on the Internet for each service.

Ports are assigned and managed by an organization known as the *Internet Corporation for Assigned Names and Numbers (ICANN)* http://www.icann.org/. Ports are broken into three categories and range in number from 1 to 65535:

- **Well-known ports**: Destination ports that are associated with common network applications are identified as well-known ports. These ports are in the range of 0 to 1023.

- **Registered ports**: Ports 1024 through 49151 can be used as either source or destination ports. Organizations can use them to register specific applications such as IM software.

- **Private ports**: Ports 49152 through 65535 are often used as source ports. Any application can use these ports.

Table 6-1 shows some of the more common well-known ports.

Table 6-1 Common Well-Known TCP/UDP Port Numbers

Destination Port Number	Abbreviation	Acronym Definition
20	FTP Data	File Transfer Protocol (for data transfer).
21	FTP Control	File Transfer Protocol (to establish connection).
23	TELNET	TELetype NETwork.
25	SMTP	Simple Mail Transfer Protocol.
53	DNS	Domain Name Service.
67	DHCP v4 Client	Dynamic Host Configuration Protocol (Client). Originally developed as Bootstrap Protocol.
68	DHCP v4 Server	Dynamic Host Configuration Protocol (Server). Originally developed as Bootstrap Protocol.
69	TFTP	Trivial File Transfer Protocol.

continued

Table 6-1   Common Well-Known TCP/UDP Port Numbers   *continued*

Destination Port Number	Abbreviation	Acronym Definition
80	HTTP	Hypertext Transfer Protocol.
110	POP3	Post Office Protocol version 3.
137	NBNS	NetBIOS Name Service (Microsoft).
143	IMAP4	Internet Message Access Protocol (version 4).
161	SNMP	Simple Network Management Protocol.
443	HTTPS	Hypertext Transfer Protocol Secure.

Interactive Activity 6-4: Match the Protocol Name to the Destination Port Number in the TCP Segment (6.2.7.2)

In this interactive activity, you match the protocol name to the destination port number in the TCP segment. Use file ia-6272 on the CD-ROM that accompanies this book to perform this interactive activity.

Layered Model and Protocols

Many protocols have been developed as the Internet has evolved. These protocols do not operate independently but work together in a layered sequence or protocol stack. This section describes two main layered models used in networking and how protocols interact to enable messages to be sent and received.

Protocol Interaction

Successful communication between hosts requires interaction between several protocols. These protocols are implemented in software and hardware that is loaded on each host and network device.

The interaction between protocols can be depicted as a protocol stack. It shows the protocols as a layered hierarchy, with each higher-level protocol depending on the services of the protocols shown in the lower levels.

Figure 6-18 shows a protocol stack with the primary protocols necessary to access a web server on an Ethernet LAN. The lower layers of the stack are concerned with moving data over the network and providing services to the upper layers. The upper layers are focused more on the content of the message being sent and the user interface. The basic protocol stack is running on the web server and the web clients.

To visualize the interaction between various protocols, it is common to use a layered model. A layered model depicts the operation of the protocols occurring within each layer, as well as the interaction with the layers above and below it.

Figure 6-18 Web Server Protocol Stack

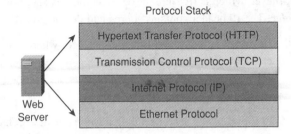

The layered model has many benefits:

- Assists in protocol design because protocols that operate at a specific layer have defined information that they act on and a defined interface to the layers above and below.

- Fosters competition because products from different vendors can work together.

- Prevents technology or capability changes in one layer from affecting other layers above and below.

- Provides a common language to describe networking functions and capabilities.

The first layered reference model for internetwork communications was created in the early 1970s and is referred to as the Internet model. It defines four categories of functions that must occur for communications to be successful. The architecture of the TCP/IP protocols follows the structure of this model. Because of this, the Internet model is commonly referred to as the *TCP/IP model*. Figure 6-19 shows the four-layer TCP/IP model.

Figure 6-19 TCP/IP Protocol Layer Interaction

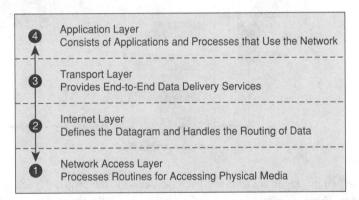

Protocol Operation of Sending and Receiving a Message

When sending messages on a network, the protocol stack on a host operates from top to bottom. In the web server example, a browser on the client requests a web page from a web server on destination port 80. This starts the process of sending the web page to the client.

As the web server replies with the requested page, the data moves down through the web server protocol stack; the application data is broken into TCP segments. Each TCP segment is given a header containing a source and destination port. Many segments are required to send an entire web page.

The TCP segment encapsulates HTTP and web page HTML user data and sends it down to the next protocol layer, which is IP. Here the TCP segment is encapsulated within an IP packet, which adds an IP *header*. The IP header contains source and destination IP addresses.

Next, the IP packet is sent to the Ethernet protocol where it is encapsulated in a frame header and trailer. Each Ethernet frame header contains a source and destination MAC address. The *trailer* contains error-checking information. Finally, the bits are encoded onto the Ethernet media (copper or fiber-optic cable) by the server NIC.

Figure 6-20 shows a web server sending a web page to a web client. Before putting any bits on the wire, the server breaks up the web page into chunks of data. Each chunk of data is encapsulated with a TCP header and numbered. The TCP header and data are then encapsulated with an IP header and finally the IP header, TCP header, and data are encapsulated within an Ethernet frame. The frame is then sent, as bits, out onto the wire toward the requesting host. The server continues sending frames until all the data in the web page has been sent to the client. This might require thousands of frames for a web page with lots of graphics.

Figure 6-20   Web Server Encapsulating Web Page Data to Send to Client

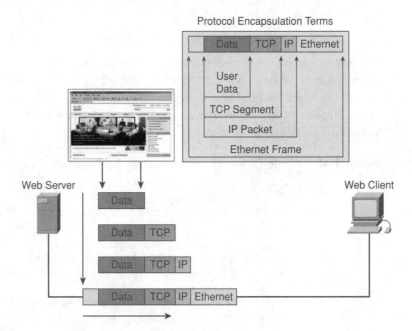

When messages are received from the network, the protocol stack on a host operates from bottom to top. Previously, we saw the process of encapsulation at each layer when the web server sent the web page to the client. The process of receiving the web page starts the unencapsulation of the message by the client.

As the bits are received by the client NIC, they are decoded and the destination MAC address is recognized by the client as its own.

The frame is sent up the web client protocol stack where the Ethernet header (source and destination MAC addresses) and trailer are removed (de-encapsulated). The remaining IP packet and contents are passed up to the IP layer.

At the IP layer, the IP header (source and destination IP addresses) is removed and the contents passed up to the TCP layer.

At the TCP layer, the TCP header (source and destination ports) is removed and the web page user data contents are passed up to the browser application using HTTP. As TCP segments are received they are reassembled to create the web page.

Figure 6-21 shows the web client receiving a web page from a web server. When the frame is received, the host strips off the Ethernet frame and then the IP header, and finally the TCP header to get to the data inside. The data is passed on to the web browser application via HTTP. After many of these frames are received and de-encapsulated, the web page sent by the server can be displayed.

Figure 6-21   Web Client De-encapsulating Web Page Data from Server

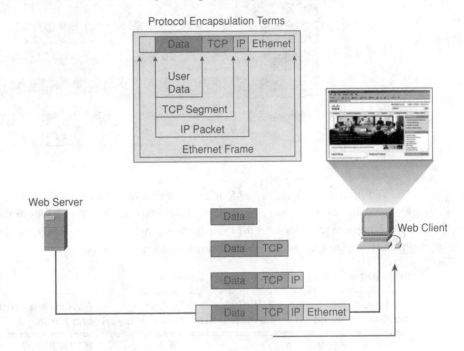

Interactive Activity 6-5: Match Networking Term with Protocol and TCP/IP Layer (6.3.2.3)

In this interactive activity, you match the host, protocol, and encapsulation terminology with the proper protocol or layer. Use file ia-6323 on the CD-ROM that accompanies this book to perform this interactive activity.

Open System Interconnection Model

The Open System Interconnection (OSI) model was developed by the International Organization for Standardization (ISO) in 1984. Unlike the TCP/IP model, it does not specify the interaction of any specific protocols. It was created as architecture for developers to follow to design protocols for network communications. Although very few protocol stacks exactly implement the seven layers of the OSI model, it is now considered the primary reference model for intercomputer communications.

NOTE

The International Organization for Standardization's name, ISO, is not an acronym or abbreviation. It is based on the Greek word *ISOS*, which means equal.

The OSI model includes all functions, or tasks, associated with internetwork communications, not just those related to the TCP/IP protocols. Compared to the TCP/IP model, which only has four layers, the

OSI model organizes the tasks into seven more specific groups. A task, or group of tasks, is then assigned to each of the seven OSI layers. The seven layers of the OSI model are shown in Figure 6-22.

Figure 6-22   OSI Model Layers

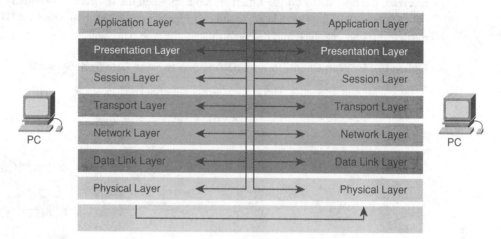

The TCP/IP model originally had four layers with layer 1 being the physical access layer. A revised version splits this layer into two, resulting in five layers. The lower layers of the revised TCP/IP model map closely to those of the OSI, as shown in Table 6-2. Basically, the TCP/IP model groups the three upper layers of the OSI model into one application layer.

Table 6-2   OSI and TCP/IP Model Layers

OSI Layer Number	OSI Layer Name	TCP/IP Layer Number	TCP/IP Name (5 layer)	Associated Protocols and Media
7	Application	5	Application	HTTP, FTP, Telnet
6	Presentation	5	Application	
5	Session	5	Application	
4	Transport	4	Transport	TCP and UDP
3	Network	3	Internetwork	IP
2	Data Link	2	Data Link	Ethernet, HDLC, PPP, Frame Relay
1	Physical	1	Physical	Media (cabling) Copper, Fiber, Wireless

The essence of protocol stacks is the separation and organization of distinct functions. The separation of functions enables each layer in the stack to operate independently of others. For example, accessing a website is feasible from a laptop computer connected to a cable modem at home, from a laptop using wireless, or from a web-enabled mobile phone. The application layer operates seamlessly, regardless of the way the lower layers are operating.

In the same way, the lower layers operate seamlessly. For example, an Internet connection functions satisfactorily when a variety of applications are running at the same time, such as e-mail, web browsing, IM, and music download.

The Packet Tracer program graphical interface allows the viewing of simulated data being transmitted between two hosts. It uses protocol data units (PDUs) to represent network traffic frames and displays protocol stack information at the appropriate layers of the OSI model.

In Figure 6-23, the request from the web client is being received by the Ethernet NIC in the web server. The following information is shown in OSI layers 1 through 4:

- **Layer 4** (Transport): TCP port numbers

- **Layer 3** (Network): IP addresses

- **Layer 2** (Data Link): Ethernet MAC addresses

- **Layer 1** (Physical): Fast Ethernet port

Figure 6-23 Packet Tracer PDU Information at Various OSI Layers

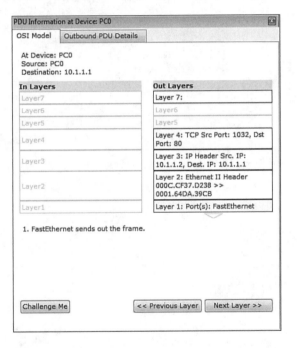

Interactive Activity 6-6: Match the Header, Address, Protocol, or Term with the Proper OSI Layer (6.3.3.3)

In this interactive activity, you match the header, address, protocol, or term to the proper layer in the network model. Use file ia-6333 on the CD-ROM that accompanies this book to perform this interactive activity.

Interactive Activity 6-7: Build an Ethernet Frame with Proper Components and Send It to Its Destination (6.3.3.4)

In this interactive activity, you build an Ethernet frame with proper components and send it to its destination. Use file ia-6334 on the CD-ROM that accompanies this book to perform this interactive activity.

Packet Tracer
☐ **Activity**

View PDU Information Being Sent Between a Client and a Server (6.3.3.5)

In this Packet Tracer activity, you use Packet Tracer to view PDU information being sent between a client and server. Use file d1-6335.pka on the CD-ROM that accompanies this book to perform this interactive activity.

Summary

This chapter discussed the client/server relationship for common network services such as HTTP, FTP, DNS, DHCP, and e-mail.

Servers are hosts that run software to enable them to provide services to other hosts over the network. Clients run software that enables them to access server services.

Protocols are divided into four main groups: applications (HTTP, FTP, Telnet, and so on); transport (TCP and UDP); Internet Protocol (IP); and network access protocols such as Ethernet, HDLC, and PPP.

DNS provides the IP address of a website URL or domain name so that a host can connect to a web server. DNS names are registered and organized on the Internet within specific high-level groups, or domains.

DHCP is a service that assigns the IP address, subnet mask, default gateway, and other information to clients.

FTP is a service that allows for the download and upload of files between a client and server.

E-mail servers use SMTP to send mail, and clients use POP3 or IMAP4 to retrieve mail. Recipients are specified using the username@domainname.domain format.

Web services transfer information between web clients and web servers. Most web pages are accessed using HTTP from servers using port 80. HTTP is not a secure service. Requests for secure HTTP are sent to port 443. These requests require the use of HTTPS.

Telnet is a service that allows administrators to log in to a host from a remote location and control the host as if they were logged in locally.

An Internet telephony client uses peer-to-peer technology similar to that used by instant messaging. IP telephony makes use of Voice over IP (VoIP) technology, which uses IP packets to carry digitized voice as data.

A protocol stack organizes the protocols as a layered hierarchy, with each higher-level protocol depending on the services of the protocols in the lower levels. Using a layered approach has many benefits.

When sending messages, the protocol stack on a host operates from top to bottom. Each layer encapsulates information and passes it to the layer below. The process is reversed on the receiving host.

Two hierarchical network models are the OSI model (seven layers) and the TCP/IP model (four or five layers). The OSI model includes all functions, or tasks, associated with internetwork communications, not just those related to the TCP/IP protocols. The OSI model is considered the primary reference model for intercomputer communications.

Activities and Labs

This summary outlines the activities and labs you can perform to help reinforce important concepts described in this chapter. You can find the activity and Packet Tracer files on the CD-ROM accompanying this book. The complete hands-on labs appear in Part II.

Interactive Activities on the CD-ROM:

Interactive Activity 6-1: Determine the Correct Service for a Client Request (6.1.1.4)

Interactive Activity 6-2: Match the Correct Transport Protocol to the Characteristics Described (6.1.3.4)

Interactive Activity 6-3: Demonstration of GUI FTP Client Use (6.2.3.2)

Interactive Activity 6-4: Match the Protocol Name to the Destination Port Number in the TCP Segment (6.2.7.2)

Interactive Activity 6-5: Match Networking Term with Protocol and TCP/IP Layer (6.3.2.3)

Interactive Activity 6-6: Match the Header, Address, Protocol, or Term with the Proper OSI Layer (6.3.3.3)

Interactive Activity 6-7: Build an Ethernet Frame with Proper Components and Send It to Its Destination (6.3.3.4)

Packet Tracer Activities on the CD-ROM:

Observing Web Requests (6.2.2.2)

View PDU Information Being Sent Between a Client and a Server (6.3.3.5)

Labs in Part II of This Book:

Lab 6-1: Observing DNS Name Resolution (6.2.1.3)

Lab 6-2: Exploring FTP (6.2.3.3)

Lab 6-3: Configuring an E-mail Client (6.2.4.4)

Check Your Understanding

Complete all the review questions listed here to test your understanding of the topics and concepts in this chapter. The "Check Your Understanding and Challenge Questions Answer Key" appendix lists the answers.

1. What happens when part of a message using TCP is not delivered to the destination host?

    A. The sender resends the entire message.

    B. The sender sends a request to find out what happened.

    C. Nothing. TCP does not check for errors and missing data.

    D. The part of the message that is missing is retransmitted.

2. A user uploads large new files to his or her website. What service is this user likely using to copy the files to the website?

3. A workstation gets its IP address, subnet mask, and default gateway automatically. What service is being employed?

4. What three main protocols do e-mail users and servers normally use to process e-mail?

    A. DHCP

    B. SMTP

    C. IMAP4

    D. DNS

    E. POP3

5. Which protocol allows you to enter www.cisco.com instead of an IP address to open the web page?

6. Match the term on the left to the definition on the right.

HTML	Hosts a web page
HTTP	Requests a web page
HTTPS	Used to create web pages
Web server	Secure protocol that uses port 443
Web client	Protocol commonly used by a web browser

7. What acronym is associated with making a phone call using the Internet?

    A. IM

    B. HTML

    C. HTTP

    D. SNMP

    E. VoIP

8. Match the port number on the left to the associated protocol on the right.

Port Numbers	Protocols
68	FTP Data
21	HTTP
23	SNMP
25	DNS
53	FTP Control
20	POP3
80	Telnet
110	HTTPS
161	SMTP
443	DHCP

9. Select three protocols that operate at the application layer on the OSI model.

   A. ARP

   B. TCP

   C. DSL

   D. FTP

   E. POP3

   F. HTTP

10. As an Ethernet frame enters the NIC of a destination host, in what order do the headers (and trailers if applicable) get removed to de-encapsulate the frame and pass the user data to the application?

   A. IP, Ethernet, TCP

   B. Ethernet, TCP, IP

   C. Ethernet, IP, TCP

   D. TCP, IP, Ethernet

   E. IP, TCP, Ethernet

11. Which of the following TCP/IP protocols is matched to the correct layer of the OSI model? (Choose all that apply.)

   A. IP, Network

   B. UDP, Network

   C. TCP, Application

   D. HTTP, Application

   E. TCP, Transport

12. What allows an FTP server to keep track of connections from multiple clients to the FTP service?

   A. The frame header source and destination MAC address

   B. The packet header destination IP and MAC addresses

   C. The packet header source IP address and TCP header source port number

   D. The TCP destination port number and the frame header source MAC address

13. A frame from a client comes into a server with a destination port of 80 in the TCP segment. What service will receive that segment on the server?

14. A UTP cable has a poorly terminated connector. With what layer of the OSI model is this problem associated?

   A. Layer 7, application

   B. Layer 3, network

   C. Layer 4, transport

   D. Layer 1, physical

   E. Layer 5, session

15. Which of the following can be contained in an Ethernet frame? (Choose all that apply.)

   A. Source and destination MAC addresses

   B. Source and destination ID numbers

   C. Source and destination port numbers

   D. Source and destination IP addresses

   E. Source and destination serial numbers

16. VoIP applications are sensitive to delay. What transport protocol is better suited to voice applications?

   A. IP

   B. UDP

   C. TCP

   D. FTP

   E. DHCP

17. When transferring a file using FTP, what is the order of protocols from the upper layers of the TCP/IP model to the lower layers?

   A. TCP uses FTP, which uses IP

   B. FTP uses TCP, which uses IP

   C. IP uses FTP, which uses TCP

   D. FTP uses UDP, which uses IP

   E. FTP uses IP, which uses UDP

Challenge Questions and Activities

These questions and activities require a deeper application of the concepts covered in this chapter. You can find the answers in the appendix.

1. Which layers of the TCP/IP model have corresponding layers in the OSI model? What is the layer number and name of the corresponding OSI layer?

2. A network user reports that she cannot access a website. The support technician can **ping** the server by its IP address but cannot connect when entering the website address in the browser. Which protocol or service is most likely to be the source of the problem?

CHAPTER 7

Wireless Technologies

Objectives

Upon completion of this chapter, you will be able to answer the following questions:

- What are benefits and limitations of wireless technology?

- Where are wireless technologies commonly used?

- How does a wireless personal-area network (WPAN) compare to a wireless local-area network (WLAN) and a wireless wide-area network (WWAN)?

- What components are required to build a WLAN and what are their functions?

- What are the current standards for WLANs and how do they compare?

- What parameters must be configured to allow a wireless client to access network resources?

- What techniques are available to help secure the WLAN?

- How is an access point and wireless client configured to allow communication to occur?

Key Terms

This chapter uses the following key terms. You can find the definitions in the Glossary.

electromagnetic wave   *page 233*

wavelength   *page 233*

spectrum   *page 233*

infrared (IR)   *page 233*

Infrared Direct Access (IrDA)   *page 233*

radio frequency (RF)   *page 234*

Industrial, Scientific, and Medical (ISM) bands
  page 234

Unlicensed National Information Infrastructure
  (UNII) bands   *page 234*

Bluetooth   *page 234*

hotspot   *page 235*

wireless personal-area networks (WPAN)   *page 236*

wireless local-area networks (WLAN)   *page 236*

wireless wide-area networks (WWAN)   *page 236*

Code Division Multiple Access (CDMA)   *page 236*

Global System for Mobile Communication (GSM)
  page 236

802.11a   *page 237*

802.11b   *page 237*

802.11g   *page 237*

802.11n   *page 237*

Wireless-Fidelity (Wi-Fi)   *page 237*

multiple-input, multiple-output (MIMO)   *page 237*

wireless client   *page 239*

STA   *page 239*

access point (AP)   *page 239*

wireless bridge   *page 239*

antenna   *page 239*

Service Set Identifier (SSID)   *page 240*

ad-hoc   *page 240*

Independent Basic Service Set (IBSS)   *page 240*

infrastructure mode   *page 240*

Basic Service Set (BSS)   *page 240*

cell   *page 240*

This chapter introduces wireless technologies, including infrared and radio frequency, and the benefits and limitations of each. You also learn about wireless technologies, with emphasis given to wireless local-area networks, also called wireless LANs (WLANs), and considerations for planning, configuring, and securing these networks. Part II of this book includes all the curriculum labs for this chapter plus an additional challenge lab.

Wireless Technology

In addition to the wired network commonly found in most LAN environments, various technologies exist that allow the transmission of information between hosts without cables. These technologies are collectively referred to as wireless.

Wireless Technologies and Devices

Wireless technologies use electromagnetic waves to carry information between devices. An *electromagnetic wave* is the same medium that carries radio signals from the broadcasting station to a receiver or supplies light from a light bulb.

The electromagnetic spectrum includes radio and television broadcast bands, visible light, x-rays, and gamma rays. Each of these has a specific range of *wavelengths* and associated energies as shown in Figure 7-1.

Figure 7-1   Electromagnetic Spectrum

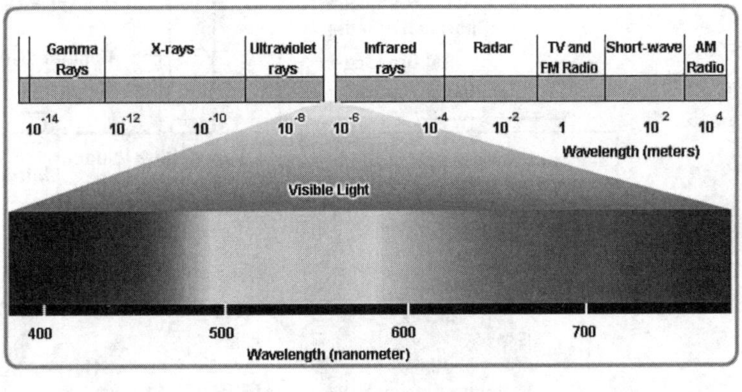

Some types of electromagnetic waves are not suitable for carrying data. Much of the electromagnetic *spectrum* is regulated by governments and licensed to various organizations for specific applications. In most countries, specific areas of the electromagnetic spectrum have been set aside to allow public use without the restriction of having to apply for special permits. The most common wavelengths used for public, unlicensed, wireless communications include the infrared and parts of the radio frequency (RF) band.

Infrared

Infrared (IR) is relatively low energy and cannot penetrate through walls or other obstacles. It is commonly used to connect and move data between devices such as personal digital assistants (PDA) and PCs or cell phones and PCs. A specialized communication port known as an *Infrared Direct Access (IrDA)* port uses IR to exchange information between devices. IR only allows a one-to-one type of connection.

NOTE

IrDA also stands for the Infrared Data Association. The goal of this nonprofit organization is to develop globally adopted specifications for infrared wireless communications.

IR is commonly used for remote control devices, wireless mice, and wireless keyboards. It is generally used for short-range, line-of-sight communications. However, reflecting the IR signal off objects to extend the range is possible. For greater ranges, higher frequencies of electromagnetic waves are required.

Radio Frequency (RF)

Radio frequency (RF) waves have a much higher energy than IR and can penetrate through walls and other obstacles, allowing RF to travel further. Even though RF can penetrate materials better than IR, it is still stopped by many materials and also affected by environmental conditions such as high humidity.

Certain areas of the RF bands have been set aside for use by unlicensed devices such as wireless LANs, cordless phones, and computer peripherals. This includes the 900 MHz, 2.4 GHz, and the 5 GHz frequency ranges. The 900 MHz and 2.4 GHz ranges are known as the *Industrial, Scientific, and Medical (ISM) bands* and can be used with very few restrictions. The 5 GHz bands most commonly used for WLAN communication are the *Unlicensed National Information Infrastructure (UNII) bands*. This is shown in Figure 7-2.

Figure 7-2   ISM and UNII Bands Used for WLAN Communication

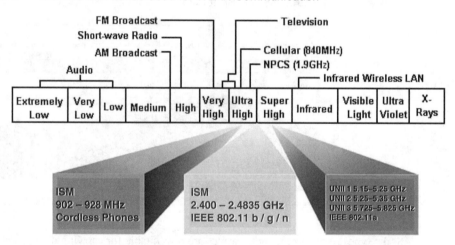

Bluetooth is a technology that makes use of the 2.4 GHz band. It uses a low output power and is therefore limited to low-speed, short-range communications. The advantage that Bluetooth has over IR is that it allows communication with many devices at the same time. This one-to-many communication has made Bluetooth technology the preferred method over IR for connecting computer peripherals such as mice, keyboards, and printers.

Other technologies that make use of the 2.4 GHz and 5 GHz bands are the modern wireless LAN technologies that conform to the various IEEE 802.11 standards. These technologies use a much higher output power than Bluetooth, which gives them a significantly greater range.

Interactive Activity 7-1: Selecting the Wireless Technology (7.1.1.4)

In this interactive activity you select the wireless technology associated with the given scenario. Use file ia-7114 on the CD-ROM that accompanies this book to perform this interactive activity.

Benefits and Limitations of Wireless Technology

Wireless technology offers many advantages compared to traditional wired networks. One of the main advantages is the capability to provide anytime, anywhere connectivity for mobile users. These users include salespeople and consultants who spend much of their time away from the office as well as anyone else who must remain in contact while away from their home network. The widespread implementation of wireless in public locations, known as *hotspots*, allows people to easily connect to the Internet to download information and exchange e-mails and files.

Wireless technology is fairly easy and inexpensive to install. The cost of home and business wireless devices continues to decrease. Yet, despite the decrease in cost, the data rate and capabilities of these devices have increased, allowing faster, more reliable, and secure wireless connections.

Wireless technology enables networks to be easily expanded, without the limitations of cabled connections. This greatly reduces costs and increases their flexibility. For example, a company that has variations in the number of employees during different times of the year need not spend the money to install wired networking capabilities for these seasonal employees. These employees can make use of a wireless connection to share the company resources. In addition, new or visiting users can also use the wireless network without any additional costs.

Some of the benefits of wireless LANs include the following:

- **Mobility**: Wireless allows for easy connection of both stationary and mobile clients.
- **Scalability**: Wireless can be easily expanded to allow more users to connect or to increase coverage area.
- **Flexibility**: Wireless provides anytime, anywhere connectivity.
- **Cost savings**: Equipment costs continue to fall as the technology matures.
- **Reduced installation time**: Installation of a single piece of equipment can provide connectivity for a large number of individuals.
- **Reliability in harsh environments**: Wireless is easy to install in emergency or environmentally unfriendly locations.

Despite the flexibility and benefits of wireless, some limitations and risks exist. First, wireless LAN (WLAN) technologies make use of the unlicensed regions of the RF spectrum. Because these regions are unregulated, many different devices make use of them. As a result, these regions are extremely congested and signals from different devices often interfere with each other. In addition, many devices such as microwave ovens and cordless phones also use these frequencies and can interfere with WLAN communications.

A second major concern with wireless is the lack of inherent security. Wireless was designed to provide ease of access to users. It does this by announcing its presence and broadcasting data in a manner that allows anyone the ability to access it. This same feature limits the amount of protection wireless can provide for the data. It allows anyone to intercept the communication stream, even unintended recipients. To address these security concerns, techniques such as authentication and encryption have been developed to help secure wireless transmissions.

Some of the limitations of wireless LANs include the following:

- **Interference**: Wireless technology is susceptible to interference from other devices that produce electromagnetic energies. This includes cordless phones, microwaves, televisions, and other wireless LAN implementations.

- **Network and data security**: Wireless LAN technology is designed to provide access to the data being transmitted, not security of the data. Additionally, it can provide unprotected access into the wired network.

- **Technology**: Wireless LAN technology continues to evolve. Wireless LAN technology does not currently provide the speed or reliability of wired LANs.

Types of Wireless Networks and Their Boundaries

Wireless networks are grouped into three major categories: *wireless personal-area networks (WPAN)*, *wireless local-area networks (WLAN)*, and *wireless wide-area networks (WWAN)*.

Despite these distinct categories, placing boundary limitations on a wireless network is difficult. This is because, unlike a wired network, a wireless network does not have precisely defined boundaries. The range of wireless transmissions can vary due to many factors. The range of wireless networks can be affected by natural and man-made interference, fluctuation in environmental conditions, as well as the composition and placement of obstacles within the wireless coverage area.

WPAN

A WPAN is the smallest wireless network used to connect various peripheral devices such as mice, keyboards, and PDAs to a computer. All of these devices are dedicated to a single host and usually use IR or Bluetooth technology.

WLAN

WLAN is typically used to extend the boundaries of the local wired network (LAN). WLANs use RF technology and conform to the various IEEE 802.11 standards. They allow many users to connect to a wired network through a device known as an access point (AP), which acts as a connection between the wireless network and the Ethernet wired network.

WWAN

WWAN networks provide coverage over extremely large areas. A good example of a WWAN is the cell phone network. These networks use technologies such as *Code Division Multiple Access (CDMA)* or *Global System for Mobile Communication (GSM)* and are often regulated by government agencies.

Interactive Activity 7-2: Selecting the Type of Wireless Network (7.1.3.3)

In this interactive activity you select the type of wireless network being used in a given scenario. Use file ia-7133 on the CD-ROM that accompanies this book to perform this interactive activity.

Wireless LANs

Wireless LANs can make use of many different components and technologies. Various standards have been developed to help ensure interoperability between different vendors' equipment and to help ensure the best possible performance from the WLAN.

Wireless LAN Standards

The main organization responsible for the creation of wireless technical standards is the Institute of Electrical and Electronics Engineers (IEEE). The IEEE has developed a number of standards to ensure that wireless LAN devices can communicate with each other. These standards specify the portion of the RF spectrum used, data rates, how the information is transmitted, and more.

The IEEE 802.11 standard governs the WLAN environment. There are currently four main amendments to the IEEE 802.11 standard that describe different characteristics for wireless communications. The currently available amendments are *802.11a*, *802.11b*, *802.11g,* and *802.11n*. The 802.11n amendment is not ratified at the time of this writing. Ratification is expected in late 2008. Collectively these technologies are referred to as *Wireless Fidelity (Wi-Fi)*. Table 7-1 provides a brief comparison of the current WLAN standards and their technology.

Table 7-1   Current WLAN Standards

Standard	Characteristics
802.11a	Uses 5 GHz RF spectrum.
	Maximum data rate of 54 Mbps.
	Not compatible with 2.4 GHz spectrum; that is, 802.11b/g/n devices.
	Range is approximately 33 percent that of the 802.11 b/g.
	Relatively expensive to implement compared to other technologies.
	Increasingly difficult to find 802.11a-compliant equipment.
802.11b	First of the 2.4 GHz technologies.
	Maximum data rate of 11 Mbps.
	Range of approximately 150 feet (46 m) indoors/300 feet (96 m) outdoors.
802.11g	Uses the 2.4 GHz RF band.
	Maximum data rate of 54 Mbps.
	Backward compatible with 802.11b.
802.11n	Newest standard still in development. Expected ratification date late 2008.
	Specifies support for both 2.4 GHz and 5 GHz technologies.
	Extends the range and data throughput.
	Uses multiple antennas, wide channels, and *multiple-input, multiple-output (MIMO)* technology.
	Designed to be backward compatible with existing 802.11a, 802.11b, and 802.11g equipment.

Another organization, known as the Wi-Fi Alliance, is responsible for testing wireless LAN devices from different manufacturers. The Wi-Fi logo on a device means that this equipment should interoperate with other devices of the same standard, which also bear the Wi-Fi logo. Figure 7-3 shows two devices bearing the Wi-Fi logo.

Figure 7-3   Interoperability Between Wi-Fi Devices

It is important to note that much of the current draft 802.11n equipment offers support only for the 2.4 GHz band. The full 802.11 draft standard does specify support for the 5 GHz band in addition. Industry demand is pushing for the development of equipment that supports both the 2.4 GHz and 5 GHz bands. Some manufacturers are already producing equipment that supports both bands.

Wireless LAN Components

After a standard is adopted, it is important that all components within the WLAN adhere to that standard or are compatible with the standard. Various components must be considered in a WLAN, including a wireless client, an access point, a wireless bridge, and an antenna. These are shown in Figure 7-4.

Figure 7-4   Wireless Devices

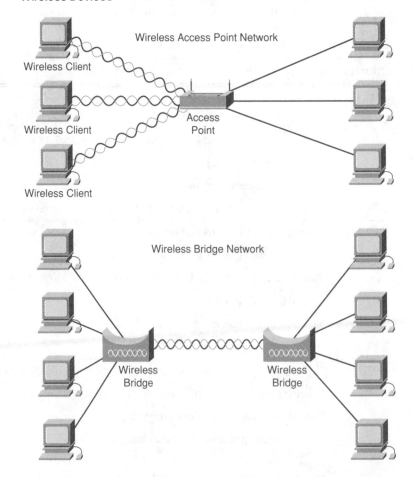

A *wireless client* is also known as an *STA* or station. STAs are any addressable host on a wireless network. Wireless, like Ethernet, uses the MAC address to identify end devices. A STA is the actual end device such as a laptop computer or a PDA. Client software runs on the STA and allows the STA to connect to the wireless network. Often this distinction is blurred and the actual end device is referred to as a client. Wireless STAs can be either stationary or mobile.

An *access point (AP)* is the device that connects the wireless network to the wired LAN. Most home and small business environments actually deploy a multi-function device that contains an AP, switch, and router among other functionality. These devices are often referred to as wireless routers. The Linksys WRT 300N shown in Figure 7-5 is an example of such a multi-function device.

Figure 7-5   Linksys WRT 300N Wireless Router

This device acts as a translational bridge by converting the frames between the 802.11 format used on the wireless network and the 802.3 format used on Ethernet networks. The AP also keeps track of all associated wireless clients and acts as an intermediary for frames addressed to or coming from the wireless clients. APs are normally used to provide wireless STAs with access to the Ethernet network. An AP supports wireless connections within a limited area known as a cell or Basic Service Set (BSS).

Wireless bridges are designed to provide long-range, point-to-point or point-to-multipoint connections. They seldom allow the connection of STAs and are designed to connect one wired LAN segment to another using wireless technology. Bridging technology on the unlicensed RF frequencies can connect networks 25 miles (40 km) or more apart.

Antennas are used on APs, STAs, and wireless bridges. The role of an antenna is to increase the output signal strength from a wireless device. The increase in output power is known as gain. Generally, the stronger the output signal, the greater the expected range. This means that an antenna with a higher gain should have a greater transmission distance than one with a lower gain.

Antennas are classified according to the way they radiate the signal. Directional antennas concentrate the signal strength into one direction. Omnidirectional antennas are designed to emit equally in all directions. APs normally deploy omnidirectional antennas in order to provide connectivity over a large area.

By concentrating all the signal strength into one direction, directional antennas can achieve great transmission distances. Directional antennas are normally used in point-to-point bridging applications where two sites must be connected together over a long distance.

Interactive Activity 7-3: Wireless Components (7.2.2.3)

In this interactive activity you match the wireless component to the appropriate description. Use file ia-7223 on the CD-ROM that accompanies this book to perform this interactive activity.

WLANs and the SSID

When building a wireless network, ensuring that the wireless components connect to the appropriate WLAN is important. This is done using a *Service Set Identifier (SSID)*. The SSID is a case-sensitive, alphanumeric string that is up to 32 characters in length. It is sent in the header of all frames transmitted over the WLAN and is used to tell wireless devices which WLAN they belong to and with which other devices they can communicate. Regardless of the type of WLAN installation, all wireless devices in a WLAN must be configured with the same SSID in order to communicate.

The two basic forms of WLAN installations are ad-hoc and infrastructure mode.

Ad-hoc

The simplest form of a wireless network is created by connecting two or more wireless clients together in a peer-to-peer network. A wireless network established in this manner is known as an *ad-hoc* network and does not include an AP. All clients within an ad-hoc network are equal. The area covered by this network is known as an *Independent Basic Service Set (IBSS)*. A simple ad-hoc network can be used to exchange files and information between devices without the expense and complexity of purchasing and configuring an AP.

Infrastructure Mode

Although an ad-hoc arrangement might be good for small networks, larger networks require a single device that controls communications in the wireless cell. If present, an AP will take over this role and control who can talk and when. When an AP is in charge of communications in a cell it is referred to as *infrastructure mode*. Infrastructure mode is the mode of wireless communication most often used in home and business environments. In this form of WLAN, individual STAs cannot communicate directly with each other. To communicate, each device must obtain permission from the AP. The AP controls all communications and ensures that all STAs have equal access to the medium. The area covered by a single AP is known as a *Basic Service Set (BSS)* or *cell* as shown in Figure 7-6.

Figure 7-7 shows the difference between an IBSS and a BSS. In a BSS the AP is in charge and controls all communication, whereas in an IBSS there is no AP to take charge.

The BSS is the smallest building block of a WLAN. Because the area of coverage of a single AP is limited, multiple BSSs are often connected together to form an *Extended Service Set (ESS)*. An ESS consists of multiple BSSs connected together through a distribution system (DS). An ESS uses multiple APs and each AP is in a separate BSS. Although there are separate BSSs, the SSID is common throughout the entire ESS.

Figure 7-6   A Wireless Cell or Basic Service Set (BSS)

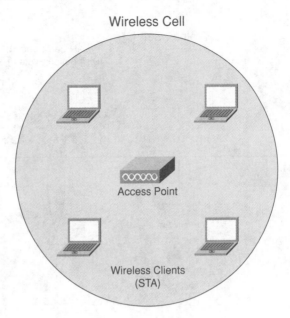

Figure 7-7   IBSS and BSS

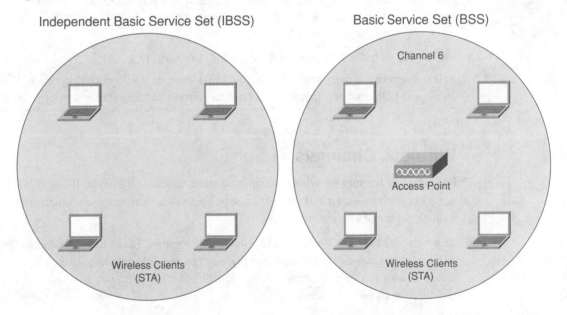

In order to allow a client to move between the cells without the loss of signal, BSSs must overlap by approximately 10 percent, as shown in Figure 7-8. This allows the client to connect to the second AP before disconnecting from the first AP.

Figure 7-8   Overlapping BSSs to Provide Seamless Roaming

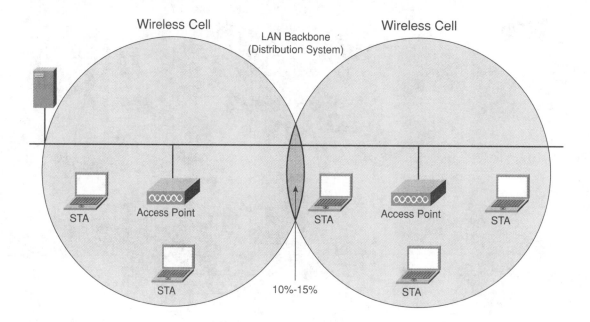

Most home and small business environments consist of a single BSS. However, as the required coverage area and number of hosts needing to connect increases, creating an ESS becomes necessary.

Interactive Activity 7-4: Linksys GUI: Setting the SSID (7.2.3.4)

In this interactive activity you configure the SSID using the Linksys GUI interface. Use file ia-7234 on the CD-ROM that accompanies this book to perform this interactive activity.

Wireless Channels

Regardless of whether the wireless clients are communicating within an IBSS, BSS, or ESS, the conversation between sender and receiver must be controlled. One way to accomplish this control is through the use of *wireless channels*.

Channels are created by dividing the available RF spectrum. Each channel is capable of carrying a different conversation. This is similar to the way that multiple television channels are transmitted across a single medium. Multiple APs can function in close proximity to one another as long as they use different channels for communication.

Unfortunately, the frequencies used by some channels overlap with those used by others. Different conversations must be carried on non-overlapping channels. The number and distribution of channels vary by region and technology. If using the 2.4 GHz spectrum in North America, there are three non-overlapping channels: 1, 6, and 11. In this spectral range, channels must be at least five apart to avoid overlap. In North America, the 5 GHz range uses three different UNII bands, each with four non-overlapping channels. When creating an ESS, ensuring that adjacent cells are using non-overlapping channels for communication is important, as shown in Figure 7-9.

Figure 7-9   Channel Assignment in an ESS

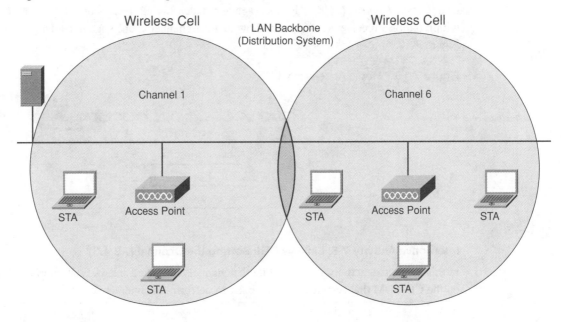

You can manually or automatically set the channel selection used for a specific conversation, based on factors such as current usage and available throughput. Normally each wireless conversation makes use of a separate channel. IEEE 802.11n combines multiple channels to create a single wide channel, which provides more bandwidth and increases the data rate.

Within a WLAN, the lack of well-defined boundaries makes detecting whether collisions occur during transmission impossible. Therefore, using an access method on a wireless network that ensures collisions do not occur is necessary. Wireless technology uses an access method called *Carrier Sense Multiple Access with Collision Avoidance (CSMA/CA)*. With CSMA/CA, stations listen to the channel to see whether it is free; if it is they start to transmit after a random period of time.

CSMA/CA creates a reservation on the channel for use by a specific conversation. While a reservation is in place, no other device may transmit on the channel, thus possible collisions are avoided. When the conversation is complete, the reservation is released and made available for others. When one station starts to send, all other stations detect the transmission and delay their transmissions for a period to allow the conversation to complete.

In some circumstances, stations might not be within range of the transmitting station and are not able to detect the transmission. In cases such as this, RTS/CTS comes into play. With RTS/CTS, a device that requires use of a specific communication channel in a BSS asks permission from the AP. This is known as a *Request to Send (RTS)*. If the channel is available, the AP will respond to the device with a *Clear to Send (CTS)* message indicating that the device may transmit on the channel. A CTS is broadcast to all devices within the BSS. Therefore, all devices in the BSS know that the requested channel is now in use and wait for the conversation to complete before transmitting. RTS/CTS is not normally used in small wireless networks such as those encountered in homes and small businesses. This is because the chances of a station being unable to detect the transmissions of another station in a small network are slim and the overhead associated with CTS/RTS would actually slow down the network performance.

When the AP receives the packet correctly, the conversation is complete. At this point, the AP issues an *acknowledgement (ACK)*. This message is broadcast to all devices on the WLAN. All devices within the BSS receive the ACK and know that the channel is once again available, as illustrated in Figure 7-10.

Figure 7-10   Media Access in a BSS

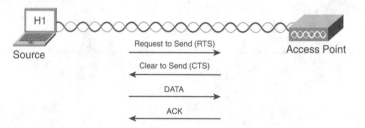

Interactive Activity 7-5: Linksys GUI: Setting the Channel (7.2.4.3)

In this interactive activity you configure the channel using the Linksys GUI interface. Use file ia-7243 on the CD-ROM that accompanies this book to perform this interactive activity.

Configuring the Access Point

The first step in any wireless network deployment is careful planning done in consultation with all the stakeholders, including anyone who will use, manage, or support the network. This step helps determine the standard to use, equipment required, network layout, and channel assignment. After these factors have been determined the next step is to configure the AP.

Most integrated routers offer both wired and wireless connectivity and serve as the AP in the wireless network. Basic configuration settings such as passwords, IP addresses, and DHCP settings are the same whether the device is being used to connect wired or wireless hosts. Basic configuration tasks, such as changing the default password, should be conducted before the AP is connected to a live network.

When using the wireless functionality of an integrated router, additional configuration parameters are required, such as setting the wireless mode, SSID, and wireless channel to be used.

Wireless Mode

Most home AP devices can support various modes, mainly 802.11b, 802.11g, and 802.11n. Although these all use the 2.4 GHz range, each uses a different technology to obtain its maximum throughput. The type of mode enabled on the AP depends on the type of host connecting to it. If only one type of host connects to the AP device, set the mode to support it. If multiple types of hosts will connect, select mixed mode. Each mode includes a certain amount of overhead. By enabling mixed mode, network performance will decrease due to the overhead incurred in supporting all modes. Figure 7-11 illustrates the different modes available on a Linksys wireless router.

Figure 7-11   Wireless Modes in a Linksys Wireless Router

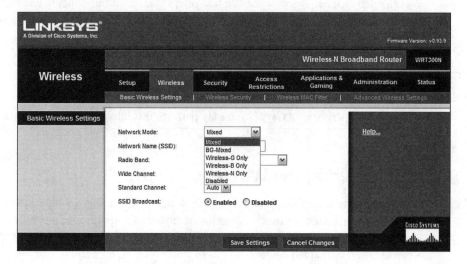

SSID

The SSID, as shown in Figure 7-12, is used to identify the WLAN. All devices that want to participate in the WLAN must use the same SSID. To allow easy detection of the WLAN by clients, the SSID is normally broadcast. It is possible to disable the broadcast feature of the SSID. If the SSID is not broadcast, wireless clients will need to have this value manually configured. Although it makes detecting a WLAN more difficult, disabling the SSID broadcast should not be considered a security feature.

Figure 7-12   SSID and Wireless Channel

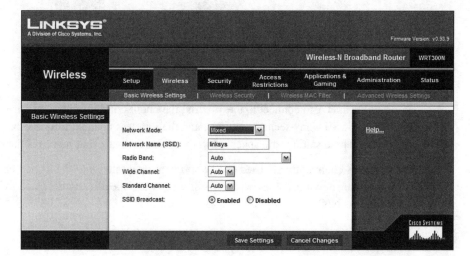

Wireless Channel

The choice of channel for an AP must be made relative to the other wireless networks around it. Adjacent BSSs must use non-overlapping channels in order to optimize throughput. Most APs now offer a choice to manually configure the channel, or allow the AP to automatically locate the least congested channel or locate the one that offers maximum throughput. The 802.11n technology also offers the ability to fuse channels together to create a wide channel that is capable of carrying data at a higher transfer rate than a standard channel.

Lab 7-1: Configuring a Wireless Access Point (7.2.5.3)

In this lab you configure an access point to allow clients to associate to. Refer to the hands-on lab in Part II of this *Learning Guide*. You may perform this lab now or wait until the end of the chapter.

Configuring the Wireless Client

A wireless host, or STA, is defined as any device that contains a wireless NIC and runs wireless client software. This client software allows the hardware to participate in the WLAN. PDAs, laptops, desktop PCs, printers, projectors, and Wi-Fi phones are all common examples of STAs. Figure 7-13 shows some wireless-enabled devices.

Figure 7-13   Wireless-Enabled Devices

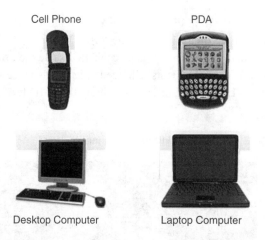

In order for a STA to connect to the WLAN, the client configuration must match that of the AP. This includes the SSID, any security settings, and the wireless channel information if it was manually set on the AP. These settings are specified in the client software that manages the client connection.

The wireless client software used can be software integrated into the device operating system, or can be standalone, downloadable, wireless utility software specifically designed to interact with the specific wireless NIC.

Integrated Wireless Utility Software

The Windows XP wireless client software is an example of a popular wireless client utility that is included as part of the device OS. This client software can control most basic wireless client configurations but is not optimized for any specific wireless NIC. It is user friendly and offers a simple connection process.

Standalone Wireless Utility Software

Wireless utility software is usually supplied with the wireless NIC and is designed to work with that specific NIC. It usually offers enhanced functionality over the Windows XP wireless utility software. It normally includes features such as

- **Link information**: Displays the current strength and quality of a wireless signal

- **Profiles**: Allows configuration options such as channel and SSID to be specified for each wireless network

- **Site survey**: Enables the detection of all wireless networks in the vicinity

Allowing both the wireless utility software and Windows XP client software to manage the wireless connection at the same time is not possible. For most situations the Windows XP wireless client software is sufficient. However, if multiple profiles must be created for each wireless network or advanced configurations settings are necessary, using the utility supplied with the NIC might be better.

Lab 7-2: Configuring a Wireless Client (7.2.6.4)

In this lab you configure a wireless client to associate to a previously configured AP. Refer to the hands-on lab in Part II of this *Learning Guide*. You may perform this lab now or wait until the end of the chapter.

After you configure the client software, you should verify the link between the client and the AP. To do so, open the wireless link information screen to display information such as the connection data rate, connection status, and wireless channel used. Figure 7-14 shows an example of typical link information. It shows the quality of the wireless signal and the current signal strength.

Figure 7-14   Linksys Wireless Client

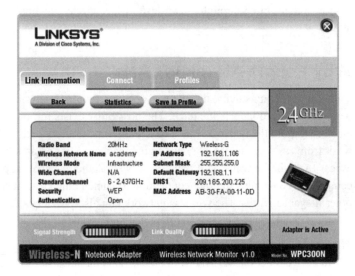

In addition to verifying the wireless connection status, verify that data can actually be transmitted. One of the most common tests for verifying successful data transmission is a simple **ping**. If the **ping** is successful, physical connectivity is present and data transmission is usually possible. If the **ping** is unsuccessful from source to destination, **ping** the AP from the wireless client to ensure that wireless connectivity is available. If this fails as well, the issue is between the wireless client and the AP, as shown in Figure 7-15. In this case, check the settings on both the client and the AP and try to reestablish connectivity.

Figure 7-15   Misconfiguration of the Wireless Client

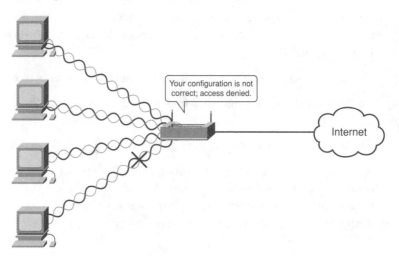

If the wireless client can successfully connect to the AP, check the connectivity from the AP to the next hop on the path to the destination. If the connection is successful, the problem is most likely not with the AP configuration, but may be an issue with another device on the path to the destination or the destination device itself.

Security Considerations on a Wireless LAN

One of the primary benefits of wireless networking is the convenience of connecting devices without the restrictions imposed by wires. Unfortunately, that ease of connectivity and the fact that the information is transmitted through the air also makes wireless technology vulnerable to interception and attacks.

Why People Attack WLANs

With wireless connectivity, the attacker does not require a physical connection to the network or networked devices to launch an attack. The possibility exists for an attacker to tune into wireless signals emanating from the network, much like tuning into a radio station. The attacker can access the network from any location the wireless signal reaches. After an attacker has access to the network he has access to all the information it contains as well as the resources it provides. For example, an intruder can use the company's Internet connection to launch attacks against other networks or to carry out other illegal activities. The wireless network can also provide access to the wired network where intruders can damage files or steal personal and private information.

The vulnerabilities in wireless networking require special security features and implementation methods to help protect the WLAN from attack. This includes steps to secure the wireless device, such as implementing secure passwords and changing all default settings, as well as more advanced security configurations such as data encryption.

War Driving and War Walking

War driving is the process of driving around an area searching for wireless LANs. When discovered, the location of the WLAN is logged and shared. The goal of war driving is to bring attention to the fact that most wireless networks are insecure and also to show the widespread acceptance and use of wireless LAN technology.

A similar process to war driving is known as war walking, in which the person walks around an area to discover wireless access. Once access is discovered, a chalk mark is placed in front of the location to indicate the status of the wireless connection. This mark allows others to easily identify open WLANs, which can be exploited.

The SSID provides a convenient way for users to gain entry into a WLAN. All computers connecting to a wireless network must know the SSID before they are able to connect. By default, wireless routers and access points announce the presence of the WLAN by broadcasting the SSID to all computers within range. With SSID broadcast activated, as shown in Figure 7-16, any wireless client can detect the network and connect to it, if no other security features are in place.

Figure 7-16   SSID and SSID Broadcast Settings

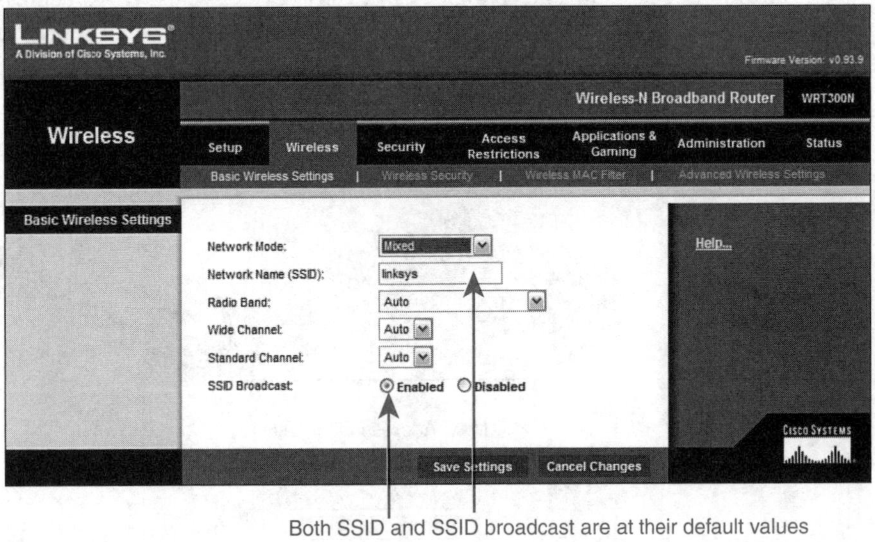

Both SSID and SSID broadcast are at their default values

The SSID broadcast feature can be turned off. When it is turned off, the fact that the network is there is no longer made public. This does not provide any real level of security but does make connecting more difficult for a client. Any computer trying to connect to the network must be manually configured with the SSID. Easily obtainable tools do exist that allow someone wanting to gain access to the wireless network to actively determine the network SSID.

Additionally, changing all default settings is important. Wireless devices are usually shipped preconfigured with settings such as SSIDs, passwords, and IP addresses in place. These default settings are public knowledge and make identifying and infiltrating a network easy for an attacker. Default information should be changed to something secure and unique before the wireless device is connected to a live network.

Even with SSID broadcasting disabled, the possibility exists for someone to gain access to a WLAN using the well-known default SSID. Additionally, if other default settings such as passwords and IP addresses are not changed, attackers can access an AP and make changes themselves by either locking out legitimate users or providing themselves and others with unauthorized access. Changing these defaults will decrease the chance of unauthorized access to the WLAN.

Disabling SSID broadcast and changing default settings, by themselves, will not protect the network. For example, SSIDs are transmitted in clear text in every 802.11 frame. Software is readily available that will allow a device to intercept wireless signals and read the SSID. Even with SSID broadcast turned off and default values changed, attackers can learn the name of a wireless network through the use of these devices. Many different techniques must be deployed to help secure a WLAN, including filtering, authentication, and encryption.

MAC Address Filtering

One way to limit access to wireless networks is to control exactly which devices can connect to the network through the filtering of the MAC address, as shown in Figure 7-17. MAC address filtering uses the MAC address embedded in every frame to identify which devices are allowed to connect to the wireless network. When a wireless client attempts to connect, or associate, with an AP it sends its MAC address information. If MAC address filtering is enabled, the wireless router or AP will look up this MAC address in a preconfigured list. Only devices whose MAC addresses have been prerecorded in the router's database are allowed to associate with the network. Frames with MAC addresses not found in the database are dropped by the AP.

Figure 7-17   MAC Address Filtering

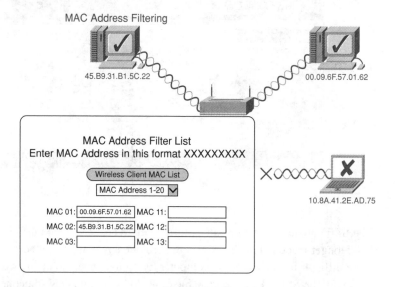

Several issues exist with MAC address filtering that hinders its usefulness. For example, it requires the MAC addresses of all devices that should have access to the network to be included in the database before connection attempts occur. A device that is not identified in the database will not be able to connect. For large, dynamic networks the administration of MAC addresses can become quite a task. Additionally, the possibility exists for an attacker to capture frames from the WLAN and then clone the address of a device that does have permission to use the network. This method is now extremely easy to do with tools that are freely available for download from the Internet.

Authentication on a WLAN

Another way to control who can connect to the WLAN is to implement *authentication*. Authentication is the process of permitting entry to a network based on a set of credentials. It is used to verify that the person or device attempting to connect to the network is who they claim to be.

The use of a username and password is the most common form of authentication. In a wireless environment, authentication ensures that the connected host is verified. Client authentication, if enabled, must occur before it is allowed to associate to the WLAN. Association is the point when the AP agrees to handle data to and from the wireless host. The three types of wireless authentication methods are open authentication, pre-shared keys (PSK), and Extensible Authentication Protocol (EAP).

Open Authentication

By default, wireless devices do not require authentication. Any and all clients are able to associate regardless of who they are. This is referred to as *open authentication*, which really means no authentication at all, as shown in Figure 7-18. Open authentication should be used only on public wireless networks such as those found in many schools and restaurants. It can also be used on networks where authentication will be done by other means once connected to the network.

Figure 7-18   Open Authentication

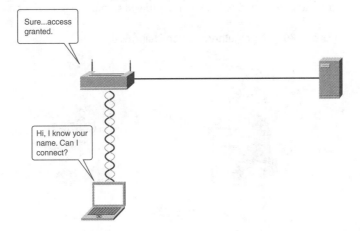

Pre-shared keys (PSK)

With *pre-shared keys (PSK)* both the AP and client must be configured with the same key or secret word, as shown in Figure 7-19. The AP sends a random string of bytes to the client. The client accepts the string and encrypts or scrambles it based on the key and an encryption algorithm. The encrypted string is then sent back to the AP. The AP also carries out the encryption process locally using the same algorithm and the same shared secret word. If the encrypted string received by the AP from the client is the same as the one generated by the client, authentication is successful and the client is allowed to connect.

One of the problems with PSK is the authentication is only one way. The host authenticates to the AP. PSK does not authenticate the AP to the host, nor does it authenticate the actual user of the host. In order to obtain mutual authentication between the user and the AP you must use Extensible Authentication Protocol (EAP).

Figure 7-19 Authentication Using Pre-shared keys

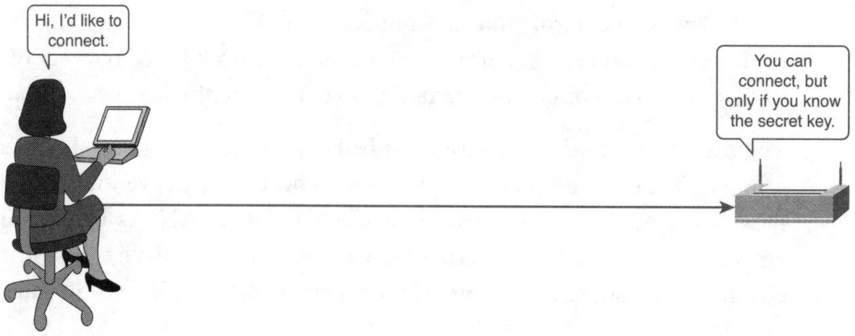

Extensible Authentication Protocol (EAP)

Extensible Authentication Protocol (EAP) provides mutual, or two-way, authentication as well as user authentication, as illustrated in Figure 7-20. When EAP software is installed on the client, the client communicates with a back-end authentication server such as *Remote Authentication Dial-in User Service (RADIUS)*. This back-end server functions separately from the AP and maintains a database of valid users who can access the network. When using EAP, the user, not just the host, must provide a username and password, which is checked against the RADIUS database for validity. If valid, the user is authenticated and allowed to make use of the network services.

Figure 7-20 User Authentication Using EAP

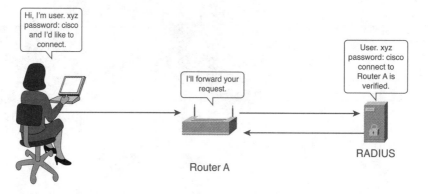

After authentication is enabled, regardless of the method used, the client must successfully pass authentication before it can associate with the AP. If both authentication and MAC address filtering are enabled, authentication occurs first. When authentication is successful, the AP then checks the MAC address against the MAC address table, as shown in Figure 7-21. When verified, the AP adds the host MAC address into its host table. The *association* of the client with the AP allows the client to connect to the network.

EAP frames are considered upper-level data by the MAC layer, so the STA must be authenticated and associated with the AP before it can commence network authentication via RADIUS. For this reason, open authentication is the normal setting when EAP is used.

Figure 7-21 Authentication and Association

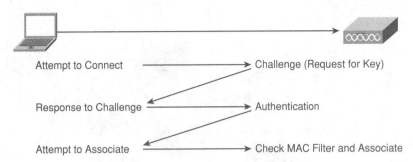

Attempt to Connect ——————————→ Challenge (Request for Key)

Response to Challenge ←—————————— Authentication

Attempt to Associate ——————————→ Check MAC Filter and Associate

Encryption on a WLAN

Authentication and MAC filtering might stop an attacker from connecting to a wireless network but it will not prevent the attacker from being able to intercept transmitted data. Because a wireless network does not have distinct boundaries and all traffic is transmitted through the air, intercepting, or sniffing, the wireless frames is easy for an attacker. *Encryption* is the process of transforming data so that even if it is intercepted it is unusable. This process is shown in Figure 7-22.

Figure 7-22 Encryption of Wireless Data

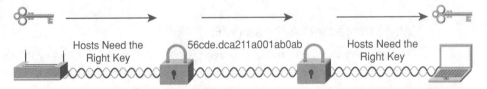

Hosts Need the Right Key

56cde.dca211a001ab0ab

Hosts Need the Right Key

Wired Equivalency Protocol (WEP)

Wired Equivalency Protocol (WEP) is a security feature that encrypts network traffic before it is transmitted. WEP uses preconfigured keys to encrypt and decrypt data.

A WEP key is entered as a string of numbers and letters and is generally 64 bits or 128 bits long. In some cases, WEP supports 256 bit keys as well. To simplify creating and entering these keys, many devices include a *passphrase* option. The passphrase is an easy way to remember the word or phrase used to automatically generate a key.

In order for WEP to function, the AP, as well as every wireless device allowed to access the network, must have the same WEP key entered. Without this key, devices will not be able to understand the wireless transmissions.

WEP makes being able to use intercepted data difficult for attackers. However, there are weaknesses within WEP, including the use of a static key on all WEP-enabled devices. If a device containing the WEP key is lost or stolen, it can be used to gain access to the network. In addition, applications are available to attackers that they can use to discover the WEP key, as illustrated in Figure 7-23. These applications are readily available on the Internet and require little knowledge to use. After the attacker has extracted the key, he has complete access to all transmitted information. For these reasons WEP is no longer recommended unless the devices are unable to support Wi-Fi Protected Access (WPA).

Figure 7-23 Cracking the WEP Key

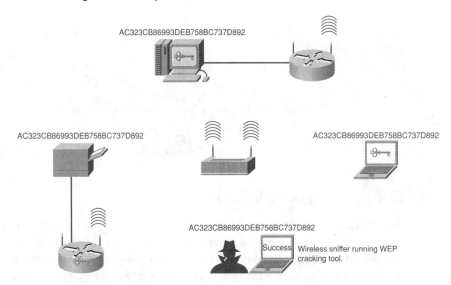

AC323CB86993DEB758BC737D892

AC323CB86993DEB758BC737D892

AC323CB86993DEB758BC737D892

AC323CB86993DEB758BC737D892

Success | Wireless sniffer running WEP cracking tool.

One way to overcome this vulnerability is to change the key frequently. Another way is to use a more advanced and secure form of encryption known as Wi-Fi Protected Access.

Wi-Fi Protected Access (WPA)

Wi-Fi Protected Access (WPA) uses encryption keys from 64 bits up to 256 bits. However, WPA, unlike WEP, generates new, dynamic keys each time a client establishes a connection with the AP. For this reason, WPA is considered more secure than WEP because it is significantly more difficult to crack.

Interactive Activity 7-6: Linksys GUI: Configuring Encryption (7.3.4.3)

In this interactive activity, you configure encryption using the Linksys GUI interface. Use file ia-7343 on the CD-ROM that accompanies this book to perform this interactive activity.

Traffic Filtering on a WAN

In addition to controlling who can gain access to the WLAN and who can make use of transmitted data, controlling the types of traffic transmitted across a WLAN is also worthwhile. This task is accomplished using traffic filtering.

Traffic filtering blocks undesirable traffic from entering or leaving the wireless network. Filtering is done by the AP as traffic passes through it. It can be used to remove traffic from, or destined to, a specific MAC or IP address. It can also block certain applications by port numbers. By removing unwanted, undesirable, and suspicious traffic from the network, more bandwidth is devoted to the movement of important traffic, which improves the performance of the WLAN. For example, traffic filtering can be used to block all Telnet traffic destined for a specific machine, such as an authentication server. Any attempts to telnet into the authentication server would be considered suspicious and blocked. Figure 7-24 shows the MAC filtering capabilities on a Linksys wireless router.

Figure 7-24   MAC Filtering on a Linksys Wireless Router

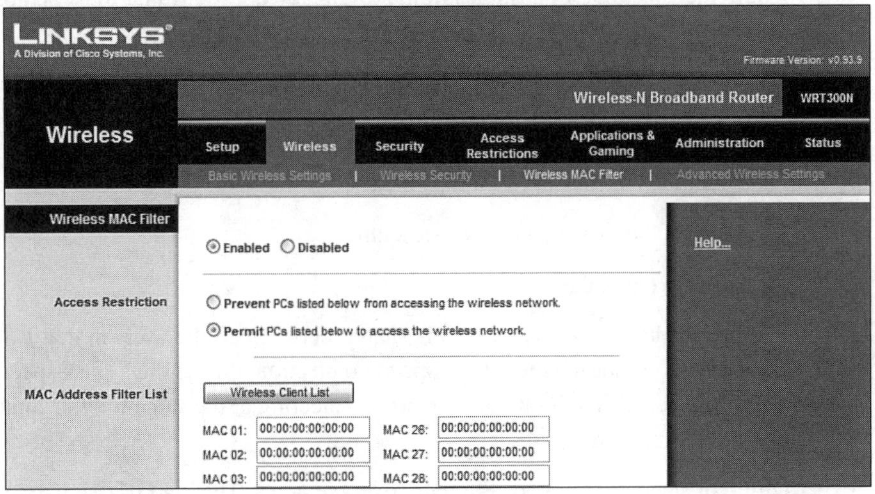

Lab 7-3: Configuring Wireless Security (7.3.5.2)

In this interactive lab you apply security measures to the WLAN to prevent unauthorized access to transmitted information. Refer to the hands-on lab in Part II of this *Learning Guide*. You may perform this lab now or wait until the end of the chapter.

Configuring an Integrated AP and Wireless Client

Before any configuration of network devices can occur, the wireless network must be carefully planned. Time spent in planning will save a great deal of time, frustration, and money later on.

Planning the WLAN

When implementing a wireless network solution, planning before performing any installation is important. This includes

- Determining the type of wireless standard to use
- Determining the most efficient layout of devices
- Devising an installation and security plan
- Documenting a strategy for backing up and updating the firmware of the wireless devices

Wireless Standards

When determining which WLAN standard to use, you must consider several factors. The most common factors include

- Bandwidth requirements
- Coverage areas
- Existing implementations
- Cost

You gather this information by determining end-user requirements. The best way to learn end-user requirements is to ask questions. Some of the key questions that must be answered before proceeding are

- What throughput is actually required by the applications running on the network?

- How many users will access the WLAN?

- What is the necessary coverage area?

- What is the existing network structure?

- What is the budget?

The bandwidth available in a BSS is shared between all the users in that BSS. Even if individual applications do not require a high-speed connection, one of the higher-speed wireless technologies might be necessary if multiple users are connecting at the same time or multiple applications are being run at the same time.

Different standards support different coverage areas. The 2.4 GHz signal, used in 802.11 b/g/n technologies, travels a greater distance than does the 5 GHz signal used in 802.11a technologies. Thus 802.11 b/g/n supports a larger BSS, which translates into less equipment and a lower cost of implementation.

The existing network affects new implementation of WLAN standards. To provide the best cost recovery, new equipment must be backward compatible with the existing network infrastructure. For example, if the existing network has been developed around the 5 GHz technologies then any new technology considered must also use these frequencies. Some of the current draft 802.11n equipment only operates at 2.4 GHz and is therefore backward compatible with 802.11g and 802.11b but not with 802.11a. Remember that the full 802.11n standard supports both 2.4 GHz and 5 GHz but not all equipment is fully compatible at the time of this writing.

Cost is also a factor. When considering cost, consider Total Cost of Ownership (TCO), which includes the purchase of the equipment as well as installation and support costs. In a medium to large business environment, TCO has a greater impact on the WLAN standard chosen than in the home or small business environment. This is because in the medium to large business, more equipment is necessary and sophisticated installation and support plans are required, increasing cost.

Installation of Wireless Devices

For home or small business environments, the installation usually consists of a limited amount of equipment, which can be easily relocated to provide optimum coverage and throughput. In the enterprise environment, equipment cannot be easily relocated and coverage must be complete. Determining the optimum number and placement of APs to provide this coverage at the least amount of cost is important.

In order to accomplish this task, a *site survey* is usually conducted. The organization or department responsible for the site survey must be knowledgeable in WLAN design and equipped with sophisticated equipment for measuring signal strengths and interference. Depending on the size of the WLAN implementation, this process can be very expensive. For small installations a simple site survey is usually conducted using wireless STAs and the utility programs packaged with most wireless NICs. Site survey modeling software is available and has improved to the point that only the most challenging enterprise environments now require detailed on-site surveys. In all cases, considering known sources of interference, such as high-voltage wires, motors, and other wireless devices, when determining the placement of WLAN equipment is necessary.

Installing and Securing the AP

After the best technology and placement of the AP are determined, install the WLAN device and configure the AP with security measures. Security measures should be planned and configured before connecting the AP to the network or ISP.

Some of the more basic security measures include

- Change default values for the SSID, usernames, and passwords.

- Disable remote management to prevent access from external networks.

- Allow connections to the device only through secure protocols such as HTTPS.

- Disable broadcast SSID.

- Configure MAC address filtering.

Some more advanced security measures include

- Configure encryption using WEP or WPA.

- Configure authentication.

- Configure traffic filtering.

Keep in mind that no single security measure will keep your wireless network completely secure. Combining multiple techniques strengthens the integrity of your security plan but cannot guarantee that the integrity of the network will never be compromised. Security merely decreases the likelihood that this might happen.

When configuring the clients, ensuring that the SSID matches the SSID configured on the AP is essential. Additionally, encryption keys and authentication keys must also match. Remember that the SSID and keys are case sensitive. If the SSIDs do not match, the client will not associate with the AP. If the authentication keys do not match, the client will also be unable to associate. Mismatched encryption keys do not normally prevent association but do render the data transferred unreadable. Many devices use the same key for both authentication and encryption purposes. In this case mismatched keys will prevent association.

Challenge Lab 7-4: Planning the Home or Small Business WLAN

In this lab you plan a WLAN installation for a home or small business. Refer to the hands-on lab in Part II of this *Learning Guide*. You may perform this lab now or wait until the end of the chapter.

Backing Up and Restoring Configuration Files

After the wireless network is properly configured and traffic is moving, a full configuration backup should be performed on wireless access points and bridges. This step is especially important if a great deal of customization has been done to the configuration.

With most integrated routers designed for the home and small business markets, performing this task is simply a matter of selecting the **Backup Configurations** option from the appropriate menu and specifying the location where the file should be saved. The integrated router provides a default name for the configuration file, which can be changed if desired. The restore process is just as simple. Select the **Restore Configurations** option. Then simply browse to the location where the configuration file was previously saved and select the file. After selecting the file, click **Start to Restore** to load the configuration file.

Sometimes returning the setting to the factory default conditions might be necessary. To accomplish this task select either the **Restore Factory Defaults** option from the appropriate menu or press and hold the **Reset** button for 30 seconds. The latter technique is especially useful if you are unable to connect to the AP of the integrated router through the network but have physical access to the device.

Interactive Activity 7-7: Linksys GUI: Backing Up and Restoring a Configuration File (7.4.3.2)

In this interactive activity you use the Linksys GUI interface to back up and restore configuration files on the wireless router. Use file ia-7432 on the CD-ROM that accompanies this book to perform this interactive activity.

Updating the Firmware

The operating system on most integrated routers is stored in firmware. As new features are developed or problems with the existing firmware are discovered, updating the firmware on the device might become necessary.

The process for updating firmware on an integrated router, such as the Linksys wireless router, is simple. However, not interrupting the process once it is started is important. If the update process is interrupted before completion, the device might be rendered inoperable.

Before attempting an update of the firmware, determine the version of the firmware currently installed on the device. This information is usually displayed on the configuration screen or the connection status screen. Next, search the manufacturer's website and related newsgroups on the Internet to discover the firmware feature set, issues that might warrant an upgrade, and whether updates are available.

Download the updated version of the firmware and store it on the hard drive of a device that can be directly connected to the integrated router. Using a machine that is directly connected to the integrated router with a cable to prevent any interruption in the update process caused by a wireless connection is best.

Select the **Firmware Upgrade** feature in the GUI as shown in Figure 7-25. Browse to the appropriate file on the directly connected device and start the upgrade.

Figure 7-25   Upgrading the Linksys Wireless Router Firmware

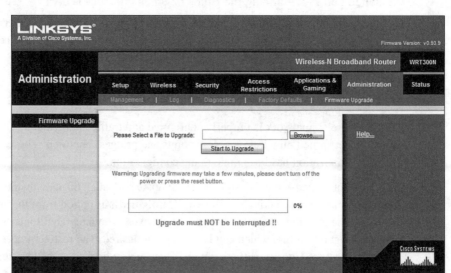

Interactive Activity 7-8: Linksys GUI: Updating the Firmware (7.4.4.2)

In this interactive activity you use the Linksys GUI interface to update the firmware on the wireless router. Use file ia-7442 on the CD-ROM that accompanies this book to perform this interactive activity.

Summary

This chapter described the various technologies that allow the transmission of information between hosts without the use of cables. It described the benefits and limitations of these technologies and some of the devices that use them.

Wireless technologies use electromagnetic waves such as infrared (IR) and radio frequency (RF) radiation to carry information between devices. IR is generally used for short range one-to-one communication whereas RF is used for longer range or one-to-many communications.

Wireless networks are grouped into three major categories: wireless personal-area networks (WPAN), wireless local-area networks (WLAN), and wireless wide-area networks (WWAN).

The main organization responsible for the creation of wireless technical standards is the IEEE. Standards that govern the WLAN environment include 802.11a, 802.11b, 802.11g, and 802.11n and are known as WiFi standards.

WLAN devices include wireless clients, access points, wireless bridges, and antennas. Wireless clients are also known as STAs and are the end, network addressable, device. APs allow wireless clients in a limited area to connect to the wired network by translating between the IEEE 802.11 wireless frame format and the standard 802.3 Ethernet frame format. Wireless bridges provide a mechanism for the connection of wired networks through wireless technology. Wireless devices use antennas to transmit and receive information. The two types of antennas are directional and omnidirectional.

WLANs are divided into two types. A small peer-to-peer network is known as an ad-hoc network and does not include an AP. A wireless network that has an AP is termed an infrastructure network. The area controlled by the AP is referred to as a cell or Basic Service Set (BSS). Many BSSs can be connected together through a Distribution System (DS) to create an Extended Service Set (ESS). Each ESS is identified by a Service Set Identifier (SSID). All wireless devices in a WLAN must be configured with the same SSID and operate using the same standards in order to communicate.

To separate conversations in a cell, the RF spectrum is divided into different channels. APs and clients uses an access method called Carrier Sense Multiple Access with Collision Avoidance (CSMA/CA) that creates a reservation on the channel for use by a specific conversation.

Because wireless technology transmits information through the open space, wireless networks are more susceptible to attacks than wired networks. An attacker can access a wireless network from any location the wireless signal reaches. Once connected, attackers can use your Internet services for free or damage files and steal private information from your network.

By combining various basic and advanced security techniques, reducing the risk of attack is possible. Some of the basic security measures include

- Change default values for the SSID, usernames, and passwords.
- Disable broadcast SSID.
- Configure MAC address filtering.

More advanced security measures include

- Configure encryption using WEP or WPA.
- Configure authentication.
- Configure traffic filtering.

Before installing a wireless network, an installation plan should be created that includes the standards to be used, the location of devices, a security plan, and a strategy for backing up configurations. In order to carry out this plan, the following steps are needed:

- Gather user requirements to determine the appropriate standard to use, bandwidth requirements, coverage areas, existing implementations, and cost.

- Perform a site survey to determine the optimum number and location of APs.

- Combine multiple security techniques to strengthen the integrity of the wireless network.

- Perform a full configuration backup of wireless devices to provide a stored copy in case of device failure.

- Upgrade the firmware, if necessary, to take advantage of enhancements to the operating system.

Activities and Labs

This summary outlines the activities and labs you can perform to help reinforce important concepts described in this chapter. You can find the activity files on the CD-ROM accompanying this book. The complete hands-on labs appear in Part II.

Interactive Activities on the CD:

Interactive Activity 7-1: Selecting the Wireless Technology (7.1.1.4)

Interactive Activity 7-2: Selecting the Type of Wireless Network (7.1.3.3)

Interactive Activity 7-3: Wireless Components (7.2.2.3)

Interactive Activity 7-4: Linksys GUI: Setting the SSID (7.2.3.4)

Interactive Activity 7-5: Linksys GUI: Setting the Channel (7.2.4.3)

Interactive Activity 7-6: Linksys GUI: Configuring Encryption (7.3.4.3)

Interactive Activity 7-7: Linksys GUI: Backing Up and Restoring a Configuration File (7.4.3.2)

Interactive Activity 7-8: Linksys GUI: Updating the Firmware (7.4.4.2)

Labs in Part II of This Book:

Lab 7-1: Configuring a Wireless Access Point (7.2.5.3)

Lab 7-2: Configuring a Wireless Client (7.2.6.4)

Lab 7-3: Configuring Wireless Security (7.3.5.2)

Challenge Lab 7-4: Planning the Home or Small Business WLAN

Check Your Understanding

Complete all the review questions listed here to test your understanding of the topics and concepts in this chapter. The "Check Your Understanding and Challenge Questions Answer Key" appendix lists the answers.

1. Which devices commonly make use of wireless technology? (Choose all that apply.)

   A. Television remote control

   B. IrDA-equipped PDA

   C. Bluetooth-enabled headphone

   D. Cellular phone

   E. Satellite radio receiver

2. Which is true of wireless technology?

   A. Wireless provides sharply defined network boundaries.

   B. Wireless is inherently a very secure technology.

   C. Wireless technology is easily scaled to provide increased coverage.

   D. Wireless technology is immune to outside sources of interference.

3. Which WLAN standard amendments use the 2.4 GHz frequency range? (Choose all that apply.)

   A. 801.11a

   B. 802.11b

   C. 802.11g

   D. 802.11n

4. Which IEEE standard applies to WLANs?

   A. 802.3

   B. 802.5

   C. 802.11

   D. 802.15

5. What is the main purpose of an SSID?

   A. Data encryption

   B. User authentication

   C. WLAN identification

   D. Secure key exchange

6. What name is given to a small wireless network that does not contain an AP?

   A. Infrastructure

   B. Ad-hoc

   C. BSS

   D. ESS

   E. IBSS

7. What is the name given to the smallest coverage area in an infrastructure WLAN? (Choose two.)

   A. Cell

   B. IBSS

   C. BSS

   D. ESS

   E. DS

8. Which occurs first in a WLAN, association or authentication?

9. What is the default authentication type on most WLAN devices?

10. Which security precautions should be implemented on a wireless AP? (Choose all that apply.)

   A. Change all default settings.

   B. Disable SSID broadcast.

   C. Encrypt data using WPA.

   D. Change the WEP key regularly.

   E. Configure security settings before connecting to a live network.

Challenge Questions and Activities

These questions require a deeper application of the concepts covered in this chapter. You can find the answers in the appendix.

1. You have just configured a WLAN for a small accounting company. The company intends to use its network to allow temporary employees to work on clients' tax returns during the peak season. The manager has asked you whether WEP will protect the clients' confidential information from being intercepted by unauthorized individuals. What would be your response?

2. A colleague has asked you why they lose wireless connectivity on their home network every time they answer their cordless phone. How would you answer this? What solution would you suggest?

CHAPTER 8

Basic Security

Objectives

Upon completion of this chapter, you will be able to answer the following questions:

- What are the main networking threats and their characteristics?

- What are the different methods of attack?

- What security procedures and applications exist to help prevent attacks?

- What is a firewall and how is it used to protect against an attack?

- What is a DMZ and how is basic DMZ architecture structured?

- How do you configure a DMZ and port forwarding with an integrated router device?

- What is vulnerability analysis software and how can it help prevent attacks?

Key Terms

This chapter uses the following key terms. You can find the definitions in the Glossary.

All over the world, people use networks to exchange sensitive information with each other. People purchase products and do their banking over the Internet. We rely on networks to be secure and to protect our identities and private information. Network security is a shared responsibility that each person must accept when he or she connects to the network. In this chapter you will learn about the threats that exist on the network and how you can do your part to protect your computers and information.

Networking Threats

Every day, home and organizational networks come under attack from inside and outside intruders. The attackers have various motivations and the attacks can take many different forms. This section describes types of attackers, the damage they can cause, and intrusion techniques.

Risks of Networking Intrusion

Whether wired or wireless, computer networks are quickly becoming essential to everyday activities. Individuals and organizations alike depend on their computers and networks for functions such as e-mail, accounting, organization, and file management. Intrusion by an unauthorized person can result in costly network outages and loss of work. Attacks on a network can be devastating and can result in a loss of time and money due to damage or theft of important information or assets.

Intruders can gain access to a network through software vulnerabilities, hardware attacks, or even through less high-tech methods, such as guessing someone's username and password. Intruders who gain access by modifying software or exploiting software vulnerabilities are often called *hackers*.

After the hacker gains access to the network, four types of threats, shown in Figure 8-1, might arise:

- **Information theft**: Breaking into a computer to obtain confidential information. Information can be used or sold for various purposes. An example is stealing an organization's proprietary information, such as research and development information. A hacker who has gained access to the network might also obtain information by intercepting data as it is transmitted.

- **Identity theft**: A form of information theft where personal information is stolen for the purpose of taking over someone's identity. Using this information, an individual can obtain legal documents, apply for credit, and make unauthorized online purchases. Identity theft is a growing problem costing billions of dollars per year.

- **Data loss/manipulation**: Breaking into a computer to destroy or alter data records. An example of data loss is a virus that reformats a computer's hard drive. An example of data manipulation is breaking into a records system to change information, such as the price of an item.

- **Disruption of service**: Preventing legitimate users from accessing services to which they should be entitled. Examples include Denial of Service (DoS) attacks to servers, network devices, or network communications links.

Interactive Activity 8-1: Identifying Security Threats (8.1.1.2)

In this interactive activity you identify the type of security threat described. Use file ia-8112 on the CD-ROM that accompanies this book to perform this interactive activity.

Figure 8-1   Types of Networking Threats

Information Theft

Data Loss and Manipulation

Identity Theft

Disruption of Service

Sources of Network Intrusion

Security threats from network intruders can come from both internal and external sources, as shown in Figure 8-2.

Figure 8-2   External and Internal Attacks

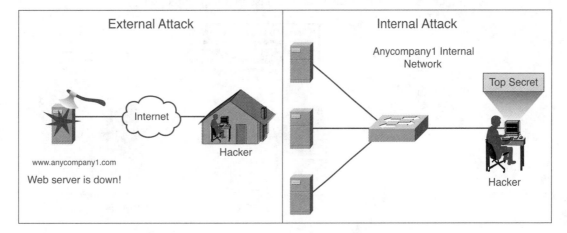

External Threats

External threats arise from individuals working outside of an organization. They do not have authorized access to the computer systems or network. External attackers work their way into a network mainly from the Internet, wireless links, or dial-up access servers.

Internal Threats

Internal threats occur when someone has either authorized access to the network through a user account or has physical access to the network equipment. The internal attacker knows the internal politics and people. This person often knows what information is both valuable and vulnerable and how to get to it.

However, not all internal attacks are intentional. In some cases, an internal threat can come from a trustworthy employee who picks up a virus or security threat while outside the company and unknowingly brings it into the internal network. Legitimate network users and administrators can inadvertently disrupt network operations and corrupt data.

Most companies spend considerable resources defending against external attacks; however, most threats are from internal sources. According to the FBI, internal access and misuse of computer systems account for approximately 70 percent of reported incidents of security breaches.

Social Engineering and Phishing

One of the easiest ways for an intruder to gain access, either internal or external, is by exploiting human behavior. One of the more common methods of exploiting human weaknesses is called social engineering.

Social engineering refers to the ability of something or someone to influence the behavior of a group of people. In the context of computer and network security, social engineering refers to a collection of techniques used to deceive internal users into performing specific actions or revealing confidential information. Figure 8-3 shows an internal hacker posing as a help desk person to obtain user ID and password information.

Figure 8-3   Social Engineer and Unsuspecting Employee

With these techniques, the attacker takes advantage of unsuspecting legitimate users to gain access to internal resources and private information, such as bank account numbers or passwords.

Social engineering attacks exploit the fact that users are generally considered one of the weakest links in security. Social engineers can be internal or external to the organization, but most often do not come face-to-face with their victims.

Three of the most commonly used techniques in social engineering are pretexting, phishing, and vishing.

Pretexting

Pretexting is a form of social engineering where an invented scenario (the pretext) is used on a victim in order to get the victim to release information or perform an action. The target is typically contacted over the telephone. For pretexting to be effective, the attacker must be able to establish legitimacy with the intended target, or victim. This often requires some prior knowledge or research on the part of the attacker. For example, if an attacker knows the target's Social Security number, he or she might use that information to gain the trust of the target. The target is then more likely to release further information.

Phishing

Phishing is a form of social engineering where the phisher pretends to represent a legitimate outside organization. A phisher typically contacts the target individual (the phishee) via e-mail. The phisher might ask for verification of information, such as password or username, in order to prevent some terrible consequence from occurring.

Figure 8-4 shows an example of phishing, where an e-mail is received that appears to be from the customer's bank. When the customer clicks on the link, it redirects the person to the phisher's website where bank account information can be entered. Legitimate banking institutions do not send these types of e-mails to customers. If you receive an e-mail such as this, read it carefully. They are frequently translated from one language to another and might have spelling or grammar errors. If you click the link, do not enter any information but take note of the URL you are redirected to. It will usually be from another country or domain.

Figure 8-4   Phisher and Phishee

Vishing

Vishing, or phone phishing, is a new form of social engineering that uses Voice over IP (VoIP). With vishing, an unsuspecting user is sent a voice mail instructing him or her to call a number that appears to be a legitimate telephone-banking service. The call might be intercepted by a thief or the number dialed might actually be the thief's number. Bank account numbers or passwords entered over the phone for verification are then stolen.

Methods of Attack

Hackers use various tools to do damage to their target networks. Some of these deliver relatively benign local threats and others can bring down a large network. Attackers might use a combination of techniques to achieve their goals. This section describes the main types of invading software and their delivery methods.

Viruses, Worms, and Trojan Horses

Social engineering is a common security threat that preys upon human weakness to obtain desired results.

In addition to social engineering, other types of attacks exist that exploit vulnerabilities in computer software. Examples of these attack techniques include viruses, worms, and Trojan horses. All of these are types of malicious software introduced onto a host. They can damage a system and destroy data, as well as deny access to networks, systems, or services. They can also forward data and personal details from unsuspecting PC users to criminals. In many cases, they can replicate themselves and spread to other hosts connected to the network.

Sometimes these techniques are used in combination with social engineering to trick an unsuspecting user into executing the attack. Figure 8-5 illustrates several software attack methods.

Figure 8-5   Software Attack Methods

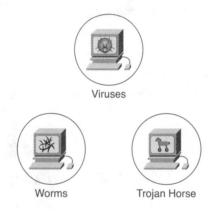

Viruses

Worms   Trojan Horse

Viruses

A *virus* is a program that runs and spreads by modifying other programs or files. A virus cannot start by itself; it needs to be activated. Once activated, a virus might do nothing more than replicate itself and spread. Although simple, even this type of virus is dangerous because it can quickly consume all available memory and bring a system to a halt. A more serious virus might be programmed to delete or corrupt specific files before spreading. Viruses can be transmitted via e-mail attachments, downloaded files, instant messages, or any type of removable media such as diskettes, CDs, and USB devices.

Worms

A *worm* is similar to a virus but, unlike a virus, does not need to attach itself to an existing program. A worm uses the network to send copies of itself to any connected hosts. Worms can run independently and spread quickly. They do not necessarily require activation or human intervention. Self-spreading network worms can have a much greater impact than a single virus. They infect local networks and large parts of the Internet quickly.

Trojan Horses

A *Trojan horse* is a non–self-replicating program that is written to appear like a legitimate program, when in fact it is an attack tool. A Trojan horse relies upon its legitimate appearance to deceive the victim into initiating the program. It might be relatively harmless or can contain code that can damage the contents of the computer's hard drive. Trojans can also create a back door into a system, allowing hackers to gain access. Figure 8-6 shows a relatively innocent-looking screen that invites the user to download and run a potentially fun computer game. If the user does this he might be downloading a Trojan or other virus that can do damage to his computer.

Figure 8-6   Space Wars 3000 Game Trojan Horse

Space Wars 3000
The Ultimate
Intergalactic Game

Click here to play

Click the Play button to download Space Wars.

Interactive Activity 8-2: Determine the Effects of a Virus, Worm, or Trojan Horse (8.2.1.3)

In this interactive activity, you determine whether the user has been infected by a virus, worm, or Trojan horse. Use file ia-8213 on the CD-ROM that accompanies this book to perform this interactive activity.

Denial of Service and Brute Force Attacks

Sometimes the goal of an attacker is to shut down the normal operations of a network. This type of attack is usually carried out with the intent to disrupt the functions of an organization.

Denial of Service Attack

Denial of Service (DoS) attacks are aggressive attacks on an individual computer or groups of computers with the intent to deny services to intended users. DoS attacks can target end-user systems, servers, routers, and network links.

In general, DoS attacks seek to

- Flood a system or network with traffic to prevent legitimate network traffic from flowing

- Disrupt connections between a client and server to prevent access to a service

Several types of DoS attacks exist. Security administrators need to be aware of the types of DoS attacks that can occur and ensure that their networks are protected. Two common DoS attacks are

- *SYN (synchronous) flood*: A flood of packets is sent to a server requesting a client connection. The packets contain invalid source IP addresses. The server becomes occupied trying to respond to these fake requests from the SYN flood and therefore cannot respond to legitimate ones.

■ *Ping of death*: **Ping** is a network connectivity testing tool used to determine whether a host is reachable. By default, a normal **ping** is only 32 bytes but can be set to be much larger. With the ping of death, a packet that is greater in size than the maximum allowed by IP (65,535 bytes) is sent to a device, which can cause the receiving system to crash. Figure 8-7 illustrates the ping of death DoS attack.

Figure 8-7   Ping of Death DoS Attack

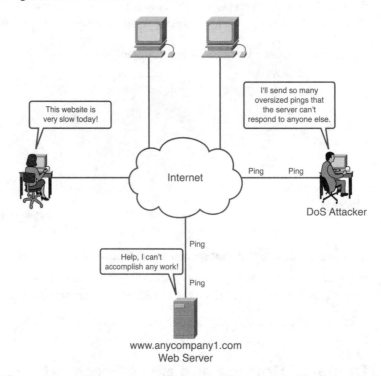

Distributed Denial of Service Attack

A *Distributed Denial of Service (DDoS)* attack is a more sophisticated and potentially damaging form of the DoS attack. It is designed to saturate and overwhelm network links with useless data. DDoS attacks operate on a much larger scale than DoS attacks. Typically hundreds or thousands of attack points attempt to overwhelm a target simultaneously. The attack points might be unsuspecting computers that have been previously infected by the DDoS code. The systems that are infected with the DDoS code attack the target site when invoked. Figure 8-8 illustrates a DDoS attack. An interesting case of a DDoS attack is a worm designed to exploit a vulnerability in an office software product. A patch that could prevent the attack was available on the publisher's website but so many people attempted to download the fix that they overloaded the web server, causing an unintentional DDoS attack on it.

Brute-Force Attack

Not all attacks that cause network outages are specifically DoS attacks. A brute-force attack is another type of attack that can result in denial of services.

With *brute-force* attacks, a fast computer is used to try to guess passwords or to decipher an encryption code. The attacker tries a large number of possibilities in rapid succession to gain access or crack the code. Brute-force attacks can cause a denial of service due to excessive traffic to a specific resource or by locking out user accounts.

Figure 8-8   DDoS Attack

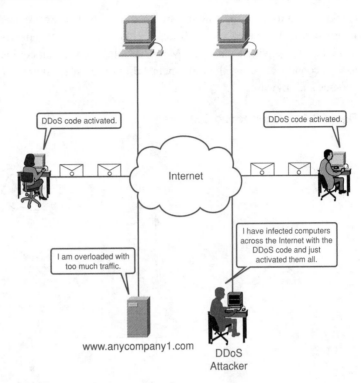

Interactive Activity 8-3: Establish a Server Connection During a DoS Attack (8.2.2.3)

In this interactive activity you attempt to establish a TCP connection to the web server during a Denial of Service (DoS) attack. Use file ia-8223 on the CD-ROM that accompanies this book to perform this interactive activity.

Spyware, Tracking Cookies, Adware, and Pop-Ups

Not all attacks do damage or prevent legitimate users from having access to resources. Many threats are designed to collect user information that can be used for advertising, marketing, and research. They can also be used for illegal purposes. These include spyware, tracking cookies, adware, and pop-ups. Although these types of software might not damage a computer, they invade privacy and can be annoying.

Spyware

Spyware is any program that gathers personal information from your computer without your permission or knowledge. This information is sent to advertisers or others on the Internet and can include passwords and account numbers.

Spyware is usually installed unknowingly when a user downloads a file, installs another program, or clicks a pop-up. It can slow down a computer and make changes to internal settings, creating more vulnerabilities for other threats. In addition, spyware can be very difficult to remove.

Tracking Cookies

Cookies are a form of spyware but are not always bad. They are used to record information about Internet users when they visit websites. Cookies can be useful or desirable by allowing personalization and other time-saving techniques. Many websites require that cookies be enabled in order to allow the user to connect or access the full functionality of the site. Figure 8-9 illustrates the difference between cookies and spyware.

Figure 8-9   Cookies and Spyware

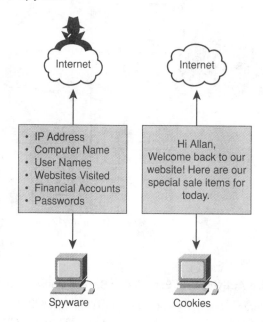

Adware

Adware is a form of spyware used to collect information about a user based on websites the user visits. That information is then used for targeted advertising. Adware is commonly installed by a user in exchange for a "free" product. When a user opens a browser window, adware can start new browser instances that attempt to advertise products or services based on a user's surfing practices. The unwanted browser windows can open repeatedly, and can make surfing the Internet very difficult, especially with slow Internet connections. These browser windows are not pop-ups and take much more time to open.

Adware can be very difficult to uninstall. Some adware companies are actually malware (bad software) disguised as anti-spyware (good software) and might ask money for ways to remove them from your computer. If you have a computer that is infected with adware, you can sometimes remove it with an anti-spyware program. You can also search the Internet for the name of the adware and obtain information on how to remove it. A frustrated user with adware on his computer is shown in Figure 8-10.

Figure 8-10   Multiple Adware Windows

Pop-Ups and Pop-Unders

Pop-ups and pop-unders are additional advertising windows that display when visiting a website. Unlike adware, pop-ups and pop-unders are not intended to collect information about the user and are typically associated only with the website being visited.

- Pop-ups open in front of the current browser window.

- Pop-unders open behind the current browser window.

They can be annoying and usually advertise products or services that are undesirable.

Spam

Another annoying by-product of our increasing reliance on electronic communications is unwanted bulk e-mail. Sometimes merchants do not want to bother with targeted marketing. They want to send their e-mail advertising to as many end users as possible, hoping that someone is interested in their product or service. This widely distributed approach to marketing on the Internet is called spam.

Spam is a serious network threat that can overload ISPs, e-mail servers, and individual end-user systems. A person or organization responsible for sending spam is called a spammer. Spammers often make use of unsecured e-mail servers to forward e-mail. Spammers can use hacking techniques, such as viruses, worms, and Trojan horses, to take control of home computers. These computers are then used to send spam without the owner's knowledge. Spam can be sent via e-mail or more recently via instant messaging software.

It is estimated that every user on the Internet receives more than 3000 spam e-mails in a year. Spam consumes large amounts of Internet bandwidth and is a serious enough problem that many countries now have laws governing spam use. Figure 8-11 shows how an open relay mail server can be used to forward spam.

Figure 8-11   Spam Sent Through an Open Relay Mail Server

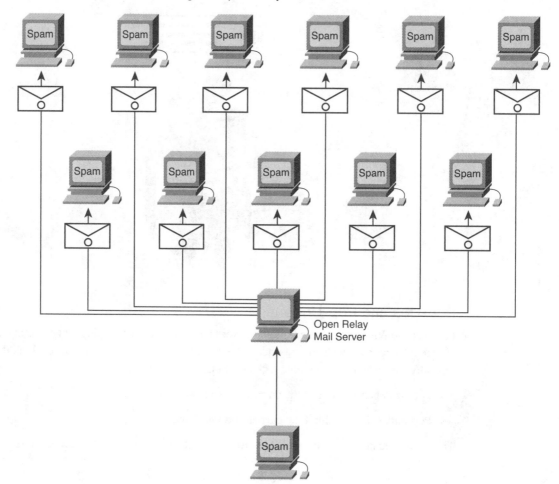

Security Policy

To help protect the network and resources, most organizations develop a security policy that provides guidelines and measures that can be taken to prevent or reduce the effects of attacks. This section describes the content of a typical security policy. It also identifies some of the more common measures that can be taken to reduce security risks, including the installation of Anti-X software and the use of firewalls. Anti-X refers to the many software packages that combat viruses, spyware and spam, and so on.

Common Security Measures

Security risks cannot be eliminated or prevented completely. However, effective risk management and assessment can significantly minimize the existing security risks. To minimize the amount of risk, it is important to understand that no single product can make an organization secure. True network security comes from a combination of products and services, combined with a thorough security policy and a commitment to adhere to that policy.

A *security policy* is a formal statement of the rules that users must adhere to when accessing technology and information assets. It can be as simple as an acceptable use policy, or it can be several hundred pages in length and detail every aspect of user connectivity and network usage procedures.

A security policy should be the central point for how a network is secured, monitored, tested, and improved upon. A key goal of the security policy is the reduction of the human factor in network security. Social engineering works only on humans and most users do not intentionally mean to harm the network. The security policy addresses the poor security habits of users because many do not realize the consequences of their actions.

Although most home users do not have a formal written security policy, as a network grows in size and scope, the importance of a defined security policy for all users increases drastically. Some things to include in a security policy are

- **Identification and authentication policies**: Specify authorized persons who can have access to network resources and how they are verified. This includes physical access to wiring closets and critical network resources such as servers, switches, routers, and access points.

- **Password policies**: Ensure that passwords meet minimum requirements and are changed regularly.

- **Acceptable use policies**: Identify network applications and usages that are and are not acceptable.

- **Remote access policies**: Identify how remote users can access a network and what is and is not accessible via remote connectivity.

- **Incident handling procedures**: Describe how security incidents will be handled.

When a security policy is developed, all users of the network need to support and follow the security policy in order for it to be effective.

Security procedures implement security policies. Procedures define configuration, login, audit, and maintenance processes for hosts and network devices. They include the use of both preventative measures to reduce risk, as well as active measures for how to handle known security threats. Security procedures can range from simple, inexpensive tasks, such as maintaining up-to-date software releases, to complex implementations of firewalls and intrusion-detection systems.

Some of the security tools and applications used in securing a network include

- **Software patches and updates**: Software applied to an OS or application to correct a known security vulnerability or add functionality

- **Virus protection**: Software installed on an end-user workstation or server to detect and remove viruses, worms, and Trojan horses from files and e-mail

- **Spyware protection**: Software installed on an end-user workstation to detect and remove spyware and adware

- **Spam blockers**: Software installed on an end-user workstation or server to identify and remove unwanted e-mails

- **Pop-up blockers**: Software installed on an end-user workstation to prevent pop-up and pop-under advertisement windows from displaying

- **Firewalls**: A security tool that controls traffic to and from a network

Figure 8-12 illustrates several security tools and applications that are available.

Figure 8-12   Security Tools and Applications

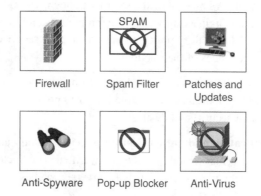

Firewall   Spam Filter   Patches and
                                    Updates

Anti-Spyware   Pop-up Blocker   Anti-Virus

Updates and Patches

One of the most common methods that a hacker uses to gain access to hosts and/or networks is through software vulnerabilities. Keeping software applications up-to-date with the latest security patches and doing updates to help deter threats is important. A patch is a small piece of code that fixes a specific software problem or "bug." An update, on the other hand, might include additional functionality to the software package as well as patches for specific issues.

OS (operating system, such as Linux, Windows, and so on) and application vendors continuously provide updates and security patches that can correct known vulnerabilities in the software. In addition, vendors often release collections of patches and updates called service packs. Fortunately, many operating systems offer an automatic update feature that allows OS and application updates to be automatically downloaded and installed on a host. The Windows XP Automatic Updates screen is shown in Figure 8-13.

Figure 8-13   Windows Automatic Updates

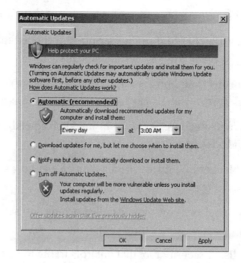

Anti-virus Software

Even when the OS and applications have all the current patches and updates, they might still be susceptible to attack. Any device that is connected to a network is susceptible to viruses, worms, and Trojan horses. These threats might be used to corrupt OS code, affect computer performance, alter applications, and destroy data.

Some of the signs that a virus, worm, or Trojan horse might be present include

- Computer starts acting abnormally

- Program does not respond to mouse and keystrokes

- Programs starting or shutting down on their own

- E-mail program begins sending out large quantities of e-mail

- CPU usage is very high

- Unidentifiable, or a large number of, processes are running

- Computer slows down significantly or crashes

Figure 8-14 shows the Windows Fatal Exception Error screen that can result from corrupted code and other problems.

Figure 8-14 Windows Fatal Exception Screen

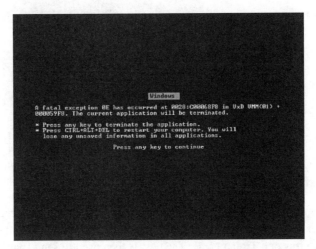

Anti-virus software can be used as both a preventative tool and as a reactive tool. It prevents infection and detects and removes viruses, worms, and Trojan horses. Anti-virus software should be installed on all computers connected to the network. Many anti-virus programs are available.

Some of the features that can be included in anti-virus programs are

- **E-mail checking**: Scans incoming and outgoing e-mails and identifies suspicious attachments.

- **Resident dynamic scanning**: Loads a memory-resident scanning program that automatically checks executable files and documents when they are accessed and warns the user.

- **Scheduled scans**: Virus scans can be scheduled to run at regular intervals and check specific drives or the entire computer.

- **Automatic Updates**: Checks for, and downloads, known virus characteristics and patterns. These programs can be scheduled to check for updates on a regular basis.

Anti-virus software relies on knowledge of the virus to remove it. Therefore, when a virus is identified, it is important to report it or any virus-like behavior to the network administrator. This step is normally done by submitting an incident report according to the company's network security policy.

Network administrators can also report new instances of threats to the local governmental agency that handles security problems. For example, one such agency in the United States, US-Cert, has a page at https://forms.us-cert.gov/report/. This agency is responsible for developing countermeasures to new virus threats as well as ensuring that those measures are available to the various anti-virus software developers. Figure 8-15 shows an anti-virus program's Security Status window and the various components that are activated by the product. These include a memory-resident shield that scans all executable files before running them, and an e-mail scanner that scans e-mails as they are received and notifies the user of any problems with an attachment. It also indicates that the internal virus database is up-to-date and when the next virus scan is scheduled to run.

Figure 8-15   Anti-virus Program Security Status Window

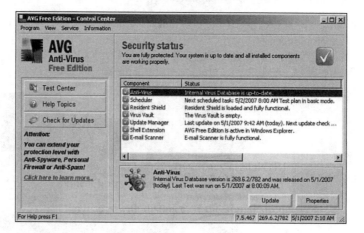

Anti-spam

Spam is not only annoying, but it can also overload e-mail servers and potentially carry viruses and other security threats. Additionally, spammers take control of a host by planting code on it in the form of a virus or a Trojan horse. The host is then used to send spam mail without the user's knowledge. A computer infected this way is known as a spam mill. Anti-spam software protects hosts by identifying spam and performing an action, such as placing it into a junk folder or deleting it. It can be loaded on a machine locally, but can also be loaded on an e-mail server, as shown in Figure 8-16. Many ISPs also offer spam filters. Anti-spam software does not recognize all spam, so it is important to open e-mail carefully. It might also accidentally identify wanted e-mail as spam and treat it as such. Some ISPs, such as EarthLink, offer a service that controls spam by monitoring e-mail received and automatically sends a response to unknown senders. They allow incoming messages only from senders that the recipient has approved beforehand. To be added to the legitimate sender list, the sender must click on a link and enter some basic information, including a code. The recipient has the option of approving the sender or not. If approved, the original message will be sent to the recipient's inbox and all future messages from that sender will be forwarded directly. This feature is a minor inconvenience for the sender but is very effective in blocking spam.

Figure 8-16   Server-Based Spam Blocker

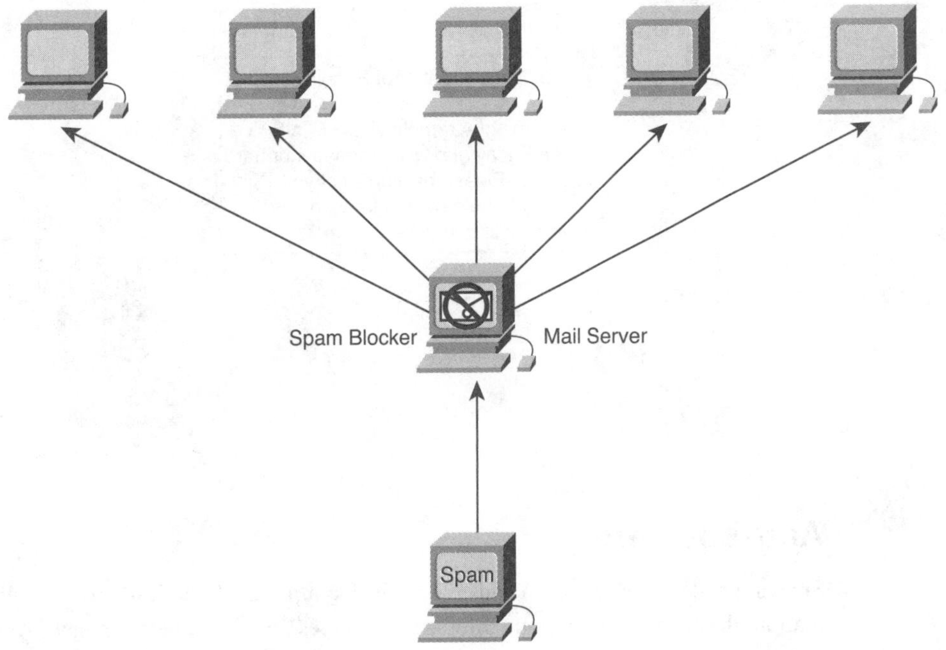

In addition to using spam blockers, other preventative actions to prevent the spread of spam include

- Apply OS and application updates when available.

- Run an anti-virus program regularly and keep it up-to-date.

- Do not forward suspect e-mails.

- Do not open e-mail attachments, especially from people you do not know.

- Set up rules in your e-mail to delete spam that bypasses the anti-spam software.

- Identify sources of spam and report these sources to a network administrator so that they can be blocked.

- Report incidents to the governmental agency that deals with spam abuse.

One of the most common types of spam forwarded is virus warnings. Although some virus warnings sent via e-mail are true, a large number of them are hoaxes and do not really exist. This type of spam can create problems because people warn others of the impending disaster and so flood the e-mail system. In addition, network administrators might overreact and waste time investigating a problem that does not exist. Finally, many of these e-mails can actually contribute to the spread of viruses, worms, and Trojan horses. Before forwarding virus warning e-mails, check to see whether the virus is a hoax at a trusted source such as http://vil.mcafee.com/hoax.asp or http://hoaxbusters.ciac.org/.

Many people forward hoax e-mails because they are afraid not to. The user receiving the hoax e-mail in Figure 8-17 might think that if he does not forward the warning, coworkers will have their computer systems compromised.

Figure 8-17   Virus E-mail Hoax

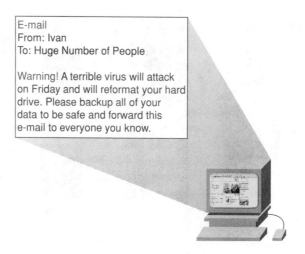

Anti-spyware

Spyware and adware can also cause virus-like symptoms. In addition to collecting unauthorized information, they can use important computer resources and affect performance. Anti-spyware software detects and deletes spyware applications, as well as prevents future installations from occurring. Many anti-spyware applications also include detection and deletion of cookies and adware. Some anti-virus packages include anti-spyware functionality.

Pop-up stopper software can be installed to prevent pop-ups and pop-unders. Many web browsers include a pop-up blocker feature by default. Note that some programs and web pages create necessary and desirable pop-ups. Most pop-up blockers offer an override feature for this purpose, such as pressing the Alt key to allow the pop-up.

Figure 8-18 shows an anti-spyware scanner after the system has been scanned and no threats were found. Although running multiple virus scanners is not recommended, you can run multiple anti-spyware scanners and one might find spyware that another does not.

Figure 8-18   Anti-spyware Scanner

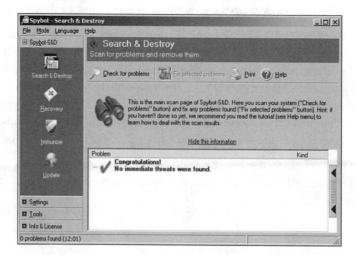

Interactive Activity 8-4: Identify the Purpose of Security Tools (8.3.5.2)

In this interactive activity, you identify the purpose of each security tool. Use file ia-8352 on the CD-ROM that accompanies this book to perform this interactive activity.

Using Firewalls

This section introduces firewalls, including common configurations in small and home networks. You also learn about vulnerability analysis and best practices to mitigate security vulnerabilities.

What Is a Firewall?

In addition to protecting individual computers and servers attached to the network, controlling traffic traveling to and from the network is important.

A *firewall* is one of the most effective security tools available for protecting internal network users from external threats. A firewall can permit some traffic while denying others, as shown in Figure 8-19.

Figure 8-19   Firewall Permits Some Traffic and Denies Other Traffic

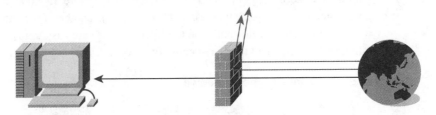

A firewall resides between two or more networks and controls the traffic between them, helping to prevent unauthorized access. Firewall products use various techniques for determining what is permitted or denied access to a network:

- **Packet filtering**: Prevents or allows access based on IP and/or MAC addresses.

- **Application/website filtering**: Prevents or allows access based on the application. Websites can be blocked by specifying a website *URL* address or keywords.

- *Stateful packet inspection (SPI)*: Incoming packets must be legitimate responses to requests from internal hosts. Incoming unsolicited packets are blocked unless permitted specifically. SPI can also include the capability to recognize and filter out specific types of attacks such as DoS.

Firewall products might support one or more of these filtering capabilities. Additionally, firewalls often perform *network address translation (NAT)*. NAT translates an internal address or group of addresses into an outside, public address that is sent across the network. This feature allows internal IP addresses to be concealed from outside users.

Firewall products come packaged in various forms, as illustrated in Figure 8-20:

- **Appliance-based firewalls**: An appliance-based firewall is a firewall that is built into a dedicated hardware device known as a security appliance. Dedicated firewall devices are specialized computers that do not have peripherals or hard drives. Appliance-based firewalls can inspect traffic very fast and are less prone to failure. They frequently come preconfigured to recognize specific types of attacks and can be tailored to the organization's needs. Dedicated devices tend to be more expensive than the other types of firewall listed here.

- **Server-based firewalls**: A server-based firewall consists of a firewall application that runs on a network operating system (NOS) such as Linux, UNIX, Windows, or Novell Netware. Firewall applications generally provide a solution that combines an SPI firewall and access control based on IP address or application. Server-based firewalls can be less secure than dedicated, appliance-based firewalls because of the security weaknesses of the general purpose OS on which they run.

- **Integrated firewalls**: An integrated firewall is implemented by adding firewall functionality to an existing device, such as a router. Most home integrated routers have built-in basic firewall capabilities that support packet, application, and website filtering. Higher-end routers that run specialized operating systems such as Cisco IOS Software also have firewall capabilities that can be configured by a network administrator. Configuring these requires knowledge of the traffic to be filtered and of the IOS commands required.

- **Personal firewalls**: Personal firewalls reside on host computers and are not designed for LAN implementations. They might be available by default from the OS or might be installed from an outside vendor. Client-side firewalls typically filter using SPI. The user might be prompted to allow certain applications to connect or might define a list of automatic exceptions. Personal firewalls are often used when a host device is connected directly to an ISP modem. It might interfere with Internet access if not properly configured. Using more than one personal firewall at a time is not recommended because they can conflict with one another. Free and low-cost personal firewalls are available for download on the Internet. They are easy to install in their default configuration and can be tuned to filter specific types of traffic if desired.

Figure 8-20   Different Types of Firewalls

Cisco Security Appliances   Server-Based Firewall

Linksys Wireless Router   Personal Firewall
with Integrated Firewall

Using a Firewall

By placing the firewall between the internal network (*intranet*) and the Internet as a border device, all traffic to and from the Internet can be monitored and controlled. This firewall creates a clear line of defense between the internal and external network. However, in situations where some external customers require access to internal resources, a *demilitarized zone (DMZ)* can be configured to accommodate them.

The term *demilitarized zone* is borrowed from the military. A DMZ is a designated area between two powers where military activity is not permitted. In computer networking, a DMZ refers to an area of the network that is accessible to both internal and external users. It is more secure than the external network but not as secure as the internal network. It is created by one or more firewalls to separate the internal, DMZ, and external networks. Web servers for public access are frequently placed in a DMZ.

Single-Firewall Configuration

A single firewall has three areas: one for the external network, the internal network, and the DMZ. All traffic is sent to the firewall from the external network. The firewall is then required to monitor the traffic and determine what traffic should be passed to the DMZ, what traffic should be passed internally, and what should be denied altogether. A single firewall configuration, as shown in Figure 8-21, is appropriate for smaller, less congested networks. However, a single firewall configuration does have a single point of failure and can be overloaded. A two-firewall configuration is more appropriate for larger, more complex networks that handle a lot more traffic. In the figure, if the traffic from the external host is destined for the web server in the DMZ, the router with the firewall will allow it. If an external host attempts to access the internal FTP server, the firewall will block it. Hosts on the internal network can access both the internal FTP server and the DMZ web server.

Figure 8-21   One-Firewall DMZ Architecture

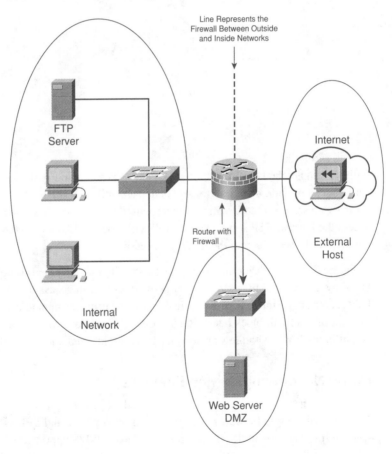

Two-Firewall Configuration

Figure 8-22 shows a typical multi-firewall DMZ setup. A two-firewall configuration has an internal and external firewall with the DMZ located between them. The external firewall is less restrictive and allows an Internet user access to the services in the DMZ. It also allows any traffic from an internal user to an outside resource, such as an external web or FTP server, to pass through. The internal firewall is more restrictive and protects the internal network from unauthorized access.

Figure 8-22   Two-Firewall DMZ Architecture

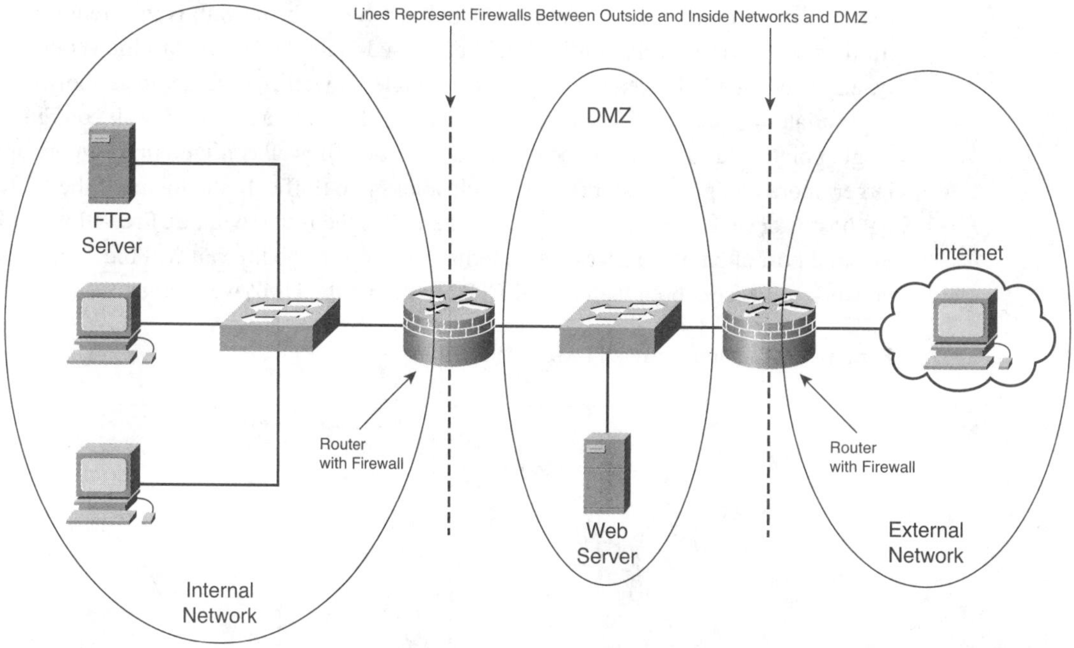

In this example, the two-firewall arrangement serves essentially the same function as the single firewall but can provide more control and better scalability. If the traffic from the external host is destined for the web server in the DMZ, the router with the firewall will allow it. If an external host attempts to access the internal FTP server, the firewall will block it. Hosts on the internal network can access both the internal FTP server and the DMZ web server.

In Figure 8-22, the PC on the external network (the Internet) is allowed access to the web server in the DMZ by the external firewall. Internal network users can access this web server in the DMZ and the FTP server on the internal network. If the external user attempts to access the internal FTP server, the internal firewall will block her. If it is necessary to give external users access to the FTP server, it can be put in the DMZ with the web server. Then both internal and external users can access it.

Home Networking Device Firewalls

Many home network devices, such as integrated routers, frequently include multi-function firewall software. This single firewall setup typically provides NAT and SPI, as well as IP, application, and website filtering capabilities. It also provides basic DMZ support capabilities.

With the integrated router, a simple DMZ can be set up that allows an internal server to be accessible by outside hosts. To accomplish this, you must specify the *static IP address* of the server in the DMZ configuration. If the server already has a dynamic address assigned, it can be reserved and made permanent. The integrated router isolates traffic destined to the IP address specified. This traffic is then forwarded only to the switch port where the server is connected. All other hosts are still protected by the firewall. The Linksys WRT300N can provide this function, which is illustrated in Figure 8-23.

Figure 8-23   Linksys Integrated Firewall

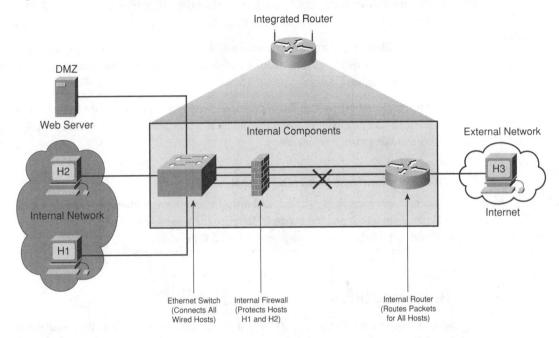

When the DMZ is enabled, in its simplest form, outside hosts can access all ports on the server, such as 80 (HTTP), 21 (FTP), and 110 (E-mail POP3). A more restrictive DMZ can be set up using the *port forwarding* capability. With port forwarding, ports that should be accessible on the server are specified. In this case, only traffic destined for those port(s) is allowed or forwarded; all other traffic is excluded.

The wireless access point within the integrated router is considered part of the internal network. It is important to realize that if the wireless access point is unsecured, anyone who connects to it is within the protected part of the internal network and is behind the firewall. Hackers can use this to gain access to the internal network and completely bypass any firewall security.

Lab 8-1: Configuring Access Policies and DMZ Settings (8.4.2.4)

In this lab you configure firewall settings and create a DMZ using the Linksys GUI. Refer to the hands-on lab in Part II of this *Learning Guide*. You may perform this lab now or wait until the end of the chapter.

Vulnerability Analysis

Many vulnerability analysis tools are available for testing host and network security. These tools are known as security scanners, and they can help identify areas where attacks might occur and offer guidance on steps that you can take. Although the capabilities of the vulnerability analysis tools can vary based on manufacturer, some of the more common features include determining the following:

- **Number of hosts available on a network**: Identifies the active hosts on the network that have services to offer. The number of hosts offering service should be limited to only those that need to advertise services. Hosts advertising services can be identified by attackers.

- **The services hosts are offering**: Indicates what services hosts are advertising. For example, a host might have the Telnet service activated and could be a target for outside attackers. Unneeded services should be disabled.

- **The operating system and versions on the hosts**: Identifies hosts with older OS versions and outdated patches. Vulnerabilities in these older unpatched OSs can be exploited by attackers.

- **Packet filters and firewalls in use**: Provides an inventory of hosts that are running filters and what they are blocking. This feature can be useful in determining whether the proper access controls are in place.

- **Applications software updates required**: Provides an analysis of applications software running on hosts and can identify those that might allow attacks. These applications can be patched to correct the security vulnerability.

Lab 8-2: Performing a Vulnerability Analysis (8.4.3.2)

In this lab you research, download, and install a security vulnerability tester and use it to determine weaknesses in a host and the network. Refer to the hands-on lab in Part II of this *Learning Guide*. You may perform this lab now or wait until the end of the chapter.

Best Practices

Several recommended practices can help mitigate security threats and the risks they pose, including the following:

- Define security policies

- Physically secure servers and network equipment

- Set login and file access permissions

- Update OS and applications

- Change permissive default network device and host settings

- Run anti-virus and anti-spyware

- Update anti-virus software files

- Activate browser tools—pop-up stoppers, anti-phishing, plug-in monitors

- Use a firewall

The first step towards securing a network is to understand how traffic moves across the network and the different threats and vulnerabilities that exist. After security measures are implemented, a truly secure network needs to be monitored constantly. Security procedures and tools need to be reviewed in order to stay ahead of evolving threats. Figure 8-24 reviews the main forms of security that can be employed to help protect against computer and network attacks.

Figure 8-24   Types of Security

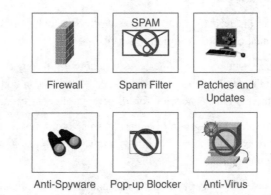

Summary

This chapter discussed various networking threats such as information theft, identity theft, data loss and manipulation, and disruption of service.

Hackers are intruders who gain access to a network through software vulnerabilities, hardware attacks, or through the carelessness of network users. Attacks can come from both internal and external sources. Internal attacks account for 70 percent of security incidents.

Social engineering is a group of techniques used to deceive internal users into performing specific actions or revealing confidential information. Three types of social engineering attacks are pretexting, phishing, and vishing.

Other threats to the security of networks and computers, in addition to social engineering attacks, include viruses, worms, and Trojan horses. Viruses are programs that when activated spread by modifying other programs or files, causing damage to files, or erasing them completely. A worm is similar to a virus except it runs independently and spreads by resending itself as an e-mail attachment or part of a network message. A Trojan horse is a program that appears legitimate, but when initiated, can damage a hard drive or create a back door into a system, allowing hackers to gain access.

Effective network security comes from a combination of products and services combined with a thorough security policy and a commitment to adhere to that policy. A security policy should include identification and authentication policies, password policies, acceptable use policies, remote access policies, and incident-handling procedures. All users of the network must support and follow the security policy in order for it to be effective.

Tools and applications used in securing a network include software patches and updates, virus protection, spam blockers, pop-up blockers, and firewalls. Keep software applications up-to-date with the latest security patches and updates to help deter threats. Anti-virus software, installed on every computer, detects and removes known viruses, worms, and Trojan horses. Anti-spam software identifies spam and places it into a junk folder or deletes it.

A firewall controls the traffic between networks and helps prevent unauthorized access. Firewall products use various techniques for determining what is permitted or denied access to a network. Firewalls perform packet filtering, which controls access based on IP or MAC addresses. They can perform application/website filtering based on the application. Firewalls also provide SPI, which ensures that incoming packets are legitimate responses to requests from internal hosts. SPI can recognize and filter out attacks such as DoS.

A DMZ is an area of the network that is accessible to both internal and external users. If the wireless access point is unsecured, anyone who connects to it is considered part of the internal network and is on the internal protected side of the firewall.

Vulnerability analysis tools (security scanners) help identify areas where attacks might occur and offer guidance on steps that can be taken.

Activities and Labs

This summary outlines the activities and labs you can perform to help reinforce important concepts described in this chapter. You can find the activity files on the CD-ROM accompanying this book. The complete hands-on labs appear in Part II.

Interactive Activities on the CD:

Interactive Activity 8-1: Identify Security Threats (8.1.1.2)

Interactive Activity 8-2: Determine the Effects of a Virus, Worm, or Trojan Horse (8.2.1.3)

Interactive Activity 8-3: Establish a Server Connection During a DoS Attack (8.2.2.3)

Interactive Activity 8-4: Identify the Purpose of Security Tools (8.3.5.2)

Labs in Part II of This Book:

Lab 8-1: Configuring Access Policies and DMZ Settings (8.4.2.4)

Lab 8-2: Performing a Vulnerability Analysis (8.4.3.2)

Check Your Understanding

Complete all the review questions listed here to test your understanding of the topics and concepts in this chapter. The "Check Your Understanding and Challenge Questions Answer Key" appendix lists the answers.

1. A hacker breaks into a server and obtains a list of users and their personal data. Using this information, the hacker applies for a credit card. What type of network threat does this represent?

    A. Data loss

    B. Identity theft

    C. Data manipulation

    D. Disruption of service

2. How does a phisher typically contact a victim?

3. A user opens an e-mail file attachment. After the user opens the attachment, her computer hard drive crashes and all information on the computer is lost. What type of attack most likely occurred?

    A. Worm

    B. Virus

    C. Trojan horse

    D. Denial of Service

4. In rapid succession, an intruder tries a large number of possibilities to guess passwords. As a result, other users on the network are locked out. What type of attack occurred?

   A. DDoS

   B. Brute force

   C. Ping of death

   D. SYN flooding

5. What type of program installs and gathers personal information, including passwords and account information, from a computer without permission or knowledge of the user?

   A. Adware

   B. Pop-ups

   C. Spyware

   D. Pop-unders

6. A network administrator is troubleshooting a computer that is operating strangely. It boots slowly, programs will not load, and the keyboard responds very slowly. What is the best action for the administrator to take?

   A. Attach a different keyboard.

   B. Attach the PC to the Internet to check its operating system website for patches.

   C. Add the PC to the network to see whether it can communicate with other PCs.

   D. Boot the PC and run anti-virus and anti-spyware applications from an external drive.

7. Identify three firewall filtering options.

   A. MAC filtering

   B. IP filtering

   C. Fragment filtering

   D. Website filtering

   E. Username filtering

8. Which of the following are firewall products commonly used to protect computers and network resources? (Choose all that apply.)

   A. Personal firewall

   B. Bandwidth-based firewall

   C. Server-based firewall

   D. Appliance-based firewall

   E. Switch-based firewall

9. What are three security features commonly found on a home or small business integrated router device?

   A. TCP

   B. DMZ

   C. POP

   D. NAT

   E. SPI

10. What two statements are true regarding a multi-firewall DMZ?

    A. The internal firewall is typically less restrictive and the external firewall is more restrictive.

    B. Servers to be accessed by external users need to be behind the internal firewall.

    C. Servers accessible by internal users can be internal, in the DMZ, or external to the network.

    D. The internal firewall is typically more restrictive and the external firewall is less restrictive.

    E. The internal firewall allows all types of external traffic to pass.

11. A user visits a website and downloads what he thinks is a free computer game. When the user begins playing the game, the computer begins acting strangely. What type of attack most likely occurred?

12. What specific type of security software can remove adware?

    A. Pop-up stoppers

    B. Anti-virus

    C. Anti-spyware

    D. Firewall

    E. Anti-spam

13. The features of anti-virus software can include all the following except:

    A. Automatic checking of virus database updates

    B. Resident shield to check executables

    C. Automatic removal of unknown viruses

    D. Scheduler to run scans on a regular basis

    E. E-mail scanner

14. What are three techniques used in social engineering?

    A. Pretexting

    B. Vishing

    C. Phishing

    D. Frying

    E. Spamming

15. What type of security attack takes advantage of software vulnerabilities and can rapidly spread across a network?

16. A hacker on the Internet sends millions of packets with invalid source IP addresses to a server. The server becomes overloaded attempting to respond to these packets. What type of attack is this?

    A. Ping of death

    B. Trojan horse

    C. SYN flooding

    D. Brute force

17. When working with a Linksys home networking device you configure it to allow external traffic to a specific server for FTP and HTTP. All other traffic is blocked. What statements are true regarding this scenario? (Choose two.)

   A. The server can only have a dynamic address assigned.

   B. The server must have a permanent static address.

   C. This is known as a simple basic DMZ.

   D. This is known as port forwarding.

18. Why is it a concern if a hacker connects to the wireless AP of a home networking device that is connected to an ISP? (Choose all that apply.)

   A. The hacker will have free access to the Internet.

   B. The hacker might be able to change configuration settings on the device.

   C. The hacker will be given the administrator password.

   D. The hacker is on the internal network behind the firewall.

Challenge Questions and Activities

This question require a deeper application of the concepts covered in this chapter. You can find the answers in the appendix.

1. You have just built a new home PC and will be connecting directly to your ISP through a DSL modem. You do not have a router with a firewall. What types of security software could you install and what other measures could you take to help secure your computer and protect it from malicious attacks or malware?

CHAPTER 9

Troubleshooting Your Network

Objectives

Upon completion of this chapter you will be able to answer the following questions:

- What are the steps involved in the troubleshooting process?

- What are some of the common troubleshooting techniques and when is it appropriate to use each?

- How can the senses be used to troubleshoot network issues?

- What utilities are available for troubleshooting connectivity issues?

- What are some of the more common issues with wired networks?

- What are some of the common issues related to WLANs?

- What are some possible sources of help when troubleshooting?

Key Terms

This chapter uses the following key terms. You can find the definitions in the Glossary.

troubleshooting   page 296

network monitoring tools   page 297

top-down troubleshooting   page 298

bottom-up troubleshooting   page 298

divide-and-conquer troubleshooting   page 300

trial-and-error troubleshooting   page 301

substitution troubleshooting   page 301

lease   page 303

echo request   page 305

echo reply   page 305

hop   page 306

DHCP server   page 314

Frequently Asked Questions (FAQ)   page 317

help desk   page 318

This chapter examines the art of troubleshooting and the procedures and processes that make troubleshooting easier and more successful. It is not meant to be an exhaustive guide to troubleshooting PC and network problems but rather an introduction with specific examples. This chapter relies on the complete understanding of all the topics and concepts presented thus far. If a concept or solution is not understood as presented, review the supporting materials covered in previous chapters of this book.

Most network troubleshooting is done based on the OSI model. This model has been introduced in this course and will be discussed in more detail in subsequent CCNA Discovery courses. Additional information on the OSI model is provided on the CD-ROM accompanying this book. Part II of this book includes the corresponding labs for this chapter.

Troubleshooting Process

Regardless of the amount of time spent designing and installing a network, problems do occur. When faced with a malfunctioning network, it is important to face the problem in a very structured manner. *Troubleshooting* is the process of identifying, locating, and correcting problems that occur. Experienced individuals often rely on instinct to troubleshoot. However, structured techniques can be used to determine the most probable cause and solution. Regardless of the approach taken, certain steps should always be followed:

How To

Step 1.   **Define the problem**: At this step the problem is defined in terms of the observed symptoms and associated causes.

Step 2.   **Gather facts**: Fact gathering is done by questioning the affected users and administrators, and using tools such as protocol analyzers to learn as much about the problem as possible.

Step 3.   **Consider the possibilities**: Systematic reasoning and diagnostic methods are used at this step to narrow down the possible causes.

Step 4.   **Create an action plan**: Based on the list of possible problems, create an action plan to troubleshoot the problem.

Step 5.   **Implement the action plan**: When you implement the action plan, be certain to document all steps. Documentation is important to provide a back-out plan in case the actions do not produce the desired result or have a negative impact on the network or device.

Step 6.   **Observe the results**: Verify that the action plan had the desired results. If not, undo any changes that were made.

Step 7.   **Repeat the problem-solving process**: If the action plan did not work repeat the problem-solving process. Troubleshooting is often an iterative process; you get closer to the actual problem with each iteration.

Step 8.   **Document facts**: The final stage of problem solving is to document the process. Documentation should actually be maintained throughout the entire process.

Documenting all steps taken during troubleshooting, even the ones that did not solve the issue, is important. Documentation becomes a valuable reference should the same or similar problem occur again. It can sometimes point to the correct solution for the problem or at least eliminate wasting time by repeating failed attempts. This documentation should include as much information as possible about the following:

- The problem encountered
- Steps taken to determine the cause of the problem
- Steps to correct the problem and ensure that it will not reoccur

This section introduces the different approaches to troubleshooting.

Gathering Information

When a problem is reported, verify it and determine the extent of its impact. Verifying the problem reported is important because many issues are not exactly as reported by the end users. After the problem is confirmed, the first step in troubleshooting is to gather as much information about the problem as possible. One of the first places to gather information is to question the individual who reported the problem as well as any other affected users. Information gathered from the end user can include

- End-user experiences

- Observed symptoms

- Error messages

- Information about recent configuration changes to devices or applications

Next, collect information about any equipment that might be affected. You can gather this information from existing documentation, which should include current configurations. A copy of all log files and a listing of any recent changes made to equipment configurations are also necessary. Other information on the equipment includes the manufacturer, make, and model of devices affected, as well as ownership and warranty information. The version of any firmware or software on the device is also important because compatibility problems might exist with particular hardware platforms.

You can gather information about the network using *network monitoring tools*. Network monitoring tools are complex applications often used on large networks to continually gather information about the state of the network and network devices. These tools might not be available for smaller networks.

A checklist is beneficial to ensure that all the required information has been collected. The types of information that you should gather before starting the troubleshooting process include the following:

- Nature of the problem
    - End-user reports
    - Problem verification reports
- Equipment
    - Manufacturer
    - Make/model
    - Firmware version
    - Operating system version
    - Ownership/warranty information
- Configuration and topology
    - Physical and logical topology
    - Configuration files
    - Log files
- Previous troubleshooting, including steps and results

Approaches to Troubleshooting

After all necessary information is gathered it is time to start the troubleshooting process. The exact technique deployed will depend on the problem and the experience level of the technician.

Inexperienced individuals should follow one of the more structured approaches but experienced individuals often prefer to rely on their knowledge and instincts and take a less structured approach. Several different structured troubleshooting techniques are available, including

- Top-down
- Bottom-up
- Divide-and-conquer

All of these structured approaches assume a layered concept of networking. An example of a layered approach is the OSI model, in which every function of communication is broken down into seven distinct layers. Using this model, a troubleshooter can verify all functionality at each layer until the problem is located and isolated. The TCP/IP model is also a layered model often used in the troubleshooting process.

The structure of these approaches makes them ideally suited for the novice troubleshooter. More experienced individuals often bypass structured approaches and rely on instinct and experience. They might use less structured techniques such as trial-and-error or substitution.

A structured approach to troubleshooting often detects problems that an unstructured method might overlook. Early detection and correction of these problems can prevent future problems with the network. For this reason, troubleshooters are encouraged to use structured approaches whenever possible.

Top-Down

The *top-down troubleshooting* approach, as shown in Figure 9-1, starts with the application layer and works down toward the physical layer. It looks at the problem from the point of view of the user and the application.

If the problem appears to be isolated to a single workstation or application, this technique is suitable. For example, if the user can access various websites on the Internet but is unable to retrieve e-mail, the top-down approach is appropriate.

Bottom-Up

The *bottom-up troubleshooting* approach, as shown in Figure 9-2, starts with the physical layer and works up toward the application layer. The physical layer is concerned with hardware and wire connections. Check to determine whether cables have been pulled out of their sockets. If the equipment has indicator lights, check to see whether they are on or off. If they are off, check the power to the devices and physical connectivity. Many network problems can be attributed to the physical layer, so this is often a good model to follow.

Figure 9-1   Top-Down Troubleshooting

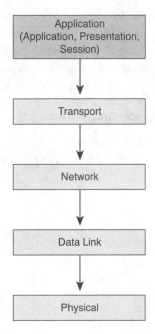

Figure 9-2   Bottom-Up Troubleshooting

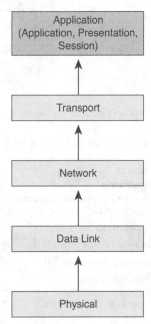

Divide-and-Conquer

The *divide-and-conquer troubleshooting* approach can begin troubleshooting at any layer, as shown in Figure 9-3, and work up or down from there. For example, the troubleshooter might begin at the network layer by verifying IP configuration information, and then decide to work upward toward the application layer or downward toward the physical layer depending on what was observed. Another example is splitting up a network and isolating a problem on one specific segment.

Figure 9-3   Divide-and-Conquer Troubleshooting

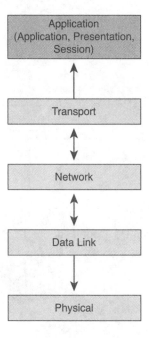

Table 9-1 provides a comparison of the three methods of structured troubleshooting.

Table 9-1   Structured Troubleshooting Methodologies

Troubleshooting Approach	How It Operates	When It Is Suitable	Advantages/ Disadvantages
Top-down	Always starts at the application layer and works its way toward the physical layer until it finds the problem.	Suitable for use when the problem is suspected to be with an application/user or upper layers.	Fast if the problem is related to the upper layers, but can waste a lot of time if problem occurs at lower layers.
Divide-and-conquer	Based on the reported problem and the troubleshooter's experience, troubleshooting can begin at any layer and work up or down.	Suitable when the problem has specific symptoms and the troubleshooter has some experience.	One of the fastest troubleshooting approaches, but requires experience to use efficiently.
Bottom-up	Always starts at the physical layer and works its way toward the application layer until the problem is located.	Suitable for complex problems.	Slow, but solid approach to troubleshooting. Can waste a lot of time if problem is related to upper layers.

Trial-and-Error

Trial-and-error troubleshooting relies on individual knowledge to determine the most probable cause of a problem. A troubleshooter makes an educated guess on the most likely solution based on past experience and knowledge of the network structure. After the solution is implemented, if it does not work, the troubleshooter uses this information to help determine the next most likely cause. This process is repeated until the problem is isolated and solved.

Although the trial-and-error approach has the potential to be extremely fast, it relies on the abilities and experiences of the troubleshooter and can result in incorrect assumptions and overlooking simple solutions. If the trial-and error approach does not determine the problem in the first few attempts, the experienced troubleshooter normally switches to a more structured approach. This technique is used in situations where downtime is extremely expensive and the goal is to re-establish connectivity and not just determine the underlying problem.

Substitution

With *substitution troubleshooting*, the problem is assumed to be caused by a specific hardware component or a configuration file. The defective part or code is replaced by a known good device or file. Although it does not necessarily locate the problem, this technique can save time and quickly restore network functionality. This method relies on the availability of substitute parts, components, and back-up configuration files, which can be very expensive to maintain.

An example of a substitution technique is when an ISP replaces a possible broken end-user device rather than send a technician out to troubleshoot and locate a specific issue. This technique is also often used for inexpensive parts such as network interface cards and patch cables.

Interactive Activity 9-1: Determining the Troubleshooting Technique (9.1.3.3)

In this interactive activity you determine the best troubleshooting technique used to solve a problem. Use file ia-9133 on the CD-ROM that accompanies this book to perform this interactive activity.

Using Utilities to Troubleshoot Connectivity Issues

A large number of tools, both software and hardware based, exist to help isolate connectivity problems in wired and wireless networks. These range from simple visual inspection to complex diagnostic hardware devices.

Detecting Physical Problems

A large proportion of networking problems are related to physical components or problems with the physical layer. Physical problems are concerned mainly with the hardware aspects of computers and networking devices and the cables that interconnect them. They do not consider the logical (software) configuration of devices.

Physical problems can occur in both wired and wireless networks. One of the best detection methods for physical problems is the use of the senses: vision, smell, touch, and hearing. Quite often, the senses can quickly pinpoint a devastating problem.

Vision

Vision can detect cabling problems such as the following:

- Cables that are not connected
- Cables connected to the wrong port
- Loose cable connections
- Damaged cables and connectors
- Wrong type of cable

Vision also allows troubleshooters to use the cues provided by LEDs about the condition and function of various networking devices. In many environments, parts of the network are covered for their protection. A simple visual inspection can often prevent unforeseen problems from occurring.

Smell

Smell can alert troubleshooters to components that are overheating. The smell of burning insulation or components is very distinct and is a sure sign that something is seriously wrong.

Touch

Troubleshooters can use touch to feel for overheated components as well as to detect mechanical problems with devices such as laptops and switches that include cooling fans. These fans usually create a small vibration in the component that you can detect using touch. The absence of this vibration or the presence of excessive amounts of vibration can indicate that the cooling fan has failed or is about to do so.

Hearing

Hearing can detect major problems such as electrical arcing and the proper operation of cooling fans and disk drives. All devices have characteristic sounds and any changes from the normal sounds usually indicate a problem of some sort. An experienced network technician gets accustomed to the sounds produced by the network and can quickly identify potential problems by deviations from the normal sound pattern.

Software Utilities for Troubleshooting Connectivity

A number of software utility programs are available that can help identify network problems. The functionality of all of these commands is available in all current operating systems, although the syntax might vary between operating systems. Most of these commands are command-line interface (CLI) utilities and include the following:

- **ipconfig**: Displays IP configuration information
- **ping**: Tests connections to other IP hosts
- **tracert**: Displays route taken to destination
- **netstat**: Displays network connections
- **nslookup**: Directly queries the name server for information on a destination domain

Troubleshooting Using **ipconfig**

The **ipconfig** command displays the current IP configuration information for a host. Issuing this command from the command prompt displays the basic configuration information, including IP address, subnet mask, and default gateway.

The command **ipconfig /all** displays additional information including the MAC address, IP addresses of the default gateway, and the DNS servers. It also indicates whether DHCP is enabled, the DHCP server address, and *lease* information. A sample output from the command is shown in Example 9-1.

Example 9-1 Output of the **ipconfig /all** Command

```
C:\>ipconfig /all

Windows IP Configuration

        Host Name . . . . . . . . . . . . : host-a
        Primary Dns Suffix  . . . . . . . : cisco.com
        Node Type . . . . . . . . . . . . : Hybrid
        IP Routing Enabled. . . . . . . . : No
        WINS Proxy Enabled. . . . . . . . : No
        DNS Suffix Search List. . . . . . : cisco.com

Ethernet adapter Local Area Connection:

        Connection-specific DNS Suffix  . : cisco.com
        Description . . . . . . . . . . . : NVIDIA nForce Networking Controller
        Physical Address. . . . . . . . . : 00-15-58-55-FF-F8
        Dhcp Enabled. . . . . . . . . . . : Yes
        Autoconfiguration Enabled . . . . : Yes
        IP Address. . . . . . . . . . . . : 192.168.1.100
        Subnet Mask . . . . . . . . . . . : 255.255.255.0
        Default Gateway . . . . . . . . . : 192.168.1.1
        DHCP Server . . . . . . . . . . . : 192.168.1.1
        DNS Servers . . . . . . . . . . . : 172.27.20.10
                                            172.27.20.11
        Lease Obtained. . . . . . . . . . : Thursday, October 11, 2007 3:07:16 PM
        Lease Expires . . . . . . . . . . : Friday, October 12, 2007 3:07:16 PM
```

This utility can help determine improper or incomplete addressing information, which can prevent network communications. Without an appropriate IP configuration, a host cannot participate in communications on a network. In addition, if the host does not know the correct location of the DNS servers it cannot translate names into IP addresses and communications using domain names is impossible.

If IP addressing information is assigned dynamically, you can use the command **ipconfig /release** to release the current DHCP bindings. You use the **ipconfig /renew** command to request fresh configuration information from the DHCP server. A host might contain faulty or outdated IP configuration information and a simple renewal of this information is all that is required to regain connectivity.

If, after releasing the IP configuration, the host is unable to obtain fresh information from the DHCP server, the problem could be that there is no network connectivity. Verify that the NIC has an illuminated link light, indicating that it has a physical connection to the network. If the link light is lit, and the host is still unable to obtain addressing information from the DHCP server, the problem might be an issue with the DHCP server or network connections to the DCHP server. Also, verify that the address has not been statically assigned to the adapter.

Packet Tracer Activity Using the ipconfig Command (9.2.3.2)

In this Packet Tracer activity you determine the IP addressing information with the **ipconfig** command. Use file d1-9232.pka on the CD-ROM that accompanies this book to perform this activity using Packet Tracer.

Troubleshooting Using **ping**

If the IP configuration appears to be correctly configured on the local host, a good next step is to test network connectivity by using the **ping** command. The **ping** command is used to test whether a destination host is reachable. The **ping** command can be followed by either an IP address or the name of a destination host, as shown in Example 9-2.

Example 9-2 Output of the **ping** Command

```
C:\>ping cisco.netacad.net

Pinging cisco.netacad.net [128.107.229.50] with 32 bytes of data:

Reply from 128.107.229.50: bytes=32 time=71ms TTL=113
Reply from 128.107.229.50: bytes=32 time=71ms TTL=113
Reply from 128.107.229.50: bytes=32 time=72ms TTL=113
Reply from 128.107.229.50: bytes=32 time=72ms TTL=113

Ping statistics for 128.107.229.50:
    Packets: Sent = 4, Received = 4, Lost = 0 (0% loss),
Approximate round trip times in milli-seconds:
    Minimum = 71ms, Maximum = 72ms, Average = 71ms

C:\>ping 128.107.229.50

Pinging 128.107.229.50 with 32 bytes of data:

Reply from 128.107.229.50: bytes=32 time=72ms TTL=113
Reply from 128.107.229.50: bytes=32 time=72ms TTL=113
Reply from 128.107.229.50: bytes=32 time=72ms TTL=113
Reply from 128.107.229.50: bytes=32 time=71ms TTL=113

Ping statistics for 128.107.229.50:
    Packets: Sent = 4, Received = 4, Lost = 0 (0% loss),
Approximate round trip times in milli-seconds:
    Minimum = 71ms, Maximum = 72ms, Average = 71ms
```

When a **ping** is sent to an IP address, a packet known as an *echo request* is sent across the network to the IP address specified. If the destination host receives the echo request, it responds with a packet known as an *echo reply*. If the source receives the echo reply, connectivity is verified. The basic **ping** command usually issues four echoes and waits for the replies to each one. It can, however, be modified to increase its usefulness. Example 9-3 shows some of the more advanced features of the **ping** command.

Example 9-3 Advanced Features of **ping**

```
C:\>ping

Usage: ping [-t] [-a] [-n count] [-l size] [-f] [-i TTL] [-v TOS]
            [-r count] [-s count] [[-j host-list] ¦ [-k host-list]]
            [-w timeout] target_name

Options:
    -t              Ping the specified host until stopped.
                    To see statistics and continue - type Control-Break;
                    To stop - type Control-C.
    -a              Resolve addresses to hostnames.
    -n count        Number of echo requests to send.
    -l size         Send buffer size.
    -f              Set Don't Fragment flag in packet.
    -i TTL          Time To Live.
    -v TOS          Type Of Service.
    -r count        Record route for count hops.
    -s count        Timestamp for count hops.
    -j host-list    Loose source route along host-list.
    -k host-list    Strict source route along host-list.
    -w timeout      Timeout in milliseconds to wait for each reply.
```

If a **ping** is sent to a name, such as www.cisco.com, a packet is first sent to a DNS server to resolve the name to an IP address. After the IP address is obtained, the echo request is forwarded to the IP address and the process proceeds. If a **ping** to the IP address succeeds, but a **ping** to the name does not, most likely a problem exists with DNS.

If **ping**s to both the name and IP address are successful, but the user is still unable to access the application, the problem most likely resides in the application on the destination host. For example, it might be that the requested service is not running.

If neither **ping** is successful, network connectivity along the path to the destination is most likely the problem. If this occurs, the common practice is to **ping** the default gateway. If the **ping** to the default gateway is successful, the problem is not local. If the **ping** to the default gateway fails, the problem resides on the local network.

Packet Tracer
☐ Activity

Using the ping Command (9.2.4.3)

In this Packet Tracer activity you examine end-to-end connectivity using the **ping** command. Use file d1-9243.pka on the CD-ROM that accompanies this book to perform this activity using Packet Tracer.

Troubleshooting Using **tracert**

The **ping** utility can only verify connectivity between end devices. However, if a problem exists and the device cannot **ping** the destination, the **ping** utility does not always indicate where the problem resides. If a router along the path drops the connection it will include the router's IP address in the destination unreachable message that is returned. Unfortunately, this occurs only if the router actually drops the packet—not if the echo request or echo reply is lost in transit. To determine the location where packets are being lost, another utility known as **tracert** is used.

The **tracert** utility output, pictured in Example 9-4, provides connectivity information about the path a packet takes to reach the destination and about every router, or *hop*, along the way. It also indicates how long a packet takes to get from source to each hop and back (round trip time). **tracert** can help identify where a packet might have been lost or delayed due to bottlenecks or slowdowns in the network.

Example 9-4 The **tracert** Command

```
C:\>tracert

Usage: tracert [-d] [-h maximum_hops] [-j host-list] [-w timeout] target_name

Options:
    -d                       Do not resolve addresses to hostnames.
    -h maximum_hops    Maximum number of hops to search for target.
    -j host-list           Loose source route along host-list.
    -w timeout             Wait timeout milliseconds for each reply.


C:\>tracert cisco.netacad.net

Tracing route to cisco.netacad.net [128.107.229.50]
over a maximum of 30 hops:

    1     1 ms    <1 ms    <1 ms  192.168.1.1
    2     8 ms     8 ms     9 ms  bas1-toronto46_lo0_SYMP.net.bell.ca [64.230.197.216]
    3     6 ms     7 ms     7 ms  dis7-toronto01_Vlan147.net.bell.ca [64.230.202.105]
    4     7 ms     7 ms     6 ms  core2-toronto01_GE11-2.net.bell.ca [64.230.204.141]
    5     7 ms     6 ms     6 ms  core4-toronto63_POS13-1.net.bell.ca [64.230.233.93]
    6    17 ms    17 ms    17 ms  core1-chicago23_pos12-0-0.net.bell.ca [64.230.147.14]
    7    18 ms    18 ms    17 ms  bx2-chicagodt_so-2-0-0-0.net.bell.ca [64.230.203.146]
    8    18 ms    17 ms    18 ms  151.164.250.241
    9    70 ms    70 ms    70 ms  ded4-g8-3-0.sntc01.pbi.net [151.164.41.165]
   10    72 ms    71 ms    71 ms  Cisco-Systems-1152786.cust-rtr.pacbell.net [64.161.0.62]
   11    70 ms    70 ms    70 ms  sjc5-dmzbb-gw1.cisco.com [128.107.224.105]
   12    71 ms    71 ms    71 ms  sjc12-dmzdc-gw1-gig1-1.cisco.com [128.107.224.14]
   13    72 ms    71 ms    71 ms  cna-prod-nv.cisco.com [128.107.229.50]

Trace complete.
```

The **tracert** command can be followed by either an IP address or the name of a destination host. If a name is used a DNS lookup must be conducted just as with **ping**.

The basic **tracert** utility only allows up to 30 hops between a source and destination device before it assumes that the destination is unreachable. This number is adjustable by using the **–h** parameter. Other modifiers are also available.

Troubleshooting Using **netstat**

Sometimes you need to know which active TCP connections are open and running on a networked host. **netstat**, shown in Example 9-5, is an important network utility that you can use to verify those connections. **netstat** lists the protocol in use, the local address and port number, the foreign address and port number, and the state of the connection.

```
Example 9-5  The netstat Command
C:\>netstat -a

Active Connections

  Proto  Local Address          Foreign Address        State
  TCP    host-a:epmap           host-a:0               LISTENING
  TCP    host-a:microsoft-ds    host-a:0               LISTENING
  TCP    host-a:2869            host-a:0               LISTENING
  TCP    host-a:25111           host-a:0               LISTENING
  TCP    host-a:25112           host-a:0               LISTENING
  TCP    host-a:1025            host-a:0               LISTENING
  TCP    host-a:1035            localhost:1036         ESTABLISHED
  TCP    host-a:1036            localhost:1035         ESTABLISHED
  TCP    host-a:1057            localhost:27015        ESTABLISHED
  TCP    host-a:4664            host-a:0               LISTENING
  TCP    host-a:11500           host-a:0               LISTENING
  TCP    host-a:11526           host-a:0               LISTENING
  TCP    host-a:11526           localhost:1102         TIME_WAIT
  TCP    host-a:11526           localhost:1103         TIME_WAIT
  TCP    host-a:11526           localhost:1104         TIME_WAIT
  TCP    host-a:11526           localhost:1105         TIME_WAIT
  TCP    host-a:11527           host-a:0               LISTENING
  TCP    host-a:11528           host-a:0               LISTENING
  TCP    host-a:11529           host-a:0               LISTENING
  TCP    host-a:11530           host-a:0               LISTENING
  TCP    host-a:11531           host-a:0               LISTENING
  TCP    host-a:11532           host-a:0               LISTENING
  TCP    host-a:11533           host-a:0               LISTENING
  TCP    host-a:27015           host-a:0               LISTENING
  TCP    host-a:27015           localhost:1057         ESTABLISHED
  TCP    host-a:62514           host-a:0               LISTENING
  TCP    host-a:netbios-ssn     host-a:0               LISTENING
  TCP    host-a:1059            twweb5.gocyberlink.com:http   ESTABLISHED
  TCP    host-a:1061            kdc.uas.aol.com:https   ESTABLISHED
  TCP    host-a:1063            twweb4.gocyberlink.com:http   CLOSE_WAIT
  TCP    host-a:1065            64.12.24.9:https       ESTABLISHED
```

```
TCP    host-a:1078             aimtoday-chi02.evip.aol.com:http  TIME_WAIT
TCP    host-a:1101             ats-ddb.dial.aol.com:5190   ESTABLISHED
TCP    host-a:2869             192.168.1.1:2448        CLOSE_WAIT
TCP    host-a:2869             192.168.1.1:2449        TIME_WAIT
UDP    host-a:microsoft-ds     *:*
UDP    host-a:1031             *:*
UDP    host-a:1041             *:*
UDP    host-a:1042             *:*
UDP    host-a:1045             *:*
UDP    host-a:3776             *:*
UDP    host-a:ntp              *:*
UDP    host-a:1060             *:*
UDP    host-a:1062             *:*
UDP    host-a:1066             *:*
UDP    host-a:1074             *:*
UDP    host-a:1900             *:*
UDP    host-a:62514            *:*
UDP    host-a:ntp              *:*
UDP    host-a:netbios-ns       *:*
UDP    host-a:netbios-dgm      *:*
UDP    host-a:1900             *:*
```

Unexplained TCP connections can pose a major security threat because they can indicate that something or someone is connected to the local host. Additionally, unnecessary TCP connections can consume valuable system resources thus slowing down the host's performance. Use **netstat** to examine the open connections on a host when performance appears to be compromised.

Many useful options are available for the **netstat** command. Detailed help on the **netstat** command is available via the help feature with the command, **netstat –h**.

Troubleshooting Using **nslookup**

When accessing applications or services across the network, humans usually rely on the DNS name instead of the IP address. When a request is sent to that name, the host must first contact the DNS server to resolve the name to the corresponding IP address. The host then uses the IP to package the information for delivery.

The **nslookup** utility allows an end user to look up information about a particular DNS name in the DNS server. When the **nslookup** utility is issued, the information returned includes the IP address of the DNS server being used as well as the IP address of the name specified. **nslookup** is often used as a troubleshooting tool for determining whether the DNS server is performing name resolution as expected. Example 9-6 shows the output of the **nslookup** command for the query shown in Figure 9-4.

Example 9-6 The **nslookup** Command

```
C:\>nslookup cisco.netacad.net
Server:  DNSTEST.svr.example.com
Address: 192.168.254.32

Non-authoratative answer:
Name:  cisco.netacad.net
Address: 209.165.200.224
```

Figure 9-4   DNS Lookup Process

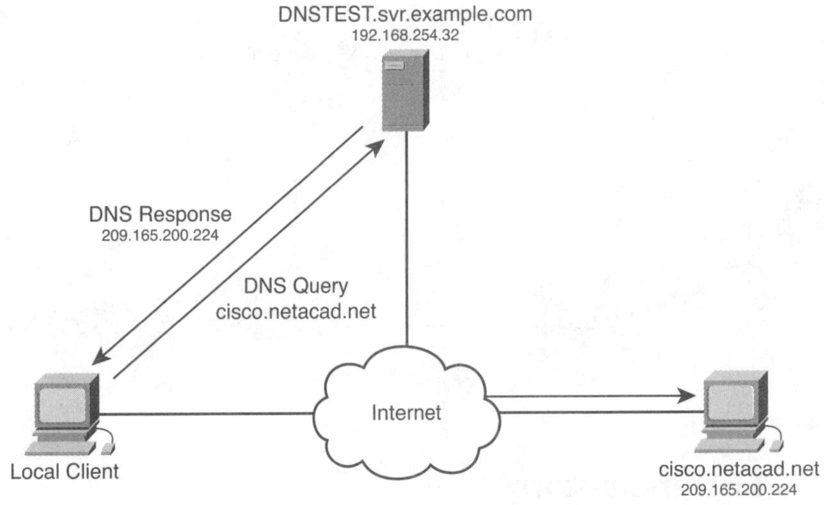

DNSTEST.svr.example.com
192.168.254.32

DNS Response
209.165.200.224

DNS Query
cisco.netacad.net

Internet

Local Client

cisco.netacad.net
209.165.200.224

Lab 9-1: Troubleshooting Using Network Utilities (9.2.7.2)

In this lab you use various network utilities to help solve connectivity issues. Refer to the lab in Part II of this *Learning Guide*. You may perform this lab now or wait until the end of the chapter.

Common Networking Issues

Although the number of potential problems with network connectivity is almost limitless, some are more common than others. Having a good understanding of the most likely problems can save a great deal of time and frustration.

Connectivity Issues

Connectivity problems occur on wireless networks, wired networks, and networks that use both, as illustrated in Figure 9-5. When troubleshooting a network with both wired and wireless connections, troubleshooting using a divide-and-conquer approach to isolate the problem to either the wired or wireless network is often best. The easiest way to determine whether the problem is with the wired or the wireless network is to perform the following steps:

Step 1.   **Ping from a wireless client to the wireless router**: This verifies whether the wireless client is connecting as expected.

Step 2.   **Ping from a wired client to the wireless router**: This verifies whether the wired client is connecting as expected.

Step 3.   **Ping from the wireless client to a wired client**: This verifies whether the wireless router is functioning as expected.

Figure 9-5   Network with Both Wired and Wireless Components

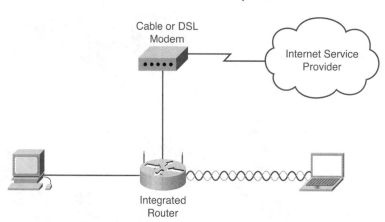

LED Indicators

Regardless of whether the fault is present on the wireless or wired network, one of the first steps of troubleshooting should be to examine the LEDs, which indicate the current state or activity of a piece of equipment or connection. LEDs might change color or flash to convey information. The exact configuration and meaning of LEDs varies among manufacturers and devices.

Figure 9-6 shows the LEDs on a Linksys wireless router. Three types of LEDs are commonly found on devices: power, status, and activity. On some devices a single LED might convey multiple pieces of information depending on the current status of the device. Checking the equipment documentation for the exact meaning of all indicators is important but some commonality does exist. If this documentation is misplaced it is normally available online at the manufacturer's website.

Figure 9-6   LED on a Linksys Wireless Router

Inactive LEDs might be an indication of a device failure, port failure, or cabling issues. Possibly the device is nonfunctional due to faulty hardware. The port itself might also have become faulty due to hardware failure or improperly configured software. Regardless of whether the network is wired or wireless, verify that the device and ports are up and functional before spending large amounts of time trying to troubleshoot other issues.

Power LED

The power LED is usually a solid green color indicating that the device is being supplied with power. No light indicates a problem with the power. In this case, check the power connections and/or the position of the power switch, if present.

Status LED

The status LED indicates the current condition of the device and can change color or flash. It is also used during device self-diagnostic testing to indicate the stage of completion.

When self-diagnostics are completed the color indicates status as follows:

- Solid green indicates the device is functioning properly.

- Amber can indicate that an error has been encountered that is correctable, such as a missing or damaged operating system.

- Red can indicate that the device has experienced a major hardware problem that will require service.

Activity LED

The activity LED is also referred to as the link light. This LED is normally associated with a specific port; under normal conditions the link light flashes, indicating that traffic is flowing through the port. The rate of flash might indicate the speed at which the port is functioning.

The link light has these indicators:

- Solid green indicates that a device is plugged into the port but no traffic is flowing.

- Amber indicates the device is making adjustments to the way the port is operating.

- No light indicates that nothing is plugged into the port, or that an issue exists with the port, transmitting device, or cable.

On wireless devices the activity light can indicate status of the radio connection; the flash rate differs depending on whether the clients are associated or searching for an association.

Wired Connectivity Problems

If the wired client is unable to connect to the wireless router, check the physical connectivity and cabling. Cabling is the central nervous system of wired networks and one of the most common issues when experiencing inactivity.

There are several issues to watch for in cabling:

- Correct type of cable for the application. Two types of UTP cables are commonly encountered in networking: straight-through cables and crossover cables. Using the wrong type of cable might prevent connectivity.

- Improper cable termination is one of the main problems encountered in networks. To avoid this, cables should be properly terminated according to standards.

- Cables should be constructed according to standards. Terminate cables via the 568A or 568B termination standard.

- Avoid untwisting too much cable during termination. This can cause crosstalk and severely degrade network performance.

- Crimp connectors on the cable jacket to provide strain relief.

- Maximum cable run lengths exist based on characteristics of the different cables. The attenuation caused by exceeding these run lengths can have a serious negative impact on network performance.

- If connectivity is a problem, verify that the correct ports are being used between the networking devices.

- Protect cables and connectors from physical damage. Support cables to prevent strain on connectors and run cable through areas that will not be in the way. Damage to the cable sheath might indicate internal damage to the cable.

Lab 9-2: Troubleshooting Physical Connectivity (9.3.3.2)

In this lab you examine and correct various physical connectivity issues. Refer to the lab in Part II of this *Learning Guide*. You may perform this lab now or wait until the end of the chapter.

Connectivity Problems in a WLAN

If the wireless client is unable to connect to the network, it might be because of wireless connectivity problems. Wireless communications rely on radio frequency signals (RF) to carry data. Many factors can affect the capability to connect hosts using RF.

The strength of an RF signal decreases with distance. If the signal strength is too low devices will be unable to reliably associate and move data. If the client cannot associate with the access point (AP), no communication can occur. The NIC client utility can be used to display the signal strength and connection quality.

RF signals are also susceptible to interference from outside sources, including other devices functioning on the same frequency. Environmental issues can also decrease the RF signal strength and limit connectivity. Factors such as high humidity, plant growth, and relocation of furniture can greatly affect the RF signal quality. A thorough site survey should be conducted before the installation of a WLAN and again if connectivity problems are encountered. The survey should scan for interference on the same frequencies as are being used by the WLAN as well as coverage patterns.

APs share the available bandwidth between devices. As more devices associate with the AP, the bandwidth for each individual device decreases, causing network performance problems such as application timeouts and slow downloads. The solution is to reduce the number of wireless clients using each channel.

Not all wireless standards are compatible. The 802.11a (5 GHz band) is not compatible with the 802.11b/g standards (2.4 GHz band). The 802.11n draft standard currently specifies operation in both frequency ranges although most current draft 802.11n equipment functions only in the 2.4 GHz range. Within the 2.4 GHz band, each standard uses different technology. Unless specifically configured, equipment that conforms to one standard might not function properly with equipment that conforms to another standard even if they both use the same frequency band.

Each wireless conversation must occur on a separate, non-overlapping channel. Some AP devices can be configured to select the least congested or highest throughput channel. Although automatic settings work, manual setting of the AP channel provides greater control and might be necessary in some environments.

Not all connectivity issues in a WLAN are related to RF problems. Modern WLANs incorporate various technologies to help secure the data. Incorrect configuration of any of these can prevent communication. Some of the most common settings that are configured incorrectly include the SSID, authentication, and encryption.

SSID

The SSID is a 32-character, case-sensitive, alphanumeric string that must match on both the AP and client. If the SSID is not broadcast, it must be manually entered onto the client. If the client is configured with the wrong SSID, it will not associate with the AP. Additionally, if another AP is present that is broadcasting the SSID, the client might automatically associate to it. Figure 9-7 shows the basic wireless setup configuration page on a Linksys wireless router.

Figure 9-7   Basic Wireless Setup

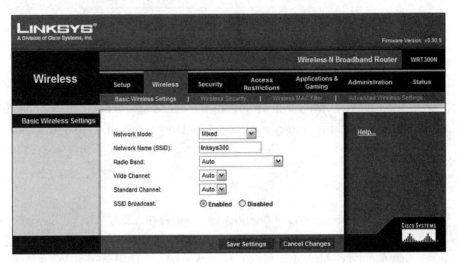

Authentication

On most APs open authentication is configured by default, allowing all devices to connect. If a more secure form of authentication is configured, a key is necessary. Both the client and the AP must be configured with the same key. If the keys do not match, authentication will fail and the devices will not associate, as illustrated in Figure 9-8.

Encryption

Encryption is the process of altering the data so that it is not usable by anyone without the proper encryption key. If encryption is enabled, the same encryption key must be configured on both the AP and the client. If the client associates with the AP but cannot send or receive data, the encryption key might be the issue.

WLAN connectivity issues can often be corrected by simply reconfiguring or relocating existing equipment. Sometimes, installing additional equipment or changing the frequency band being used in the WLAN might be necessary.

Figure 9-8   Association Failure

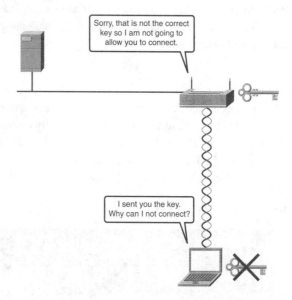

Interactive Activity 9-2: Effect of Channel Assignment on Throughput (9.3.4.2)

In this interactive activity you construct a Basic Set Service (BSS) to examine the effect of channel assignment on throughput. Use file ia-9342 on the CD-ROM that accompanies this book to perform this interactive activity.

Troubleshooting WLAN Connectivity Issues (9.3.5.2)

In this Packet Tracer activity you determine reasons why a wireless STA is unable to connect and then correct the problem. Use file d1-9352.pka on the CD-ROM that accompanies this book to perform this activity using Packet Tracer.

DHCP Issues

If the physical connection of the wired or wireless host appears to be correct, the next step is to check the IP configuration of the client. The IP configuration can have a major impact on the capability of a host to connect to the network. The ISR or wireless router often acts as a *DHCP server* for local wired and wireless clients. It provides them with all the IP configuration information required to participate on the network, including IP address, subnet mask, default gateway, and possibly even IP addresses of DNS servers. The DHCP server binds the IP address to a client's MAC address and stores that information in a client table. On the home wireless router, this table can be examined through the Status | Local Network page in the GUI, as shown in Figure 9-9.

The DHCP client table information should match the local host information, which can be obtained from the **ipconfig /all** command. Additionally, the IP address on the client must be on the same network as the LAN interface of the wireless router. The wireless router's LAN interface should be set as the default gateway. If the client configuration information does not agree with information in the client table, the address should be released (**ipconfig /release**) and renewed (**ipconfig /renew**) to form a new binding.

Figure 9-9 DHCP Settings on a Wireless Router

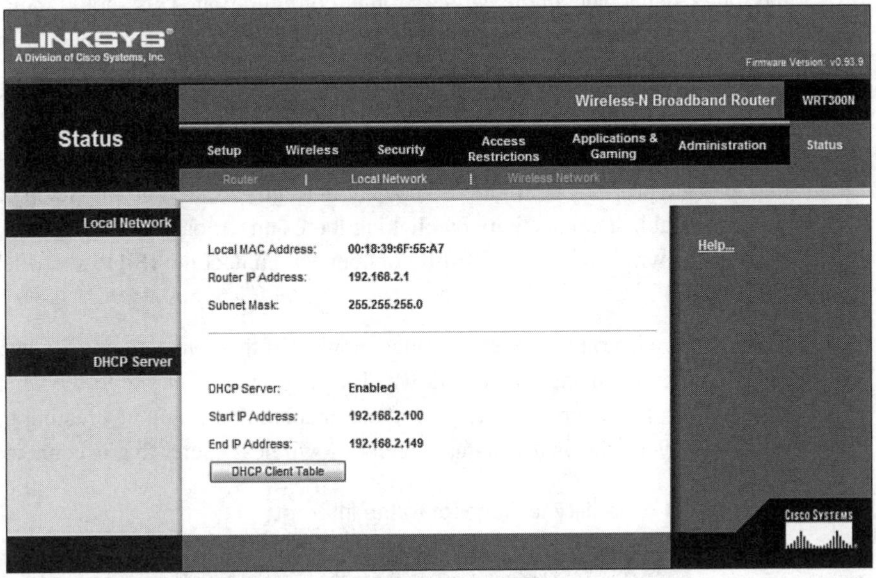

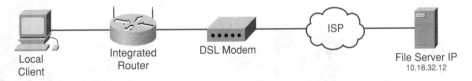

Troubleshooting the Wireless Router to ISP Connection

If both the wired and wireless clients are obtaining the correct IP configuration and can connect to the wireless router, but are unable to **ping** each other, the problem is most likely occurring on the wireless router. Check all configurations to ensure that no security restrictions could be causing the issue.

If hosts on the wired and wireless local network can connect to the wireless router and with other hosts on the local network, but not to the Internet, the problem might be in the connection between the wireless router and the ISP. Example 9-7 shows the output from the **ping** command for Figure 9-10 when the Internet is not reachable.

Figure 9-10 Inability to Connect to the Internet

Local Client — Integrated Router — DSL Modem — ISP — File Server IP 10.18.32.12

Example 9-7 Network Unreachable

```
C:\>ping 10.18.32.12

Pinging 10.18.32.12 with 32 bytes of data:

Request timed out.
Request timed out.
Request timed out.
Request timed out.

Ping statistics for 10.18.32.12:
    Packets: Sent = 4, Received = 0, Lost = 4 (100% loss),
```

Many ways exist to verify connectivity between the wireless router and the ISP. One way is to check the router status page in the wireless router configuration. This should indicate that the connection is good. It should also show the IP address assigned to the wireless router from the ISP.

If this page shows no connection, the wireless router might not be connected. Check all physical connections and LED indicators on the wireless router. If the DSL or cable modem is a separate device, check those connections and indicators as well. If the ISP requires a login name and password, check that they are properly configured. They are normally located on the Setup configuration page. Next, try to re-establish connectivity by clicking the Connect, or IP Address Renew, button on the Status page. If the wireless router will still not connect, contact the ISP to see whether the issue is occurring from its end.

If the status page on the wireless router shows that the connection is up, but a **ping** to an Internet site fails, the individual site might be down. Try pinging another site to see whether that is successful. If it is not, check for security measures that are enabled that might be creating the issue, such as port filtering. Figure 9-11 shows the Status screen of a wireless router that is connected to the ISP.

Figure 9-11   Inability to Connect to the Internet

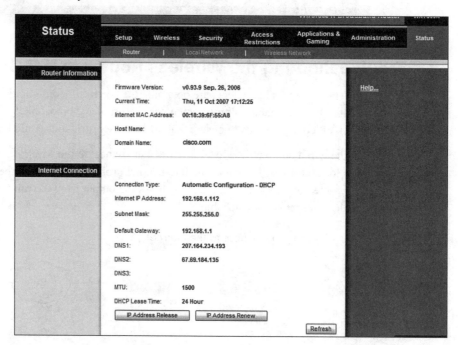

Interactive Activity 9-3: Determining Where a Problem Exists (9.3.6.2)

In this interactive activity you determine the area of a network where a problem could exist. Use file ia-9362 on the CD-ROM that accompanies this book to perform this interactive activity.

Troubleshooting and the Help Desk

Following a structured troubleshooting process can help to quickly and accurately locate and isolate issues. Networks continue to grow and technology evolves rapidly. It is impossible for any one individual to be an expert on all the technologies and equipment that make up the modern network. In addition, networks are becoming increasingly interconnected and issues on one network might affect users on another. For these reasons, outside sources of help are often required during the troubleshooting process.

Documentation

Network documentation is an important part of any troubleshooting process. Network documentation should include a normal or baseline measurement of network performance against which potential problems can be judged.

The performance baseline can include the types of traffic normally expected, as well as the volume of traffic to and from servers and network devices. The baseline should be documented just after the network is installed, when it is running optimally. Baseline performance should be re-established after any major changes to the network are implemented.

Additionally, documentation such as topology maps, network diagrams, and addressing schemes can provide valuable information when a troubleshooter is trying to understand the physical layout of the network and the logical flow of information.

Documentation should be maintained during the troubleshooting process. This documentation can be a valuable reference and can be used when future issues arise. Good troubleshooting documentation should include

- Initial problem
- Steps taken to isolate the problem
- Results of all steps taken, both successful and unsuccessful
- Final determined cause of the problem
- Final problem resolution
- Preventative measures

Using Outside Sources of Help

If, during the troubleshooting process, the troubleshooter is unable to determine the problem and its resolution, obtaining assistance from outside sources might be necessary. Some of the most common sources for help include

- Previously kept documentation
- Online *frequently asked questions (FAQ)*
- Colleagues and other network professionals
- Internet forums

Good documentation can save a great deal of time and effort by directing the troubleshooter to the most likely cause of the problem. It can also provide the technical information required to isolate, verify, and correct the issue. Documentation provided with many networking devices, however, often does not provide sufficient information to troubleshoot anything except the most basic issues.

Most manufacturers provide a series of FAQs about their product or technology on their website. These FAQs are usually based on previous requests for help. FAQs are a good source of current information and should be consulted whenever possible.

Colleagues and forums often provide a wealth of information; there is no substitute for troubleshooting experience. These individuals might be within the company or people who share the same interests and responsibilities. With the increased availability of the Internet and the development of support forums, troubleshooters can now obtain assistance from people around the world in real time.

Using the Help Desk

Although many sources of help are available, the *help desk* is often the end user's first stop for timely assistance. The help desk is a group of individuals with the knowledge and tools required to help diagnose and correct common problems. This group provides assistance for the end user to determine whether a problem exists, the nature of the problem, and the problem resolution.

Many companies and ISPs establish help desks to assist their users with networking problems. Most large IT companies run help desks for their individual products or technologies. For example, Cisco offers help desk assistance for problems integrating Cisco equipment into a network, or problems that might occur after installation. Some help desk support is offered free of charge but an increasing number of sites charge for this service.

Many ways exist for contacting a help desk, including e-mail, live chat, and phone. Although e-mail is good for non-urgent problems, phone or live chat is better for network emergencies. This availability is especially important in organizations such as banks where small amounts of downtime can cost large amounts of money. Unfortunately, with more companies switching to VoIP, outages in the network can prevent voice communications with the help desk. For this reason many companies retain a regular phone line into their IT area.

If necessary, the help desk can take control of a local host through remote access software. This capability allows help desk technicians to run diagnostic programs and interact with the host and network without having to physically travel to a job site. This greatly reduces the wait time for problem resolution and allows the help desk to assist more users.

As an end user, giving the help desk as much information as possible is important. The help desk will require information on any service or support plans that are in place along with specific details of the affected equipment. This can include make, model, and serial number along with the version of firmware or operating system running on the device. The help desk might also require the IP and MAC address of the malfunctioning device. The help desk will require information specific to the problem, including the following:

- Symptoms encountered
- Who encountered the problem
- When the problem manifests
- Steps taken to identify the problem
- Results of steps taken

For a follow-up call, be prepared to provide the date and time of the previous call, the ticket number, and name of the technician who handled the initial call. Be at the affected equipment, and be prepared to provide the help desk staff with access to the equipment if requested.

A help desk is generally organized in a series of levels of experience and knowledge. If the first-level help desk staff is unable to solve the problem they might escalate the problem to a higher level. Higher-level staff are generally more knowledgeable and have access to resources and tools that the first-level help desk staff does not.

Record all information regarding the interaction with the help desk, such as

- Time/date of call
- Name/ID of technician
- Problem reported
- Course of action taken
- Resolution/escalation
- Next steps (followup)

By working together with the help desk, most problems can be resolved quickly and easily. When it is resolved, be sure to update all documentation accordingly for future reference.

Summary

This chapter examined what to do when things go wrong in a network. It outlined the process of identifying, locating, and isolating problems that occur. Regardless of the troubleshooting technique deployed, the first step in the troubleshooting process is the collection of information from various sources.

After sufficient information is gathered, various troubleshooting techniques can be deployed. Some of these, such as the top-down, bottom-up. and divide-and-conquer techniques are very structured. Some, such as substitution and trial-and-error, are much less structured but can be faster depending on the experience level of the troubleshooter. More experienced troubleshooters often use less structured approaches, relying more on their experience and knowledge level to quickly determine the cause of a problem and make the necessary corrections.

Many connectivity problems can be attributed to the physical layer. Problems at this layer involve hardware devices and cabling only and do not extend to logical configurations. Different senses can be used to help locate and diagnose these physical layer problems.

A number of software utilities exist to assist in troubleshooting connectivity problems. These utilities allow the logical configuration of the host to be examined as well as trace the path that data takes between source and destination. These utilities include **ipconfig**, **ping**, **tracert**, **netstat**, and **nslookup**.

LED indicators can be used to visually determine the state of a connection or hardware device. They also provide information about connection speed and the association of wireless clients to APs.

For wired clients many problems can be traced to improper or defective cabling, including connecting the cable to the wrong port. For wireless clients the major issues are misconfiguration of SSID and encryption or authentication keys, incompatible standards, wrong or overused channels, and RF issues such as interference and signal strength.

Many sources of help are available to assist with the troubleshooting process. These include documentation, FAQs, online forums, and colleagues. Most large companies and equipment manufacturers also provide a help desk to assist clients with issues.

Help desks are normally structured with different levels of technical expertise and access to information. If the first-level techs are unable to assist, the problem is escalated to second-level techs; if they are unable to assist the problem might be escalated to the top level of technical support. When interacting with the help desk, having as much information available on the problem and equipment as possible is important. By fully using the resources available, most problems can be remedied quickly.

Activities and Labs

This summary outlines the activities and labs you can perform to help reinforce important concepts described in this chapter. You can find the activity and Packet Tracer files on the CD-ROM accompanying this book. The complete hands-on labs appear in Part II.

Interactive Activities on the CD-ROM:

Interactive Activity 9-1: Determining the Troubleshooting Technique (9.1.3.3)

Interactive Activity 9-2: Effect of Channel Assignment on Throughput (9.3.4.2)

Interactive Activity 9-3: Determining Where a Problem Exists (9.3.6.2)

Packet Tracer Activities on the CD-ROM:

Using the **ipconfig** Command (9.2.3.2)

Using the **ping** Command (9.2.4.3)

Troubleshooting WLAN Connectivity Issues (9.3.5.2)

Labs in Part II of This Book:

Lab 9-1: Troubleshooting Using Network Utilities (9.2.7.2)

Lab 9-2: Troubleshooting Physical Connectivity (9.3.3.2)

Check Your Understanding

Complete all the review questions listed here to test your understanding of the topics and concepts in this chapter. The "Check Your Understanding and Challenge Questions Answer Key" appendix lists the answers.

1. A secretary calls to report that she cannot access a shared directory on the network and desperately requires a document in that directory. What is the first step that should be taken?

    A. Collect additional information on the problem from the secretary.

    B. Tell the secretary to use a backup copy of the file.

    C. Copy the file to a USB memory key and deliver it to the secretary.

    D. Tell the secretary that you will investigate the issue and get back to her.

2. Which troubleshooting technique would an experienced network technician most likely use first?

    A. Top-down

    B. Bottom-up

    C. Divide-and-conquer

    D. Trial-and-error

3. An employee is experiencing problems with printing from a word processing application. The technician first checks that the printer is connected to the network and powered up. He next verifies that he is able to **ping** the printer from the workstation and then finally checks that the word processing software is properly installed and configured. What troubleshooting technique was used?

   A. Top-down

   B. Bottom-up

   C. Divide-and-conquer

   D. Trial-and-error

4. A technician suspects that the reason a colleague cannot connect to the Internet is because of misconfigured IP address settings. The technician checks the settings and makes the appropriate corrections. What troubleshooting technique was used?

   A. Top-down

   B. Bottom-up

   C. Divide-and-conquer

   D. Trial-and-error

5. A technician checks the settings on a desktop and notices that the IP address on the machine is different from that listed in the DHCP bindings table on the DHCP server. What step should the technician take to correct the issue?

   A. Test network connectivity with **tracert**.

   B. Test network connectivity with **ping**.

   C. Release and renew the IP address with **ipconfig**.

   D. Assign the machine a manual IP address.

6. A technician attempts to connect to a web page using the DNS name of the site. This connection fails, but when the IP address is substituted, the page is displayed. What utility could the technician use to verify the IP address being supplied by the DNS process?

   A. **ping**

   B. **tracert**

   C. **netstat**

   D. **ipconfig**

   E. **nslookup**

7. Users are complaining that connecting to a certain website is extremely slow. You verify that nobody is having any issues with any other sites and that the complaint is valid. What utility would be appropriate to determine whether a problem does exist?

   A. **ping**

   B. **tracert**

   C. **netstat**

   D. **ipconfig**

   E. **nslookup**

8. What does a flashing green port activity LED normally indicate?

  A. There is an error on the network port.

  B. The port is functioning normally but there is a problem with the connected host.

  D. The port is functioning normally but there is no data moving through the port.

  E. The device is functioning normally and data is moving through the port.

9. Which parameter(s), if misconfigured, will prevent an STA from associating with an AP? (Choose all that apply.)

  A. SSID

  B. Authentication key

  C. Encryption key

  D. Association key

10. Which are possible sources of help when troubleshooting? (Choose all that apply.)

  A. Colleagues

  B. Internet

  C. Help desk

  D. Documentation

  E. FAQs

Challenge Questions and Activities

These questions require a deeper application of the concepts covered in this chapter. You can find the answers in the appendix.

1. AnyCompany has just rearranged its office environment with the addition of many new plants and large metal filing cabinets. Users of the WLAN are now complaining that they no longer have access at their desks, but the manager is not convinced because the company did not alter the WLAN structure. What steps would you take to isolate and correct the problem? Which troubleshooting technique is most appropriate?

2. A friend calls you and says that he can no longer connect to the Internet from his home office. Knowing that you are a very good troubleshooter he asks you what he should do. What would you tell him?

CHAPTER 10

Putting It All Together

Networking is an exciting and dynamic career choice. Business requirements continue to change and information technology must evolve to support these needs. New technologies and services are continually developed and existing ones refined to support the enterprise.

This course and *Learning Guide* have provided the skills and information necessary to understand the basics of networking technology and apply it to solutions for the home and small business environments. Large organizations and service providers expand on this basic technology and provide a wide range of services not only to the home and small business user, but also to enterprise-level customers.

Regardless of the career path you choose, exposure to these new and evolving technologies and services occurs daily. This is only the beginning in the discovery of the power of the network.

Summary Activity

Throughout this course, you have learned about computer hardware and software, wired and wireless networking components, protocols and applications, and techniques for securing a network.

In this summary activity, use the knowledge you have gained to plan and implement a technical solution for a small business. Your solution should be based on the needs and requirements of the business environment.

Activities and Labs

This chapter does not include Interactive and Packet Tracer activities. The complete hands-on Lab appears in Part II.

Labs in Part II of This Book:

Lab 10-1: Capstone Project—Putting It All Together

Check Your Understanding and Challenge Questions Answer Key

Chapter 1

Check Your Understanding

1. A, D, F. Spreadsheet, word processing, and database programs are all application programs designed to accomplish a specific task. Windows XP, Windows Vista, and Linux are all operating systems.

2. D. Basic input output system (BIOS) is the instructions used to test the hardware and load the OS when the machine is first powered on. The BIOS code is stored in a memory chip and is therefore known as firmware. BIOS is only one type of firmware.

3. A. Network applications have two portions. One portion runs on the local machine while the other portion runs on a remote machine. Spreadsheet, word processing, and database software normally run on a local machine while e-mail runs as a client on the local machine and connects to a remote server, making it a network application.

4. A. The mainframe computer is normally a large centralized computer found in enterprise environments. Servers can also perform some of the same functions as mainframes but are normally not large and are often distributed around the enterprise.

5. D. Workstations are high-end machines designed to run graphics and engineering type applications.

6. C, D. Both workstations and desktop computers are normally used by a single individual. Mainframes and servers are designed to provide services to multiple individuals at any given time.

7. B. Estimated download time is calculated as follows: (600 KB × 1024 B/KB × 8 b/B)/(1000 b/kb × 256 kbps) = 19.2 seconds.

8. C. A pixel is the unit of measure for a computer monitor. It is an abbreviation of the term *pic*ture *el*ement and indicates the number of distinct points that make up the image. Gigahertz is a measure of analog frequency, KB is a measure of storage capacity, and kbps is a measure of data transfer rate.

9. C, D. Pre-built machines offer adequate performance at a reasonable price. The end user has no control over the components used to assemble the machine and cannot optimize its performance for any one application.

10. B. Before upgrading any components that are located on-board with expansion cards, it is necessary to disable the onboard component to avoid conflict.

11. A, B, C, D. All the stated factors are important criteria when selecting a motherboard.

12. A. The CPU should be the first component selected based on its speed and structure. Once the CPU is selected then the motherboard can be picked to support the CPU. RAM and HDD are secondary considerations once the motherboard and CPU are selected.

13. C. All programs must be run from system memory (RAM). The program may be stored on a HDD but it must first be moved from the HDD to RAM before the CPU can communicate with it.

14. A, B, C, D, E. All of these devices are considered input devices because they accept information and convert it into a form that can be used by the computer.

15. C. Before working on any system components always unplug the computer and properly ground it and yourself.

16. A. By touching hands, the charges on both individuals become the same and no charge will pass through the component. All other mentioned techniques would be ineffective in equalizing the charges and allow a charge to move from one individual to the other through the component, possibly causing damage to it.

17. B. With PnP-compliant devices the driver is installed before the device is connected to the computer and powered on. When the printer is powered on, the computer detects the device and finishes the installation.

Challenge Questions and Activities

1. In her haste Charlene did not take proper precautions against ESD. While inserting the memory, a static discharge could have occurred rendering the memory inoperable. The only recourse Charlene has is to replace the memory and adhere to best practices for the prevention of ESD when she installs the new memory.

2. These advanced features may be available only with the latest driver. You should advise Juri to go to the manufacture's website to download and install the latest driver. These features should then be available.

Chapter 2

Check Your Understanding

1. ext2 and ext3. Modern versions of Linux will use the ext2 file system for a basic installation and ext3 if file system journaling is required.

2. B. An upgrade will replace the old OS files with the new and leave applications and data intact. A clean install would overlay applications and data. Multiboot would install a new OS to another partition, making applications and data in another unavailable. Virtualization is not appropriate for this task.

3. IP address, subnet mask, and default gateway address. The three basic IP parameters needed are the IP address for the computer, a subnet mask to go with it, and the IP address of the default gateway (router interface on the local network).

4. A and B. Device type and location are most useful because they provide information that a network admin can use to troubleshoot problems.

5. Redirector. The redirector takes requests for remote resources and sends them out onto the network through the computer NIC so that they can reach the server that has the resources.

6. Kernel. The kernel and its drivers deal with hardware and translate requests made by the shell and applications into language the computer components can understand.

7. C and D. Linux and BSD are open source OSs released under the GPL. Windows, Mac OS, and UNIX are commercial OSs that are proprietary and do not allow users to modify code.

8. B, C, and E. The OS selected must be able to support the desired user applications. The computer hardware must support the OS, and knowledgeable support staff is needed.

9. All the answers are correct. If there is no upgrade path, she must do all the answer items to convert to Vista while retaining her data and applications.

10. A. Prompt for permission allows the admin to be notified either before the updates are downloaded or after they have been downloaded but before they are installed. Automatic installation downloads them and installs them without user intervention, and manual installation requires the admin to identify the updates desired and download them and install them manually.

Chapter 3

Check Your Understanding

1. B, C. The web camera and printer attached to a PC are considered peripherals. Components attached to network devices, such as hubs and switches, are normally considered hosts.

2. B, D, E. The printer attached to a hub and the server and IP phone attached to a switch are hosts. Components attached to network devices, such as hubs and switches, are normally considered hosts.

3. A, D. Peer-to-peer networks are easy to set up and generally cost less than server-based networks but do not scale well or provide centralized security and administration.

4. B, E. Logical topology maps do not show details of hardware location or cabling runs. They are intended to show higher-level information such IP addresses, naming, and network applications.

5. D. A unicast is sending to a single host, a multicast is sending to multiple hosts, and a broadcast is sending to all hosts. A simulcast is not a form of computer messaging.

6. B. The web browser and e-mail reader are both only client applications.

7. D. The e-mail reader is a client application. When sharing a folder, the computer acts as a server, so it is playing both roles.

8. D. Encapsulation on an Ethernet network involves placing an IP packet inside an Ethernet frame.

9. B. The Windows **ipconfig /all** command displays the IP address, subnet mask, default gateway, and MAC address, as well as the IP address of DNS and DHCP servers. The other commands are not valid.

10. C. Switches do not pass collision fragments, so each port on a switch is considered a separate collision domain.

11. C, D. Both switches and routers examine the transmitted information and can determine whether the message has been damaged by a collision. Neither of these devices will forward a collision fragment, thus limiting the size of the collision domain.

12. C. When a frame is to be delivered to a MAC address that is not in the switch's MAC address table, the switch will flood the frame out all ports in an attempt to deliver it.

13. B. ARP requests are sent out to a broadcast MAC address (FFFF:FFFF:FFFF). All devices in the broadcast domain will hear this request but only the device to which the request is addressed in the segment will respond.

14. D. ARP replies are sent as a unicast to the device making the request. Only the requesting device hears this reply.

15. A, B, C, and D. All the answers are criteria that can be used to break up a network into multiple access layer networks.

16. D. The distribution layer connects multiple access layer networks. Routers are the most common device found in the distribution layer.

17. A. Routers do not pass broadcasts unless specifically configured to do so. This keeps broadcast traffic local to where it is generated and improves overall network performance.

18. B. A LAN is either a single local network or a group of interconnected local networks under the control of a single administrator.

19. D. The physical topology is concerned only with the physical layout of the network and devices. It is not concerned with the flow of information that is recorded as the logical configuration.

20. B. The physical MAC address, also known as the hardware address, identifies the NIC of a specific host. The logical IP address also identifies a host but includes information that indicates the network on which the host resides. Both are required to deliver a message in an Ethernet/IP local network.

21. A default gateway is used when information must be sent to a host on another network. The message is sent to the router using the default gateway address. After the router has the message it can examine the destination IP address to determine how to forward the message toward the host.

22. A switch is not a shared-bandwidth device and provides a dedicated circuit for communication between hosts. Switches will not forward collision fragments but will pass broadcasts. Because hosts generate broadcasts as part of their activity, adding more hosts will increase the number of broadcasts and degrade network performance.

Challenge Questions and Activities

1. Because the desktop computer is able to connect to the Internet, the home network appears to be functioning properly. The difference between the school and home networks is the network address. It is likely that the laptop has a static IP address configured that places it on the school's network. To allow it to function in Tebuc's home network it would have to be configured with the network address in use on that network. Configuring the laptop to acquire an address via DHCP or setting a static address on the home network should correct the problem.

2. The increased numbers of computers are generating more broadcasts. Because the computers are all connected to a single access layer device these broadcasts are not contained and are consuming valuable bandwidth. The simplest solution would be to segment the network using a router to contain broadcast traffic.

Chapter 4

Check Your Understanding

1. C, D. IP packets are also called datagrams and they have a header that contains IP addresses. A frame contains an additional header with MAC addresses and encapsulates a packet. Packets can contain segments, which is a term for a piece of TCP data. Packets (datagrams) do not have MAC addresses in them, only a frame does.

2. A. Only **tracert** (and **traceroute** with UNIX/Linux) shows hops and it also shows successful transmission. Some graphical **tracert** and **ping** utilities are available but the basic CLI commands display only textual output.

3. Correct answers are as follows:

   EMI: Noise created by an electrical environment

   Coax cable: Uses a BNC or F-series connector

   ScTP: Expensive type of twisted-pair cabling

   Fiber-optic circuit: Uses two fibers: one to transmit, one to receive

   Cladding: Used inside fiber-optic cabling to reflect light

   Crosstalk: Signal from one cable interferes with another

   Attenuation: Signal weakening over distance after it is transmitted

4. D. ISPs obtain address blocks from local, national, or regional Internet registries. The ISP is then responsible for assigning these addresses to their customers.

5. A, D, E. Fiber-optic cabling uses light to transmit data over long distances and is commonly used between buildings because it is immune to EMI and RFI. Nearby lightning strikes and voltage differentials between buildings do not affect it. It uses only two conductors and is not used to connect to the customer's cable modem.

6. B, E, F. UTP uses electrical pulses to transmit data. It is unshielded and highly susceptible to interference and so is not suitable for use between buildings. It is very easy to work with and is by far the most common type of network cabling.

7. A, C, E. ISPs support large numbers of users and provide transport connections from customers and to other ISPs. ISP POPs and NOCs contain many different types of robust equipment. They do not purchase access connectivity from end users.

8. A, D. Coax is heavier, stiffer, and more difficult to install than UTP. Fiber connectivity in home networking is not unheard of, but is not common. Category 5 (and 5e) is commonly used for UTP data connectivity. Multimode and single mode are types of fiber network cable, and Category 6 can support Gigabit speeds with Ethernet. In fact, Cat 5 can also support Gigabit speeds.

9. DSL and cable modem are by far the most common types of high-speed service for home users. T1 is a business class service. Dial-up is quite common but is not high-speed. The same is true of cellular modem. Satellite provides moderate speeds but is not nearly as widely used as DSL and cable.

10. F. All of these are correct. A Linksys WRT300N integrated router provides all of these functions.

11. Asymmetric service provides higher download speeds than upload speeds and is primarily for home and small business. Symmetric service provides equal download speeds and upload speeds and is common in larger businesses or those where users from the Internet will be accessing internal servers.

12. E. Connections between like devices require a crossover cable. Of the possible answers, only the PC-to-switch connection is between unlike devices and would use a straight-through cable.

13. D. A Cable Modem Termination System (CMTS) is a service provider device that combines the signals from the cable modems of many customers. It does not relate to the other technologies listed.

14. C. Open, short, reversed, and split pairs are all wiring problems that can occur with UTP. Close is not.

15. C. The RJ-45 (8-wire) connector is used with Ethernet UTP. BNC and F-Series are used with coax and RJ-11 (four-wire) is used with telephone systems. ST-45 does not exist.

16. B, D. Crosstalk is when the signal from one wire bleeds into an adjacent wire. Attenuation is the degradation of a signal as it moves along a conductor. Crossfire, overload, and aggregation are not UTP data transmission problems.

17. C. The data must travel from the PC to the Linksys integrated router (switch portion) and then to the DSL modem (unless the DSL modem is integrated into the Linksys). From there it travels through the phone line to the ISP POP (to a DSLAM) and then to the server (probably through an Ethernet switch). Any answer referring to cable or CMTS is wrong because the user has DSL service.

18. E. Each router that a packet passes through is considered a hop. A port or interface is a connection point on a switch or router. There is usually only one NOC per ISP, and IXP is an Internet Exchange Point where ISPs connect.

19. A, B, C. An IP packet header contains control information, source IP address, and destination IP address. It cannot contain all intermediate router IP addresses. The street address of the ISPs headquarters would not help the packet reach its destination.

Challenge Questions and Activities

1. Answers will vary and will be localized. Services could be obtained from multiple independent providers or from a single provider.

   Phone service options:

   Land line or cell service from a local telco

   Cell service from a national provider

   Satellite phone from national provider

   Cable phone service from a cable provider

   TV service options:

   Off-air broadcast TV reception (via antenna)

   Television service from a local telco

   Satellite TV from a national provider

   Cable TV from a cable provider

Internet service options:

Dial-up service from local telco

DSL service from a local or other telco

Cell Internet from a national provider

Satellite Internet from a national provider

Cable Internet from a cable provider

Chapter 5

Check Your Understanding

1. B. The decimal value of 37 is actually 32 + 4 + 1. To represent the number in binary format these values are turned on and all others are turned off resulting in a binary value of 0010 0101.

2. C. The bit values from most significant to least significant are 128, 64, 32, 16, 8, 4, 2, and 1. In this example the bits that are turned on are the 32, 16, and 2 bits. 32 + 16 + 2 = 50.

3. B. The subnet mask is all ones in the first and second octet indicating that these octets make up the network portion of the address. To find the network number turn all host bits off. This results in a value of 172.16.0.0.

4. B. Because the IP address starts with a value of 129 we know it is a Class B address. In a Class B address the first two octets represent the network portion and the last two represent the host portion.

5. D. To calculate the number of hosts possible use 2 raised to the number of host bits. In this example we would have $2^6 = 64$ possible hosts. Because we cannot use either the first or last address in the range we must subtract 2 leaving 62 usable hosts.

6. B and C. The bits that are on in the subnet mask indicate which bits represent the network portion of the address. Only 137.16.3.4 and 137.16.7.1 have the same network address portion.

7. E. Class B addresses start with an octet value from 128 to 191 and in this range the first two octets represent the network portion and the last two octets represent the host portion. For a valid IP address the host bits cannot be all zeros or all ones because these would represent the network number and network broadcast address respectively. The only address that meets all of these requirements is 163.15.17.2.

8. A, B, C, and D. The RFC 1918 private address space includes all addresses in the networks 10.0.0.0, 172.16.0.0 to 172.31.0.0, and 192.168.0.0 to 192.168.255.0. All the addresses, with the exception of 23.14.2.6 fall into these ranges.

9. B. The default subnet masks for the Class A, B, and C networks are 255.0.0.0, 255.255.0.0, and 255.255.255.0, respectively.

10. D. The MAC broadcast address achieved by turning on all 48 bits. Because Mac addresses are normally represented in hexadecimal format this would be FF:FF:FF:FF:FF:FF

11. B. Unicast messages are one-to-one, multicast are one-to-many, and broadcast are one-to-all.

12. B. MAC multicast addresses start with the pattern 01:00:5E.

13. A and D. DHCP relieves the network administrator from the tedious task of manually configuring IP addresses. It also allows IP addresses to be reused but does not allow addresses to be shared between machines. Each machine still requires a separate and unique IP address. DHCP will work with any type of IP address, private or public.

14. A. The correct sequence is the host must first discover a DHCP server. Once the server is discovered it makes an offer to the host of an available IP address. If the host decides it would like to use the offered address it must request the address for the server. If this address is still available the server binds it to the host's IP address and then acknowledges that the host can now use that address.

15. C. Because the host does not know where the server is, it sends out a broadcast message.

16. A. The DHCP Client Table supplies the requested information.

17. C. Because the router would receive an address on its WAN interface from the ISP it is acting as a DHCP client. Because it will also provide IP addressing information to the internal hosts it is also acting as a DHCP server.

18. B. NAT is used in both the home/small business worlds as well as the enterprise environment to allow internal hosts to be configured with a private IP address and at the same time be able to reach destinations on the Internet. NAT normally converts internal private addresses to public addresses as the traffic moves out of the network.

19. DHCP provides a mechanism for the automatic assignment of IP address information. In most small home networks the multi-function unit receives IP addressing information from the ISP which puts the outside or Internet interface on the ISP's network. The multi-function device then acts as a DHCP server to provide IP addressing information to internal hosts.

20. APIPA provides a mechanism for the automatic configuration of IP addresses on an interface if the DHCP server is not reachable. The configured addresses are on the same network and therefore allow APIPA configured devices to communicate. APIPA is used by newer Microsoft operating systems.

Challenge Questions and Activities

1. The problem is that the server and the hosts are on different networks. Because the subnet mask used is 255.255.255.0, the first three octets are being used to indicate the network address. The server is on the 172.27.16.0 network, whereas the hosts all reside on the 172.27.17.0 network. The easiest way to remedy the problem is to change the IP address of the server to put it on the same network as the hosts. Care must be used to assign an address that is not part of the DHCP pool or a conflict will result.

2. NAT is network address translation and is normally used to convert private address space used on internal networks to public addresses that can be routed on the Internet. If NAT is not functioning on the multi-function device this translation is not occurring and the private addresses are being blocked from traveling on the Internet. Because all hosts on the internal network are using private addresses they are able to communicate.

Chapter 6

Check Your Understanding

1. D. The sending host receives acknowledgments from the destination host to determine if the destination host has received all segments. Unacknowledged segments are re-transmitted.

2. File Transfer Protocol (FTP) is normally used to transfer large files.

3. DHCP is used to automatically configure IP hosts. DNS translates a domain name to an IP address.

4. B, C, E. SMTP is a mail-sending protocol and POP3 and IMPA4 are mail server protocols. DHCP is used to automatically configure IP hosts. DNS translates a domain name to an IP address.

5. DNS translates a domain name to an IP address.

6. Explanation:

HTML	Used to create web pages
HTTP	Protocol commonly used by a web browser
HTTPS	Secure protocol that uses port 443
Web server	Hosts a web page
Web client	Requests a web page

7. E. Voice over IP (VoIP) allows voice phone calls to be carried over the Internet. IM is an instant-messaging application. HTML is used to compose web pages. HTTP is used to request web pages and DNS translates a domain name to an IP address. SNMP is Simple Network Management Protocol.

8. Explanation:

Port Numbers	Protocols
20	FTP Data
21	FTP Control
23	Telnet
25	SMTP
53	DNS
68	DHCP
80	HTTP
110	POP3
161	SNMP
443	HTTPS

9. D, E, F. FTP, POP3, and HTTP operate at the application layer (layer 7). ARP is Address Resolution Protocol and operates at the network layer (layer 3). TCP operates at the transport layer (layer 4). Digital subscriber line (DSL) operates primarily at the physical layer (layer 1).

10. C. The Ethernet frame header and trailer are removed first, and then the IP header, and finally the TCP header.

11. A, D, E. UDP and TCP are transport layer protocols, not network or application. IP is network and HTTP is application layer.

12. C. The incoming packet source IP address and the source port number from the client create a socket for the server to keep track of.

13. Web service or HTTP (port 80).

14. D. Cable-related issues are associated with OSI layer 1, physical. The other layers have nothing to do with cabling.

15. A, C, D. Source and destination MAC addresses, source and destination IP addresses, and source and destination port numbers are all part of an Ethernet frame. Source and destination ID numbers and source and destination serial numbers are bogus.

16. B. The only transport protocols here are TCP and UDP. UDP does not use acknowledgments as TCP does and so it is better suited to voice.

17. B. FTP rides on top of TCP, which rides on top of IP, the foundation of the Internet.

Challenge Questions and Activities

1. The TCP/IP network access layer 1 is comparable to the OSI physical and data link layers 1 and 2. The TCP/IP Internet layer 2 is comparable to OSI network layer 3. TCP/IP transport layer 3 is comparable to OSI transport layer 4. TCP/IP application 4 is comparable to OSI layer 7. The TCP/IP model does not have a session (OSI layer 5) or presentation (OSI layer 6) layer.

2. DNS translates a domain name to an IP address. If you can **ping** a server by its IP address but not its domain name, the problem may be that the DNS server is down or unreachable and cannot translate the name to an IP address.

Chapter 7

Check Your Understanding

1. A, B, C, D, E. All the stated devices make use of different types of wireless technology.

2. C. Wireless scales easily. Wireless network boundaries vary with conditions such as temperature and humidity. They are not sharply defined. Wireless is sensitive to sources of interference and is inherently insecure.

3. B, C, D. IEEE 802.11b, g, and n all use the 2.4 GHz range. In addition, 802.1n also provides for compatibility with the 802.11a technology at 5 GHz.

4. C. 802.11 applies to WLANs. IEEE 802.3 is Ethernet, 802.5 is Token Ring, and 802.15 is WPAN.

5. C. The Service Set Identifier (SSID) is used to identify the wireless LAN.

6. B. A wireless network without an AP is known as an ad-hoc network. When the AP is present the network is referred to as an infrastructure network. IBSS, BSS, and ESS are all coverage areas in an infrastructure network.

7. A, C. The cell or Basic Service Set (BSS) is the smallest area covered by a single AP. An Independent Basic Service Set (IBSS) is the area coverage area in an ad-hoc network. The Extended Service Set (ESS) is a collection of BSSs linked together through a Distribution System (DS).

8. Authentication. Authentication verifies client credentials to ensure that they are who they claim to be. After a client is authenticated it is allowed to associate with the WLAN. The process occurs in this order to prevent unauthorized clients from associating with the AP. Once the client is associated, additional authentication techniques may be used to authenticate the user.

9. Open is the default authentication method and allows all clients to authenticate.

10. A, B, C, D, E. All are valid precautions when working with an AP. Not all of these precautions would be implemented in every installation.

Challenge Questions and Activities

1. WEP does not stop the data from being intercepted but does encrypt the data to make it unusable if it is intercepted. Unfortunately, WEP is not a secure technology and various tools can be easily downloaded from the Internet that will extract the WEP key from the data stream. When the WEP key is known, all data can be read. For security purposes the accounting firm should use WPA, which provides a stronger (longer) key and a more robust encryption algorithm.

2. Both cordless phones and WLAN technology use the same radio frequencies to carry information. When the cordless phone is used, its signal interferes with the WLAN and causes the signal to be unusable. When the call is completed the interference stops and wireless NIC is able to reconnect to the network. The best solution would be to change the frequency of either the cordless phone or the WLAN. If they are both operating at 2.4 GHz, one should be changed to the 5 GHz range.

Chapter 8

Check Your Understanding

1. B. By stealing personal user data a thief can impersonate another and apply for credit or make illegal purchases.

2. E-mail. Phishers attempt to trick email recipients into divulging personal information.

3. B. This is most likely a virus because it activates when opened and did not attempt to trick the user or propagate itself.

4. B. Using a powerful computer and software to determine a password or crack a code is known as brute force.

5. C. Spyware gathers personal information without permission or knowledge of the user.

6. D. The problems described are symptoms of an infected computer. Booting the PC and running anti-virus and anti-spyware applications from an external drive is the safest way to detect and correct problems.

7. A, B, D. Most firewalls can filter based on the source IP and MAC address as well as specific website URLs or domains. Fragment filtering and user name filtering are not firewall features.

8. A, C, D. Personal firewalls are common on home PCs; Server-based and appliance-based firewalls are common in larger organizations. Bandwidth-based do not exist and while switch-based firewalls are possible, they are not common.

9. B, D, E. Demilitarized zones (DMZ), network address translation (NAT), and stateful packet inspection (SPI) are common firewall features on a home or small business integrated router device. TCP is a transport protocol and POP is Post Office Protocol.

10. C, D. Internal users can typically access internal servers as well as those in the DMZ or external ones. The internal firewall is typically more restrictive and the external firewall is less restrictive because it must allow external users to access DMZ resources.

11. Trojan or Trojan horse. When a program is masquerading as something else and does damage to the computer it is most likely a Trojan horse.

12. C. Adware is a form of spyware and can be detected and removed by an anti-spyware program.

13. C. All of these are features of anti-virus software except automatic removal of unknown viruses. A virus that is unknown may not be detectable and most will likely not be removed. This is why it is so important to download the latest virus signature database for the anti-virus software being used.

14. A, B, C. Pretexting, vishing, and phishing are all forms of social engineering. Frying is not a techniques used in social engineering and spamming is sending large quantities of unsolicited email.

15. Worm. A worm can self propagate and spread quickly to many computers, rapidly infecting large parts of the Internet.

16. C. This is an example of SYN flooding where many packets with invalid source IP addresses are sent to a server.

17. B, D. When the ports to which packets will be forwarded are limited to one or more specific ones, this is known as port forwarding. The server can start with a dynamic address but it must then be reserved to make it static. It does not require a dynamic address. The server must have a permanent static address. A basic simple DMZ will forward all ports to the server, not just specific ones.

18. A, B, and D. A wireless user that can gain access to an unprotected AP will have free access to the Internet. If the owner of the AP has not changed the ID and password from the default, the hacker may be able to change configuration settings on the device. The hacker is on the internal network behind the firewall and will potentially have access to all internal hosts. The hacker will not be given the administrator password. He must know it already or be able to guess it.

Challenge Questions and Activities

1. Answers will vary but could include: Install a personal firewall, anti-virus, anti-spyware and anti-pop-up software (or packages that contain a combination of these). Set up a user login account with a password. Ensure that you have the latest OS and application software updates. Run a security scanner to help identify potential vulnerabilities.

Chapter 9

Check Your Understanding

1. A. The first step is to gather as much information on the problem as possible. The other items are steps that may be taken but only after appropriate information is gathered.

2. D. Experienced troubleshooters often use less structured troubleshooting techniques relying more on their experience. Trial-and-error is the only unstructured technique listed.

3. B. This is an example of a bottom-up approach starting at the physical layer and then moving to the network and finally application layers.

4. D. This is an example of trial-and-error. The technician relied on previous knowledge and experience to guess at the problem.

5. C. The most appropriate course of action is to release and renew the IP address, forcing the machine to obtain a new address from the DHCP server.

6. E. The **nslookup** utility is used to directly query the DNS server.

7. B. The most appropriate utility would be **tracert**. Because the site does load it must be accessible and because users are not experiencing problems with any other sites the problem cannot be internal to the organization. **tracert** will provide information as to where the slowdown in the network connectivity is located.

8. E. A flashing green activity LED indicated that everything is normal and data is moving through the port. If the LED was off, amber or red it would indicate problems. A solid green light indicates all is well but there is no data flowing through the port.

9. A, B. The SSID and authentication key must be properly configured for association to occur. A misconfigured encryption key will not prevent associate but will prevent meaningful communications. There is no such thing as an association key.

10. A, B, C, D, E. All of these are possible sources of help during the troubleshooting process.

Challenge Questions and Activities

1. The first step would be to gather as much information from the end users as possible. When are they unable to connect? Can they connect to local resources but not remote ones? If they cannot connect to either local or remote resources then it would be appropriate to connect one of their machines directly to the wired network to see if the problems persisted (divide-and-conquer approach). If the problems persist, the issue is not with the WLAN. If connectivity is fine from the wired network but not from the WLAN then the WLAN is suspect and must be investigated.

The WLAN uses RF to move information. RF can be absorbed by plants due to their high water content. In addition the metal filing cabinets will absorb, reflect, and possibly scatter the RF energy completely changing the coverage pattern in the office. A site survey would have to be conducted and WLAN equipment rearranged to compensate for the new office geometry.

2. The first step is to collect as much information about the problem as possible. You might ask the following questions:

- What sites did he try to connect to?

- Is it affecting just web or is other traffic such as email and FTP also affected?

- When did this happen?

- What changes did he make before the problem occurred?

From this information you could deduce the most probably cause. Have the user ping the Internet and the gateway to try and determine if the problem is with the home network or the ISP. Check the network address information on the computer to verify that it is correct for the network. Release and renew the IP address if it is obtained dynamically. Also check the address settings on the home networking device and possibly renew them as well. If all else fails call the ISP and ask if there is a possible outage in the area.

CHAPTER 1

Labs: Personal Computer Hardware

The lab exercises included in this chapter cover all the Chapter 1 online curriculum labs to ensure that you have mastered the practical, hands-on skills needed to understand the basics of computer hardware and storage. As you work through these labs, use Chapter 1 in Part I of this book or use the corresponding Chapter 1 in the Networking for Home and Small Businesses course of the CCNA Discovery online curriculum for assistance.

Lab 1-1: Determining Data Storage Capacity (1.3.2.2)

Objectives

- Determine the amount of RAM (in MB) installed in a PC.

- Determine the size of the hard disk drive (in GB) installed in a PC.

- Determine the used and available space on the hard disk drive (in GB).

- Check other types of storage devices (floppy, CD-ROM, DVD).

Background/Preparation

The storage capacity of many PC components is measured in megabytes (MB) and gigabytes (GB). These components include RAM, hard disk drives, and optical media, such as CDs and DVDs. In this lab, you determine the capacity and space available for various computer components.

To perform this lab, you need to use a computer with Windows XP installed.

Task 1: Identify the Amount of RAM in a Computer

Step 1.   Windows XP offers two ways to view control panels: Classic View and Category View. The options available depend on which one of these two views you are using. If you see the Switch to Category View option on the left, you are currently in the Classic View mode. If Switch to Classic View is displayed, you are currently in Category View mode. For this task, be sure that you are in Classic View mode, shown in Figure 1-1.

Figure 1-1   Control Panel Category and Classic Views

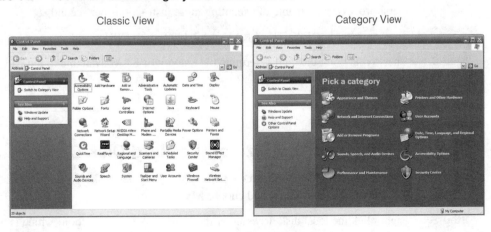

Step 2. From the Start menu, select **Control Panel**. In the Control Panel, choose **System** to open the System Properties dialog box. Alternatively, you can get this information by clicking the **Start** button and right-clicking the **My Computer** icon. Next, choose **Properties** from the drop-down menu.

Note that if you are using Windows XP in Classic View, you need to select **Settings** from the Start menu and then **Control Panel**. To switch to the standard XP view, right-click the Start button and select **Properties**. Select **Start Menu** and then click **OK**.

The computer operating system and service pack information are listed in the upper part of the dialog box. The computer processor type, speed, and memory are listed in the lower portion, as shown in Figure 1-2.

Figure 1-2   My Computer Information Screen

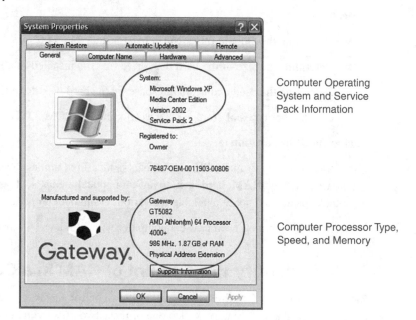

In Figure 1-2, the computer processor is an AMD Athlon 64 processor with a clock speed of 986 megahertz (MHz). Clock speed is a measurement of the number of cycles per second that a processor is capable of doing. The number of cycles impacts the number of instructions per second that the CPU can process. A higher clock speed generally means that a processor is capable of executing more instructions per second.

The computer has 1.87 GB of RAM available for the CPU.

Step 3. Check your computer and determine the amount of RAM available to the CPU. How much RAM is in your computer?

Task 2: Determine the Size of the Hard Disk Drive

Step 1. Double-click the **My Computer** icon on your computer desktop. If you do not have a My Computer icon, click **Start** and choose **My Computer**.

Step 2. Right-click the local disk drive under the Hard Disk Drives section (which is usually the C drive), and select **Properties**. The Local Disk Properties dialog box opens. The total capacity of the hard drive is shown above the Drive C icon, as illustrated in Figure 1-3.

Figure 1-3   Hard Disk Drive Capacity

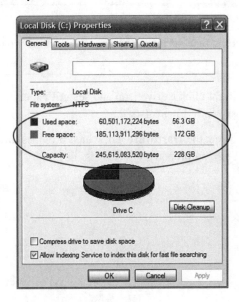

Step 3.   Determine the size of the hard drive on your computer. What is the total size of the hard drive in GB?

Step 4.   Keep the Local Disk Properties dialog box open for Task 3.

Task 3: Determine the Free Space and Used Space on the Hard Drive

In the Local Disk Properties dialog box, the used and free space are shown in both bytes and GB above the capacity information, as shown in Figure 1-4.

Figure 1-4   Hard Disk Free Space

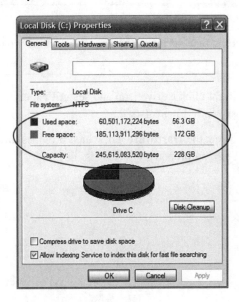

What is the used space of your hard drive in GB?

_____

What is the free space of your hard drive in GB?

_____

Task 4: Check for Other Storage Devices

Step 1.   Right-click the **Start** button and select **Explore**. Select **My Computer** in the left pane, as shown in Figure 1-5.

Figure 1-5   Available Storage Devices

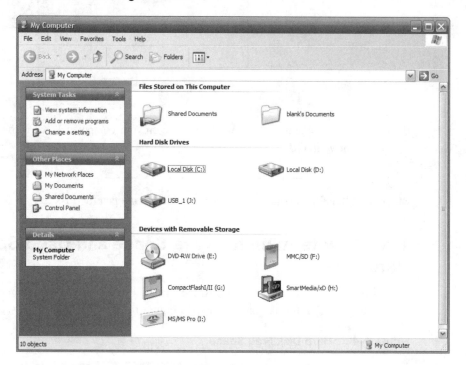

How many drive letters are shown in the window that appears?

_____

Step 2.   Right-click a drive icon and select **Properties**. The Disk Properties window appears, as shown in Figure 1-6.

Step 3.   Select the **Hardware** tab, which provides information about each device and whether it is working properly.

Figure 1-6   Disk Properties

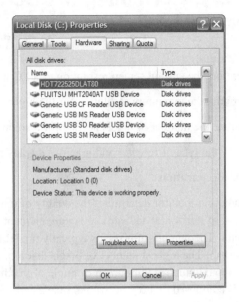

Task 5: Reflection

1. Why is it important to know the amount of RAM in your computer?

    _____

    _____

    _____

    _____

2. Why is it important to know the size of a hard drive as well as the space being used?

    _____

    _____

    _____

    _____

Lab 1-2: Determining the Screen Resolution of a Computer (1.3.3.4)

Objectives

- Determine the current screen resolution of a PC monitor.

- Determine the maximum resolution for the highest color quality.

- Calculate the number of pixels needed for resolution settings.

- Identify the type of monitor and graphics display adapter installed.

Background/Preparation

The resolution of a monitor determines the quality of the screen display. The resolution is determined by the number of horizontal and vertical picture elements (pixels) that are used to produce the image on the monitor. The number of pixels is typically predefined by the manufacturers of graphics cards and PC monitors. The highest number of pixels that a monitor and graphics card can support is referred to as maximum resolution. An example of maximum resolution is 1280 x 1024, which means the display is composed of 1280 horizontal pixels and 1024 vertical pixels. The higher the resolution is set, the sharper the display image. Two factors determine the maximum resolution of a PC monitor and the number of colors the monitor can display:

- Capability of the monitor

- Capability of the graphics card, especially the amount of onboard memory

To perform this lab, you need to use a computer with Windows XP installed.

Task 1: Determine the Current Screen Resolution

Step 1.   To view the current screen resolution and color quality settings, right-click any empty space on the desktop and select **Properties** from the context menu. In the Display Properties window, click the **Settings** tab.

You can also access Display Properties by opening the **Control Panel** and clicking the **Display** icon.

Figure 1-7 shows the Display Properties window.

Step 2.   Use the Display Properties Settings tab to record the current settings on your PC:

The screen resolution is_____

The horizontal resolution is_____

The vertical resolution is _____

The color quality value is _____

Step 3.   Keep the Display Properties Settings dialog box open for Task 2.

Figure 1-7   Windows XP Display Properties

Task 2: Determine the Maximum Resolution for the Highest Color Quality

The slide bar under Screen Resolution is used to configure the desired resolution.

Step 1.   Move the slide bar to see the range of screen resolutions that are available on your PC. (The range is determined by the operating system when it identifies the display adapter and the monitor.)

Step 2.   Use the Display Properties Settings tab to fill out Table 1-1 for the current settings on your PC.

Table 1-1   PC Display Settings

Minimum screen resolution	_____
Maximum screen resolution	_____
Available color quality settings	_____

Task 3: Calculate the Pixels for Current and Maximum Resolution Settings

The display on the screen consists of rows of pixels. The number of pixels in each row is the horizontal resolution. The number of rows is the vertical resolution. To determine the total number of pixels in a screen resolution, you multiply the horizontal resolution by the vertical resolution. For example, if the current resolution is 1280×1024, the total number of pixels is 1280 times 1024, or 1,310,720.

Step 1.   Calculate the total number of pixels for the lowest resolution:

Step 2.   Calculate the total number of pixels for the maximum resolution:

Task 4: Identify the Type of Graphics Card Installed

You can get detailed information about the graphics card (also called the display adapter) in the Display Properties screen.

Step 1.   In the Display Properties screen, click the **Advanced** button.

Step 2.   Select the **Adapter** tab, as shown in Figure 1-8.

Figure 1-8   Windows XP Advanced Adapter Properties

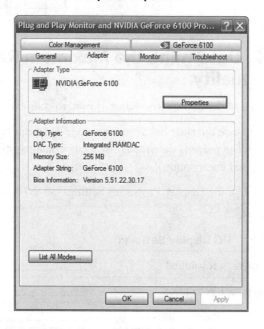

Step 3.   Use the information found in the Adapter tab to complete Table 1-2.

Table 1-2   Graphics Card Information

Graphics card manufacturer and model (Adapter Type)	_____
Graphics memory on card (Memory Size)	_____

Task 5: Identify the Type of Monitor and Available Refresh Rates

You can get detailed information about the monitor in the Display Properties screen. The screen refresh rate determines the number of times per second the screen is illuminated or redrawn. A refresh rate of 60 hertz means the screen is illuminated 60 times per second. Higher refresh rates provide less screen flicker, which reduces eye strain, but may adversely affect the monitor. You should set the refresh rate to the highest level the monitor can safely support.

Step 1. Click the **Monitor** tab to see the monitor type and current refresh rate, as shown in Figure 1-9.

Figure 1-9   Windows XP Monitor Properties

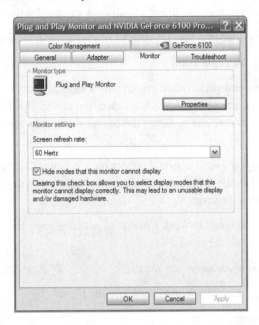

Step 2. Use the information found in the Monitor tab to complete Table 1-3.

Table 1-3   PC Monitor Information

Monitor type	_____
Supported refresh rates	_____

What can occur if you select a refresh rate that is higher than what the monitor can safely display? Do not actually change the refresh rate.

_____

_____

_____

Lab 1-3: Installing a Printer and Verifying Its Operation (1.5.3.4)

Objectives

- Manually install a printer using the default Windows XP driver.
- Verify printer and driver installation and troubleshoot any problems.
- Download and install the most recent driver from the printer manufacturer.

Background/Preparation

Many home and small office printers are Plug-and-Play, which means that Windows XP automatically discovers the printer and installs a functional driver. However, if you know the process for manually installing a printer and updating the printer driver, you have the knowledge to troubleshoot many types of printer problems.

In this lab, you install a virtual printer on a Windows XP workstation. You also compare the features available with the Windows default printer driver with those available with the latest driver available from the manufacturer.

This lab is designed to work without an actual printer, but most steps are exactly the same for connecting a physical printer.

The following resources are required:

- Computer with Window XP installed
- Internet connection

Task 1: Add a Printer

Step 1.   From the Start menu, select **Control Panel**. If working in Classic view, select **Settings** and then **Control Panel**. Double-click the **Printers and Faxes** icon. If this icon is not shown, click **Switch to Classic View** in the left pane.

Step 2.   In the Printers and Faxes window, click the **Add Printer** icon to open the Add Printer Wizard, shown in Figure 1-10. Click **Next**.

Figure 1-10   Windows Add Printer Wizard

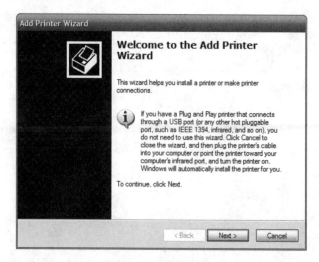

Step 3.   In the Local or Network Printer window shown in Figure 1-11, click the **Local printer attached to this computer** radio button and uncheck **Automatically detect and install my Plug and Play printer**. Click **Next**.

Figure 1-11   Windows Local or Network Printer Selection

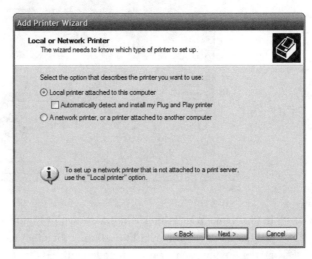

Step 4.   In the Select a Printer Port window shown in Figure 1-12, click the **Use the following port** radio button and choose **LPT1: (Recommended Printer Port)**. Click **Next**.

Figure 1-12   Windows Printer Port Selection

Step 5.   Note: In this step, you choose a driver provided by Windows XP for an HP LaserJet 2200, a common home or small office, black-and-white laser printer. You do not have to physically have the printer to do these steps. However, if you are installing a printer that is actually attached to your computer, choose the manufacturer and printer model corresponding to your printer instead of the HP LaserJet 2200.

In the Install Printer Software window shown in Figure 1-13, select **HP** from the Manufacturer list. In the Printers list, locate HP LaserJet 2200 Series PCL and click to select it. Click **Next**.

Figure 1-13   Selecting a Printer to Install

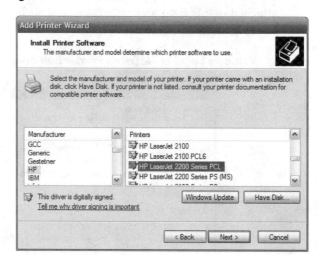

Step 6.   In the Name Your Printer window shown in Figure 1-14, choose a descriptive name for the printer. In an environment like a large office that has several printers of the same make and model, giving each printer a unique name so that it can easily be identified is helpful. Click **No** under Do You Want to Use This Printer as the Default Printer? (If you are connecting an actual printer, click **Yes** if you want Windows applications to use this printer by default.) Click **Next**.

Figure 1-14   Entering a Printer Name

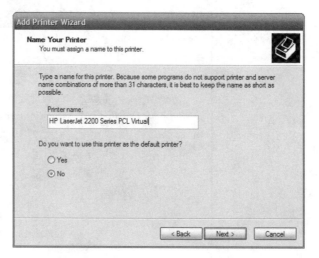

Step 7.   In the Printer Sharing window, click **Next** to accept the default option to not share this printer.

Step 8.   If you are actually installing a printer, click **Next** in the Print Test Page window to print a test page. If you are installing a virtual HP LaserJet 2200, click the **No** radio button before clicking **Next**.

Step 9.   In the Completing the Add Printer Wizard window shown in Figure 1-15, review the printer settings and then click **Finish**.

Figure 1-15   Completing the Add Printer Wizard

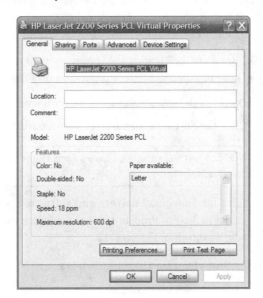

Task 2: Verify the Printer Installation

Step 1.   Select **Printers and Faxes** in the Control Panel and check to see that the printer you installed and named is shown. If it is not shown, repeat Task 1.

Step 2.   Right-click the icon for the new printer (HPLJ 2200 Series PCL Virtual) and then click **Properties**. The dialog box shown in Figure 1-16 opens.

Figure 1-16   Viewing Printer Properties

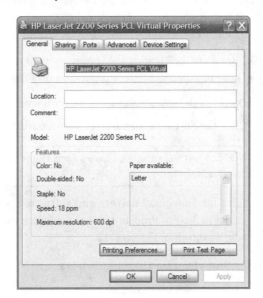

Step 3.   Click the **Advanced** tab and record the name of the driver shown in the Driver text box.

_____

Step 4.   Click the **Device Settings** tab and examine the available options for the printer using this driver, as shown in Figure 1-17. To close the window, click **Cancel**.

Figure 1-17   Printer Device Settings

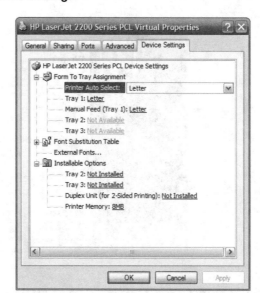

Task 3: Download and Install an Updated Printer Driver

When you use the Add Printer Wizard to manually install a printer, the driver that is installed by default allows the device to function, but the Windows-installed driver does not always allow all features of the device to be used. The most full-featured drivers are usually those provided by the device manufacturer.

Updating a printer driver is one of the best ways to troubleshoot problems and to increase printer functionality. Most manufacturers continue to update drivers to improve compatibility with operating systems, so periodically checking for driver updates and installing them if they are available is a good idea.

In this Task, you go to the Hewlett-Packard website to obtain an updated driver for the HP LaserJet 2200. If you have installed a different printer, modify these instructions as needed.

Step 1.   Open a web browser and go to **http://www.hp.com**.

Step 2.   Click the **Software and Driver Downloads** link.

> **NOTE:** Many manufacturers have a support link on their home page that leads to drivers and other downloads.

Step 3.   Click the **Download drivers and software (and firmware)** radio button. Enter the printer model in the For Product text box and click the double-arrow link to the right of the text box, as shown in Figure 1-18.

Figure 1-18   Searching for Updated Drivers

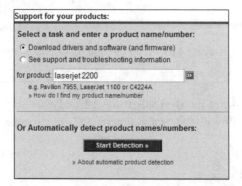

Step 4. The search displays the available products, as shown in Figure 1-19. Click **HP LaserJet 2200 Printer** or the model of the printer for which you are downloading a driver.

Figure 1-19   Selecting the Correct Printer

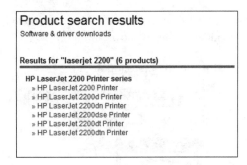

Step 5. Click **Microsoft Windows XP** in the list of operating systems. In the list of drivers shown, click **Download** for the HP LaserJet 2200 PCL6 driver option shown in Figure 1-20.

Figure 1-20   Downloading an Updated Driver

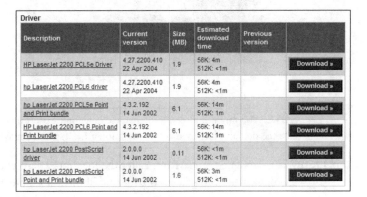

Step 6. In the download dialog box shown in Figure 1-21, click **Save.**

Figure 1-21   Saving the Updated Driver

Step 7. In the Save As dialog box, click the **Desktop** icon in the left pane to save the driver installation file to your desktop. You can save the file anywhere, but it is important that you know where you have saved it.

Step 8.   Write the name of the file:

_____

Step 9.   Click the **Save** button. Close the browser and any other open applications.

Step 10.   Navigate to the location where you downloaded the driver. Double-click the icon for the downloaded file, as shown in Figure 1-22.

Figure 1-22   Starting the Installation

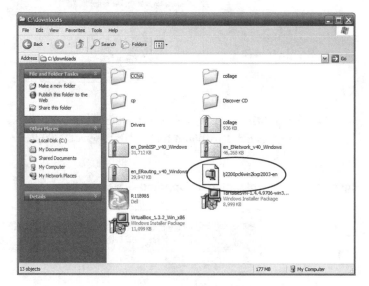

NOTE: You might not see the filename extension (.exe). File extensions are visible only if you disable the default **Hide extensions for known file types** from Windows Explorer.

Step 11.   When prompted, click **Run**. Enter the location where you want the files to be extracted to and click **Unzip** to unpack the files, as shown in Figure 1-23. If you selected the default location, the files are now stored in c:\lj2200. Click **Close** to finish the WinZip self-extractor.

Figure 1-23   Extracting and Saving the Installation Files

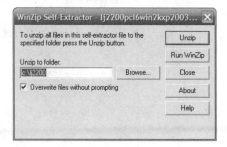

Step 12.   Repeat Task 2, Steps 1 and 2, to open the Properties page of the new printer. Click the **Advanced** tab. Click the **New Driver** button and then click **Next** to begin the Add Printer Driver Wizard.

Step 13.   Click **Have Disk** in the Printer Driver Selection window shown in Figure 1-24.

Figure 1-24   Selecting the Printer to Install

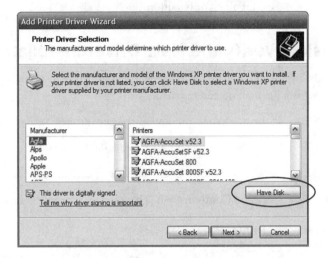

Step 14.   In the Install From Disk window shown in Figure 1-25, click **Browse** and locate the folder created earlier in this task by navigating to **My Computer > Local Disk(C:) > lj2200**. Click **Open**, and you return to the **Install From Disk** window. Click **OK**.

Figure 1-25   Installing the Printer

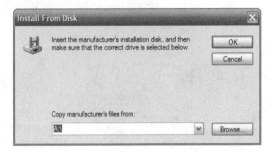

Step 15.   In the Printer Driver Selection window shown in Figure 1-26, select **HP LaserJet 2200 Series PCL 6** and then click **Next**. Click **Finish** in the window that follows.

Figure 1-26   Selecting the Printer Model

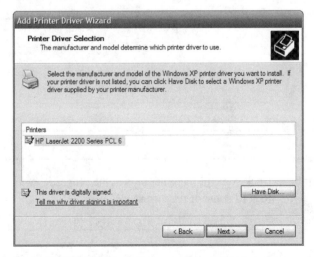

Step 16.   When the process is finished, return to the properties window of the printer (refer to Task 2), click the **Apply** button, and then click **OK**.

Task 4: Verify the New Driver Installation

In this Task, you compare the Windows default driver installed in the first Task to the newly installed driver from the manufacturer website.

Step 1.   In the properties window of the new printer, verify that the Apply button is dimmed.

Step 2.   Click the **Advanced** tab. What is the name of the driver?

_____

Step 3.   Click the **Configure** tab. The window for the HP LaserJet 2200 is shown in Figure 1-27.

Figure 1-27   Printer Properties

Step 4.   Compare the Configure tab to the Device Settings tab in Step 4 of Task 2. What are the differences?

_____

_____

_____

_____

_____

_____

_____

Step 5.   Click some of the other tabs in the properties window to compare the new and old drivers. Record some of the differences here.

_____

_____

CHAPTER 2

Labs: Operating Systems

The lab exercises included in this chapter include the Chapter 2 online curriculum lab and a challenge lab to ensure that you have mastered the practical, hands-on skills needed to determine the OS and application version and potential for an OS upgrade. As you work through these labs, use Chapter 2 in Part I of this book or use the corresponding Chapter 2 in the Networking for Home and Small Businesses course of the CCNA Discovery online curriculum for assistance.

 ## Lab 2-1: Examining Operating System and Application Versions (2.3.3.2)

Objectives

- Determine the operating system (OS) version and revision.
- Examine the method used for configuring Windows XP updates.
- Determine the revision number of a particular application.

Background/Preparation

Keeping operating systems and applications up to date to ensure stable operation and to address security vulnerabilities is important. These updates are called revisions, updates, patches, or hot fixes. The three ways to update the Windows XP operating system are automatic updating, downloading patches automatically and manually determining when they are installed, or manually downloading and installing the patches.

This lab can be done individually, in pairs, or in teams. To perform this lab, you need to use a computer with Windows XP and an application such as Microsoft Word installed.

Task 1: Determine the Windows XP Version and Revision Number

Step 1. Click **Start > All Programs > Accessories > Windows Explorer**. Alternatively, right-click **Start** and select **Explore**.

Step 2. From the **Help** menu, choose **About Windows**.

Which version of Windows XP and service pack is installed on your computer?

_____

How much physical memory (RAM) is available to Windows XP?

_____

Why is memory important to an operating system?

_____

_____

_____

_____

Step 3.   Click the **End-User License Agreement** link on the About Windows screen. According to the license agreement, how many backup copies of Windows XP can you legally make?

_____

Step 4.   According to the license agreement, what is the maximum number of devices you can connect to this workstation to use file or print services?

_____

Step 5.   Close the end-user license agreement window. Close the About Windows window.

Task 2: Configure Windows XP for Updates

Step 1.   Click the **Start** button and select the **Control Panel** option. If using the Classic Start menu, choose **Start > Settings > Control Panel**.

Step 2.   If the right window pane shows Pick a Category, select the **Switch to Classic View** link in the left pane. Double-click the **Automatic Updates** icon.

Which four options are available for automatic updates?

_____

_____

Step 3.   Click the **How Does Automatic Updates Work?** link. Expand the **How Are Updates Downloaded**? section by clicking the **+** (plus sign) beside the option.

Based on the information presented, what happens if you are using your computer, updates are being downloaded, and you disconnect from the Internet?

_____

Step 4.   Expand the **How Are Updates Installed?** section. Based on the output shown, what is the default time for when updates are installed?

_____

Step 5.   Close the **How Does Automatic Updates Work?** window and return to the Automatic Updates window.

What is the current setting for automatic updates, and why do you think the person who set up the computer chose this option?

_____

_____

_____

Step 6.   Close the **Automatic Updates** window.

Step 7.   Another way of configuring a system for automatic updates is through the System icon in Control Panel. Click the **Start > Control Panel**, and double-click the **System** icon. The System Properties window opens. Click the **Automatic Updates** tab.

Are the options the same as before?

_____

Step 8.   Close the **System Properties** window.

Task 3: Determine an Application Version

Step 1.   Open any Windows-based application such as Microsoft Word.

Step 2.   From the application **Help** menu option, choose the **About** option.

What is the application version?

_____

Step 3.   If this is a Microsoft application, you might see a **System Info** button. If there is a button, click it. If there is no button, skip to the next step. Explore the different options available under System Info, including information related to your specific application. System Info provides similar information to that provided by winmsd.exe.

Step 4.   Click the **Help** menu again. If there are double down arrows at the bottom of the menu, click them to show all the menu options. Some applications have a Check for Updates option. Does the application have this option?

_____

Do you think that Internet access is required for an application that has a Check for Updates option? Why or why not?

_____

_____

_____

Step 5.   Close the application.

Task 4: Reflection

When is it important to get an update for an application or an operating system?

_____

_____

_____

List one instance when you might need to know which version of the operating system or application is being used.

_____

_____

Challenge Lab 2-2: Evaluating an OS Upgrade

Objectives

- Inspect the hardware installed in a computer using the Control Panel and the winmsd.exe utility.
- Determine whether a computer can accommodate a specific OS.

Background/Preparation

As an OS evolves, it typically requires additional system resources to support new capabilities and features. In this lab, you use the Microsoft website to look up the minimum requirements of the Windows Vista Home Basic edition. You also evaluate the existing hardware of a Windows XP computer and determine whether it can support an upgrade to Windows Vista.

The minimum requirements address CPU type and speed, the amount of RAM and hard disk space needed, graphics capabilities, and other items. The minimum hardware requirements for an OS allow the system to boot and function and are not necessarily the recommended requirements. Ensuring that the system on which the OS is to be installed or upgraded has resources over the minimum for it to perform at a level that is satisfactory to the end user is important.

Regardless of the hardware platform, not all existing Microsoft OSs can be upgraded to Windows Vista. Some, such as Windows 2000, require a clean install. In this case, all data must be backed up, and applications must be reinstalled after the new OS is installed. For a list of the Windows versions that can be upgraded to Windows Vista, go to http://www.microsoft.com/windows/products/windowsvista/buyorupgrade/upgradepaths.mspx.

To perform this lab, you need a computer with Windows XP installed, access to the command prompt, and Internet connectivity.

Task 1: Locate Minimum Requirements for Windows Vista

Step 1.   Open a web browser and go to http://www.microsoft.com.

In the search text box, which words do you think would give you the best result if you are searching for the requirements for installing Windows Vista?

_____

_____

Step 2.   Locate the link that describes the specific minimum hardware requirements to install Windows Vista Home Basic edition.

_____

NOTE: The requirements for Windows Vista Home Basic edition are significantly less than those for Windows Vista Home Premium, Windows Vista Business, Windows Vista Enterprise, and Windows Vista Ultimate. You might want to use the requirements for these other versions as your minimum requirements.

List the minimum hardware requirements: _____

Processor type/speed (in MHz): _____

System memory (RAM): _____

Graphics card: _____

Graphics memory: _____

Hard disk size: _____

Hard disk free space: _____

Optical drive:_____

Task 2: Determine the Hardware Information for the Computer Using winmsd.exe

One way to determine system information is with the winmsd.exe utility. You must have access to the **run** command to use it. Winmsd is an abbreviation for Windows Microsoft Diagnostics. The utility provides a considerable amount of information, but it is not always easy to interpret. Microsoft support personnel use winmsd to diagnose problems with the Windows OS because it centralizes all system information.

Step 1.   Click **Start > Run**.

Step 2.   Type **winmsd.exe** in the **Open** box, and then click **OK**.

Step 3.   In the System Information window, compare your computer against the minimum hardware requirements for Windows Vista Home Basic edition or one of the other Vista editions.

Task 3: Determine CPU Type and Amount of RAM Using System Properties

Another way to determine system information is to use the individual Windows GUI utilities, such as the System Properties window.

Click **Start > Control Panel**, and double-click the **System** icon.

In the System Properties dialog box, OS and service pack information are listed in the upper part of the General tab. The computer processor type, speed, and memory are listed in the lower portion.

How much RAM does your computer contain? Does it meet the minimum requirements for Windows Vista?

Check the processor. Does it meet the minimum requirements for Windows Vista?

Task 4: Determine Hard Disk Capacity and Amount of Free Disk Space Using My Computer Properties

Step 1.   Double-click the **My Computer** icon on your computer desktop. If there is no **My Computer** icon, click **Start > My Computer**.

Step 2.   Right-click the local disk drive under the Hard Disk Drives section (usually the C drive) and select **Properties**. In the General tab, Capacity lists the total capacity of the hard drive.

What is the total size in GB of the hard drive on your computer?

Will the hard disk capacity meet the minimum requirements to install Windows Vista?

In the Local Disk Properties dialog box, the used and free space is shown in both bytes and GB above Capacity.

What is the used space of your hard drive in GB?

_____

What is the free space of your hard drive in GB?

_____

Will the amount of space available meet the minimum requirements to install Windows Vista?

_____

Task 5: Check for Other Drives (Floppy, CD-ROM, DVD)

Right-click the **Start** button and select **Explore**. Click the + (plus sign) to expand the **My Computer** folder and – (minus sign) to contract the **Local Disk (C:)** folder if necessary to see the drive letters and icons more easily.

How many drive letters are shown in the window that appears?

_____

_____

Does the computer have a DVD-ROM drive?

_____

Task 6: Verify the Monitor and Graphics Capabilities

Step 1.   Click **Start > Control Panel** and double-click the **Display** icon.

Step 2.   Click the **Settings** tab in the Display Properties dialog box.

Step 3.   Examine the information for Screen Resolution to see whether the resolution of at least 800 x 600 is an option. If so, this meets SVGA standards. Does the monitor meet the minimum requirements to install Windows Vista?

_____

Task 7: Download and Run Windows Vista Upgrade Advisor

Step 1.   If your current OS is Windows XP with Service Pack 2, you can use the Windows Vista Upgrade Advisor to help you to determine whether you can run Windows Vista and which editions can be supported. To download and run the Upgrade Advisor, go to the Microsoft website at the following URL. When the download is complete, run the installation program and allow the program icon to be placed on your desktop.

http://www.microsoft.com/windows/products/windowsvista/buyorupgrade/upgradeadvisor.mspx

Step 2.   Click **Run** when the installation is complete or click the icon on the desktop to start the application. Click **Start Scan** to check your computer system for Windows Vista compatibility.

Step 3.   When the scan is complete, click the **See Details** button and then click the version of Windows Vista you are considering installing. The Upgrade Advisor program examines three categories: System Requirements, Devices, and Programs. Click the **Details** button for each of these categories to see the issues identified.

Task 8: Reflection

Why is it important to verify that the hardware meets the minimum requirements of the operating system *before* you try to install a new version?

_____

_____

_____

_____

_____

_____

CHAPTER 3

Labs: Connecting to the Network

The lab exercises included in this chapter cover all the Chapter 3 online curriculum labs to ensure that you have mastered the practical, hands-on skills needed to build a simple network, examine network addressing, and share resources. As you work through these labs, use Chapter 3 in Part I of this book or use the corresponding Chapter 3 in the Networking for Home and Small Businesses course of the CCNA Discovery online curriculum for assistance.

 ## Lab 3-1: Building a Peer-to-Peer Network (3.1.5.3)

Objectives

- Design and build a simple peer-to-peer network using a crossover cable supplied by the instructor.
- Verify connectivity between the peers using the **ping** command.

Background/Preparation

In this hands-on lab, you plan and build a simple peer-to-peer network using two PCs and an Ethernet crossover cable.

The following resources are required:

- Two Windows XP Professional PCs, each with an installed and functional network interface card (NIC)
- An Ethernet crossover cable

Task 1: Diagram the Network

Step 1. A network diagram is a map of the logical topology of the network. In the following space, sketch a simple peer-to-peer network connecting two PCs. Label one PC with IP address 192.168.1.1 and the other PC with IP address 192.168.1.2. Use labels to indicate connecting media and any necessary network devices.

Step 2. A simple network like the one you designed can use a hub or switch as a central connecting device, or the PCs can be directly connected. Which type of cable is required for a direct Ethernet connection between the two PCs?

_____

_____

_____

_____

Task 2: Document the PCs

Step 1.   Check the computer name settings for each PC and make adjustments as necessary. For each PC, click **Start > Control Panel.** Double-click the **System** icon, and then click the **Computer Name** tab, as shown in Figure 3-1. Alternatively, right-click **My Computer** and click **Properties**. In Table 3-1, write down the computer name that is displayed following Full Computer Name.

Figure 3-1   Computer Name in Windows XP

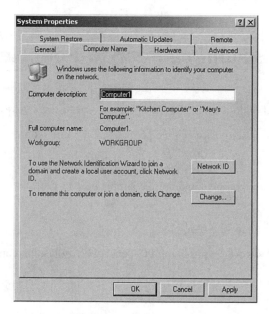

Table 3-1   Computer Names

Computer	Computer Name
PC1	
PC2	

Step 2.   Check to see whether the two PCs have the same name. If they do, change the name of one PC by clicking the **Change** button, typing a new name in the **Computer name** field, and then clicking **OK**.

Step 3.   Click **OK** to close the System Properties window.

Why is it important that each PC on a network have a unique name?

_____

_____

_____

_____

Task 3: Connect the Ethernet Cable

Step 1. Use the Ethernet crossover cable provided by the instructor. Plug one end of the cable into the Ethernet NIC of PC1.

Step 2. Plug the other end of the cable into the Ethernet NIC of PC2. As you insert the cable, you should hear a click, which indicates that the cable connector is properly inserted into the port. If you do not hear or feel a click, pull lightly on the cable. If it comes out too easily, the clip might need to be carefully bent slightly outward to provide resistance so that it will not come out of the port on the NIC. If the clip is broken off, the cable should be replaced.

Task 4: Verify Physical Connectivity

Step 1. After the Ethernet crossover cable is connected to both PCs, take a close look at each Ethernet port. A light (usually green or amber) indicates that physical connectivity has been established between the two NICs. Try unplugging the cable from one PC and then reconnecting it to verify that the light goes off then back on.

Step 2. Click **Start > Control Panel**, double-click the **Network Connections** icon, and confirm that the local area connection is established. If physical connectivity problems exist, you will see a red X over the Local Area Connection icon with the words "Network cable unplugged."

Step 3. If the local area connection does not indicate that it is connected, troubleshoot by repeating Tasks 3 and 4. You might also want to ask your instructor to confirm that you are using an Ethernet crossover cable.

Task 5: Configure IP Settings

Step 1. Configure the logical addresses for the two PCs so that they are able to communicate using TCP/IP. On one of the PCs, click **Start > Control Panel**, double-click the **Network Connections** icon, and then right-click the connected **Local Area Connection** icon. Choose **Properties** from the drop-down menu.

Step 2. Using the scroll bar in the Local Area Connection Properties window, scroll down to highlight **Internet Protocol (TCP/IP)**. Click the **Properties** button to open the window shown in Figure 3-2.

Step 3. Select the **Use the following IP address** radio button and enter the following information for PC1:

IP Address: **192.168.1.1**

Subnet Mask: **255.255.255.0**

Step 4. Click **OK**, which closes the Internet Protocol (TCP/IP) Properties window. Click the **Close** button to exit the Local Area Connection Properties window.

Step 5. Repeat Steps 1–4 for PC2 using the following information:

IP Address: **192.168.1.2**

Subnet Mask: **255.255.255.0**

Figure 3-2   Windows XP TCP/IP Properties

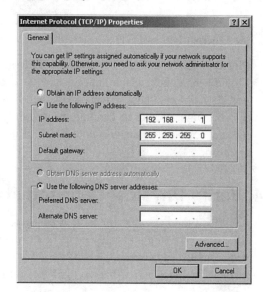

Task 6: Verify IP Connectivity Between the Two PCs

To test TCP/IP connectivity between the PCs, you must disable Windows Firewall temporarily on both PCs. Be sure to re-enable Windows Firewall after you complete the tests.

Step 1.   On PC1, on the Windows XP desktop, click **Start > Control Panel**, and double-click **Network Connections**.

Step 2.   Right-click the **Local Area Connection** icon and select **Properties**. Click the **Advanced** tab. Locate and click the **Settings** button.

Step 3.   Make a note of whether the firewall settings are Enabled (On) for the Ethernet port or Disabled (Off) for the Ethernet port.

Step 4.   If the firewall settings are enabled, click the **Off (not recommended)** radio button to disable the firewall. You will re-enable the setting in a later Task. Click **OK** in this dialog box and the following one to apply this setting.

Step 5.   Now that the two PCs are physically connected and configured correctly with IP addresses, you need to make sure they communicate with each other. The **ping** command is a simple way to accomplish this task. The **ping** command is included with the Windows XP operating system.

Step 6.   Repeat Steps 1–4 on the second PC. The second PC will **ping** 192.168.1.1.

Step 7.   On PC1, click **Start > Run**. Enter **cmd**, and then click **OK**. A Windows command prompt window appears.

Step 8.   At the prompt, enter **ping 192.168.1.2** and press **Enter**. A successful **ping** will verify the IP connectivity. It should produce results similar to those shown in Example 3-1.

Example 3-1:   Successful ping Output
```
C:\>ping 192.168.1.2

Pinging 192.168.1.2 with 32 bytes of data:

Reply from 192.168.1.2: bytes=32 time<1ms TTL=64
Reply from 192.168.1.2: bytes=32 time<1ms TTL=64
Reply from 192.168.1.2: bytes=32 time<1ms TTL=64
Reply from 192.168.1.2: bytes=32 time<1ms TTL=64

Ping statistics for 192.168.1.2:
    Packets: Sent = 4, Received = 4, Lost = 0 (0% loss),
Approximate round trip times in milli-seconds:
    Minimum = 0ms, Maximum = 0ms, Average = 0ms
```

Step 9.   Close the **Windows command prompt** window on both PCs.

Task 7: Verify Connectivity Using My Network Places

Step 1.   A PC can share its resources with other PCs on the network. PCs with shared resources should be visible through My Network Places. On PC1, click **Start > My Network Places** and then click **View workgroup computers** in the left panel.

Do you see an icon for the other PC in your peer-to-peer network?

_____

What is the name of the other PC?

_____

Is it the same name you recorded in Task 2?

_____

Step 2.   Repeat Step 1 on the second PC.

Step 3.   Close any open windows.

Task 8: (Optional) Re-enable the Firewall

Perform this task only if the firewall was originally enabled.

Step 1.   If you disabled Windows Firewall in Task 6, click **Start > Control Panel**, and open the **Network Connections** control panel.

Step 2.   Right-click the Ethernet network connection icon and select **Properties**. Click the **Advanced** tab. Locate and click **Settings**.

Step 3.   If the firewall settings are disabled (and they were enabled before this lab began), click the **On** radio button to enable the firewall. Click **OK** in this dialog box and the following one to apply this setting.

Lab 3-2: Determine the MAC Address of a Host (3.3.3.2)

Objective

- Determine the MAC address of a Windows XP computer on an Ethernet network using the **ipconfig /all** command.

Background/Preparation

Every computer on an Ethernet local network has a Media Access Control (MAC) address that is burned into the NIC. Computer MAC addresses are usually displayed as six sets of two hexadecimal numbers separated by dashes or colons (for example, 15-EF-A3-45-9B-57). The **ipconfig /all** command displays the computer MAC address. You may work individually or in teams.

The following resources are required:

- Windows XP workstation with at least one Ethernet NIC.

- Access to the **Run** command.

Task 1: Open a Windows Command Prompt Window

Step 1.   From the Windows XP desktop, click **Start > Run.**

Step 2.   Enter **cmd** in the Run dialog box then click **OK**.

Task 2: Use the ipconfig /all Command

Enter the **ipconfig /all** command at the command prompt and press **Enter**. (Typical results are shown in Example 3-2, but your computer will display different information.)

Example 3-2   ipconfig /all Command Output
```
C:\>ipconfig /all


Windows IP Configuration


        Host Name . . . . . . . . . . . . : Computer1
        Primary Dns Suffix  . . . . . . . :
        Node Type . . . . . . . . . . . . : Hybrid
        IP Routing Enabled. . . . . . . . : No
        WINS Proxy Enabled. . . . . . . . : No
        DNS Suffix Search List. . . . . . : cisco.com


Ethernet adapter Local Area Connection:


        Connection-specific DNS Suffix  . : cisco.com
        Description . . . . . . . . . . . : Intel(R) PRO/100 VE Network Connection
        Physical Address. . . . . . . . . : 00-07-E9-63-CE-53
        Dhcp Enabled. . . . . . . . . . . : Yes
        Autoconfiguration Enabled . . . . : Yes
        IP Address. . . . . . . . . . . . : 192.168.1.103
```

```
Subnet Mask . . . . . . . . . . : 255.255.255.0

Default Gateway . . . . . . . . : 192.168.1.1

DHCP Server . . . . . . . . . . : 192.168.1.1

DNS Servers . . . . . . . . . . : 172.16.7.3

                                  172.16.7.6

Lease Obtained. . . . . . . . . : Tuesday, September 25, 2007 1:40:58 PM

Lease Expires . . . . . . . . . : Wednesday, September 26, 2007 1:40:58 PM
```

Task 3: Locate the MAC (Physical) Address(es) in the Output from the ipconfig /all Command

Use Table 3-2 to fill in the description of the Ethernet adapter and the physical (MAC) address.

Table 3-2   Ethernet MAC Address(es)

Description	Physical Address
Example: VIA Rhine II Fast Ethernet Adapter	Example: 00-50-2C-A5-F5-73

Task 4: Reflection

Why might a computer have more than one MAC address?

The sample output from the **ipconfig /all** command shown previously in Example 3-2 had only one MAC address. Suppose that the output was from a computer that also had wireless Ethernet capability. How might the output change?

Try disconnecting the cable(s) to your network adapter(s) and use the **ipconfig /all** command again. What changes do you see? Does the MAC address still display? Will the MAC address ever change?

What are other names for the MAC address?

Lab 3-3: Determine the IP Address of a Computer (3.3.6.2)

Objective

- Use the **ipconfig /all** command to determine the IP address of a Windows XP host on an Ethernet network.

Background/Preparation

Every computer connected to the Internet has a unique identifier, called an IP address. IP addresses are displayed as four numbers, known as octets, separated by periods (for example, 192.168.1.4). The **ipconfig /all** command displays your computer's IP address and information about the network. The following resources are required:

- A workstation that is attached to the local network and that has its IP address already configured
- Access to the **Run** command

In this lab you locate your computer's IP address to discover its unique number.

Task 1: Determine the IP Address of the Computer

Step 1.   From the Windows XP desktop, click **Start > Run**.

Step 2.   In the Run dialog box, enter **cmd** then click the **OK** button.

Step 3.   At the command prompt, enter **ipconfig /all** and press **Enter**.

The **ipconfig /all** command then displays a list of information about your computer's IP configuration, as shown in Example 3-3. The information displayed for your computer will be different.

Example 3-3   Sample ipconfig /all Output

```
C:\>ipconfig /all


Windows IP Configuration


        Host Name . . . . . . . . . . . . : Computer1

        Primary Dns Suffix  . . . . . . . :

        Node Type . . . . . . . . . . . . : Hybrid

        IP Routing Enabled. . . . . . . . : No

        WINS Proxy Enabled. . . . . . . . : No

        DNS Suffix Search List. . . . . . : cisco.com


Ethernet adapter Local Area Connection:


        Connection-specific DNS Suffix  . : cisco.com

        Description . . . . . . . . . . . : Intel(R) PRO/100 VE Network Connection

        Physical Address. . . . . . . . . : 00-07-E9-63-CE-53

        Dhcp Enabled. . . . . . . . . . . : Yes

        Autoconfiguration Enabled . . . . : Yes
```

```
IP Address. . . . . . . . . . . : 192.168.1.103
Subnet Mask . . . . . . . . . . : 255.255.255.0
Default Gateway . . . . . . . . : 192.168.1.1
DHCP Server . . . . . . . . . . : 192.168.1.1
DNS Servers . . . . . . . . . . : 172.16.7.3
                                  172.16.7.6
Lease Obtained. . . . . . . . . : Tuesday, September 25, 2007 1:40:58 PM
Lease Expires . . . . . . . . . : Wednesday, September 26, 2007 1:40:58 PM
```

Step 4.   Locate the IP address and record the finding.

IP address _____

Why is it important that a computer get an IP address?

_____

_____

Lab 3-4: IP Addresses and Network Communication (3.5.2.2)

Figure 3-3   A Simple Peer-to-Peer Network

Objectives

- Build a simple peer-to-peer network and verify physical connectivity.

- Assign various IP addresses to hosts and observe the effects on network communication.

Background/Preparation

In this lab, you build a simple peer-to-peer network using two PCs and an Ethernet crossover cable. You also assign various compatible and non-compatible IP addresses to the hosts and determine the effects on their capability to communicate.

NOTE: You may use the small peer-to-peer network that was built in Lab 3-1.

The following resources are required:

- Two Windows XP Professional PCs, each with an installed and functional NIC

- An Ethernet crossover cable to connect the PCs (provided by instructor)

- (Optional lab setup) A hub or switch and two straight-through cables to connect the PCs (provided by instructor)

Task 1: Connect the PCs to Create a Peer-to-Peer Network

Step 1.   Obtain an Ethernet crossover cable provided by the instructor to connect the two PCs.

NOTE: (Optional lab setup.) The PCs may be connected to a hub (or switch) using two straight-through cables. The following instructions assume you are using a crossover cable.

Step 2.   Plug one end of the cable into the Ethernet NIC of PC1. Plug the other end of the cable into the Ethernet NIC of PC2. As you insert the cable, you should hear a click, which indicates that the cable connector is properly inserted into the port.

Task 2: Verify Physical Connectivity

Step 1.   After the Ethernet crossover cable is connected to both PCs, take a close look at each Ethernet port. A link light (usually green or amber) indicates that physical connectivity has been established between the two NICs. Try unplugging the cable from one PC and then reconnecting it to verify that the light goes off then back on.

Step 2.   Click **Start > Control Panel**, double-click the **Network Connections** icon, and confirm that the local area connection is established. If physical connectivity problems exist, you will see a red X over the Local Area Connection icon with the words "Network cable unplugged."

Step 3. If the local area connection does not indicate that it is connected, troubleshoot by repeating Tasks 1 and 2. You might also want to ask your instructor to confirm that you are using an Ethernet crossover cable.

Task 3: Configure IP Settings for the Two PCs

Step 1. Configure the logical IP addresses for the two PCs so that they are able to communicate using TCP/IP. On PC1, go to the **Control Panel**, double-click the **Network Connections** icon, and then right-click the connected **Local Area Connection** icon. Choose **Properties** from the drop-down menu.

Step 2. Using the scroll bar in the Local Area Connection Properties window, scroll down to highlight **Internet Protocol (TCP/IP)**. Click the **Properties** button.

Step 3. Select the **Use the following IP address** radio button and enter an IP address of **192.168.1.1** and a subnet mask of **255.255.255.0**, as shown in Figure 3-4. With this IP address and subnet mask, the network number the host is on is 192.168.1.0 and 192.168.1.1 is the first host on the 192.168.1.0 network.

Figure 3-4   Internet Protocol Properties for PC1

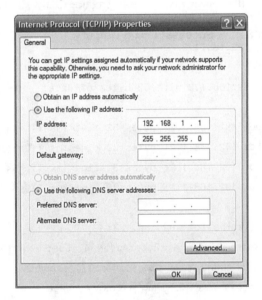

Step 4. Click **OK**, which closes the Internet Protocol (TCP/IP) Properties window. Click the **Close** button to exit the Local Area Connection Properties window.

Step 5. Repeat Steps 1–4 for PC2 using an IP address of 192.168.1.2 and a subnet mask of 255.255.255.0. The network number this PC is on is 192.168.1.0, and 192.168.1.2 is the second host on the 192.168.1.0 network.

Task 4: Verify IP Connectivity Between the Two PCs

To test TCP/IP connectivity between the PCs, you must temporarily disable Windows Firewall on both PCs. Windows Firewall should be re-enabled after the tests have been completed.

Step 1. On each PC, on the Windows XP desktop, click **Start > Control Panel** and double-click **Network Connections**.

Step 2. Right-click the **Local Area Connection** icon and select **Properties**. Click the **Advanced** tab. Locate and click the **Settings** button.

Step 3. Make a note of whether the firewall settings are Enabled (On) for the Ethernet port or Disabled (Off) for the Ethernet port.

Step 4. If the firewall settings are enabled, click the **Off (not recommended)** radio button to disable the firewall. The setting will be re-enabled in a later Task. Click **OK** in this dialog box and the following one to apply this setting. Repeat Steps 1–4 on the second PC.

Step 5. Now that the two PCs are physically connected and configured correctly with IP addresses, you need to make sure they communicate with each other. The **ping** command is a simple way to accomplish this task. The **ping** command is included with the Windows XP operating system.

Step 6. Repeat this procedure for PC2.

Step 7. On PC1, click **Start > Run**. Enter **cmd**, and then click **OK**.

Step 8. At the prompt, enter **ping 192.168.1.2** and press **Enter**. A successful **ping** will verify the IP connectivity. It should produce results similar to those shown in Example 3-4.

Example 3-4   Successful ping Output
```
C:\>ping 192.168.1.2

Pinging 192.168.1.2 with 32 bytes of data:

Reply from 192.168.1.2: bytes=32 time<1ms TTL=64
Reply from 192.168.1.2: bytes=32 time<1ms TTL=64
Reply from 192.168.1.2: bytes=32 time<1ms TTL=64
Reply from 192.168.1.2: bytes=32 time<1ms TTL=64

Ping statistics for 192.168.1.2:
    Packets: Sent = 4, Received = 4, Lost = 0 (0% loss),
Approximate round trip times in milli-seconds:
    Minimum = 0ms, Maximum = 0ms, Average = 0ms
```

Step 9. Close the **Windows command prompt** window on both PCs.

Task 5: Change IP Address for PC2

Step 1. On PC2, click **Start > Control Panel**, double-click the **Network Connections** icon, and then right-click the connected **Local Area Connection** icon. Choose **Properties** from the drop-down menu.

Step 2. Using the scroll bar in the Local Area Connection Properties window, scroll down to highlight **Internet Protocol (TCP/IP)**. Click the **Properties** button.

Step 3. Change the logical IP address for PC2 from 192.168.1.2 to **192.168.2.2** and leave the subnet mask set to 255.255.255.0. On what network is PC2 now?

_____

Step 4. Click **OK**, which closes the Internet Protocol (TCP/IP) Properties window. Click the **Close** button to exit the Local Area Connection Properties window.

Step 5. Refer back to Task 3. On what network is PC1?

_____

The two PCs are still on the same physical Ethernet network. Are they on the same logical IP network?

_____

Task 6: Test Network Connectivity Between the Two PCs

Step 1. On PC1, click **Start > Run**. Enter **cmd**, and then click **OK**. A Windows command prompt window appears.

Step 2. At the prompt, enter **ping 192.168.2.2** and press **Enter**. An unsuccessful **ping** is shown in Example 3-5.

Example 3-5   Unsuccessful ping Output
```
C:\>ping 192.168.2.2

Pinging 192.168.2.2 with 32 bytes of data:

Request timed out.
Request timed out.
Request timed out.
Request timed out.

Ping statistics for 192.168.2.2:
    Packets: Sent = 4, Received = 0, Lost = 4 (100% loss),
```

Why was the ping not successful?

_____

What type of networking device would allow the PCs to communicate?

_____

Task 7: Change IP Address for PC1

Step 1. Using the procedure described in Task 5, change the logical IP address for PC1 from 192.168.1.1 to 192.168.2.99 and leave the subnet mask set to 255.255.255.0. On what network is PC1 now?

_____

Step 2.   Click **OK**, which closes the Internet Protocol (TCP/IP) Properties window. Click the **Close** button to exit the Local Area Connection Properties window.

The two PCs are still on the same physical Ethernet network. Are they on the same logical IP network now?

Task 8: Test Network Connectivity Between the Two PCs

Step 1.   On PC2, click **Start > Run**. Enter **cmd**, and then click **OK**. A command prompt window appears.

Step 2.   At the prompt, enter **ping 192.168.2.99** and press **Enter**. Was it successful? Why or why not?

Task 9: (Optional) Re-enable the Firewall

Perform this task only if the firewall was originally enabled.

Step 1.   If you disabled Windows Firewall in Task 4, click **Start > Control Panel** and double-click **Network Connections**.

Step 2.   Right-click the **Ethernet** network connection icon and select **Properties**. Click the **Advanced** tab. Locate and click **Settings**.

Step 3.   If the firewall settings are disabled (and they were enabled before this lab began), click the **On** radio button to enable the firewall. Click **OK** in this dialog box and the following one to apply this setting.

Lab 3-5: Connect and Configure Hosts (3.6.4.3)

Objectives

- Connect a PC to a router using a straight-through cable.

- Configure the PC with an appropriate IP address.

- Configure the PC with a NetBIOS computer name.

- Verify the PC configuration using Windows XP and through a command prompt.

Background/Preparation

In order for the PC to participate in the local network and the Internet, it must be connected to a network device. The following resources will be required:

- Linksys Model WRT300N wireless router or equivalent SOHO router

- Two computers with Ethernet NICs and Windows XP Professional installed on both

- Two straight-through cables

Task 1: Identify Ethernet Ports

Step 1.   On the Linksys router, locate the Ethernet LAN (Local Area Network) ports. The Ethernet LAN ports connect your network hosts and devices. The four LAN ports are grouped together in the center of the router as shown in Figure 3-5.

Figure 3-5   Linksys Router LAN Ports

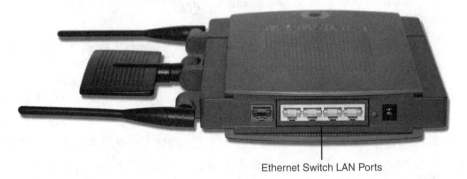

Ethernet Switch LAN Ports

Step 2.   On the PC, locate the Ethernet NIC port. The port could be integrated into the motherboard or it could be an adapter. In either case, the port will be an RJ-45 connector. Figure 3-6 shows an Ethernet port on an adapter.

Figure 3-6   PCI Ethernet Adapter

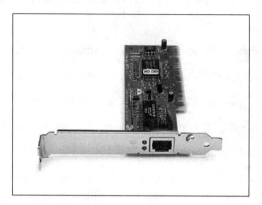

Task 2: Connect the Cable Between the PC and the Router

Step 1. Connect one end of the straight-through Ethernet cable to an Ethernet LAN port on the router. These ports are also referred to as switch ports to differentiate them from the Internet port, which is connected to the router portion of the wireless router.

Step 2. Connect the other end of the cable to the PC Ethernet port.

Step 3. Repeat this procedure for the second PC.

Task 3: Assign the PCs an IP Address and Default Gateway

Step 1. In order to assign an IP address and default gateway to a Windows XP host, click **Start > Control Panel.**

Step 2. There are two ways to view Control Panels: Classic View and Category View. The options available depend on which one of these two views you are using. If you see the Switch to Category View option on the left, you are currently in the Classic view mode. If you see the Switch to Classic View option on the left, you are currently in Category view mode. Ensure that you are in **Classic View** mode.

Step 3. Locate and double-click the **Network Connections** control panel icon.

Step 4. Right-click the **Local Area Connection** icon that represents your NIC and click the **Properties** menu option.

Step 5. In the middle window, scroll down until you see and can click the **Internet Protocol (TCP/IP)** option.

Step 6. Click the **Properties** button; the Internet Protocol (TCP/IP) Properties window appears. Next, click the **Use the following IP address** button, which activates the IP address, subnet mask, and default gateway text boxes.

Step 7. In the IP address field, enter **192.168.1.2**. Configure the subnet mask to **255.255.255.0**. Configure the default gateway to **192.168.1.1**. Figure 3-7 shows these settings. (DNS server information is not necessary at this time, so you do not need to fill out the fields under Use the Following DNS Server Addresses.) When finished, click **OK**.

Figure 3-7   Internet Protocol Properties

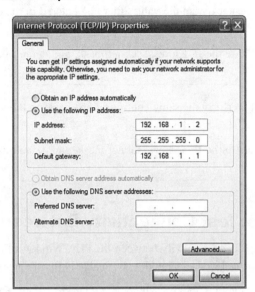

Step 8.   From the Internet Protocol (TCP/IP) Properties window, click **OK** to apply the changes. Be patient because this step might take some time. After the changes are applied, you are returned to the Network Connections window.

Step 9.   Because the two computers are on the same network, their IP addresses will be similar, their subnet masks will be identical, and their default gateways will be identical. Perform the same procedures on the second PC to assign an IP address, subnet mask, and default gateway using the following information:

IP address: **192.168.1.3**

Subnet mask: **255.255.255.0**

Default gateway: **192.168.1.1**

Why do you think the IP addresses are different, but the subnet masks and default gateways are the same?

_____

_____

_____

_____

_____

Task 4: Verify the IP Address Configuration

Step 1.   On the Windows XP desktop, click **Start > Run**.

Step 2.   In the **Open** text box, enter **cmd** and press **Enter**.

Step 3.   In the command-line prompt, enter **ipconfig /all**. Verify that the IP address and the default gateway are the values that you entered in the earlier Tasks. If they are incorrect, repeat Tasks 3 and 4.

Are the IP address, subnet mask, and default gateway correct for the first PC?

_____

Step 4.   Perform the same configuration check on the second PC. If the values are incorrect, repeat Tasks 3 and 4.

Are the IP address, subnet mask, and default gateway correct for the second PC?

_____

Task 5: Test Connectivity Between the Two PCs

To test TCP/IP connectivity between the PCs, Windows Firewall must be disabled temporarily on both PCs. Windows Firewall should be re-enabled after the tests have been completed.

Step 1.   On PC1, on the Windows XP desktop, click **Start > Control Panel** and double-click **Network Connections**.

Step 2.   Right-click the **Local Area Connection** icon and select **Properties**. Click the **Advanced** tab. Locate and click the **Settings** button.

Step 3.   Make a note of whether the firewall settings are Enabled (On) for the Ethernet port or Disabled (Off) for the Ethernet port.

_____

Step 4.   If the firewall settings are enabled, click the **Off (not recommended)** radio button to disable the firewall. You re-enable the setting in a later Task. Click **OK** in this dialog box and the following one to apply this setting. Use the same process on PC2 to disable the firewall if necessary.

Step 5.   From the same command prompt on the first PC, enter **ping 192.168.1.3** to test connectivity with the second PC.

Step 6.   If the **ping** is not successful, perform the appropriate troubleshooting steps such as checking the cabling and checking your IP address, subnet mask, and default gateway assignments.

Step 7.   From the command prompt on the second PC, enter **ping 192.168.1.2 to** check connectivity to the first PC. The **ping** should succeed.

Task 6: Configure the NetBIOS Name

Step 1.   Right-click **Start** and choose the **Explore** option.

How many drive letters are shown in the window that appears?

_____

_____

Which drive letters are shown?

_____

_____

Step 2.   Right-click the **My Computer** icon on your Windows XP desktop and choose the **Properties** option. The System Properties window appears.

> **NOTE:** If the My Computer icon does not appear on the desktop, click **Start**, right-click **My Computer**, and select the **Properties** option.

Step 3.   Click the **Computer Name** tab.

Step 4.   Click **Change**. Make a note of the current computer name.

_____

Step 5.   In the **Computer Name** text box, enter **PC1**. Ensure that the **Member of** radio button or field is set to **Workgroup**.

Step 6.   Make a note of the **Workgroup** name.

_____

Step 7.   Click **OK**. If prompted to restart the computer, click **OK** to restart and follow the directions on the screen.

Step 8.   Use the same process to name the second computer **PC2**. Also ensure that the **Workgroup** name is set to the same value as PC1.

Task 7: Verify Configuration

Step 1.   To verify the new configuration, open a command prompt on each computer. If you forgot how, refer to Task 4, Steps 1–3.

Step 2.   Use the **nbtstat** command to view and gather information about remote computers. At the command prompt, enter **nbtstat** and press **Enter**. The letters shown are options called switches that you can use with the **nbtstat** command.

Step 3.   On PC1, enter **nbtstat –n** and press **Enter** to see the local NetBIOS name of PC1.

Step 4.   On PC2, enter the same command to verify the NetBIOS name is set to PC2.

Step 5.   The **nbtstat –a** command can be used to look at a remote computer's name table. Enter **nbtstat** again from the command prompt. Notice in the output that when you use the **–a** switch, you have to put a space and then enter a remote computer's name (RemoteName).

Step 6.   From PC1, enter **nbtstat –a PC2** and press **Enter**. The **nbtstat** information for PC2 shows on PC1's monitor.

What command would you use from the command prompt on PC2 to view information about PC1?

_____

Step 7.   From PC2, enter the appropriate command to view PC1's **nbtstat** information.

Step 8.   The **nbtstat –A** (notice that the switch is a capital *A* this time) can be used to view the same information using an IP address rather than a name. If you enter **nbtstat** again, you can see that the command syntax tells you that you use **–A** followed by an IP address. The IP address is that of the remote computer.

From PC1, enter **nbtstat –A 192.168.1.3** to see the same information that was returned by the **nbtstat –a PC2** command.

Write the command that you would type on PC2 to view information about PC1, using the IP address of PC1 instead of the NetBIOS name.

_____

Step 9.   From PC1, you can use the **ping** command to verify connectivity. However, instead of using an IP address, you can use the NetBIOS name. From the PC1 command prompt, enter **ping PC2** (notice the capitalization). The result should be successful.

Step 10.   From PC1, enter **ping pc2** (notice the capitalization).

Does the **ping** succeed using lowercase letters?

_____

Step 11.   You can use the **nbtstat –r** command to see NetBIOS names that have been resolved (they are known). From the PC1 and PC2 command prompts, enter **nbtstat –r** to see that the remote computer is known using NetBIOS.

Step 12.   Close the command prompt window.

Task 8: (Optional) Re-enable the Firewall

Perform this task only if the firewall was originally enabled.

Step 1.   If the answer to Task 5, Step 3 was On or Enabled on PC1, click **Start > Control Panel**, and open the **Network Connections** control panel.

Step 2.   Right-click the **Ethernet** network connection icon and select **Properties**. Click the **Advanced** tab. Locate and click **Settings**.

Step 3.   If the firewall settings are disabled (and they were enabled before this lab began), click the **On** radio button to disable the firewall. Click **OK** in this dialog box and the following one to apply this setting.

Task 9: Return IP Address and NetBIOS Name to Original Values

Step 1.   Return to Task 3 to change the IP address back to the original.

Step 2.   Return to Task 6, Step 5 to change the NetBIOS name back to the original.

Task 10: Reflection

Check two or three computers in your lab at school. Complete Table 3-3.

Table 3-3   Computer Information

	Computer Name	IP Address and Subnet Mask	Default Gateway
1			
2			
3			

Share this information with a classmate.

In your opinion, are the names descriptive?

Are all the computers in the classroom part of the same local network? How could you prove that?

Lab 3-6: Sharing Resources (3.6.5.3)

Objectives

Use Windows XP to complete the following tasks:

- Share files and folders.

- Map network drives.

Background/Preparation

One of the key benefits of having PCs networked together is that it provides access for sharing information with other connected users. Whether it is a song, a proposal, or your holiday pictures, there are many situations where you need to share data with friends or business colleagues.

Mapping drives goes hand-in-hand with sharing folders because drive mappings provide quick access to commonly used folders. They also provide an easier way for users to navigate and find the files and/or folders they are looking for. Drive mappings redirect a local resource (drive letter) to a shared network resource (hard drive or folder on the network).

This task requires two configured Windows XP Professional workstations connected via a local network. Note: Use the previously configured network from Lab 3-5.

Task 1: Share a Folder

Step 1.   Click **Start > All Programs > Accessories > Windows Explorer**.

Step 2.   In the Folders pane, click the **+** (plus sign) beside **My Computer**. Click the **C** drive. Choose **File > New,** and select the **Folder** option. Enter **Share** as the name of the folder. (See Figure 3-8.)

Figure 3-8   Windows Explorer

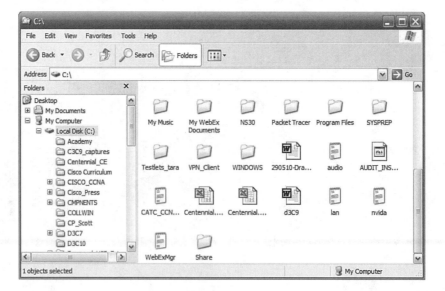

Step 3.   Right-click the new **Share** folder and choose **Properties.**

NOTE: The Sharing option is not available for the Documents and Settings, Program Files, and Windows system folders.

Step 4.   Click the **Sharing** tab, as shown in Figure 3-9. In the Share Properties dialog box, click the **Share this folder** radio button to share the folder with other users on your network. The default name for the shared folder is the same name as the original folder name.

NOTE: To change the name of the folder on the network, enter a new name for the folder in the Share name text box. This will not change the name of the folder on your computer.

Figure 3-9   Sharing a Folder in Windows

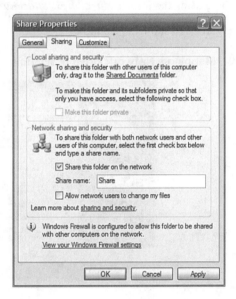

Step 5.   Click **Apply** and then **OK**.

Step 6.   Create a text file using Notepad and save it to the Share folder. On the Windows XP desktop, click **Start > All Programs > Accessories > Notepad**.

In the Notepad application, enter the message **Hello World!**.

Choose **File > Save**. In the **File name** field, enter **Test message**. Click the icon with the folder and up arrow.

Step 7.   Double-click **My Computer**, and then double-click drive **C:**. Locate and double-click the **Share folder**, and then click **Save**.

Step 8.   Close the Notepad application.

Step 9.   Repeat Steps 1–5 for the second Windows XP Professional machine with the following exceptions:

Share name: **Share2**

Text file contents: **Hello planet!**

Text filename: **Test Message 2**

Task 2: Map Network Drives to Provide Quick and Easy Access to Shared Folders

Step 1.   On the first Windows XP workstation, click **Start > All Programs > Accessories > Windows Explorer**.

Step 2.   In the Folders pane, click **My Computer**. Choose **Tools > Map Network Drive**.

Step 3.   In the **Drive** text box, select an unused drive letter using the drop-down menu.

What drive letter did you choose?

_____

Step 4.   In the **Folder** field, enter the IP address of the remote PC and the name of the remote share using the format *ip_address**sharename*.

Figure 3-10 shows an example.

Figure 3-10   Mapping a Network Drive in Windows

Step 5.   Click **Finish**.

A window appears with the message Attempting to connect to \\192.168.1.3\share2. A window opens to display the contents of the shared folder called Share2 that has now been assigned a drive letter.

_____

NOTE: The IP address can be replaced by the computer name.

_____

Step 6.   Double-click the **Test Message 2** text document. Add the words **Techs rule** to the document. Choose **File > Save.**

What message is displayed? Why do you think this happened?

_____

_____

Step 7.   The files within a shared folder are automatically protected in the Windows XP Professional version. Click **OK** in the message box. Click **Cancel**, and then click **Close** for the Test Message 2 document.

Step 8.   In the message box, click **No** to close the document without saving the changes.

Step 9.   Repeat Steps 1–5 in Task 2 to map a drive on the second Windows XP workstation. This drive should be mapped to the share you configured in Task 1.

Task 3: Verify Work

Step 1.   From the first Windows XP Professional machine, click **Start > All Programs > Accessories > Windows Explorer**.

Step 2.   Expand **My Computer** by clicking on the **+** (plus sign) beside the option.

The Windows Explorer list should display a drive with the drive letter label that you chose for the remote share.

Step 3.   Repeat Steps 1 and 2 for the second Windows XP Professional machine.

If the drive letter appears on both computers, the folders are shared and drives are mapped properly on both Windows XP workstations. You can perform the same steps on any folder. When a drive is properly mapped to shared folders, all files and folders within the shared folder will be accessible from the workstations.

Task 4: Reflection

What are some of the benefits of mapped drives and shared folders in a home or small office network?

_____

_____

_____

Which folders cannot be shared? Can you think of reasons why an operating system might not allow certain types of folders to be shared?

_____

_____

_____

A mapped drive provides a pointer to a network resource, but mapped drive letters are said to be locally significant only. What do you think is meant by _locally significant_?

_____

_____

_____

CHAPTER 4

Labs: Connecting to the Internet Through an ISP

The lab exercises included in this chapter include all the Chapter 4 online curriculum labs to ensure that you have mastered the practical, hands-on skills needed to use a **traceroute** utility and to build and test Ethernet cables. As you work through these labs, use Chapter 4 in Part I of this book or use the corresponding Chapter 4 in the Networking for Home and Small Businesses course of the CCNA Discovery online curriculum for assistance.

 ## Lab 4-1: Tracing Internet Connectivity (4.2.3.3)

Objectives

- Use software that shows how data travels through the Internet.

- Use the **ping** utility to test connectivity to a remote network.

- Construct a visual map of connectivity from your network to a remote network.

Background/Preparation

In order to perform this lab, Internet connectivity is required. On a PC, open a web browser to ensure that connectivity exists before beginning this lab.

This lab has an optional first step of downloading and installing a free program that can be used to determine the path a packet takes through the Internet. This program might be free, but it also might be copyrighted. Also, you may not be permitted to download and install software on a campus computer. Check with the instructor or student assistant if you are unsure.

The following resources will be required:

- Windows-based computer with Internet connectivity

- Ability to download and install freeware software (optional)

- Access to the **Run** command and/or the command prompt

Task 1: (Optional) Download and Install a Free Program

Step 1.   Open a search engine such as Google (http://www.google.com), Yahoo! (http://www.yahoo.com), or Search (http://search.com).

Which words do you think would give you the best result if you are searching for a visual program that allows you to trace how data (a packet) travels through the Internet? Write your search words.

_____

_____

Step 2.   Enter the words you chose in the search field. Locate and download the software and install it. Usually, the website has a link to the download site or you can click the words **Download** or **Download Now**. When you download any freeware, remember the location on the hard drive, flash drive, or disk media where you saved the program. Write down where the download is saved:

_____

What is the name of the program you installed?

_____

_____

_____

Task 2: Locate Websites

Step 1.   Using the search engine again, locate five businesses with a web server located in a country different from your own.

_____

_____

Write the names of the five business websites.

_____

_____

_____

_____

Step 2.   Using the search engine again, locate a business in your own country that has a website that is accessible.

Write the URL of the website. An example URL is http://www.cisco.com.

_____

Task 3: (Optional) Use Downloaded Visual Trace Route Tool

Step 1.   Using the software you have downloaded and installed, determine the path the packet takes to reach one of the remote country destinations. Each tool normally allows you to enter a URL. The program should either list or visually display the path taken by the packet.

How many hops does the packet take to get from your computer to the destination computer?

_____

If your tool also provides time information, write down how long it took for the packet to reach the first hop:

_____

Step 2.   Use the tool to determine the path to another foreign country site.

How many hops does the packet take to get from your computer to the destination computer?

_____

Step 3.   Use the tool to determine the path to a website in your own country.

Was the time it took to reach a website in your own country shorter or longer?

_____

Write down an instance where the time it takes to reach a web server in your own country would be longer than it takes to reach another country's web server.

_____

_____

_____

_____

Task 4: Use the tracert Command

The Windows **tracert** command is issued from the command prompt and provides textual output of each hop of the route taken by the packets.

Step 1.   Click **Start > Run**, enter **cmd** in the Open text box, and press **Enter**. An alternative way to get to the command prompt is to click **Start > All Programs > Accessories > Command Prompt**.

Step 2.   From the command prompt, enter **tracert** and press **Enter**. Options that can be used with the **tracert** command are shown. Items shown in square brackets [ ] are optional. For example, the first option that can be used with the **tracert** command is **–d**. Entering **tracert –d www.cisco.com** issues the command to the computer to trace the route to http://www.cisco.com, but do not try to resolve IP addresses to names. The *target_name* parameter is mandatory (it does not have brackets around it) and it is replaced with the destination network. In the previous example of **tracert –d www.cisco.com**, www.cisco.com is the *target_name*.

Which **tracert** option would be used to designate that only five hops could be used to search for the device address on the destination network?

_____

Write the full command for tracing a route to http://www.cisco.com, instructing the computer to not search for it after seven hops.

_____

Step 3.   Using one of the remote country destination addresses (use the same address as the one you used with the visual tool if possible), use the **tracert** command to determine how many hops it takes to reach the remote web server. Write the number of hops and the destination:

_____

The **tracert** command uses Internet Control Message Protocol (ICMP) echo request messages to determine the path to the final destination. The path displayed is a list of IP addresses assigned to routers that connect to one another to form the path. The ICMP packets contain a value called a Time To Live (TTL). The TTL value is 30 by default on a Microsoft-based PCs, and each router through which the packet passes decrements that value by 1 before sending the packet on to the next router in the path. When the TTL value reaches 0, the router that has the packet sends an ICMP time exceeded message back to the source.

The **tracert** command determines the path by sending the first ICMP echo request message with a TTL of 1 and then increases that TTL value by 1 until the target responds or the maximum number of hops is reached. The path is determined by examining the ICMP time exceeded messages that are sent back by routers along the way and by the ICMP echo reply message that is returned from the destination. Routers that do not return the ICMP time exceeded messages are shown by a row of asterisks (*).

Step 4.   Perform another **tracert** to one of the websites used earlier. How many hops does your **tracert** command show that the packet went through?

Task 5: Use the pathping Command

Another route-tracing command that can be used on a Windows XP computer is **pathping**. This command combines the abilities of the **tracert** command with the **ping** command. From the command prompt, use the **pathping** command to determine the IP addresses of the routers used to create the packet path to another foreign country address. An example of the **pathping** command used to trace the path to Cisco is **pathping www.cisco.com**.

How many hops did the **pathping** command display to your remote destination?

When do you think that you would ever use commands like **pathping** or **tracert**?

Task 6: (Optional) Use the whois Function

Some of the freeware route-tracing tools include an option to perform a **whois** function. **whois** is a separate program, or it might be integrated with a tool similar to **tracert** or **pathping**. It displays (and sometimes has a link to) who owns the web link of either the destination URL (such as http://www.cisco.com) or any of the links along the path. Explore the freeware tool that you have downloaded and installed and determine whether it has a **whois** function. If it does, use it to determine who owns the domain name of one of the previous destinations used.

Why would you want to use the **whois** function?

_____

_____

_____

_____

_____

_____

Task 7: Reflection

With a classmate, compare all the commands used in this lab. Describe the purpose and benefit of each one. Which do you think is the most useful command?

_____

_____

_____

_____

_____

_____

_____

Lab 4-2: Building Straight-Through and Crossover UTP Cables (4.5.3.2)

Objectives

Build and test straight-through and crossover unshielded twisted-pair (UTP) Ethernet network cables.

Background/Preparation

In this lab, you build and terminate Ethernet straight-through patch cables and crossover cables. With a straight-through cable, the color of wire used by pin 1 on one end is the same color used by pin 1 on the other cable end, as is the case for the remaining seven pins. You will construct the cable using either TIA/EIA T568A or T568B standards for Ethernet, which determine which color wire is used on each pin. Straight-through patch cables are normally used to connect a host directly to a hub or switch or to a wall plate in an office area.

With a crossover cable the second and third pairs on the RJ-45 connector at one end of the cable are reversed. The pinouts for the cable are the T568A standard on one end and the T568B standard on the other end. Crossover cables are normally used to connect hubs and switches or can be used to directly connect two hosts to create a simple network. This two-part lab can be done individually, in pairs, or in groups.

The following resources will be required:

- Two 2 to 3 ft (0.6 to 0.9 m) lengths of cable, Category 5 or 5e
- A minimum of four RJ-45 connectors (more might be needed if miswiring occurs)
- An RJ-45 crimping tool
- An Ethernet cable tester
- Wire cutters

Use Tables 4-1 and 4-2 as references when building cables, depending on whether you are building a T568A or T568B cable.

Table 4-1   T568A Standards

Pin No.	Pair No.	Wire Color	Function
1	2	White/Green	Transmit
2	2	Green	Transmit
3	3	White/Orange	Receive
4	1	Blue	Not used
5	1	White/Blue	Not used
6	3	Orange	Receive
7	4	White/Brown	Not used
8	4	Brown	Not used

Table 4-2   T568B Standards

Pin No.	Pair No.	Wire Color	Function
1	2	White/Orange	Transmit
2	2	Orange	Transmit
3	3	White/Green	Receive
4	1	Blue	Not used
5	1	White/Blue	Not used
6	3	Green	Receive
7	4	White/Brown	Not used
8	4	Brown	Not used

Part A: Build and Test an Ethernet Straight-Through Patch Cable

In this part of the lab, you build a straight-through Ethernet patch cable. Patch cables are normally used to connect workstations and servers to an RJ-45 jack in a work area or directly to a hub or switch in some cases. They are also used to connect a router to a hub or switch.

Task A1: Obtain and Prepare the Cable

Step 1.   Determine the length of cable required. This measurement could be that from a device such as a computer to the device to which it connects (such as a hub or switch) or between a device and an RJ-45 outlet jack. Add at least 12 inches (30.48 cm) to the distance. The TIA/EIA standard states the maximum length for a patch cable is 16.4 feet (5 m). Standard Ethernet cable lengths are usually 2 feet (.6 m), 6 feet (1.83 m), or 10 feet (3.05 m).

Which length of cable did you choose and why did you choose this length?

_____

Step 2.   Cut a piece of cable to the desired length. Stranded UTP cable is commonly used for patch cables (the cables between an end network device such as a PC and an RJ-45 connector) because it is more durable when bent repeatedly. It is called *stranded* because each of the wires within the cable is made up of many strands of fine copper wire, rather than a single solid wire. Solid wire is used for cable runs that are between the RJ-45 jack and a punch-down block.

Step 3.   Using wire strippers, remove 2 inches (5.08 cm) of the cable jacket from both ends of the cable.

Task A2: Prepare and Insert the Wires

Step 1.   Determine which wiring standard will be used. Circle the standard.

[T568A | T568B]

Step 2.   Use either Table 4-1 or 4-2, depending on the wiring standard to be used.

Step 3.   Spread the cable pairs and arrange them roughly in the desired order based on the standard chosen.

Step 4.   Untwist a short length of the pairs and arrange them in the exact order needed by the standard. It is very important to *untwist as little as possible*. The twists are important because they provide noise cancellation.

Step 5.   Straighten and flatten the wires between your thumb and forefinger.

Step 6.   Ensure that the cable wires are still in the correct order as the standard.

Step 7.   Cut the cable in a straight line to within 1/2 to 3/4 inches (1.25 to 1.9 cm) from the edge of the cable jacket. If it is longer than this, the cable will be susceptible to crosstalk (the interference of bits from one wire with an adjacent wire).

Step 8.   The tang (the prong that sticks out from the RJ-45 connector) should be on the underside pointing downward when you insert the wires. Making sure that pin 1 (wire 1) is on the left, insert the wires firmly into the RJ-45 connector until all wires are pushed as far as possible into the connector.

Task A3: Inspect, Crimp, and Reinspect

Step 1.   Visually inspect the cable and ensure that the right color codes are connected to the correct pin numbers.

Step 2.   Visually inspect the end of the connector. The eight wires should be pressed firmly against the end of the RJ-45 connector. Some of the cable jacket should be inside the first portion of the connector. This provides strain relief for the cable. If the cable jacket is not far enough inside the connector, it might eventually cause the cable to fail.

Step 3.   If everything is correctly aligned and inserted properly, place the RJ-45 connector and cable into the crimper. The crimper will push plungers down on the RJ-45 connector, as shown in Figure 4-1. The rear plunger pushes into the cable sheathing to prevent it from pulling out and leaving the wires exposed. This also helps to provide stress relief for the wires inside the sheathing. The front plunger pushes the copper connector blades into the eight wires to make electrical contact.

Figure 4-1   Crimper Plungers Attach Connector to Cable

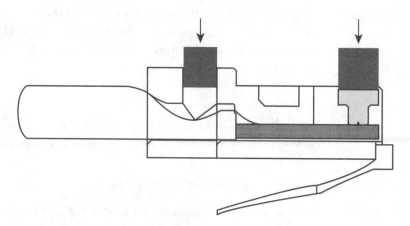

Step 4.   Visually reinspect the connector. If it's improperly installed, cut the end off and repeat the process.

Task A4: Terminate the Other Cable End

Step 1.   Use the steps in Task A3 to attach an RJ-45 connector to the other end of the cable.

Step 2.   Visually reinspect the connector. If it is improperly installed, cut the end off and repeat the process.

Step 3.   Which standard is used for patch cables in your school?

[T568A | T568B]

Task A5: Test the Cable

Step 1.   Using a cable tester, test the straight-through cable for functionality. If it fails, repeat the lab.

Step 2.   (Optional) Use the cable to connect a PC to a network.

Step 3.   (Optional) Click **Start > Run**.

Step 4.   (Optional) Enter **cmd** in the Open text box and press **Enter**.

Step 5.   (Optional) From the command prompt, enter **ipconfig**.

Step 6.   (Optional) Write down the default gateway IP address.

Step 7.   (Optional) From the command prompt, enter **ping** followed by the default gateway IP address. If the cable is functional, the **ping** should be successful (provided that no other network problem exists and the default gateway router is connected and functional).

Part B: Build and Test an Ethernet Crossover Cable

In this part of the lab, you build a crossover Ethernet cable. Crossover cables are normally used to connect like devices, such as switch to switch or hub to switch. The use of a crossover cable can save time and equipment in a testing environment. If using a crossover cable to connect one workstation to another or a PC to a router, you do not need a hub or switch.

Task B1: Obtain and Prepare the Cable

Step 1.   Determine the length of cable required. This measurement could be that from a hub to a hub, a hub to a switch, a switch to a switch, a computer to a router, or from one computer to another computer. Add at least 12 inches (30.48 cm) to the distance. Which length of cable did you choose and why did you choose this length?

Step 2.   Cut a piece of cable to the desired length and, using wire strippers, remove 2 inches (5.08 cm) of the cable jacket from both ends of the cable.

Task B2: Prepare and Insert the T568A Wires

Step 1.   Locate the T568A table (Table 4-1) at the beginning of this lab.

Step 2.   Spread the cable pairs and arrange them roughly in the desired order based on the T568A standard.

Step 3. Untwist a short length of the pairs and arrange them in the exact order needed by the standard. It is very important to *untwist as little as possible*. Twists are important because they provide noise cancellation.

Step 4. Straighten and flatten the wires between your thumb and forefinger.

Step 5. Ensure the cable wires are in the correct order based on the standard.

Step 6. Cut the cable in a straight line to within 1/2 to 3/4 inches (1.25 to 1.9 cm) from the edge of the cable jacket. If it is longer than this, the cable will be susceptible to crosstalk (the interference of bits from one wire with an adjacent wire).

Step 7. The tang (the prong that sticks out from the RJ-45 connector) should be on the underside pointing downward when you insert the wires. Insert the wires firmly into the RJ-45 connector until all wires are pushed as far as possible into the connector.

Task B3: Inspect, Crimp, and Reinspect

Step 1. Visually inspect the cable and ensure the right color codes are connected to the correct pin numbers.

Step 2. Visually inspect the end of the connector. The eight wires should be pressed firmly against the RJ-45 connector. Some of the cable jacket should be inside the first portion of the connector. This provides for cable strain relief, which can eventually cause the cable to fail.

Step 3. If everything is correctly aligned and inserted properly, place the RJ-45 connector and cable into the crimper. The crimper will push plungers down on the RJ-45 connector.

Step 4. Visually reinspect the connector. If it is improperly installed, cut the end off and repeat the process.

Task B4: Terminate the T568B Cable End

Step 1. On the other end, use the steps in Tasks B2 and B3 (but use the T568B table [Table 4-2] and standard) to attach an RJ-45 connector to the cable.

Step 2. Visually reinspect the connector. If it is improperly installed, cut the end off and repeat the process.

Step 3. Which standard would you rather use at home if you have or would like to have a home network?

[T568A | T568B]

_____

_____

Task B5: Test the Cable

Step 1. Using a cable tester, test the crossover cable for functionality. If it fails, repeat the lab.

Step 2. Use the cable to connect two PCs.

Step 3. On both computers, click **Start > Run**.

Note: If the **Run** command is unavailable on your PC, visually check the LED status lights on the NIC card. If they are on (usually green or amber), the cable is functional.

Step 4.   On both computers, enter **cmd** and press **Enter**.

Step 5.   On both computers from the command prompt, enter **ipconfig**.

Step 6.   Write down the IP address of both computers. The IP addresses should be on the same network and have the same subnet mask.

Computer 1:

_____

Computer 2:

_____

Step 7.   From the command prompt of one computer, enter **ping** followed by the IP address of the other computer. If the cable is functional, the **ping** should be successful. Do the **ping** on the other computer as well.

Note: Windows Firewall on the target computer must be temporarily disabled for the **ping** to be successful. Refer to Lab 3.1.5.3 if you need help with this. If you disable the firewall, be sure to re-enable it.

Task B6: Reflection

Which part of making these cables did you find the most difficult? Compare your views with a classmate.

_____

_____

_____

Are all four pairs of cables twisted the same amount? Discuss the reasons why or why not.

_____

_____

_____

Ask a local business or check a site such as http://www.workopolis.com/ to see how much a beginning cable installer earns and what criteria employers look for in a cable installer. Write down the information you discover in the space provided.

_____

_____

Many technicians keep a crossover cable in their toolkit. When do you think that you would use a crossover cable and when do you think a network technician would use this cable?

_____

_____

_____

Lab 4-3: Terminating UTP Cables (4.5.4.4)

Objectives

- Use a punchdown tool to terminate an RJ-45 wall jack.

- Install an RJ-45 jack in a wall plate.

- Use a punchdown tool to terminate a UTP cable at a patch panel.

Background/Preparation

In this lab, you wire an RJ-45 data jack for installation in a wall plate using a punchdown tool. This task is done frequently when installing cabling in an office environment. The punchdown tool is also used to terminate the other end of the cable at a patch panel punchdown block. The punchdown tool uses spring-loaded action to push wires between metal pins, while at the same time skinning the sheath away from the wire. This ensures that the wire makes a good electrical connection with the pins inside the jack. The punchdown tool also cuts off any extra wire.

A Category 5/5e straight-through patch cable with an RJ-45 connector normally plugs into a data jack or outlet to connect a PC to the network. It is important to use Category 5- or 5e-rated jacks and patch panels with Category 5 or 5e cabling in order to support Fast Ethernet (100 Mbps) and Gigabit Ethernet (1000 Mbps). The process of punching down wires into a data jack in an office area is the same as punching them down at a patch panel in a wiring closet. This lab can be performed individually, in pairs, or in groups.

The following resources are required:

- 2 to 3 feet (60 to 90 cm) length of cable, either Category 5 or 5e.

- RJ-45 data jack. If RJ-45 data jacks are installed on both ends of the cable, two jacks will be needed and the installation can be tested by inserting cable with RJ-45 connectors and a simple cable continuity tester. More jacks might also be needed if errors are made.

- Category 5/5e wall plate.

- Patch panel.

- Punchdown tool, type 110.

- UTP cable stripper.

- Wire cutters.

- Two known-good straight-through patch cables for testing (optional).

Task 1: Strip the Sheath

Remove the cable sheath 1 inch (2.54 cm) from the end of the cable.

Task 2: Position Wires in Data Jack

Step 1.   Position wires in the proper channels on the RJ-45 jack maintaining the twists as close to the jack as possible.

Step 2.   A number of different types of jacks are available. Most jacks have the channels color-coded to indicate where the wires go. Make sure that the colors on the wires match the colors on jack. The jack in Figure 4-2 shows one model. Jacks are typically stamped to indicate whether they are T568A or T568B.

Figure 4-2   RJ-45 Jack

Task 3: Punch Down the Data Jack

Step 1.   Use the punchdown tool, similar to the one shown in Figure 4-3, to push conductors into the channels. Make sure to position the cutting side of the punchdown tool so that it faces the outside of the jack. Not doing so will cause the tool to cut the wire being punched. Try tilting the handle of the punchdown tool a little to the outside, so it will cut better.

Figure 4-3   Punchdown Tool

Step 2.   If any wire remains attached after you use the punchdown tool, simply twist the ends gently to remove them. Then place the clips on the jack and tighten them. Make sure that no more than 1/2 inch (1.27 cm) of untwisted wire is between the end of the cable jacket and the channels on the jack. Attach the faceplate.

Step 3.   Snap the jack into the faceplate by pushing it from the back side. Make sure when you do this that the jack is right-side up so the clip faces down when the wall plate is mounted.

Step 4.   Use the screws to attach the faceplate to either the box or to the bracket. Keep in mind that a surface-mounted box might hold 1 to 2 feet (30 to 60 cm) of excess cable, in which case it will be necessary to either slide the cable through the tie-wraps, or pull back the raceway that covers it, in order to push the excess cable back into the wall. For a flush-mounted jack, all that is needed is to push the excess cable back into the wall.

Task 4: Punch Down the Patch Panel

Step 1.   On the opposite end of the cabling, remove the sheath 1 inch (2.54 cm) from the cable.

Step 2.   Lay the wires down in the patch panel so that the colors of the wires correspond exactly to the colors indicated on the pin locations in the same manner as the data jack was punched down.

Step 3.   Keep the sheath within 1/4 inch (.64 cm) of where the wires begin branching out to their pin locations.

Step 4.   Do not untwist the wires more than necessary to lay them down at the pin locations, as shown in Figure 4-4. A good way to keep from untwisting too much is to hold down the wires next to the patch panel with one finger while using the other hand to pull apart each end as you lay it across the connector.

Figure 4-4   Patch Panel Connector

Figure 4-5 shows a large punchdown patch panel with carefully routed cabling.

Figure 4-5   Large Punch Down Patch Panel with Cabling

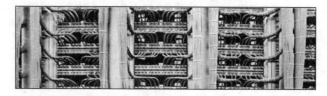

Task 5: Test the Data Jack and Patch Panel Terminations with a Basic Cable Tester (Optional)

Step 1.   Obtain two straight-through Ethernet patch cables and verify they both function properly using a simple cable tester.

Step 2.   Connect one end of one of the straight-through Ethernet patch cables to the data jack outlet and one end of the other straight-through cable to the jack at the patch panel.

Step 3.   Insert the opposite ends of the two cables into a simple cable tester and check for continuity from end to end through both patch cables, the data jack, and the patch panel. Did the cable run test good from end to end?

_____

_____

Task 6: Reflection (Optional)

Take a tour of a wiring closet that contains patch panels and punchdown blocks. Were there any other types of devices that might use similar techniques to attach wires? What do you think attaches to these cables?

_____

What do you think are some of the drawbacks and advantages of having a job installing network cabling?

_____

_____

Lab 4-4: Testing UTP Cables (4.5.5.4)

Objectives

Explore the wire-mapping features of the Fluke 620 LAN CableMeter, Fluke MicroScanner, or equivalent. Figure 4-6 shows a picture of a cable meter.

Figure 4-6   Cable Meter

- Explore the Cable Test feature: the Pass/Fail features of the Fluke 620 LAN CableMeter or equivalent.

- Explore the Cable Length feature of the Fluke 620 LAN CableMeter or equivalent.

- Use a cable tester to check for the proper installation of unshielded twisted-pair (UTP) Category 5/5e according to TIA/EIA-568 cabling standards in an Ethernet network.

Background/Preparation

Wire maps can be very helpful in troubleshooting cabling problems with UTP cable. A wire map allows the network technician to verify which pins on one end of the cable are connected to which pins on the other end.

Basic cable tests can be very helpful in troubleshooting cabling problems with UTP. The cabling infrastructure or cable plant in a building is expected to last at least ten years. Cable-related problems are one of the most common causes of network failure. The quality of cabling components used, the routing and installation of the cable, and the quality of the connector terminations will be the main factors in determining how trouble-free the cabling will be.

_____

_____

_____

_____

_____

This lab can be performed individually, in pairs, or in groups.

The following resources are required:

- Good Category 5 straight-through cables of different colors

- Good Category 5 crossover cables (T568A on one end and T568B on the other end)

- Category 5 straight-through cables of different colors and different lengths with open connections in the middle, or one or more conductors shorted at one end

- Category 5 straight-through cable with a split pair miswire

- Fluke 620 LAN CableMeter or similar instrument to test cable length, continuity, and wire map

Task 1: Set Up the Fluke 620 LAN CableMeter

Step 1. On the Fluke 620 meter, turn the rotary switch selector on the tester to the WIRE MAP position.

> **Note:** If you are using the Fluke MicroScanner, which is the current recommended replacement for the recently retired 620 LAN CableMeter, go to Task 6.

Step 2. Press the **SETUP** button to enter the setup mode and observe the LCD screen on the tester. Press the **UP** or **DOWN** arrow buttons until the desired cable type of UTP is selected. Press **ENTER** to accept that setting and go to the next one. Continue pressing the **UP** and **DOWN** arrows and pressing **ENTER** until the tester is set to the cabling characteristics in Table 4-3.

Table 4-3   Cable Meter Setup Options

Tester Option	Desired Setting - UTP
CABLE:	UTP
WIRING:	10BASE-T OR EIA/TIA 4PR
CATEGORY:	CATEGORY 5
WIRE SIZE:	AWG 24
CAL TO CABLE?	NO
BEEPING:	ON or OFF
LCD CONTRAST:	From 1 through 10 (brightest)

Step 3. After the meter is set up, press the **SETUP** button to exit setup mode.

Task 2: Test Cabling Procedure

For each cable to be tested use the following procedure:

Step 1. Place one end of the cable into the RJ-45 jack labeled UTP/FTP on the tester.

Step 2. Place the other end of the cable into the RJ-45 female coupler, and then insert the cable identifier into the other side of the coupler. The coupler and the cable identifier, shown in Figure 4-7, are accessories that come with the Fluke 620 LAN CableMeter.

Figure 4-7   Cable Identifier and Coupler

Task 3: Use the Wire Map Meter Function

The Wire Map function and a Cable ID Unit can be used to determine the wiring of both the near and far end of the cable. The top set of numbers displayed on the LCD screen is the near end, and the bottom set is the far end. Perform a Wire Map test on each of the cables provided. Fill in Table 4-4 based on the testing results for each Category 5 cable. For each cable, write down the identifying number of the cable and the cable color. Also write down whether the cable is straight-through or crossover, the tester screen test results, and a description of the problem.

Table 4-4   Cable Wire Map Test Results

Cable No.	Cable Color	Straight-through or Crossover	Displayed Test Results (Note: Refer to the Meter Manual for Detailed Descriptions of Test Results for the Wire Map Test.)	Problem/Description
			Top: Bot:	
			Top: Bot:	
			Top: Bot:	
			Top: Bot:	
			Top: Bot:	

Task 4: Use the Length Meter Function

Using the tester **LENGTH** function, perform a basic cable test on the same cables used previously. Fill in Table 4-5 with the additional information for each cable.

Table 4-5   Cable Length Test Results

Cable No.	Cable Length	Tester Test Results (Pass/Fail)

Task 5: Test Data Jack and Patch Panel Terminations for Wire Map, Length, and Miswire (Optional)

Step 1. Using the data jack and patch panel cable from Lab 4-3, connect one end of one of the straight-through Ethernet patch cables to the data jack outlet and one end of the other straight-through cable to the jack at the patch panel.

Step 2. Insert the opposite end of one of the cables into the Fluke 620 and the other into the coupler and cable identifier. Check for wire map, length, and miswire from end to end through the patch cables, the data jack, and the patch panel. Did the cable run test good from end to end? What were the results?

Wire map:

_____

Total cable run length:

_____

Any miswires?

_____

If there are problems, analyze where the problem is by testing each component and then repeat the connections if possible.

Task 6: Set Up and Test a Cable Using the Fluke MicroScanner

Step 1. Turn on the MicroScanner using the green power button on the right lower portion of the face plate.

Step 2. Remove the blue cap to expose the RJ-45 test ports. There will be one attached to the base unit and one inside the removable cap, which is known as the remote wiremap adapter.

Step 3.   Insert one end of the Cat5 cable's RJ-45 connector into the base unit and the other end into the remote wiremap adapter port inside the removable blue cap.

Step 4.   You might have to press the port button to select the RJ-45 adapter port instead of the F type port for coax.

The MicroScanner does the rest for you. It displays the wiremap and length. By default, if the wiremap fails to appear for a particular wire pair, continuity has failed, and the MicroScanner might report the distance to the fault in some circumstances. It also reports shorts and splits.

Although the MicroScanner is capable of other functions, this concludes the instructions for this particular lab.

Task 7: Reflection

If you were on a job and did not have a cable meter to test, what other methods could you use?

_____

_____

_____

CHAPTER 5

Labs: Network Addressing

The lab exercises included in this chapter cover the Chapter 5 online curriculum lab and a challenge lab to ensure that you have mastered the practical, hands-on skills needed to understand the basics of network addressing. As you work through these labs, use Chapter 5 in Part I of this book or use the corresponding Chapter 5 in the Networking for Home and Small Businesses course of the CCNA Discovery online curriculum for assistance.

Lab 5-1: Using the Windows Calculator with Network Addresses (5.1.4.3)

Objectives

- Switch between the two Windows Calculator modes.

- Use the Windows Calculator to convert between decimal, binary, and hexadecimal.

- Use the Windows Calculator to determine the number of hosts in a network with powers of 2.

Figure 5-1 shows the Windows Calculator.

Figure 5-1   Windows Calculator

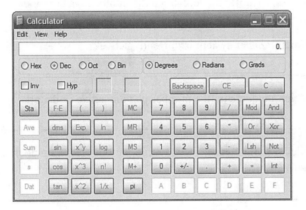

Background/Preparation

Network technicians work with binary, decimal, and hexadecimal numbers with computers and networking devices. In this lab, you use the Windows Calculator application to convert between the binary, decimal, and hexadecimal number systems. You also use the powers function to determine the number of hosts that can be addressed based on the number of bits available.

A PC with Windows XP installed and functional is the required resource for this lab.

Task 1: Access Windows Calculator and Determine Mode of Operation

Step 1. Click Start > **All Programs** > **Accessories**, and click **Calculator**. An alternative method of starting the Calculator application is to click **Start** > **Run**, type **calc** in the Open text box, and press **Enter**. Try both methods.

Step 2. When the Calculator application opens, select the **View** menu option.

Which mode is currently active?

[Standard | Scientific]

_____

Step 3. Select the standard mode, which is a basic mode for simple calculations. How many mathematical functions are available in this mode?

_____

Step 4. From the **View** menu option, select the scientific calculator mode.

How many mathematical functions are available in this mode?

_____

Task 2: Convert Between Number Systems

Step 1. Access scientific mode. Notice the number system modes available: **Hex** (Hexadecimal), **Dec** (Decimal), **Oct** (Octal), and **Bin** (Binary).

Which number system is currently active?

_____

Which numbers on the number pad are active in decimal mode?

_____

Step 2. Click the **Bin** (binary mode) radio button. Which numbers on the number pad are now active?

_____

Why do you think the other numbers are dimmed?

_____

Step 3. Click the **Hex** (hexadecimal mode) radio button.

Which characters on the number pad are now activated?

_____

Step 4. Click the **Dec** radio button. Using your mouse, click the number **1** followed by the number **5** on the number pad. The decimal number 15 has now been entered. Click the **Bin** radio button.

What happened to the number 15 listed in the text box at the top of the window?

_____

Step 5. By selecting different modes, numbers are converted from one number system to another. Select **Dec** mode again. The number in the window converts back to decimal. Select the **Hex** mode.

Which hexadecimal character (0 through 9 or A through F) represents decimal 15?

_____

Step 6. Clear the number 15 in the window. Select **Dec** again. Not only can the mouse be used to enter numbers, but the numerical keypad on the keyboard as well as numbers on the keyboard can also be used. Using the numerical keypad to the right of the **Enter** key, enter **22**. Note that if the number does not enter into the calculator, press the **Num Lock** key to enable the numeric keypad. While the number 22 is showing in the calculator, use the number keys across the top of the keyboard to add a 0 to the number 22. (220 should now be on the calculator.) Select **Bin**.

What is the binary equivalent of 220?

_____

Step 7. Clear the number 220 in the window. From binary mode, enter the following binary number: **11001100**. Select the **Dec** radio button.

What is the decimal equivalent to the binary number of 11011100?

_____

Step 8. Convert the decimal numbers in Table 5-1 to binary.

Table 5-1   Decimal to Binary Conversions

Decimal	Binary
86	_____
175	_____
204	_____
19	_____

Step 9. Convert the binary numbers in Table 5-2 to decimal.

Table 5-2   Binary to Decimal Conversions

Binary	Decimal
11000011	_____
101010	_____
111000	_____
10010011	_____

Task 3: Convert Host IP Addresses

Step 1.   Computer hosts usually have two addresses: an Internet Protocol (IP) address and an Ethernet Media Access Control (MAC) address. For the benefit of humans, the IP address is normally represented as a dotted-decimal notation, such as 135.15.227.68. Each of the decimal octets in the address or a mask can be converted to 8 binary bits. Remember that the computer understands only binary bits. If all four octets were converted to binary, how many bits would there be?

_____

Step 2.   IP addresses are normally shown with four decimal numbers ranging from 0 to 255 and separated by a period. In Table 5-3, convert the four parts of the IP address 192.168.10.2 to binary using the Windows Calculator.

Table 5-3   Binary Conversion of an IP Address

Decimal	Binary
192	_____
168	_____
10	_____
2	_____

Notice how the 10 converted to only four digits and the number 2 converted to only two digits when using the Windows Calculator. When IP addresses can have any number from 0 to 255 in each position, eight digits are normally used to represent each number. In the previous example, eight digits were needed to convert 192 and 168 to binary, but 10 and 2 did not need as many digits. Normally 0s are added to the left of the digits to have eight digits in binary for each IP address number. The number 10 would be shown as 00001010. Four extra zeros are added to the front of the other four binary digits.

Step 3.   On the calculator in binary mode, enter the digits **00001010** and select the **Dec** radio button.

Which decimal number is equivalent to 00001010?

_____

Did adding "leading" zeros affect the number?

_____

What would the number 2 (in the previous example) be if you were to make it eight digits?

_____

Task 4: Convert Host IP Subnet Masks

Step 1.   Subnet masks, such as 255.255.255.0, are also represented as dotted decimal. A subnet mask will always consist of four 8-bit octets, each one represented as a decimal number. With the exception of decimal 0 (all eight binary zeros) and decimal 255 (all eight binary ones), each octet will have some number of ones on the left and some number of zeros on the right. Convert the nine possible decimal subnet octet values in Table 5-4 to binary.

Table 5-4   Binary Conversion of Decimal Subnet Values

Decimal	Binary
0	_____
128	_____
192	_____
224	_____
240	_____
248	_____
252	_____
254	_____
255	_____

Step 2.   Convert the four parts of the subnet mask 255.255.255.0 in Table 5-5 to binary.

Table 5-5   Binary Conversion of Subnet Mask

Decimal	Binary
255	_____
255	_____
255	_____
0	_____

Task 5: Convert Broadcast Addresses

Computer hosts and network devices use broadcast addresses to send messages to all hosts. Convert the broadcast addresses in Table 5-6 to binary.

Table 5-6   Binary Conversion of Broadcast Address

Address	Binary
IP broadcast 255.255.255.255	_____
MAC broadcast FF:FF:FF:FF:FF:FF	_____

Task 6: Convert IP and MAC Addresses for a Host

Step 1.   Click **Start > Run**, enter **cmd**, and press **Enter**. From the command prompt, enter **ipconfig /all**.

Step 2.   Make a note of the IP address and physical address (also known as a MAC address).

IP address: _____

MAC address: _____

Step 3.   Using the calculator, convert the four numbers contained in the IP address to binary and record them in Table 5-7.

Table 5-7   Binary Conversion of an IP Address

Decimal	Binary
	_____
	_____
	_____
	_____

Step 4.   The MAC or physical address is normally represented as 12 hexadecimal characters, grouped in pairs and separated by dashes (-). Physical addresses on a Windows-based computer are shown in a format of xx-xx-xx-xx-xx-xx, where each x is a number from 0 to 9 or a letter from a to f. Each of the hex characters in the address can be converted to four binary bits which is what the computer understands. If all 12 hex characters were converted to binary, how many bits would there be?

_____

Convert each of the hexadecimal pairs to binary in Table 5-8. For example, if the number CC-12-DE-4A-BD-88-34 was the physical address, convert the hexadecimal number CC to binary (11001100). Then convert the hexadecimal number 12 to binary (00010010) and so on. Be sure to add the leading zeros for a total of eight binary digits per pair of hex digits.

Table 5-8   Binary Conversion of a MAC Address

Hexadecimal	Binary
	_____
	_____
	_____
	_____
	_____
	_____

Task 7: Manipulate Powers of 2 to Determine the Number of Hosts on a Network

Binary numbers use two digits: 0 and 1. When you calculate how many hosts can be on a subnetwork, you use powers of 2 because binary is being used. As an example, we have a subnet mask that leaves six bits in the host portion of the IP address. In this case, the number of hosts on that network is 2 to the 6th power minus 2 (because you need a number to represent the network and a number that can be used to reach all the hosts—the broadcast address). The number 2 is always used because we are working in binary. The number 6 is the number of bits that are used for the host bits.

Step 1. On the calculator, in **Dec** mode, input the number **2**. Select the x^y key, the key that raises a number to a power. Input the number **6**. Click the = key, press **Enter** on the keyboard, or press the = key on the keyboard—all give the total. The number 64 appears in the output. To subtract two, click the minus (-) key and then the **2** key followed by the = key. The number 62 appears in the output. This means 62 hosts could be utilized.

Step 2. Using the previously described process, determine the number of hosts using the number of bits used for hosts in the four examples in Table 5-9.

Table 5-9   Determining Possible Number of Hosts

No. of Bits Used for Hosts	No. of Hosts
5	
14	
24	
10	

Step 3. Using a techniques similar to Step 1, determine what 10 to the 4th power equals.

_____

Step 4. Close the Windows Calculator application.

Task 8: (Optional) Determine the Network Number and Number of Hosts Based on Subnet Mask

Given the IP network address of 172.16.203.56 and a subnet mask of 255.255.248.0, determine the network portion of the address and calculate how many hosts can be created from host bits left using these steps:

Step 1. Start by converting the four octets of the decimal IP address to binary, and then convert the decimal subnet mask to binary. Remember to include leading zeros when converting to binary in order to make a total of eight bits per octet. Write your answers in Table 5-10.

Table 5-10   Binary Conversion of IP Address and Subnet Mask

Decimal IP Address and Subnet Mask	Binary IP Address and Subnet Mask
172.16.203.56	
255.255.248.0	

Step 2.   Align the 32 bits of the subnet mask to the 32 bits of the IP address and compare them. The bits in the IP address that align with the ones bits in the subnet mask represent the network number. What is the binary and decimal network number for this IP address? Determine the binary address first (include all 32 bits) and then convert it to decimal.

Binary network address: _____

_____

Decimal network address: _____

_____

How many ones bits are in the subnet mask?

_____

How many bits are left for host bits?

_____

How many hosts can be created with the bits left?

_____

Task 9: Reflection

List one other thing for which you might use the Windows Calculator scientific mode. It does not have to be related to networking.

_____

_____

_____

_____

_____

Challenge Lab 5-2: Exploring IP Address Functions on an Multi-function Device

Objectives

- Create a simple DHCP server/client network using four PCs and a multi-function device.

- Access and observe automatic IP addressing through the management GUI on a multi-function device.

- Test connectivity using the **ping** and **tracert** commands.

- Determine and describe the boundaries of private and public IP addresses in the network.

Background/Preparation

The design of the network determines which device(s) provide IP addresses to hosts. Although the multi-function device provides automatic IP addressing to its attached clients, its default gateway IP can be assigned automatically by the ISP. NAT can be employed by the multi-function device or the ISP in order to route private addresses on the Internet.

The following resources will be required:

- Linksys Model WRT300N wireless router or equivalent SOHO router

- A network jack with Internet access or that is connected to a configured DHCP server

- Four computers with Ethernet NICs and either Windows 2000 or Windows XP installed on them

Task 1: View Current IP Settings

Be sure to write down existing IP settings so that they can be restored at the end of the lab. These settings include IP address, subnet mask, default gateway, and DNS servers. If the workstation is a DHCP client, it is not necessary to record the settings.

Windows 2000 users should do the following:

Step 1.   Click **Start > Settings > Control Panel** and then open the **Network and Dial-up Connections** folder.

Step 2.   Click and open the **Local Area Connection** icon.

Step 3.   Select the TCP/IP protocol icon that is associated with the NIC in this PC.

Step 4.   Click **Properties** and view the existing IP configuration.

Windows XP users should do the following:

Step 1.   Click **Start > Settings > Control Panel** and then click the **Network Connection** icon.

Step 2.   Select the **Local Area Network Connection** and then click **Properties**.

Step 3.   Select the TCP/IP protocol icon that is associated with the NIC in this PC.

Step 4.   Click **Properties** and view the existing IP configuration.

Task 2: Configure TCP/IP Settings for DHCP

Step 1.   In the TCP/IP protocol Properties window, select **Obtain an IP address automatically** and **Obtain DNS server address automatically**.

Step 2.   Click **OK**.

Step 3.   Click **OK** on the Local Area Network Connection screen.

Task 3: Connect PCs to the Multi-function Device

Step 1.   Plug in the multi-function device power supply.

Step 2.   Check the LEDs on the front of the multi-function device to verify that the power is on.

Step 3.   Connect the PCs to the Ethernet ports on the back of the multi-function device using straight-through cables.

Step 4.   Reboot each of the host PCs.

Task 4: Verify the Physical Connection

Are link lights lit for each PC on the front of the multi-function device?

Task 5: Access the Command Prompt on a Client PC

Step 1.   Click **Start > Programs > Accessories > Command Prompt**.

What command will display the IP configuration, including DHCP and DNS servers, for the host PC?

Step 2.   Record the following information from the output of the command used:

IP address: _____

Subnet mask: _____

Default gateway: _____

DHCP server: _____

DNS servers: _____

Date/time lease obtained: _____

Date/time lease expires: _____

Where did the PC get its IP configuration?

What IP address would you expect to find associated with the switch ports on the multi-function device?

Task 6: Access the Multi-function Device Configuration Through a Web Browser

Step 1.   Open a web browser on the PC.

> **Note:** Internet Explorer users should choose **Tools > Internet Options > LAN Settings**, and verify that **Use a proxy server for your LAN** is unchecked.

Step 2.   Enter **http://** followed by the IP address of the default gateway in the browser address block.

Step 3.   Click **Go**.

Step 4.   Log in using no username and the password **admin**.

Check the local IP address displayed. This is the address associated with the internal network. Was your last answer in the previous task correct?

_____

Task 7: Examine the Multi-function Device Configuration

What is the range of addresses the multi-function device can assign to DHCP clients?

_____

What is the first IP address that can be assigned by DHCP?

_____

Compare the IP addresses assigned to the four client PCs. Were they assigned randomly within the range, or is there a pattern to the assignments?

_____

Click the **Status** menu button. What information appears under Internet Connection?

_____

Why is the Internet Connection showing these values?

_____

Task 8: Connect the Multi-function Device to the Internet

Step 1.   Use a straight-through cable to connect one end to the Internet port on the back of the multi-function device, and the other end to a network jack with Internet access.

Step 2.   Click the **Status** menu button.

Step 3.   Click **Refresh**.

Step 4.   Record the information that appears next to Internet Connection:

Connection type: _____

Internet IP address: _____

Subnet mask: _____

Default gateway: _____

DNS 1: _____

DNS 2: _____

Has the information changed?

_____

Where did the multi-function device get this configuration?

_____

Task 9: Verify Connectivity Using the ping Command

Step 1.   Click the **Administration** menu button on the multi-function device screen.

Step 2.   Click **Diagnostics** under the main menu bar.

Step 3.   Enter the IP address of one of the attached PCs next to **Ping Test**.

Step 4.   Click **Start to Ping**.

Was the ping successful?

_____

Step 5.   Close the Ping Test window.

Step 6.   Access the command prompt on one of the attached PCs.

Step 7.   Enter **ping** followed by the IP address of the multi-function device.

Was the **ping** successful?

_____

Step 8.   On the multi-function device, enter www.cisco.com next to Ping Test.

Step 9.   Click **Start to Ping.**

Was the **ping** successful?

_____

_____

_____

Step 10.   Close the Ping Test window.

Step 11.   If the **ping** to the Cisco site was not successful, explain why.

_____

_____

Task 10: Verify Connectivity Using the tracert Command

Step 1. On the multi-function device's Diagnostics screen, enter the IP address of one of the attached PCs next to **Traceroute Test**.

Step 2. Click **Start** to begin the **traceroute**.

Was the **traceroute** successful?

_____

Step 3. Close the **traceroute** window.

Step 4. Access the command prompt on one of the attached PCs.

Step 5. Enter **tracert** followed by the IP address of the multi-function device.

Was the **traceroute** successful?

_____

Step 6. On the multi-function device, enter www.cisco.com next to Traceroute test.

Step 7. Click **Start** to begin the **traceroute.**

Was the **traceroute** successful?

_____

_____

_____

Step 8. Close the Traceroute window.

Step 9. If the **traceroute** to the Cisco site was not successful, explain why.

_____

_____

_____

Why would most networks be set up to block **ping** and **traceroute** from getting out of the local network?

_____

_____

Task 11: Verify Internet Connectivity

Step 1. Open a browser window on a PC attached to the multi-function device.

Step 2. Enter http://www.cisco.com in the address block and click **Go**.

Does the page load?

_____

Why did the web page load, whereas the **ping** and **traceroute** failed?

_____

_____

Task 12: Determine the Network Boundaries

Are the IP addresses assigned to the client PCs routable on the Internet?

_____

Is the IP address assigned to the multi-function device Internet interface routable on the Internet?

_____

How did your network obtain a routable IP address in order to load the Cisco web page?

_____

Where did the packet get a routable IP address?

_____

_____

Task 13: Restore All Original Network Connections

Return all PCs to their original network connections and IP configurations.

Task 14: Reflection

How do DHCP and NAT work together to protect network security?

_____

_____

React to this statement: Without DHCP and NAT, the Internet would have collapsed long ago.

_____

CHAPTER 6

Labs: Network Services

The lab exercises included in this chapter cover all the Chapter 6 online curriculum labs to ensure that you have mastered the practical, hands-on skills needed to work with DNS, FTP, and e-mail clients. As you work through these labs, use Chapter 6 in Part I of this book or use the corresponding Chapter 6 in Networking for Home and Small Businesses course of the CCNA Discovery curriculum for assistance.

Lab 6-1: Observing DNS Name Resolution (6.2.1.3)

Objectives

- Observe the conversion of a URL to an IP address.
- Observe DNS lookup using the **nslookup** command.

Background/Preparation

Domain Name System (DNS) is invoked when you type a Uniform Resource Locator (URL), such as http://www.cisco.com, into a web browser. The first part of the URL describes which protocol is being used. Common protocols are Hypertext Transfer Protocol (HTTP), Hypertext Transfer Protocol over Secure Socket Layer (HTTPS), and File Transfer Protocol (FTP).

DNS translates the domain name, which in this example is www.cisco.com, to an IP address in order to allow the source host to reach the destination host. Work in pairs to complete this lab.

The following resources are required:

- Windows-based computer with Internet connectivity
- Access to the Run command or command prompt

Task 1: Observe DNS Conversion

Step 1. Click the **Start** button, select **Run**, enter **cmd,** and then click **OK**. The command prompt window appears.

Step 2. At the command prompt, enter **ping www.cisco.com**. The computer needs to translate www.cisco.com into an IP address so that it knows where to send the Internet Control Message Protocol (ICMP) packets. **Ping** is a type of ICMP packet.

Step 3. The first line of the output shows www.cisco.com converted to an IP address by DNS. You should be able to see the effect of DNS even if your school has a firewall that prevents **pinging**, or if Cisco has prevented people from **pinging** its web server.

Example 6-1   ping Output
```
C:\>ping www.cisco.com

Pinging www.cisco.com [198.133.219.25] with 32 bytes of data:

Request timed out.

Request timed out.
```

```
Request timed out.
Request timed out.
Ping statistics for 198.133.219.25:
    Packets: Sent = 4, Received = 0, Lost = 4 (100% loss),
```

Which IP address is shown on the screen?

_____

Work together with another student and discuss one or two other instances (besides the **ping** command) in which the computer would use DNS.

_____

_____

_____

_____

Task 2: Verify DNS Operation Using the nslookup Command

Step 1.   At the command prompt, enter the **nslookup** command, as shown in Example 6-2.

Example 6-2   The nslookup Command
```
C:\>nslookup
Default Server:  dns001.cisco.com
Address:  172.27.234.17
>
```

What is the default DNS server being used?

_____

Notice how the command prompt changed. This is the NSLOOKUP prompt. From this prompt, you can enter commands related to DNS.

Step 2.   At the prompt, enter **?** to see a list of all the available commands that you can use in NSLOOKUP mode.

What are three commands that you can use with NSLOOKUP?

_____

_____

Step 3.   At the NSLOOKUP prompt, enter **www.cisco.com**. Example 6-3 shows the output.

Example 6-3   Enter www.cisco.com at the Prompt

```
> www.cisco.com
Server:   dns001.cisco.com
Address:  172.27.234.17


Non-authoritative answer:
Name:     www.cisco.com
Address:  192.168.26.227
```

What is the translated IP address?

_____

Is it the same as the IP address shown with the **ping** command?

_____

Step 4.   At the prompt, enter the IP address of the Cisco web server that you just found. You can use NSLOOKUP to get the domain name of an IP address if you do not know the URL.

Using the previous procedures, find an IP address associated with http://www.google.com.

_____

_____

_____

Task 3: Identify Mail Servers Using the nslookup Command

Step 1.   At the prompt, enter **set type=mx** to have NSLOOKUP identify mail servers.

Step 2.   At the prompt, enter **www.cisco.com**.

What is the primary name server, the responsible mail address, and the default Time to Live (TTL)?

_____

_____

_____

_____

_____

_____

_____

_____

_____

Step 3.   At the prompt, enter **exit** to return to the regular command prompt.

Step 4.   At the prompt, enter **ipconfig /all**.

Write the IP addresses of all the DNS servers that your school uses, or those assigned by the ISP if your school does not have a local DNS server.

_____

Step 5.   Enter **exit** to close the command prompt window.

Task 4: Reflection

If your school did not have a local DNS server and was using one from the ISP, what effect would this have on name/address resolution response time?

_____

_____

Some companies do not dedicate a single server for DNS. Instead, the DNS server provides other functions as well. Which functions do you think might be included on a DNS server? Use the **ipconfig /all** command to help with this.

_____

Lab 6-2: Exploring FTP (6.2.3.3)

Objectives

Demonstrate how to use FTP from the command prompt and GUI.

Background/Preparation

File Transfer Protocol (FTP) is part of the TCP/IP suite. FTP is used to transfer files from one network device to another network device. Windows includes an FTP application that you can execute from the command prompt. Many free GUI versions of FTP software are also available that you can download. The GUI versions are easier to use than entering text from a command prompt.

When using FTP, one computer is normally the server and the other computer is the client. When accessing the server from the client, you need to provide a username and password. Some FTP servers have a user ID named *anonymous*. You can access these types of sites by simply entering **anonymous** for the user ID, without a password. Usually, the site administrator has files that can be copied but does not allow files to be posted with the anonymous user ID.

If your class does not have an FTP server available, you can download and install a freeware version, such as Home FTP Server or Cerberus FTP server. The FTP server on a computer running the CCNA Discovery Live CD can also be used, if available. Another computer will act as the FTP client by using FTP from the command line or a web browser, or you can download a freeware version of an FTP client, such as SmartFTP Client or Core FTP LE client. Work in teams of two to complete this lab.

The following resources are required:

- Windows-based computer with an FTP client

- Access to the Run command or command prompt

- FTP server (existing FTP server, downloaded freeware, or use Live CD)

Task 1: Examine FTP from the Command Prompt

Step 1.   Click the **Start** button, select **Run**, enter **cmd** on the command line, and then click **OK**.

Step 2.   At the prompt, enter **ftp** to start the FTP application. The prompt changes.

Step 3.   From the **ftp** prompt, enter **?** to see a list of the commands that can be used in this mode.

List three FTP commands.

_____

_____

_____

_____

Step 4.   At the prompt, enter **help put** (or **? put**) to see a short description of the **put** command.

What is the purpose of the **put** command?

_____

Step 5.   Use the **help** command again to find the purpose of the **get**, **send**, and **recv** commands. Write down your findings.

_____

_____

_____

_____

_____

_____

_____

_____

Step 6.   Partner with another student. If you installed FTP server software on one PC and an FTP GUI client on the other, write down the names and IP addresses of your computer and your partner's computer. If using the FTP server on a computer running the CCNA Discovery Live CD, contact your instructor for the server name and IP address. Getting the names and IP addresses correct is very important. Some FTP applications allow you to use either the IP address or the computer name.

_____

_____

Task 2: Use a GUI FTP Client or Web Browser

Step 1.   If you are using a web browser as the FTP client, open the web browser and enter **ftp://**_ip_address_of_FTP_server_ (using the IP address previously recorded). If the FTP server is configured to use an anonymous user ID, connect directly to the FTP server. Using the FTP client, download an available file from the server.

Step 2.   If you are using a GUI FTP client, open the application. For most FTP clients, you must configure a new connection by giving it a name, the IP address of the FTP server, and a username and password. You might have to enter **anonymous** if the FTP server allows this type of connection. Some applications have a check box that allows an anonymous login. When you have configured the connection, connect to the FTP server and download a file.

What is the name of the file you downloaded from the FTP server?

_____

List one example of when FTP might be beneficial to a computer technician.

_____

_____

_____

_____

Task 3: (Optional) Use Both an FTP Server and Client

Step 1.   If you control both the FTP server and client, practice sending files to and getting files from the client and the server.

Step 2.   Show your transferred files to another group of students.

Step 3.   Close the FTP server and client applications.

Lab 6-3: Configuring an E-mail Client (6.2.4.4)

Objectives

- Set up an e-mail client.

- Send and receive mail from a mail server.

- Add an e-mail account or change an existing one.

Background/Preparation

An e-mail application gives the user the ability to send and receive messages from another user located on the same local network or on the Internet. The messages are sent by the sending client and stored on an e-mail server. Another e-mail client with a mailbox on the server can then access the server at any time to receive stored messages that are destined for that client.

The following resources are required:

- Windows-based computer with Internet connectivity

- Microsoft Outlook or other e-mail client software

Task 1: Open Microsoft Outlook

Step 1.   From the **Start** menu, select **All Programs.** Locate the Microsoft Office software.

Step 2.   Select Microsoft Office Outlook as the e-mail program. If your computer does not have the Microsoft Office software, many free e-mail software packages are available on the Internet for both the Linux and Windows OS. Search the Internet to find a free e-mail client that can be installed on your computer. The following instructions might vary depending on your e-mail client.

Task 2: Set Up an E-mail Account

Step 1.   When you first start Microsoft Outlook, a screen appears with E-mail Upgrade Options. You can choose to import e-mail messages or address books from another account. Because this is your first e-mail account, click the **Do Not Upgrade** button.

Step 2.   Next, the E-mail Accounts screen asks whether you want to configure an e-mail account. Click **Yes.**

Step 3.   If Outlook has already been installed and set up for e-mail previously, you can start the Outlook application and choose **Tools, E-Mail Accounts** and then select **View or change existing e-mail account** to see how the existing account is set up.

Task 3: Enter POP3 E-mail Account Information

Step 1.   The next screen requires the user of the new account to fill in information. If you are establishing a real new e-mail account, enter your name and e-mail address. You can get your e-mail address from your ISP.

NOTE: If you are not creating a real ISP e-mail account, you can treat this step as a simulation. Just enter the information requested to become familiar with the process of creating an e-mail account.

Step 2.   Enter your server information. Contact your Internet provider to locate the server information for the incoming and outgoing mail servers. Usually, Internet providers put this information on their website in their help section.

What is your incoming (POP3) mail server?

_____

What is your outgoing (SMTP) mail server?

_____

Step 3.   Enter your username and password. Do *not* check the box to remember your password. This option is used when only one person uses the computer. If anyone else were to use the computer, that person could easily gain access to all the information in your e-mail.

Step 4.   Click the **Test Account Settings** button. If everything is correct, the screen displays that the test was successful. If it is not, correct your information and try again.

_____

NOTE: If this is a simulation, the test will not be successful and you can go to Tasks 4 and 5.

_____

Step 5.   Test your new account by sending an e-mail to a friend in class.

Task 4: (Optional) Add Another Account or Change an Account

Open Microsoft Outlook. Choose **Tools**, **E-mail Accounts.** In the screen that appears, you can add another e-mail account or change information in an existing account.

Task 5: Reflection

What are the advantages or disadvantages of using e-mail instead of regular postal mail?

_____

_____

_____

_____

_____

What are the advantages or disadvantages of using e-mail instead of an instant messaging program?

_____

_____

_____

_____

_____

With a partner, discuss five recommendations for e-mail etiquette that should be considered when e-mailing friends and business colleagues.

- ■   _____
- ■   _____
- ■   _____
- ■   _____
- ■   _____

CHAPTER 7

Labs: Wireless Technologies

The lab exercises included in this chapter cover all the Chapter 7 online curriculum labs plus an additional challenge lab, "Planning the Home or Small Business WLAN." Complete these labs to ensure that you have mastered the practical, hands-on skills needed to understand the basics of wireless networking. As you work through these labs, use Chapter 7 in Part I of this book or use the corresponding Chapter 7 in the Networking for Home and Small Businesses course of the CCNA Discovery online curriculum for assistance.

 ## Lab 7-1: Configuring a Wireless Access Point (7.2.5.3)

Objective

Configure the wireless access point (AP) portion of a multi-function device to allow access to a wireless client.

Background/Preparation

The Linksys WRT300N includes an integrated four-port switch, a router, and a wireless AP. In this lab, you configure the AP component of the multi-function device to allow access for wireless clients. The basic wireless capabilities of the multi-function device will be configured but this wireless network will not be secure. Setting up a secure wireless network is covered in Lab 7-3, "Configuring Wireless Security."

The following resources are required:

- Windows XP–based computer
- Straight-through UTP cables
- Linksys WRT300N with default settings

Task 1: Verify Connectivity Between the Computer and the Multi-function Device

Step 1. The computer used to configure the AP should be attached to one of the multi-function device's switch ports.

Step 2. On the computer, click the **Start** button and select **Run**. Enter **cmd** and click **OK** or press **Enter**.

Step 3. At the command prompt, **ping** the multi-function device using the default IP address 192.168.1.1 or the IP that has been configured on the multi-function device's port. Do not proceed until the **ping** succeeds.

Write down the command used to **ping** the multi-function device.

_____

If the **ping** is not successful, try these troubleshooting options:

- Check whether the multi-function device has power.
- Make sure that the cable is a known-good straight-through cable. Test to verify.
- Verify that the link light for the port where the computer is attached is lit.

■ Verify that the Linksys multi-function device has been reset to the default settings. Use the reset button to restore factory defaults.

■ Check to make sure that the IP address of the computer is on the 192.168.1.0 network. The computer must be on the same logical network as the multi-function device to be able to **ping** it. The DHCP service of the multi-function device is enabled by default. If the computer is configured as a DHCP client it should have a valid IP address and subnet mask. If the computer has a static IP address, it must be on the 192.168.1.0 network and the subnet mask must be 255.255.255.0.

If none of these steps correct the problem, check with your instructor.

Task 2: Log In to the Multi-function Device and Configure the Wireless Network

Step 1.   Open a web browser. In the address line, enter **http://**ip_address, where ip_address is the IP address of the wireless router (the default is 192.168.1.1). If the IP address has been changed from the default setting, use the address that worked in Task 1, Step 3. Once connected, you will be prompted for a username and password. At the prompt, leave the username text box empty, but enter the password assigned to the router. The default password is **admin**. Click **OK**.

Step 2.   In the main menu, click the **Wireless** tab.

Step 3.   In the Basic Wireless Settings window, shown in Figure 7-1, the **Network Mode** dropdown shows Mixed by default, because the AP supports 802.11b, g, and n wireless devices. You can use any of these standards to connect to the AP. If the wireless portion of the multi-function device is *not* being used, the network mode would be set to Disabled. Leave the default of Mixed selected.

Figure 7-1   Basic Wireless Settings

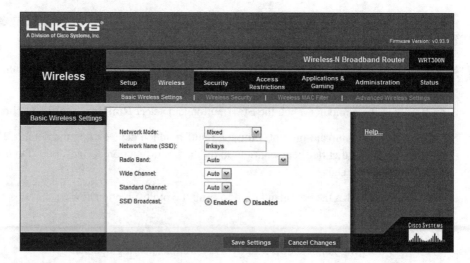

Step 4.   Delete the default SSID (linksys) in the Network Name (SSID) text box. Enter a new SSID using your last name or name chosen by your instructor. SSIDs are case sensitive.

Step 5. Write down the exact SSID name that you are using.

_____

Step 6. Click the **Radio Band** drop-down menu and write down the two options.

_____

Step 7. For a wireless network that can use 802.11b, g, or n client devices, the default is Auto. Auto allows the Wide Channel option to be chosen and gives the best performance. The Standard Channel option is used if the wireless client devices are 802.11b or g, or both b and g. The Wide Channel option is used if only 802.11n client devices are being used. Leave the default of Auto selected. SSID Broadcast is set to Enabled by default, which enables the AP to periodically send out the SSID using the wireless antenna. Any wireless devices in the area can detect this broadcast. This is how clients detect nearby wireless networks.

Step 8. Click the **Save Settings** button. When the settings have been successfully saved, click **Continue.**

The AP is now configured for a wireless network with the name (SSID) that you gave it.

Task 3: Reflection

How many wireless networks do you think could be configured in one classroom? What would limit this?

_____

_____

What do you see as a potential security problem when you broadcast your SSID from the AP?

_____

_____

_____

Lab 7-2: Configuring a Wireless Client (7.2.6.4)

Objectives

- Install and configure a driver for a wireless USB NIC for a wireless client computer.

- Determine the version of the driver installed and check the Internet for updates.

Background/Preparation

In this lab you install a driver for a wireless USB NIC in a computer. The driver is a type of software that controls the wireless NIC. The driver comes on a CD with the NIC or can be downloaded from the Internet. Many manufacturers require that the driver be installed before the adapter is connected. The procedure described in this lab is for a Linksys USB 802.11g wireless NIC, but it is similar to the procedures for other wireless NICs. You should always follow the procedure recommended by the wireless NIC manufacturer.

The following resources are required:

- Windows XP–based computer with an available USB port

- Wireless USB NIC and associated driver

- Administrator rights to install the driver

- Linksys WRT300N with wireless access configured from Lab 7-1

Task 1: Install the Wireless NIC Driver

Insert the CD that contains the wireless NIC driver into the CD/DVD drive and install the driver according to the manufacturer's recommendations. Most USB devices require that the driver be installed before the device is physically attached. Note that you may do part of the installation process now and part of it after the wireless NIC is installed. Figure 7-2 shows the Wireless NIC Setup wizard.

Figure 7-2   Wireless NIC Setup Wizard

Who is the manufacturer of the wireless NIC?

_____

_____

Describe how you installed the wireless NIC driver.

_____

_____

_____

Task 2: Connect the Wireless NIC

When prompted, connect the cable from the USB NIC to an available USB port, as shown in Figure 7-3. Click **Next** to continue.

Figure 7-3   Connecting the USB Wireless NIC

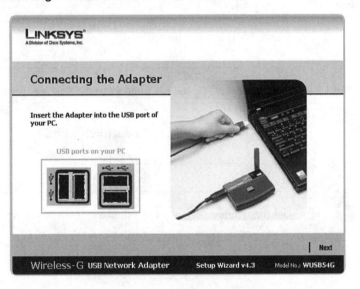

Task 3: Attach to the Wireless Network

Step 1.   Most wireless NIC adapters have client software to control the NIC. The software shows any wireless networks that are discovered, as shown in Figure 7-4. Select the SSID of the wireless network that you configured on the AP in Lab 7-1.

Figure 7-4   Available Wireless Networks

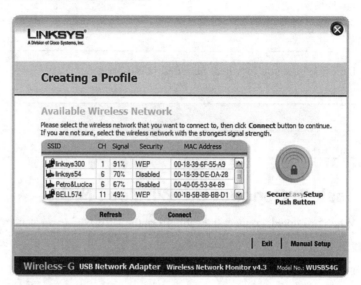

Which SSID are you using?

_____

Step 2.   If the wireless NIC did not connect to the wireless network, perform the appropriate troubleshooting.

What is the signal strength for the wireless NIC?

_____

_____

Did the wireless NIC see any other wireless networks in the area? Why or why not?

_____

_____

_____

What are some of the other SSIDs that are visible?

_____

_____

What is another name for a wireless host?

_____

Is it better to use the client software from the wireless NIC manufacturer or let Windows XP control the wireless NIC?

_____

_____

_____

_____

Task 4: Determine the NIC Driver Version

Hardware manufacturers continually update drivers. The driver that ships with a NIC or other piece of hardware might not be the most current.

To check the driver version for the NIC you installed, click **Start**, select **Control Panel** and then **Network Connections**. Right-click the wireless connection and select **Properties**. Click the **Configure** button for the NIC and then click the **Driver** tab, as shown in Figure 7-5.

Figure 7-5   Checking the Driver Version

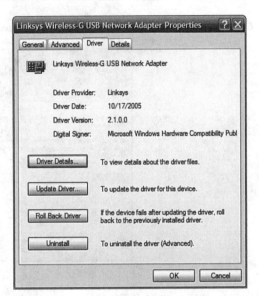

What is the name and version of the driver you installed?

_____

Task 5: Determine If the NIC Driver Is the Most Current

Search the NIC manufacturer website for drivers that support the wirelss NIC you installed. Are there more current ones available?

_____

What is the most current driver listed?

_____

If there is a more current driver, how would you apply it?

_____

_____

_____

_____

Task 6: Verify Connectivity

After you have installed the NIC, it is time to verify connectivity with the Linksys WRT300N.

Step 1.   Open a web browser such as Windows Internet Explorer or Mozilla Firefox.

Step 2.   In the address line enter **http://192.168.1.1**, which is the default setting on the AP.

Step 3.   In the Connect to 192.168.1.1 dialog box, shown in Figure 7-6, leave the Username text box empty, and enter **admin** in the Password text box. Leave the Remember my password check box unchecked. Click **OK**.

Figure 7-6   Connecting to the Multi-function Device

If you receive the Linksys Setup screen, you have established connectivity with the AP. The Setup screen can take quite some time to appear, so be patient. If you do not establish connectivity, you will have to troubleshoot the connection by checking to ensure that the devices are turned on and the IP addresses on all devices are correct. Which IP address should be configured on the wireless NIC?

_____

_____

Task 7: Reflection

Do you think the process of setting up a wireless network at a food store or bookstore is any different from what you just did? Why or why not?

_____

_____

_____

_____

_____

Do you think the AP model that you are using would be sufficient for your nearest grocery store? Why or why not?

_____

_____

_____

_____

_____

Lab 7-3: Configuring Wireless Security (7.3.5.2)

Objectives

- Create a security plan for a home or small business network.

- Configure the wireless access point (AP) portion of a multi-function device using security best practices.

Background/Preparation

A well-planned security implementation is critical to the safety of a wireless network. This lab reviews the steps that you must take to ensure the safety of the network using the following scenario.

You have just purchased a Linksys WRT300N wireless router, and you want to set up a small network in your home. You selected this router because the IEEE 802.11n specification claims that it has 12 times the speed of an 802.11g and 4 times the range. Because the 802.11n uses 2.4 GHz, it is backward compatible with both the 802.11b and 802.11g and uses multiple-in, multiple-out (MIMO) technology.

You should enable security mechanisms *before* connecting your multi-function device to the Internet or any wired network. You should also change the default values provided because they are well-known values that are easily obtainable on the Internet.

The following resources are required:

- Windows-based computer

- Linksys WRT300N

- Straight-through Ethernet cable

Task 1: Plan the Security for Your Home Network

List at least six security best practices that you should implement to secure your multi-function device and wireless network.

_____

_____

_____

_____

_____

_____

_____

_____

Describe what the security risk is for each best practice.

_____

_____

_____

_____

_____

_____

_____

_____

_____

Task 2: Connect a Computer to the Multi-function Device and Log In to the Web-Based Utility

Step 1.   Connect your computer (Ethernet NIC) to the multi-function device (port 1 on the Linksys WRT300N) by using a straight-through cable.

Step 2.   The default IP address of the Linksys WRT300N is 192.168.1.1, and the default subnet mask is 255.255.255.0. The computer and Linksys device must be on the same network to communicate with each other. Change the IP address of the computer to 192.168.1.2, and verify that the subnet mask is 255.255.255.0. Enter the internal address of the Linksys device (192.168.1.1) as the default gateway. Do this by clicking **Start > Control Panel > Network Connections**. Right-click the wireless connection and choose **Properties**. Select the Internet Protocol (TCP/IP) and enter the addresses, as shown in Figure 7-7.

Figure 7-7   Setting the IP Address on the Computer

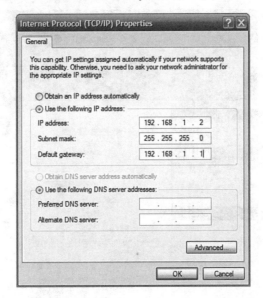

Step 3.   Open a web browser, such as Internet Explorer, Netscape, or Firefox and enter the IP address of the Linksys device (192.168.1.1 if reset to defaults) into the address field and press **Enter**.

A screen appears, requesting your username and password, as shown in Figure 7-8.

Figure 7-8   Connecting to the Linksys WRTG300N

Step 4.   Leave the Username field blank and enter **admin** for the password. It is the default password on the Linksys device. Click **OK.** Remember that passwords are case sensitive.

NOTE: As you make the necessary changes on the Linksys device, click **Save Settings** on each screen to save the changes or click **Cancel Changes** to keep the default settings.

Task 3: Change the Linksys Device Password

Once authenticated, the initial screen displayed is the **Setup > Basic Setup** screen, as shown in Figure 7-9.

Figure 7-9   Linksys WRTG300N Basic Setup Screen

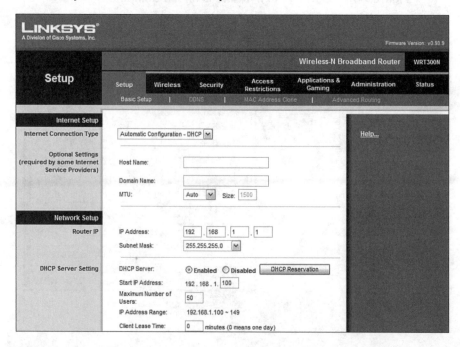

Step 1.   Click the **Administration** tab. The Management tab is selected by default.

Step 2.   Enter a new password for the Linksys device, and then confirm the password. The new password must not be more than 32 characters and must not include any spaces. The password is required to access the Linksys device web-based utility and setup wizard. Be sure to record the password you used.

Step 3.   The Web Utility Access via Wireless option is enabled by default, as shown in Figure 7-10. This option should be disabled or configured only to accept connections through secure protocols if security is of concern.

Figure 7-10   Changing the Administrative Password

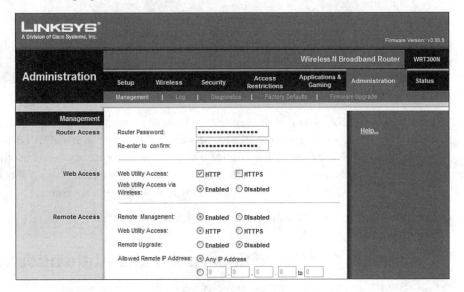

Step 4.   Click the **Save Settings** button to save the information.

NOTE: If you forget your password, you can reset the Linksys device to the factory defaults by pressing the Reset button for 5 seconds and then releasing it. The default password is admin.

Task 4: Configure the Wireless Security Settings

Step 1.   Click the **Wireless** tab, as shown in Figure 7-11. The Basic Wireless Settings tab is selected by default. The Network Name is the SSID shared among all devices on your network. It must be identical for all devices in the wireless network. It is case sensitive and must not be more than 32 characters.

Step 2.   Verify the SSID in use. If the SSID is set to the default value of **linksys,** change it to a unique name. Record the name you have chosen:

Step 3.   Leave the Radio Band set to Auto. This setting allows your network to use all 802.11n, g, and b devices.

Figure 7-11 Basic Wireless Settings

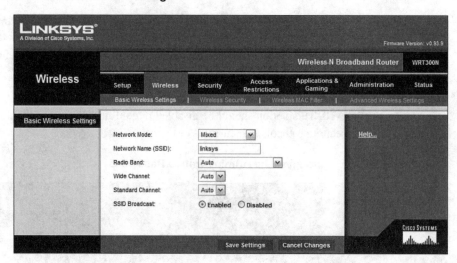

Step 4. For SSID Broadcast, click the **Disabled** button to disable the SSID broadcast. Wireless clients survey the area for networks to associate with and will detect the SSID broadcast sent by the Linksys device. For added security, do not broadcast the SSID. Please note that there are utilities and techniques to discover the SSID even if it is not broadcast. This should be used in conjunction with other security measures.

Step 5. Save your settings before going to the next task.

Task 5: Configure Encryption and Authentication

Step 1. Click the **Wireless Security** tab on the Wireless screen.

This router supports four types of security mode settings:

- Wired Equivalent Privacy (WEP)

- Wi-Fi Protected Access (WPA) Personal, which uses a pre-shared key (PSK)

- WPA2 Personal

- WPA Enterprise, which uses Remote Access Dial-In User Service (RADIUS)

- WPA2 Enterprise

- RADIUS

WPA is based on a draft version of IEEE 802.11i and offers a subset of the features finally contained in the approved version. WPA2 is based on the approved version of IEE802.11i and offers improved performance and many advanced features.

Step 2. Select WPA Personal in the Security Mode drop-down menu, as shown in Figure 7-12.

Step 3. On the next screen, shown in Figure 7-13, choose an encryption algorithm.

Figure 7-12   Setting the Wireless Security Mode

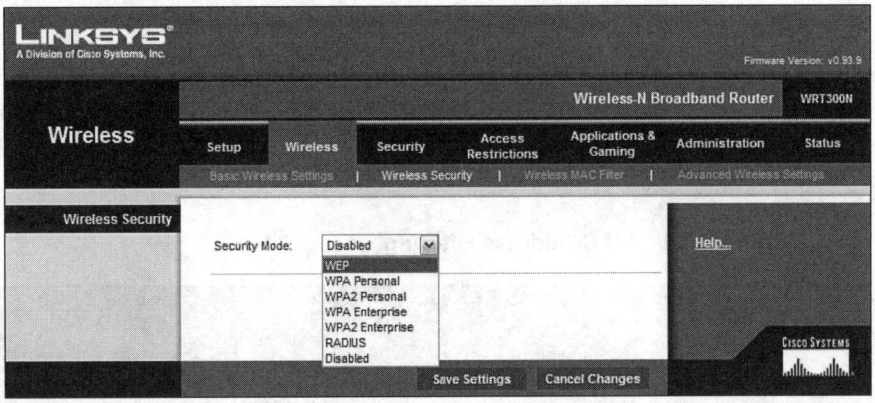

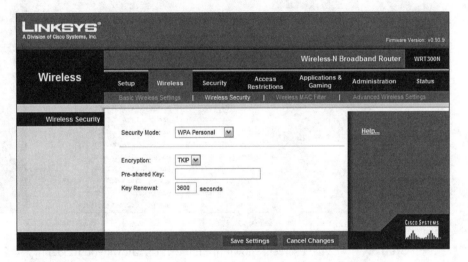

Figure 7-13   Selecting the Wireless Encryption Algorithm

To secure a network, use the highest level of encryption possible within the Selected Security mode. The following security modes and encryption levels are listed from least secure (WEP) to most secure (WPA2 with AES):

- WEP

- WPA, including Temporal Key Integrity Protocol (TKIP) and Advanced Encryption System (AES)

- WPA2, including TKIP and AES

AES is supported only by newer devices that contain a co-processor. To ensure compatibility with all devices, select **TKIP**.

Step 4.   For authentication, enter a pre-shared key between 8 and 63 characters. This key is shared by the Linksys device and all connected devices. Record the pre-shared key that you used.

Step 5.   Choose a key renewal period between 600 and 7200 seconds. The renewal period is how often the Linksys device changes the encryption key. The shorter the key renewal period, the more secure the connection. Unfortunately, shorter key renewal periods also increase the network overhead.

Step 6.   Save your settings before exiting the screen.

Task 6: Configure MAC Address Filtering

Step 1. Click the **Wireless MAC Filter** tab on the Wireless screen.

Step 2. MAC address filtering allows only selected wireless client MAC addresses to have access to your network. Select the **Permit PCs listed below to access the wireless network** radio button. Click the **Wireless Client List** button to display a list of all wireless client computers on your network, as shown in Figure 7-14.

Figure 7-14 MAC Address Filtering

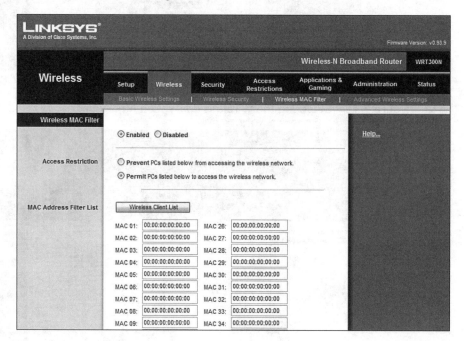

Step 3. The next screen, shown in Figure 7-15, allows you to identify which MAC addresses can have access to the wireless network. Check the **Save to MAC Address Filter List** check box for any client device you want to add, and then click the **Add** button. Any wireless clients, other than those in the list, will be prevented from accessing your wireless network. Save your settings before exiting the screen.

Figure 7-15 Selecting the MAC Addresses to Filter

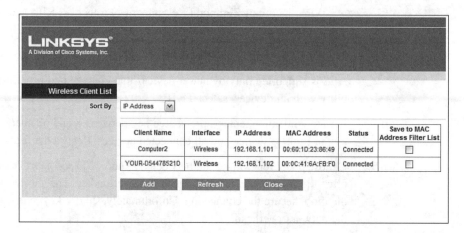

Task 7: Reflection

Which feature that you configured on the Linksys WRT300N makes you feel the most secure and why?

_____

_____

_____

_____

_____

Make a list of other items that you could do to make your network even more secure.

_____

_____

_____

_____

Challenge Lab 7-4: Planning the Home or Small Business WLAN

Objectives

- Evaluate user needs
- Use a WLAN implementation checklist
- Conduct a mini-site survey
- Plan WLAN implementation

Background/Preparation

Various wireless technologies exist each with specific characteristics. Before you can determine the most appropriate technology and WLAN implementation strategy, having a good understanding of end-user requirements as well as the physical environment where the network is to be installed is necessary. For a large-scale implementation a thorough site survey must be conducted. This requires a good understanding of radio frequency (RF) technology and access to equipment such as spectrum analyzers.

For the home and small business environments, a formal site survey is impractical. In these environments a very simplified process is often sufficient to determine which equipment should be installed and where. This process consists of an implementation checklist as well as a mini-site survey.

In this lab your friend needs to implement a home wireless network with four computers. He has chosen you to perform a mini-site survey of his home because he knows you are a student in the Networking Academy and have a good understanding of WLANs. Use the implementation checklist and site survey documents to help you plan the home network.

Find a friend in class to become your partner. Interview this person to plan and implement the home network.

Requirements for this lab include the following:

- Windows-based computer with Internet connectivity
- Linksys 300N broadband router
- Implementation checklist
- Site survey document

Task 1: Plan the WLAN

Step 1.   Use the following implementation checklist to interview your friend and find out the necessary information needed to plan the WLAN.

Implementation Checklist

❏ Determine end-user requirements. Talk with users and determine what applications are being used or will be used. Also speak with managers and any technical support people who might be present. Determine the following information:

  ■ Number of users

  ■ User locations

  ■ Applications being used

  ■ Required speed: 11 Mbps, 54 Mbps, or more

  ■ Whether all end users require the same throughput

  ■ What level of security is acceptable

❏ Determine and rank possible choices based on the following factors:

  ■ Sources of interference

  ■ Cost of possible solutions

  ■ Technical support staff, if needed

❏ Determine availability of financial resources. Are the financial resources available to implement the preferred solution? If not, one of the less preferred solutions might have to be considered.

❏ Determine whether human, technical, and financial resources are available to install and maintain selected wireless technology. Include the following:

  ■ Integration with existing wired or wireless network, if present. Can the planned wireless network be used with the existing network and resources?

  ■ Technical support staff, if needed.

Step 2.   List any items that you feel should be added to or deleted from this checklist. Justify your opinions.

_____

_____

_____

_____

_____

Step 3.   Record and keep all the information in notes.

Step 4.   Use the following mini-site survey document to find out the necessary information to plan the implementation of the WLAN.

Mini-Site Survey

1. Make a diagram of the site. The diagram should show the floor plan that depicts walls, doors, furniture, electrical outlets, and so on. The diagram should also include any existing wired or wireless network components and be drawn to scale. The more information that is contained the better.

2. Visually inspect the facility. A visual inspection will uncover obstacles such as metal racks and freezers already installed in the home.

3. Identify user areas. Mark fixed and mobile users.

4. Determine preliminary access point locations. Consider the location of wireless users and range estimations of the wireless LAN product you are using.

5. Identify the best locations for access point placement so that the network can provide optimal wireless coverage and maximum performance.

6. Document findings. Once you are satisfied that the planned location of access points will provide adequate coverage, identify them on the diagram.

Step 5.   List any items that you feel should be added to or deleted from this survey. Justify your opinions.

_____

_____

_____

_____

_____

Task 2: Use Internet for Research

Step 1.   Use the Internet to do any research required to help you implement the network. This might include specific information on wireless standards, network design best practices, signal absorption in different materials, and possible sources of interference.

Step 2.   Write down any websites you used to help you in this project. Record any sites visited and the information that you found.

_____

_____

_____

_____

_____

Step 3.   If you did not use any websites, did you use your engineering journal or the curriculum to guide you in the process?

_____

_____

_____

_____

_____

Task 3: Document Your Findings

Use a software program such as Microsoft Office or Visio to prepare a report of your findings. Include a diagram of the proposed network, including the location of any wireless devices. Add it to the original site survey diagram. The report should be specific enough that someone else could use it to install the proposed network.

_____

Task 4: Reflection

Find a classmate to discuss your report. Based on your classmate's feedback, write down at least two things that might have been completed differently during the installation of the WLAN.

_____

_____

_____

_____

_____

_____

_____

CHAPTER 8

Labs: Basic Security

The lab exercises in this chapter include the Chapter 8 online curriculum labs to ensure that you have mastered the practical, hands-on skills needed to set up a demilitarized zone (DMZ) on a Linksys multi-function device and use vulnerability analysis tools. As you work through these labs, use Chapter 8 in Part I of this book or use the corresponding Chapter 8 in the Networking for Home and Small Businesses course of the CCNA Discovery online curriculum for assistance.

Lab 8-1: Configuring Access Policies and DMZ Settings (8.4.2.4)

Figure 8-1   Lab 8-1 Topology

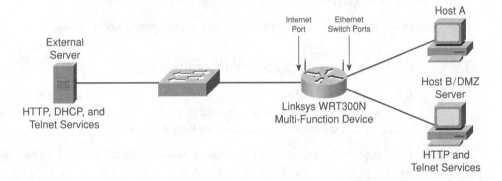

Objectives

- Log in to a multi-function device and view security settings.

- Set up Internet access policies based on IP address and application.

- Set up a DMZ for an open access server with a static IP address.

- Set up port forwarding to limit port accessibility to only HTTP.

- Use the Linksys WRT300N Help features.

Background/Preparation

This lab provides instructions for configuring security settings for the Linksys WRT300N. The Linksys provides a software-based firewall to protect internal, local-network clients from attack by external hosts. Connections from internal hosts to external destinations can be filtered based on the IP address, destination website, and application. The Linksys can also be configured to create a DMZ to control access to a server from external hosts. This lab is done in teams of two, and two teams can work together to test each other's access restrictions and DMZ functionality. The lab is divided into two parts:

- Part A: Configuring Access Policies

- Part B: Configuring a DMZ on the Multi-function Device

The following resources are required:

- Linksys WRT300N or other multi-function device with the default configuration

NOTE: If you are unsure of whether the device is in the default configuration, ask your instructor or perform the steps in Part B, Task 3 ("Restore the Multi-function Device to Its Default Settings") before beginning.

- User ID and password for the Linksys device if different from the default
- Computer running Windows XP Professional to access the Linksys GUI
- Internal PC to act as a server in the DMZ with HTTP and Telnet servers installed (preconfigured or Discovery Live CD server)
- External server to represent the ISP and Internet (with preconfigured DHCP, HTTP, and Telnet servers running [real server with services installed or Discovery Live CD server])
- Cabling to connect the PC hosts, Linksys WRT300N, or multi-function device, and switches

Part A: Configuring Access Policies

In this part of the lab, you work through the process of configuring access policies.

Task 1: Build the Network and Configure the Hosts

Step 1. Connect the host computers to switch ports on the multi-function device as shown in the topology diagram. Host-A is the console and is used to access the Linksys GUI. Host-B is initially a test machine but later becomes the DMZ server.

Step 2. Configure the IP settings for both hosts using Windows XP Network Connections and TCP/IP properties. Verify that Host-A is configured as a DHCP client. Assign a static IP address to Host-B in the 192.168.1.x range with a subnet mask of 255.255.255.0. The default gateway should be the internal local network address of the Linksys device.

NOTE: If Host-B is already a DHCP client, you can reserve its current address and make it static using the DHCP Reservation feature on the Linksys Basic Setup screen.

Step 3. Use the **ipconfig** command to display the IP address, subnet mask, and default gateway for Host-A and Host-B and record them in Table 8-1. Obtain the IP address and subnet mask of the external server from the instructor and record it in the table.

Table 8-1   Host IP Address Information

Host	IP Address	Subnet Mask	Default Gateway
Host-A			
Host-B/DMZ Server			
External Server			

Task 2: Log In to the User Interface

Step 1.   To access the Linksys or multi-function device web-based GUI, open a browser on Host-A and enter the default internal IP address for the device; normally, **192.168.1.1**.

Step 2.   Log in using the default user ID (no user ID entered) and password (**admin**), or check with the instructor if they are different. Figure 8-2 shows the Linksys login screen.

Figure 8-2   Linksys Login Screen

The multi-function device should be configured to obtain an IP address from the external DHCP server. After logging in to the Linksys device, the default screen displayed is **Setup > Basic Setup**. What is the Internet connection type?

_____

What is the default router (internal) IP address and subnet mask for the multi-function device?

_____

Step 3.   Verify that the multi-function device has received an external IP address from the DHCP server by clicking the **Status > Router** tab.

What is the external IP address and subnet mask assigned to the multi-function device?

_____

_____

Task 3: View Multi-function Device Firewall Settings

The Linksys WRT300N provides a basic firewall that uses network address translation (NAT). In addition, it provides additional firewall functionality using stateful packet inspection (SPI) to detect and block unsolicited traffic from the Internet.

Step 1.   From the main screen, click the **Security** tab to view the firewall and Internet filter status. Figure 8-3 shows the Security tab window in a default configuration.

Figure 8-3   Security Tab Window

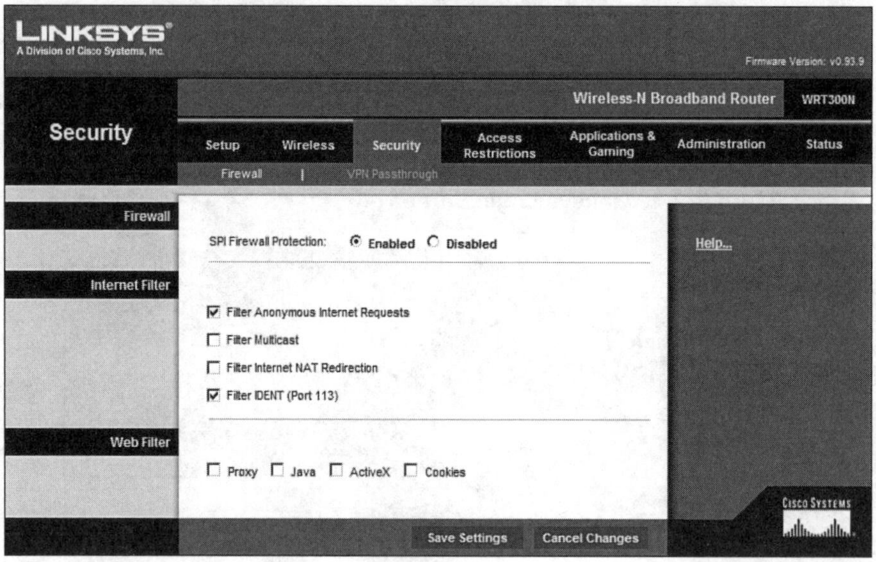

What is the status of SPI firewall protection?

_____

_____

Which Internet filter check boxes are selected?

_____

_____

Step 2.   Click **Help** to learn more about these settings. What benefits does filtering IDENT provide?

_____

_____

Task 4: Set Up Internet Access Restrictions Based on IP Address

In Lab 7-3 you saw that wireless security features can control which wireless client computers can access the multi-function device, based on MAC address. This prevents unauthorized external computers from connecting to the wireless access point (AP) and gaining access to the internal local network and the Internet.

The Linksys multi-function device can also control which internal users can get out to the Internet from the local network. You can create an Internet access policy to deny or allow specific internal computers access to the Internet based on the IP address, MAC address, and other criteria.

Step 1.   From the main multi-function device screen, click the **Access Restrictions** tab to define Access Policy 1.

Step 2.   Enter **Block-IP** as the policy name. Select **Enabled** to enable the policy, and then select **Deny** to prevent Internet access from a specified IP address.

Step 3.   Click the **Edit List** button and enter the IP address of Host-B. Click **Save Settings** and then **Close**. Click **Save Settings** to save Internet Access Policy 1 – Block-IP.

Step 4.   Test the policy by attempting to access the external web server from Host-B. Open a browser and enter the IP address of the external server in the address area. Are you able to access the server?

_____

Step 5.   Change the status of the block-IP policy to **Disabled** and click **Save Settings**. Are you able to access the server now?

_____

What other ways can access policies be used to block Internet access?

_____

_____

Task 5: Set Up an Internet Access Policy Based on an Application

You can create an Internet access policy to block specific computers from using certain Internet applications or protocols on the Internet.

Step 1.   From the main Linksys GUI screen, click the **Access Restrictions** tab to define an Internet access policy.

Step 2.   Enter **Block-Telnet** as the policy name. Select **Enabled** to enable the policy, and then click **Allow** to permit Internet access from a specified IP address as long as it is not one of the applications that is blocked.

Step 3.   Click the **Edit List** button and enter the IP address of Host-B. Click **Save Settings** and then **Close**.

What other Internet applications and protocols can be blocked?

_____

Step 4.   Select the **Telnet** application from the list of applications that can be blocked and then click the double right arrow to add it to the Blocked List. Click **Save Settings**.

Step 5.   Test the policy by opening a command prompt; click **Start > All Programs > Accessories > Command Prompt**.

Ping the IP address of the external server from Host-B using the **ping** command.

Are you able to **ping** the server?

_____

Step 6.   Telnet to the IP address of the external server from Host-B using the command **telnet** *A.B.C.D* (where *A.B.C.D* is the IP address of the external server).

Are you able to telnet to the server?

If you are not going to perform Part B at this time, skip to "Task 3: Restore the Multi-function Device to Its Default Settings" of Part B so that it is ready for the next student.

Part B: Configuring a DMZ on the Multi-function Device

In Part B of this lab you work with the DMZ capabilities of the Linksys multi-function device. First you set up a simple DMZ that allows access to any service that is running on the DMZ server. Next you limit access to the server to specific services using port forwarding.

Task 1: Set Up a Simple DMZ

Allowing access to a computer from the Internet while still protecting the other, internal local network computers is sometimes necessary. To accomplish this, you can set up a demilitarized zone (DMZ) that allows open access to any ports and services running on the specified server. Any requests made for services to the outside address of the multi-function device will be redirected to the server specified.

Step 1.   Host-B will act as the DMZ server and should be running HTTP and Telnet servers. Verify that Host-B has a static IP address or, if Host-B is a DHCP client, you can reserve its current address and make it static using the DHCP Reservation feature on the Linksys device Basic Setup screen.

Step 2.   From the main Linksys GUI screen, click the **Applications & Gaming** tab and then click **DMZ.**

Step 3.   Click **Help** to learn more about the DMZ. For what other reasons might you want to set up a host in the DMZ?

Step 4.   The DMZ feature is disabled by default. Select **Enabled** to enable the DMZ. Leave the **Source IP Address** selected as **Any IP Address,** and enter the IP address of Host-B in **Destination IP address**. Click **Save Settings** and click **Continue** when prompted.

Note: Any requests (for example, web or Telnet) sent from an outside host (the external server) to the external interface of the Linksys will be directed to the DMZ server.

Step 5.   Test basic access to the DMZ server by **pinging** from the external server to the outside address of the multi-function device. Open a command prompt by clicking **Start > All Programs > Accessories > Command Prompt** and use the **ping –a** command to verify that what is responding is actually the DMZ server and not the multi-function device. Are you able to **ping** the DMZ server?

Step 6.   Test HTTP access to the DMZ server by opening a browser on the external server and pointing to the external IP address of the multi-function device. Try the same thing from a browser on Host-A to Host-B using the internal addresses of the DMZ server (Host-B). An HTTP request to the external interface of the multi-function device from outside the network should be redirected to the DMZ server providing web services. A web request from internal Host-A to the DMZ server (Host-B) can be made directly to the internal DMZ server's address because Host-A is behind the firewall.

Are you able to access the web page?

_____

Step 7.   Test Telnet access to the DMZ server from the external server by opening a command prompt at **Start > All Programs > Accessories > Command Prompt**. Telnet to the outside IP address of the multi-function device using the command **telnet** *A.B.C.D* (where *A.B.C.D* is the outside address of the multi-function device). A Telnet request to the external interface of the multi-function device from outside the network should be redirected to the DMZ server providing Telnet services.

Are you able to telnet to the DMZ server?

_____

Step 8.   Test Telnet access to internal Host-A from the external server by opening a command prompt at **Start > All Programs > Accessories > Command Prompt**. Telnet to the inside IP address of Host-A using the command **telnet** *A.B.C.D* (where *A.B.C.D* is the inside address of Host-A).

Are you able to telnet to internal Host-A?

_____

_____

Task 2: Set Up a Host with Single Port Forwarding

The basic DMZ hosting set up in Task 1, Step 4 allows open access to all ports and services running on the server, such as HTTP, FTP, and Telnet. If a host is to be used for a particular function, such as FTP or web services, access should be limited to the type of services provided. Single port forwarding can accomplish this and is more secure than the basic DMZ, because it only opens the ports needed. Before completing this step, disable the DMZ settings from Task 1.

Host-B is the server to which ports are forwarded, but access is limited to only HTTP (web).

Step 1.   From the main screen, click the **Applications & Gaming** tab, and then click **Single Port Forwarding** to specify applications and port numbers.

Step 2.   Click the pull-down menu for the first entry under **Application Name** and select **HTTP**. This is the web server protocol port 80.

Step 3.   In the first **To IP Address** field, enter the IP address of Host-B and select **Enabled**. Click **Save Settings**.

Step 4.   Test HTTP access to the DMZ host by opening a browser on the external server and pointing to the outside address of the multi-function device. Try the same thing from a browser on Host-A to Host-B.

Are you able to access the web page?

_____

Step 5.   Test Telnet access to the DMZ server by opening a command prompt on the external server. Attempt to telnet to the outside IP address of the multi-function device using the command **telnet** *A.B.C.D* (where *A.B.C.D* is the outside IP address of the multi-function device).

Are you able to telnet to the DMZ server?

_____

Task 3: Restore the Multi-function Device to Its Default Settings

Step 1.   To restore the Linksys to its factory default settings, click the **Administration > Factory Defaults** tab.

Step 2.   Click the **Restore Factory Defaults** button. Any entries or changes to settings will be lost.

_____

NOTE: The current settings can be saved and restored at a later time using the **Administration > Management** tab and the **Backup Configuration** and **Restore Configuration** buttons.

_____

Lab 8-2: Performing a Vulnerability Analysis (8.4.3.2)

Caution: The procedures in this lab might violate legal and organizational security policies if performed on a live network. The security analyzer downloaded in this lab should only be used for instructional purposes in a lab environment. Before using a security analyzer on a live network, check with your instructor and network administration staff regarding internal policies concerning the use of these tools.

Figure 8-4   Lab 8-2 Topology

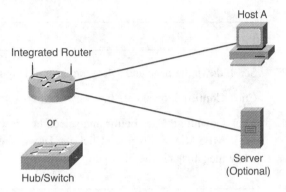

Objectives

- Download and install security analyzer software.

- Test a host to determine potential security vulnerabilities.

Background/Preparation

Security analyzers are valuable tools used by network administrators and auditors to identify network and host vulnerabilities. Many vulnerability analysis tools, also known as security scanners, are available to test host and network security. In this lab, you download and install the Microsoft Baseline Security Analyzer (MBSA). MBSA is designed to identify potential security issues related specifically to Microsoft operating systems, updates, and applications. It also identifies unnecessary services that might be running, as well as any open ports.

MBSA runs on Windows Server and Windows XP systems and scans for common security misconfigurations and missing security updates for the operating system as well as most versions of Internet Information Server (IIS), SQL Server, Internet Explorer (IE), and Office products. MBSA offers specific recommendations to correct potential problems.

This lab can be done individually or in teams of two.

The following resources are required:

- Computer running Windows XP Professional to act as the test station.

- High-speed Internet connection for downloading MBSA (unless pre-installed).

- Computer must be attached to the integrated router switch or a standalone hub or switch.

- Optionally, you can have a server running a combination of DHCP, HTTP, FTP, and Telnet (preconfigured).

Task 1: Download and Install MBSA

Step 1.   Open a browser and go to the MBSA web page at http://www.microsoft.com/technet/ security/tools/mbsa2/default.mspx.

What is the latest version of MBSA available?

_____

What are some of the features MBSA provides?

_____

_____

Step 2.   Scroll down the page and select the desired language to begin the download process.

Step 3.   Click **Continue** to validate the copy of Microsoft Windows you are running.

Step 4.   Click **Download Files below** and select the file you want to download. (The English setup file is MBSASetup-EN.msi.) Click the **Download** button on the right of this file. How many megabytes is the file to download?

_____

Step 5.   When the File Download – Security Warning dialog box displays, click **Save** and download the file to a specified folder or the desktop. You can also run it from the download website.

Step 6.   After the download is complete, make sure that all other applications are closed. Double-click the downloaded file. Click **Run** to start the Setup program, and then click **Run** if you are prompted with a security warning. Click **Next** on the MBSA Setup screen.

Step 7.   Select the radio button to accept the license agreement and click **Next**. Accept the defaults as the install progresses, and then click **Finish**. Click **OK** on the final MBSA Setup screen, and close the folder to return to the Windows desktop.

Task 2: Build the Network and Configure the Hosts

Step 1.   Connect the host computer(s) to the integrated router, a hub, or a switch as shown in the topology diagram. Host-A is the test station where MBSA will be installed. The server is optional.

Step 2.   Set the IP configuration for the host(s) using Windows XP Network Connections and TCP/IP properties. If the host is connected to the integrated router, configure it as a DHCP client; otherwise go to Step 3.

Step 3.   If the host is connected to a hub or switch and a DHCP server is not available, manually assign the host a static IP address.

Which IP address and subnet mask does Host-A and the server (optional) have?

_____

_____

_____

Task 3: Run MBSA on a Host

Double-click the desktop icon for MBSA or run it from **Start > All Programs**. Figure 8-5 shows the welcome screen.

Figure 8-5   Baseline Security Analyzer Welcome Screen

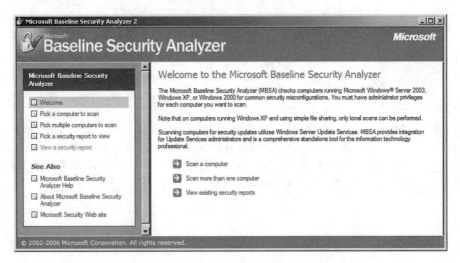

When the main screen displays, which options are available?

_____

_____

Task 4: Select a Computer to Scan

Step 1.   On the left side of the screen, click **Pick a computer to scan**. The computer shown as the default is the one on which MBSA is installed.

What are the two ways to specify a computer to be scanned?

_____

Step 2.   Accept the default computer to be scanned. Deselect checking for IIS and SQL administrative vulnerabilities because these services are not likely to be installed on the computer being scanned. Click **Start Scan**.

Task 5: View Security Update Scan Results

Step 1.   View the security report. What are the results of the security update scan?

_____

_____

Step 2. If there are any red or yellow Xs, click **How to correct this**. Which solution is recommended?

_____

_____

Task 6: View Windows Scan Results in the Security Report

Step 1. Scroll down to view the second section of the report that shows **Windows Scan Results**. Were there any administrative vulnerabilities identified?

_____

Step 2. In the Additional System Information section of the screen, in the Issue column for Services, click **What was scanned,** and click **Result details** to get a description of the check that was run. What did you find? When finished, close both pop-up windows to return to the security report.

_____

_____

Task 7: View Desktop Application Scan Results in the Security Report

Scroll down to view the last section of the report that shows **Desktop Applications Scan Results**. Were there any administrative vulnerabilities identified?

_____

How many Microsoft Office products are installed?

_____

Were there any security issues with macro security for any of them?

_____

Task 8: Scan a Server, If Available

If a server with various services is available, click **Pick a computer to scan** from the main MBSA screen, enter the IP address of the server, and then click **Start Scan**. Which security vulnerabilities were identified?

_____

_____

Were there any potentially unnecessary services installed? Which port numbers were they on?

_____

_____

Task 9: Uninstall MBSA Using Control Panel Add/Remove Programs

This step is optional, depending on whether the host will be automatically restored later by a network process.

To uninstall MBSA, click **Start > Control Panel > Add/Remove Programs**. Locate the MBSA application and uninstall it. It should be listed as Microsoft Baseline Security Analyzer 2.0.1. Click **Remove**, and then click **Yes** to confirm removal of the MBSA application. When finished, close all windows to return to the desktop.

Task 10: Reflection

The MBSA tool is designed to identify vulnerabilities for Windows-based computers. Search the Internet for other tools that might exist. List some of the tools discovered.

_____

Which tools might there be for non-Windows computers? Search the Internet for other tools that might exist and list some of them here.

_____

Which other steps could you take to help secure a computer against Internet attacks?

_____

CHAPTER 9

Labs: Troubleshooting Your Network

The lab exercises in this chapter include the Chapter 9 online curriculum labs. Complete these labs to ensure that you have mastered the practical, hands-on skills needed to understand the basics of network troubleshooting. As you work through these labs, use Chapter 9 in Part I of this book or use the corresponding Chapter 9 in the Networking for Home and Small Businesses course of the CCNA Discovery online curriculum for assistance.

Lab 9-1: Troubleshooting Using Network Utilities (9.2.7.2)

Objectives

- Use network utilities and the wireless router GUI to determine device configurations.

- Select the appropriate network utilities to help troubleshoot connectivity problems.

- Diagnose accessibility problems with web, FTP, Telnet, and DNS servers.

- Identify and correct physical problems related to cable types and connections.

Background/Preparation

In this lab, you use the browser and various troubleshooting utilities, such as **ipconfig**, **ping**, **tracert**, **netstat**, and **nslookup** to diagnose and correct connectivity problems. These command-line interface (CLI) utilities are available on most current operating systems, although the exact command and syntax might vary. Windows XP commands and syntax are used in this lab.

Your instructor will set up a network topology similar to the one shown in Figure 9-1 and will preconfigure the client computer, wireless router, server, and external router for each scenario in the lab. Various software and hardware connectivity problems will be introduced, and you will diagnose the cause from the client computer.

Figure 9-1   Lab 9-1 Setup

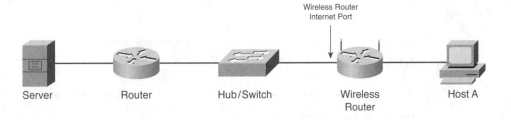

There are six scenarios. Work in teams of three, with each person taking the lead in two of the scenarios, and the other team members assisting.

The following resources are required:

- Computer running Windows XP Professional with web, FTP, and Telnet clients (CLI or GUI). This is Host-A.

- Server running a combination of DNS, HTTP, FTP, and Telnet services (preconfigured). This server will simulate Internet connections and can be a server with these services actually installed and running or a server running the Discovery Server Live CD.

- Wireless router configured as a DHCP server and client (default configuration).

- Router with two Ethernet interfaces configured as a DHCP server to a wireless router (preconfigured).

- Ethernet Cat-5 (minimum) straight and crossover cabling to connect hosts and network devices.

- Hub/switch for connecting the router to the wireless router.

Task 1: Build the Network and Configure the Hosts

Step 1.   Have your instructor set up a network topology similar to the one shown in Figure 9-1 with the Host-A client computer, wireless router, server, and router preconfigured.

Step 2.   Work from Host-A to issue commands to troubleshoot problems introduced by the instructor.

Step 3.   All commands are issued from a command prompt window. Open a command prompt window by clicking **Start > All Programs > Accessories > Command Prompt**. Keep the window open for the duration of the lab.

Task 2: Record the Baseline IP Address Information for Computers and Wireless Router

Note: Perform this task before the instructor introduces problems.

Step 1.   Host-A configuration: Issue the command that displays the IP address information for Host-A, including the DNS server, and record the information. Which command did you use?

_____

IP address:

_____

Subnet mask:

_____

Default gateway IP address:

_____

DNS server IP address:

_____

DHCP server IP address:

_____

How did Host-A obtain its IP address?

_____

Step 2.   Wireless router configuration: From Host-A, open a browser and go to the wireless router GUI by entering 192.168.1.1 as the URL address. Log in to the wireless router using the default user ID and password (check with your instructor if necessary). Check the internal and external IP address information and record it.

Internal IP address:

_____

Subnet mask:

_____

Is the DHCP server enabled?

_____

External (Internet) IP address:

_____

Subnet mask:

_____

Default gateway IP address:

_____

DNS server IP address:

_____

Step 3.   Server configuration: Obtain the server IP configuration from your instructor and record the information.

IP address:

_____

Subnet mask:

_____

Default gateway IP address:

_____

Web Server 1 protocol and name:

_____

Web Server 2 protocol and name:

_____

FTP Server 1 protocol and name:

_____

FTP Server 2 protocol and name:

_____

Task 3: Scenario 1—Diagnose Web Server Access

After your instructor sets up the problem for this scenario, use various utilities to diagnose the problem.

Step 1.   Open your browser and enter the name of Web Server 1 from Task 2. What happened?

_____

Step 2.   Try pinging the server using the name. Was it successful?

_____

Step 3.   Report the problem or suspected problem to the instructor. What was the problem? Include your reasoning.

_____

_____

_____

Step 4.   What did you do to correct the problem, if anything?

_____

_____

Step 5.   You might need to contact the instructor to correct the problem. When the problem is corrected, retest and verify access to the server.

Task 4: Scenario 2—Diagnose Web Server Access

After your instructor sets up the problem for this scenario, use various utilities to diagnose the problem.

Step 1.   Open your browser and enter the name of Web Server 2 from Task 2. (If the Discovery Server Live CD is being used this will be http://server-2.discovery.ccna.) What happened?

_____

Step 2.   Try browsing to the IP address of the web server. If the Discovery Server Live CD is being used this will be http://172.17.1.1.

_____

Step 3.   Ping the web server using the name. If the Discovery Server Live CD is being used this will be **ping server-2.discovery.ccna**. Try pinging the server by the IP address. Was the ping successful?

_____

Step 4.   The **nslookup** utility allows you to determine the IP address that DNS is providing for a specific name. Use the **nslookup** utility to query the IP address for the web server. If the Discovery Server Live CD is being used the command is **nslookup server-2.discovery.ccna**. What did this command reveal?

_____

_____

Step 5.   Report the problem or suspected problem to the instructor. What was the problem? How did you determine this?

_____

_____

_____

_____

_____

Step 6.   What did you do to correct the problem, if anything?

_____

_____

_____

_____

_____

Step 7.   You might need to contact the instructor to correct the problem. When the problem is corrected, retest and verify access to the server.

Task 5: Scenario 3—Diagnose FTP Server Access

After your instructor sets up the problem for this scenario, use various utilities to diagnose the problem.

Step 1.   Use your FTP client (CLI or GUI) to connect to FTP Server 1 from Task 2. If the Discovery Server Live CD is being used the command is **ftp://server-1.discovery.ccna**. Were you able to connect?

_____

Step 2.   Use FTP, **ping**, **nslookup**, **ipcconfig**, **tracert**, and visual inspection to determine the problem. What was the result of each of these actions?

_____

_____

_____

Step 3.   Report the problem or suspected problem to the instructor. What was the problem and how did you reason this out?

_____

_____

_____

_____

Step 4.   What did you do to correct the problem, if anything?

_____

Step 5.   You might need to contact the instructor to correct the problem. When the problem is corrected, retest and verify access to the server.

Task 6: Scenario 4—Diagnose FTP Server Access

After your instructor sets up the problem for this scenario, use various utilities to diagnose the problem.

Step 1.   Use your FTP client (CLI or GUI) to connect to FTP Server 2 from Task 2. If the Discovery Server Live CD is being used, this will be server-2.discovery.ccna. What happened?

_____

Step 2. Use FTP, **ping**, **nslookup**, **ipcconfig**, **tracert** and visual inspection to determine the problem. What was the result of each of these actions?

_____

_____

_____

_____

Step 3. Report the problem or suspected problem to the instructor. What was the problem and how did you determine it?

_____

_____

_____

_____

Step 4. What did you do to correct the problem, if anything?

_____

Step 5. You might need to contact the instructor to correct the problem. When the problem is corrected, retest and verify access to the server.

Task 7: Scenario 5—Diagnose Telnet Server Access Problem

After your instructor sets up the problem for this scenario, use various utilities to diagnose the problem.

Step 1. Use a Telnet client (CLI or GUI) to connect to the name of Server 1 identified in Task 2. If the Discovery Server Live CD is being used this will be server-1.discovery.ccna. What happened?

_____

Step 2. Which commands and tools will help you diagnose this problem? Try the commands, recording what information they supply.

_____

_____

_____

_____

Step 3. Report the problem or suspected problem to the instructor. What was the problem and how did you determine it?

_____

_____

_____

_____

_____

_____

Step 4. What did you do to correct the problem, if anything?

_____

_____

Step 5. You might need to contact the instructor to correct the problem. When the problem is corrected, retest and verify access to the server.

Task 8: Scenario 6—Analyze TCP Connections to Host-A

Step 1. Ask your instructor to verify that all problems introduced with the lab setup have been corrected. Using the appropriate clients, connect to the web, FTP, and Telnet servers simultaneously from Host-A. Use the server-1.discovery.ccna address for all connections.

Step 2. From the command line, issue a command to display the current active TCP connections to Host-A with the names of the servers and protocols. Which command did you use?

_____

Step 3. Which named connections did you see?

_____

Step 4. From the command line, issue a command to display the current active TCP connections to Host-A with IP addresses and protocol port numbers. Which command did you use?

_____

Step 5. Which IP addresses and port numbers did you see?

_____

_____

Step 6. From the command line, issue a command to display the current active TCP connections to Host-A, along with the program that created the connection. Which command did you use?

_____

Which program executable (filename with an .exe extension) is listed for each of the connections?

_____

_____

Task 9: Reflection

When troubleshooting the problem scenarios during this lab, which troubleshooting technique did you use in each scenario (top-down, bottom-up, or divide and conquer)? Was this technique appropriate? Why or why not?

_____

_____

_____

_____

Which utility or command do you feel was the most useful for network troubleshooting? Why?

_____

_____

_____

_____

Lab 9-2: Troubleshooting Physical Connectivity (9.3.3.2)

Objectives

- Examine device LEDs to determine proper Ethernet connectivity.

- Select the correct Ethernet cable for use between various types of devices.

- Visually inspect cables for potential problems.

- Use a cable tester to help identify cabling problems.

Background/Preparation

Physical cabling is one of the most common sources of network problems. This lab focuses on connectivity issues related to network cabling. You will visually inspect cabling and LED link lights to evaluate physical connections and to determine whether the correct type of cable is being used based on the devices they interconnect. You will also use a cable tester to identify problems with cables.

The instructor will set up a network topology similar to the one in Figure 9-2 and will preconfigure the hosts and network devices. The instructor will introduce various connectivity problems, and you will diagnose the cause of these problems by inspecting link lights and testing cables between devices. Various cable types, both good and bad, will be used to interconnect devices for each scenario in the lab.

Figure 9-2   Lab Setup

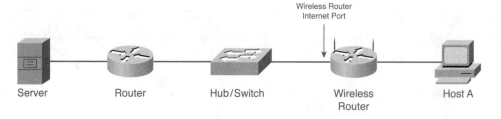

Work in teams of two, with each person taking the lead in half of the problem scenarios.

The following resources are required:

- Computer running Windows XP Professional (preconfigured)

- Server (preconfigured with the Discovery Server Live CD)

- Wireless router configured as a DHCP server and client (default configuration)

- Router with two Ethernet interfaces configured as the DHCP server to the wireless router (preconfigured)

- Hub/switch for connecting the router to the wireless router

- Mix of Ethernet Cat-5 (minimum) straight-through and crossover cabling, both good and bad, to connect hosts and network devices

- Basic Cat-5 Ethernet cable tester (RJ-45 pin-to-pin continuity checker)

- Advanced cable tester (optional), such as Fluke 620 (or similar)

Task 1: Build the Network and Configure the Hosts

Ask your instructor to set up a network topology similar to the one shown in Figure 9-2 with a pre-configured Host-A client computer, wireless router, server, and router. Initially, correct and properly functioning cabling is used so that end-to-end connectivity can be verified. The instructor then introduces cabling problems in each scenario.

Problems can consist of using the wrong type of cable between two devices (straight-through or crossover) or using a defective cable (miswired or improperly terminated). Observe device interface link lights, visually inspect cables, and use a cable tester to determine the problems.

Complete Tasks 2 and 3 of this lab before the instructor introduces problems.

Task 2: Record the Correct Cable Types Used Between Devices

Refer to the topology in Figure 9-2 and record the cable type that should be used (straight-through or crossover) based on the devices being connected. Have your instructor verify this information before proceeding.

Which type of cable should be used from Host-A to Wireless Router?

_____

Which type of cable should be used from Wireless Router (router portion) to Hub/Switch?

_____

Which type of cable should be used from Hub/Switch to Router?

_____

Which type of cable should be used from Router to Server?

_____

Task 3: Record the IP Address Information for the Computers

Step 1.   Use the **ipconfig** command, or obtain the IP address of Host-A from your instructor, and record it here.

Host-A IP address:

_____

Step 2.   Obtain the server IP address from your instructor and record it here.

Server IP address:

_____

Step 3.   Before starting on problem scenarios, verify end-to-end connectivity by pinging from Host-A to the server. If you do not get a reply from the server, check with your instructor. There may be a problem with the initial hardware or software setup.

Task 4: Scenario 1

After your instructor sets up the problem, use utilities, visual inspection, and a cable tester to isolate the problem.

Step 1.   Ping from Host-A to Server. What happened?

_____

Step 2.   Check the LED link lights on the various device interfaces. Write down any that are not lit.

_____

_____

Step 3.   Disconnect and inspect the cable connecting the network interfaces that were not lit. Describe the problem and how you were able to identify it.

_____

_____

_____

_____

_____

_____

Step 4.   What did you do to correct the problem?

_____

Step 5.   When the problem is corrected, retest and verify end-to-end connectivity by pinging from Host-A to the server. Was the ping successful?

_____

Task 5: Scenario 2

After your instructor sets up the problem, use utilities, visual inspection, and a cable tester to isolate the problem.

Step 1.   Ping from Host-A to Server. What happened?

_____

Step 2.   Check the LED link lights on the various device interfaces. Write down any that are not lit.

_____

Step 3.   Disconnect and inspect the cable connecting the network interfaces that were not lit. Describe the problem and how you were able to identify it.

_____

_____

_____

_____

_____

_____

Step 4.   What did you do to correct the problem?

_____

Step 5.   When the problem is corrected, retest and verify end-to-end connectivity by pinging from Host-A to Server. Was the ping successful?

_____

Task 6: Scenario 3

After your instructor sets up the problem, use utilities, visual inspection, and a cable tester to isolate the problem.

Step 1.   Ping from Host-A to Server. What happened?

_____

Step 2.   Check the LED link lights on the various device interfaces. Write down any that are not lit.

_____

Step 3.   Disconnect and inspect the cable connecting the network interfaces that were not lit. Describe the problem and how you were able to identify it.

_____

_____

_____

_____

_____

_____

Step 4.   What did you do to correct the problem?

_____

Step 5.   When the problem is corrected, retest and verify end-to-end connectivity by pinging from Host-A to Server. Was the ping successful?

_____

Task 7: Scenario 4

After your instructor sets up the problem, use utilities, visual inspection, and a cable tester to isolate the problem.

Step 1.   Ping from Host-A to Server. What happened?

_____

Step 2.   Check the LED link lights on the various device interfaces. Write down any that are not lit.

_____

_____

Step 3.   Disconnect and inspect the cable connecting the network interfaces that were not lit. Describe the problem and how you were able to identify it.

_____

_____

_____

_____

_____

_____

Step 4.   What did you do to correct the problem?

_____

Step 5.   When the problem is corrected, retest and verify end-to-end connectivity by pinging from Host-A to the server. Was the ping successful?

_____

Task 8: Reflection

What are some general rules to help you determine which type of Ethernet cable (straight-through or crossover) to use to connect different types of network hosts and devices?

_____

_____

_____

_____

_____

_____

Which types of problems can a cable tester detect that might not be determined by visual inspection?

_____

_____

_____

CHAPTER 10

Capstone Project: Putting It All Together

This lab is a final summative exercise based on the concepts and tools you have learned throughout this book. Complete this lab to ensure that you have mastered the practical, hands-on skills presented in the Networking for Home and Small Businesses course of the CCNA Discovery curriculum.

Objectives

- Understand the steps involved in planning and implementing a technical solution for a small business.
- Gather relevant information to help devise a technical solution to a problem.
- Devise a technical solution for a small office environment.
- Prototype a proposed technical solution using Packet Tracer 4.1.
- Plan the installation of a technical solution for a small business environment.
- Prepare and present a technical report to a diverse group.
- Configure a wireless router to support the requirements of a small business environment.

Background/Preparation

You have just successfully completed the first course in the CCNA Discovery curriculum and have obtained a contract position at a small advertising company called AnyCompany Corporation to help it update its IT resources. The company originally started with two partners who produced print flyers for local businesses. The company's list of customers has greatly expanded, and its customers are demanding more interactive advertising media, including video presentations. The partners recognize the business potential in this new market and have hired you to review their existing IT resources and produce a proposal that allows the company to take advantage of this new market. The partners have stated that if the proposal meets their requirements, they might hire you full-time to implement and manage these new resources.

The following resources are required to complete this project:

- Access to the Internet and course curriculum for research
- Office application suite for the preparation and presentation of the report
- Packet Tracer 4.1 for prototyping
- Linksys WRT300N wireless router or equivalent
- A Windows XP computer to act as wired host
- A Windows XP computer to act as wireless host
- Straight-through and crossover Category 5 Ethernet cables for testing (quantity variable)

Task 1: Gather Information and Determine Customer Requirements

You now have an idea of the scope of the project that you have undertaken, but do not have all the information required to proceed. The first step in any IT project is to gather information. You need to be able to answer the following questions:

- What is really required?

- What are the budget and the time frame to complete this project?

- What restrictions, if any, are there in equipment and resource selection?

- What resources are currently in place?

The more information that you gather at the beginning of any project, the better.

A good way to start the information-gathering process is to conduct interviews with the key individuals within the company, who are usually divided into three main groups: managers, end users, and IT support. Each group can provide valuable information.

Managers can answer questions regarding budget, expectations, and future plans. Any IT solution must take into account the plans that the company might have for growth, either in the number of employees or the technology being deployed. Managers can also provide you with information regarding company policies that might affect the proposed solution. Policies could include access, security, and privacy requirements.

The following information is normally gathered from managers:

- Budget

- Requirements and expectations

- Restrictions

- Staffing

- Future growth

End users are the people directly affected by the solution you design. Although managers are also end users, their requirements might differ drastically from the majority of the employees. Talking to as many employees from as many departments or work areas as possible to determine their requirements in speed, accessibility, and reliability is important. Determining the actual, rather than perceived, requirements is also important. From a customer service perspective, including employees in the initial discussions improves their buy-in and acceptance of the final solution.

The following information is normally gathered from end users:

- Requirements and expectations

- Current perceived performance of the equipment

- Applications used

- Work patterns

Most small businesses do not have an IT department and responsibilities might fall on one or more individuals, depending on their job role and expertise. Larger businesses might have a separate IT department. Those individuals who handle the IT can provide you with more technical information. For example, an end user might complain that an existing network has become slow, but an IT person can provide the technical information to determine whether performance has been degraded.

The following information is normally gathered from IT:

- Applications used

- Work patterns

- Hardware resources

- Network infrastructure (physical and logical topology)

- Network performance and issues

AnyCompany Corporation has provided a written summary, a floor plan, and a verbal interview with a company manager. For this task, gather as much information as possible from these three sources to help you plan a technical solution for AnyCompany Corporation.

AnyCompany Corporation Information Summary

Because AnyCompany Corporation is a very small business, it has no IT department. All employees have taken care of their own equipment and software. If they could not fix the problem, they would call in an outside service technician.

The machines are connected together through a 10 Mbps hub using Category 3 cable. The two partners and the secretary all have P2-300 MHz machines with 256 MB of RAM and 13 GB hard disk drives. The systems are all running Windows 98SE, and each has a low-capacity, monochrome laser printer attached. These machines are not capable of running the software required for video development.

What important information have you learned about the company's existing computer hardware and support mechanism?

_____

_____

_____

_____

The office will be reorganized, and additional employees will be hired to handle the new video production work. The company will have the following employees:

- **Administrative manager (currently the secretary)**: Duties include scheduling work, hiring and managing part-time workers, weekly payroll, and project tracking. The administrative manager uses spreadsheet and database software and must be able to use web-based e-mail provided by the ISP. The manager uses file sharing to allow employees to access important information. The administrative manager is also responsible for the final delivery of videos to the end user and maintains copies of all production videos for archival purposes.

What information does this provide you with regarding the hardware and software required by the administrative manager?

_____

_____

_____

- **Film and graphics production editor (one of the partners)**: Requires special editing software that uses very high-resolution graphics and requires at least 2 GB of memory to run effectively. The software also interfaces with a video capture interface board that uses a PCI-e slot in the computer. This specialized software only works in a Windows XP environment. Ensuring that the computer purchased for this position supports high-resolution video and has enough memory and a fast CPU to enable the editor to work quickly is important. The production editor produces the final copies of the films and works within very tight deadlines. The editor must also be able to use web-based e-mail provided by the ISP.

What type of computer is appropriate for the production editor?

_____

_____

_____

- **Film crew**: The other six employees are mobile workers, consisting of two production assistants, two camera people, a production manager (one of the partners), and a film director. They are in the office an average of two days per week. The rest of the time is spent either at customer sites or on film locations.

Because all the mobile workers are required to have access to e-mail and production schedules, both at the office and while on location, it is important for them to be able to connect to the main office from anywhere. They have no special software requirements, but they do need a large hard drive to store the film files for review. The mobile workers must work at various locations and might not always be able to plug into a data port. Ensuring that they are able to connect to the internal network wirelessly is important.

What type of machine would be appropriate for these workers? Do these workers require any specialized computer hardware or software?

_____

_____

_____

Because of the sensitive nature of some of the documents and records required by the administrative manager, a private color laser printer must be installed in the manager's office. A combination color copier/printer and high-resolution scanner must also be purchased and shared among all employees.

What type of interface would be appropriate for the private color laser printer and the shared copier/printer? Why?

_____

_____

_____

_____

For the purposes of training and compatibility, all the computers should use the same operating system and applications, if possible.

Which operating system should be used in the company? Why?

_____

No budget has yet been established for the completion of this project. The company is moving into this area to prevent bankruptcy, so it is important that the project be completed with the lowest possible expenditures.

_____

_____

Office Floor Plan

Figure 10-1 presents the floor plan for AnyCompany Corporation.

Figure 10-1   Office Floor Plan

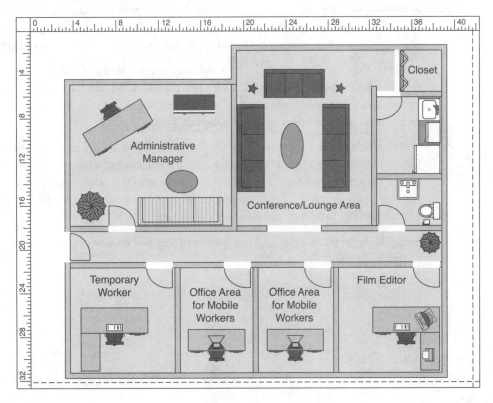

What information does the floor plan provide? What can it be used for?

_____

_____

_____

_____

_____

_____

_____

Interview with the Administrative Manager

After reviewing all the provided information speaking with an informed individual to clear up any outstanding issues or expectations is important. Susan Roberts, the new administrative manager, has agreed to meet with you for this purpose. A transcript of the interview follows:

Susan Roberts: I am the new administrative manager for AnyCompany Corporation. I am very glad that we have hired you to help us plan our IT requirements and would like to discuss them with you. I understand that you have already been supplied with a list of our planned staff and some information about how they use their computers. I have some details that might be important as you select equipment and media for our new facilities.

You: It is nice to meet you, Susan. Yes, I received a letter that listed the numbers and types of employees working at the redesigned office. It is my understanding that there will be eight employees: two office employees and six mobile workers. Any information you can provide about how these workers will use the network can help me prepare the proposal for your local network.

Roberts: Both Fred Michaels, the film and graphics production editor, and I are in our offices during regular business hours. We need access to e-mail, which we currently get from our ISP. The e-mail system that they provide uses a web client that we can access over the Internet. We are also able to access this e-mail from our home computers.

It is necessary for both of us to share files between ourselves and also with the mobile workers. These files are usually spreadsheets and documents, but sometimes, when we are close to deadlines, we have to send large film files back and forth between the mobile workers and the office. Files must be available for download during the day, and also at night, when we are away from the office. These film files are usually between 512 MB and 2 GB in size.

You: The information I received also indicated that you require a shared printer. How do you plan on using this printer?

Roberts: We want to have a color printer that is also capable of making copies. Because we expect this printer to be expensive, it is necessary for everyone to be able to print to it when they are in the office. Some of our storyboard documents are more than 100 pages, with lots of graphics.

You: How often are the mobile workers in the office? What do they need access to when they are in the office?

Roberts: Our mobile workers can be in the office anytime, day or night. They usually work out of their homes or on location, but when we are near a deadline, they can be in the office for 24 hours at a time. When they are in the office, they need to be able to use the printer and scanner. I do not want to keep files that the mobile workers need to use on my computer because they might need them at times when I am not in the office, and the computer is not turned on. I also need to share files with Fred while we are working in the office. These files can be kept on my computer or his.

You: I understand that your e-mail accounts are provided over the Web by your ISP. Do you see a need for locally hosted web or e-mail accounts?

Roberts: We also employ temporary, part-time employees when we need them. We want to be able to set up e-mail accounts for them to use while they are working with us. We usually don't have more than five or six temporary employees at any one time. All of them work from their homes and use their own computers.

You: Thank you for your time. I think I have enough information to get started. Are you the contact person if I have any further questions?

Roberts: Yes, please call me if you need more information. Thank you.

What information has this interview provided?

_____

_____

_____

_____

_____

_____

_____

_____

_____

_____

_____

_____

_____

_____

_____

_____

At this point, reviewing the notes and information that you have gathered and clearly summarizing the requirements is a good idea. If something is not clear, go back to the information-gathering task. Do not guess or assume anything because mistakes can be very costly.

Task 2: Select the Appropriate Services and Equipment

After you have gathered all the appropriate information, it is time to do some research. You must now use your knowledge and research skills to propose an appropriate technical solution for this company's limited budget and time requirements. Proposing a solution that is beyond the financial capabilities is of no benefit. However, it can be helpful to propose a solution within the current budget, and offer suggestions that would improve network performance or productivity if additional funding becomes available. If you can justify these extra expenditures, the company might consider them for later implementation or might even find the extra funding needed.

When developing a plan, starting at the end user and then working back toward the network and any shared resources, and then finally toward any external connections to the Internet or other networks is often the easiest. This allows the planner to develop a plan from the perspective of the data. Many different forms have been developed to help with planning and equipment selection. Using one of these forms or designing your own to keep everything organized is a good idea.

You have been asked to plan the network for AnyCompany Corporation from a user-centric perspective.

Step 1.   Use the Computer System Planning form to develop a proposed computer system for each of the employees at AnyCompany Corporation. Search the Internet or local sources for availability and pricing information. Use the same form to propose a server that can support their e-mail and FTP requirements.

Computer System Planning Form

Job Role:

Location:

Component	Recommendation
Processor (manufacturer/model/speed)	
Memory (type, amount)	
Hard drive (type, capacity)	
CD-ROM/DVD (R, R/W, speed)	
USB ports (number, location)	
Video card (manufacturer, model, video RAM)	
Sound card (manufacture, model)	
Modem (internal/external, speed, standard)	
Network card(s) (Ethernet: speed, wireless, standard)	
Operating system (manufacturer, version, compatibility)	
Monitor (size, resolution, refresh)	
Printer (manufacturer, model, type, speed)	
Speakers (manufacturer, model, type)	
Internet connection (USB/Ethernet/wireless)	

After the required hardware is determined the company must decide whether the systems should be built in-house or whether an outside company should be contracted to build the system. If an outside company is used, who is responsible for system maintenance? What are the terms and duration of the warrantee period? In addition, what is the final cost of the system delivered and installed at the end user site? Record this information below.

Step 2.   Using the Internet and locally available resources, select a high-speed, color copier/printer for the AnyCompany Corporation office. Document your selection including costs, specifications, and warranty.

Step 3.   Propose a network layout for AnyCompany Corporation. Because the company has limited funds available for this project, using only equipment designed for the small business and home markets is important.

Step 4.   Planning the Internet connectivity, including which services are provided by the ISP and which services must be provided in-house, is important. Larger companies usually provide services in-house whereas small businesses and individuals normally rely on an ISP to provide these services. Most ISPs offer a variety of services and service levels. Selecting an ISP is complicated, and not all technologies and services are available in all regions of the world. A number of excellent online tools are available to assist in the selection process. One such tool has been produced by the Australian government and is available at http://toolkit.acma.gov.au/internet/form.asp.

Using the curriculum and other available resources, select a local ISP to provide connectivity for AnyCompany Corporation. It will rely upon this ISP for DNS and web mail, and also needs the ISP to provide 99.999% uptime for access to the internal FTP/e-mail server. Because you are the only IT person at AnyCompany Corporation, ensuring that the ISP provides a high level of technical support is also important. Create a comparison worksheet for several local ISPs, including costing. Obtain as much information as possible.

Which internal services must be offered by AnyCompany Corporation, and which devices provide these services?

Step 5.   Complete the following network planning form as it relates to the proposed AnyCompany Corporation network.

Feature	Details
Are wired connections required?	Number:
Are wireless connections required?	Number:
Wireless standard	Choice of a/b/g/n
Firewall required?	Yes/No
ISP connectivity required?	Yes/No
Type of ISP connectivity	Choice of DSL, cable, serial, dialup
Internal or external modem required?	Yes/No (if Yes, then type of modem)
Cables required?	Yes/No (if Yes, then type of cable)
Battery backup required?	Yes/No

Task 3: Plan the Installation

After the equipment has been selected and the required services planned, the physical and logical installation is planned out. Physical installation includes the location of equipment and devices, along with how and when these devices are to be installed. In the business environment, minimizing disruption of the normal work processes is important. Therefore, most installations, changes, and upgrades are done during hours of minimal business activity. For the home, this is less important but should still be considered. Physical installation should also consider such things as adequate power outlets and ventilation, as well as the location of any necessary data drops.

You must now plan the installation of the AnyCompany network, taking care to minimize disruption to the normal business operations.

Step 1.   Using the provided floor plan and other appropriate information, plan the physical layout of all equipment data drops and power outlets. In addition, devise an implementation schedule that takes into account the work practices within AnyCompany Corporation.

Step 2. Equally as important as planning the physical layout of the network and equipment is planning the logical layout. This includes such things as addressing, naming, data flow, and security measures. Servers and network devices are assigned static IP addresses to allow them to be easily identified on the network and to also provide a mechanism for controlling access to these devices. Most other devices can be assigned addresses using DHCP.

Devise an addressing scheme for AnyCompany Corporation. The scheme must provide all network devices and servers with a static address and allow all other hosts to be configured via DHCP. Assign all devices an appropriate name. Record as much information on the floor plan from Step 1 as possible.

Step 3. AnyCompany Corporation is concerned that its files and resources might be vulnerable through the wireless network. Provide a security plan that allows only AnyCompany Corporation employees to connect to the wireless network and gain access to company information and resources.

Step 4.   After the network is planned, verifying that it works as expected is important. This is the prototyping stage and is not normally done for home or small business installations. Many different prototyping tools exist in the enterprise world.

Use Packet Tracer to prototype the planned network. Test various scenarios such as traffic coming from the Internet to the internal servers and host traffic moving to the Internet. Also confirm that the wireless network behaves as expected. Not all features of the designed network will be able to be tested using Packet Tracer.

Task 4: Prepare and Present the Proposal

All the gathered information and the proposed technical solution must be assembled into a format that makes sense to the company or individual who has asked you to provide a solution. In the small business and home markets, this might be simply a summary report that lists the key points in a manner that is easily understood. In the enterprise market, this process becomes much more structured and formal. The formal report usually contains many different sections, including

- Cover letter
- Title page and table of contents
- Executive summary
- Project proposal, comprising needs statement, goals and objectives, methodology and timetable, evaluation, budget summary, detailed budget, future funding plans
- Appended information

The report is often presented to various groups for approval. When presenting the report, present it in a confident, professional, and enthusiastic manner. This includes dressing appropriately for the target audience. The report and presentation must be technically accurate and free from spelling and grammatical errors. Always proofread your report and presentation before delivery. Have it reviewed by peers as well. A good technical solution does not overcome a bad proposal or presentation.

Prepare a proposal for AnyCompany Corporation that includes all the components listed earlier. Be sure to include all cost information and network diagrams. After preparing the report, have it reviewed by a peer. When you are confident in the proposal, present it to the class for consideration.

Task 5: Install and Configure the Network

AnyCompany Corporation has decided to accept your proposal for the installation of its new network. All the recommended equipment is on order and scheduled for delivery within a month. Planning is important for the installation stage. Preconfiguring and testing devices before installation saves a great deal of time and frustration.

Create a series of checklists for the installation and configuration the AnyCompany network. Once done, configure the multifunction device to support the planned network.

Step 1.   Create the necessary checklists, as follows:

- Create a checklist for the installation of the PCs at the customer site. This checklist should include all steps and items that must be checked, connected, or configured before the machine is ready for the end user.

_____

_____

_____

_____

_____

_____

_____

- Create a checklist for the configuration and installation of the network equipment at the customer site. This checklist should include all steps and items that must be checked, connected, or configured before the network device is considered fully functional.

_____

_____

_____

_____

_____

_____

_____

_____

■ Create a checklist for the implementation of the standard security necessary at a small business. This will be different for all devices but should include a list of all security measures on a device.

_____

_____

_____

_____

_____

_____

_____

Step 2.   Configure the multifunction device per the proposed plan.

_____

_____

_____

_____

Task 6: Test and Troubleshoot

During the installation, testing the network under as many diverse situations as possible is important. Use the various troubleshooting tools available in most operating systems and network devices to ensure that the network behaves as expected under the normal workflow that it will be exposed to. Document all tests.

For this task, test all aspects of the wireless router configuration and document your results. Test as much of the functionality as possible. Record your results in the following space. Show the results to your instructor before moving on. The instructor might ask you to demonstrate additional functionality.

Task 7: Document and Sign-Off

Sign-off is when the customer indicates satisfaction that the solution performs as promised. This is usually the point that payment is made. Many internal IT departments also request sign-off when a job is completed to the end users' satisfaction.

When sign-off occurs, printed copies of the performance and testing reports are delivered, along with the configuration information. For larger networks, much more information is required at sign-off, including physical and logical topology maps.

For this task, prepare documentation for sign-off from the manager at AnyCompany Corporation. In large installations, it can amount to several hundred pages of technical information and performance data. This includes the testing and performance documentation generated, along with any other prepared documentation.

For the purpose of this task, the required documentation is minimal. Prepare a cover page for signatures from AnyCompany stating that it agrees the network is performing at an acceptable level and it is now willing to accept responsibility for it. Attach this page to the network diagram and your test results. Have this information reviewed by a peer and then submit it to your instructor for final sign-off.

Task 8: Support

The final task in any solution is the provision of ongoing technical support. This requires a thorough understanding of the solution, technology, and customer requirements. The more thorough the documentation, the easier this stage is. Equally as important at this stage is an excellent grasp of customer service skills.

For this task, take turns playing the technical support and customer roles. The customer contacts the technical support person and reports a problem with the newly implemented AnyCompany Corporation network. The problem should be realistic. The support person tries to determine the problem by interacting with the customer.

802.11a   IEEE standard for wireless LANs that operate in 5 GHz band; uses 52-subcarrier orthogonal frequency-division multiplexing (OFDM) with a maximum raw data rate of 54 Mbps.

802.11b   The first widely accepted IEEE wireless networking standard. Because it operates in the 2.4 GHz band, other devices that operate in the same band can cause interference.

802.11g   An extension of the IEEE 802.11 standard. 802.11g applies to wireless LANs and provides up to 54 Mbps. Because it operates in the 2.4 GHz band, other devices that operate in the same band can cause interference.

802.11n   A proposed new extension to the IEEE 802.11 standard. 802.11n applies to wireless LANs and provides up to 540 Mbps in the 2.4 or 5 GHz band.

A

Accelerated Graphics Port (AGP)   Dedicated high-speed bus that supports the high demands of graphical software. This slot is reserved for video cards only.

access layer   The first point of entry into the network for all hosts. The access layer provides a physical connection to the network, as well as authentication and traffic control. A component of the Cisco three-layer network design approach that also includes a distribution layer and a core layer. The access layer provides entry to the network closest to end users.

access method   A set of rules used by LAN hardware to direct traffic on the network. It determines which host or device uses the LAN next.

access point (AP)   Wireless LAN transmitter/receiver that acts as a connection between wireless clients and wired networks.

Acknowledgement (ACK)   A transmission control character (or a transmission frame) that confirms a transmitted message was received uncorrupted or without errors or that the receiving station is ready to accept transmissions.

adapter card   A circuit board installed in a computer or networking device that provides an interface to another device or network. Common examples include a video adapter or network interface card (NIC).

Address Resolution Protocol (ARP)   A TCP/IP Layer 3 protocol that allows a host that knows another IP address on the same LAN to dynamically discover that other host's MAC address.

Address Resolution Protocol (ARP) table   A logical storage area in a host's RAM to store ARP entries. Also known as ARP cache.

ad-hoc   A Latin phrase that means "for this purpose." It refers to a custom designed or one-of-a-kind solution. Ad-hoc also means a peer-to-peer network in wireless LANs.

Advanced Encryption Standard (AES)   A symmetric 128-bit block cipher that replaces DES as a cryptographic standard. The algorithm must be used with key sizes of 128 bits, 192 bits, or 256 bits, depending on the application security requirement.

Advanced Interactive eXecutive (AIX)   An operating system based on UNIX. Recent versions of AIX can support up to 64 central processing units and two terabytes of random access memory. AIX is a propriety operating system developed by IBM.

adware   A software program that, once installed, automatically displays advertising material on a computer.

always-on   Term used to describe an Internet access service that does not require a number to be dialed. Examples include DSL and cable modem.

American Standard Code for Information Interchange (ASCII)   8-bit code for character representation (7 bits plus parity). Each letter of the alphabet is assigned a number from 0 to 127.

antenna   A device for transmitting or receiving a radio frequency (RF). Antennas are designed for specific and relatively tightly defined frequencies and are quite varied in design.

AOL instant messenger (AIM)   Instant message service that supports text chat, photo sharing, online gaming, and computer-to-computer voice using OSCAR instant message protocol and the TOC protocol.

Apache web server   A public-domain, open-source web server developed by the Apache Software Foundation for various operating systems such as UNIX, Linux, Microsoft Windows, Novell NetWare, and other operating systems.

application software   A software program designed to perform a specific task or group of tasks.

application layer   Layer 7 of the OSI model. It interfaces directly to and performs common application services for the application processes. It also issues requests to the presentation layer (layer 6).

association   The point when a wireless access point (AP) agrees to handle data to and from the wireless host.

asynchronous   Without respect to time. In terms of data transmission, asynchronous means that no clock or timing source is needed to keep both the sender and the receiver synchronized.

attenuation   The reduction of signal energy during transmission.

authentication   A process implemented on a network to verify the identity of a user.

Automatic Private IP Addressing (APIPA)   With APIPA, a DHCP client automatically self-configures an IP address and subnet mask when a DHCP server is not available. The IP address range used for APIPA is 169.254.0.1 through 169.254.255.254. The client configures itself with an address from this range and a default Class B subnet mask of 255.255.0.0. A client uses the self-configured IP address until a DHCP server becomes available.

Automatic Update   A software update service for Microsoft Windows operating systems located on the Microsoft website. The types of software updates available include critical system component updates, service packs, security fixes, patches, and free upgrades to Windows components. The Automatic Update service automatically detects the type of existing hardware.

B

backup   A copy of data saved onto storage media for the purpose of restoring the data and computer operations in case of data loss. Types of backup include full, incremental, and differential. A backup should be physically removed from the source data.

baseband   Characteristic of a network technology where only one carrier frequency is used. Ethernet is an example of a baseband network. Also called narrowband.

baseline   A quantitative expression of planned costs, schedules, and technical requirements for a defined project. A baseline is established to describe the "normal" status of network or computer system performance. The status can then be compared with the baseline at any point to measure the variation from the "normal" operation condition.

basic input/output system (BIOS)   Program stored in a ROM chip in the computer that provides the basic code to control the computer's hardware and to perform diagnostics on it. The BIOS prepares the computer to load the operating system.

Basic Service Set (BSS)   A group of 802.11 devices connected to an access point.

binary   Digital signals that are typically expressed as 1 or 0. A numbering system used in computers that is based on two values (0 and 1).

binary digit   A digit with only 1 and 0 as possible values; 1 = on and 0 = off.

bit   The smallest unit of data in a computer. A bit can take the value of either 1 or 0. A bit is the binary format in which data is processed by computers. A bit is also known as a binary digit.

bits per second (bps)   Unit of measure used to express data transfer rate of bits.

blade   A server component or individual port card that can be added to a network router or switch for additional connectivity.

blaster worm   Also known as Lovsan or Lovesan. A Distributed Denial of Service (DDoS) worm that spread during August 2003 on computers running the Microsoft Windows 2000/XP operating system.

blog   A web page that serves as a publicly accessible personal journal for an individual.

Bluetooth   Wireless industry standard that uses an unlicensed radio frequency for short-range communication enabling portable devices to communicate over short distances.

Blu-ray   High-density optical disc format used to store digital media, such as high-definition video.

boot sector   A sector of a data storage device, typically the hard drive, that contains code for booting the operating system when starting the computer.

botnet   Refers to any group of bots. Typically a collection of compromised machines that distribute worms, Trojan horses, or backdoor viruses.

bots   Software applications that run automated, simple and repetitive tasks over the Internet.

bottom-up troubleshooting   A troubleshooting technique in a layered concept of networking that starts with the physical or lowest layer and works up.

broadband   Transmission system that multiplexes multiple independent signals onto one cable. In Internet terminology a broadband connection generally refers to access technologies with download speeds of 500 Kbps or greater.

broadcast   A method for sending data packets to all devices on a network. Broadcasts are identified by a broadcast address and rely on routers to keep broadcasts from being sent to other networks.

broadcast domain   Devices within a group that receive the same broadcast frame originating from one of the devices. Broadcast domains are typically bounded by routers because routers do not forward broadcast frames.

broadcast MAC address   Hardware address reserved for frames that are intended for all hosts on a local network segment. Generally, a broadcast address is a MAC destination address of all 1s. A broadcast MAC address has the hexadecimal form of FF:FF:FF:FF:FF:FF.

browser   GUI-based hypertext client application used to access hypertext documents and other services located on innumerable remote servers throughout the Web and Internet.

brute force   A method used to gain access to a network or decrypt a message by systematically entering all possible combinations.

business software   An application designed for use in specific industries or markets.

byte   A unit of measure that describes the size of a data file, the amount of space on a disk or other storage medium, or the amount of data being sent over a network. One byte consists of 8 bits of data.

C

Cable Modem Termination System (CMTS)   A component located at the local cable television company that exchanges digital signals with cable modems on a cable network.

Carrier Sense Multiple Access with Collision Avoidance (CSMA/CA)   Basic media access method for 802.11 wireless networks.

Carrier Sense Multiple Access with Collision Detection (CSMA/CD)   Basic access method for Ethernet networks.

case   Container in which a PC or other networking device is enclosed.

catastrophic failure   In computer and networking device components, a failure that makes them nonfunctional.

cell   With wireless local networks, area controlled by the AP is referred to as a cell or Basic Service Set (BSS).

cellular phone   Telephone that uses cellular wireless technologies to communicate.

central processing unit (CPU)   Chip contained on a single integrated circuit, called the microprocessor, which interprets and processes software instructions and data. The CPU contains two basic components, a control unit and an Arithmetic/Logic Unit (ALU).

channel   Provides the pathway over which the message can travel from source to destination. In networking a channel can be a physical medium or a frequency.

chipset   Integrated circuits on a motherboard that enable the CPU to communicate and interact with the other components of the computer.

circuit   The communication path between two or more points that a current or data transmission follows.

Class A   A Class A address has four octets. The first octet is between 1 and 127, although 127 is reserved for loopback testing. The other three octets are used for host addressing. A Class A network can have 16,777,214 hosts.

Class B   A Class B address has four octets. The first octet is between 128 and 191. The first two octets identify the network. The last two octets are for host addressing. A Class B network can have 16,384 networks and 65,534 hosts.

Class C   A Class C address has four octets. The first octet is between 192 and 223. The first three octets identify the network. The last octet is for host addressing. A Class C network can have 2,097,152 networks and 254 hosts.

Class D   A Class D address has four octets. The first octet is between 224 and 239. Class D is used for multicasting.

Class E   A Class E address has four octets. The first octet is between 240 and 255. Class E IP addressing is reserved.

classful   The division of IP addresses into five classes: A, B, C, D, and E. A fixed number of networks and hosts is associated with each class.

classless   System of IP addressing that does not rely on class boundaries but instead treats all address space as being equal. Any number of bits can be assigned to represent the network portion of an address, leaving the rest to represent hosts.

classless interdomain routing (CIDR)   Technique supported by border gateway protocols and based on route aggregation. CIDR allows routers to group routes together to reduce the quantity of routing information carried by the core routers. With CIDR, several IP networks appear to networks outside the group as a single, larger entity. With CIDR, IP addresses and their subnet masks are written as four octets, separated by periods, followed by a forward slash and a two-digit number that represents the subnet mask.

Clear to Send (CTS)   Along with request to send (RTS), CTS is used by the 802.11 wireless networking protocol to reduce frame collisions introduced by the hidden terminal problem and exposed node problem.

client   A network device that participates in a client/server relationship by requesting a service from a server. When a computer is used to access the Internet, the computer is the client and the website is the service requested from the server.

cloud   A symbol that refers to connections in service provider networks.

Code Division Multiple Access (CDMA)   A communication channel access method that uses spread-spectrum technology and a special coding scheme. Cell phones and wide area wireless networks use technologies such as CDMA.

collaboration suite   Applications designed to allow the sharing of resources and information within and between organizations.

collision   In Ethernet, the result of two or more devices transmitting simultaneously. The frame from each device is damaged when they meet on the physical media. All computer networks require a mechanism to prevent collisions or to recover quickly when they occur.

collision domain   In Ethernet, the network area where data that is being transmitted simultaneously from two or more computers could collide. Repeaters and hubs propagate collisions; LAN switches, bridges, and routers do not.

command-line interface (CLI)   User interface to a computer operating system or application that depends on textual commands being entered by the user.

command.com   Command-line interpreter for DOS and 16/32-bit versions of Windows (95/98/98 SE/Me). command.com is the first program run after boot and sets up the system by running the autoexec.bat configuration file.

compact disc   An optical disk that uses a laser to record and retrieve information. Used primarily for sound or data recording.

components   Elements that make up a system such as a computer system or network.

computer   Electrical machine that can execute a list of instructions and perform calculations based on those instructions.

computer name   Identity of a computer on a wired or wireless network.

connection-oriented   Protocol to establish an end-to-end connection before data is sent so that data arrives in the proper sequence. TCP is a connection-oriented protocol.

content filtering   Blocking specific types of web content using content-control or spam-blocking solutions.

continuity   State or quality of being continuous or unbroken. End-to-end continuity tests on cable media can verify that there are no opens or shorts.

controller card   A board that interfaces between the motherboard and a peripheral.

converged network   A network capable of carrying voice, video, and digital data.

convergence   Speed and capability of a group of internetworking devices running a specific routing protocol to agree on the topology of an internetwork after a change in that topology.

core layer   One of three basic layers in the hierarchical design of Ethernet networks. The core layer is a high-speed backbone layer designed to move large amounts of data quickly. High-speed switches or routers are examples of core layer devices.

cracker   A person who creates or modifies computer software or hardware with the intent to cause harm.

crossover cable   A cable that reverses the send and receive pairs from one end to the other. Used to connect similar networking device interfaces, such as two hubs, two switches, or a PC and a router.

crosstalk   Source of interference that occurs when cables are bundled together for long lengths. The signal from one cable can leak out and enter adjacent cables.

Customer Premises Equipment (CPE)   Terminating equipment, such as terminals, telephones, and modems, supplied by the telephone company, installed at customer sites, and connected to the telephone company network.

cuteFTP   Series of FTP client applications, developed by GlobalSCAPE, which provide a simple file transfer interface for Windows-based or Mac-based systems.

D

daemon   Software that is normally loaded on a server and running, waiting for clients to request its services.

data loss The accidental or willful destruction of information on a hard disk or any other storage medium.

datagram Another term for an IP packet containing user data.

de facto standard An unoffical standard that evolves over time to become more common than the others. Ethernet is an example of a de facto standard.

default gateway The default gateway address is the address of the router interface connected to the same local network as a source host. All hosts on the local network use the default gateway address as a means of sending data outside the LAN.

default route The interface through which the router forwards a packet containing an unknown destination IP network address. The default route usually connects to another router that can forward the packet toward its final destination network.

demilitarized zone (DMZ) This term is borrowed from the military. A DMZ is a designated area between two powers where military activity is not permitted. In computer networking, a DMZ refers to an area of the network that is accessible to both internal and external users. It is more secure than the external network but not as secure as the internal network. It is created by one or more firewalls to separate the internal, DMZ, and external networks. Web servers for public access are frequently placed in a DMZ.

Denial of Service (DoS) An attack by a single system on a network that floods the bandwidth or resources of the targeted system, such as a web server, with the purpose of shutting it down.

destination The target host for a message. Ethernet/IP frames contain a destination MAC and IP address.

DHCP Dynamic Host Configuration Protocol requests and assigns an IP address, default gateway, and DNS server address to a network host automatically.

DHCP Acknowledgement The server response to a DHCP request from a client. This informs the client that it has permission to start using the offered IP configuration information.

DHCP client A host that receives its IP configuration dynamically from a DHCP server.

DHCP Discover A client that needs an IP address will send a DHCP Discover message to try and locate a DHCP server. This is a broadcast message sent to all hosts on the network, but only a DHCP server will reply. These DHCP messages are sent to port 67. Only DHCP servers are configured to listen on port 67.

DHCP Offer The server response to a DHCP Discover issued by a client, suggesting an IP address for the client.

DHCP range The group of IP addresses that a DHCP server can provide to DHCP clients.

DHCP Request The response from a host to the offer by a server, asking to use the suggested IP address.

DHCP server A server that listens on port 67 for client DHCP Discover messages and provides IP configuration dynamically to clients. Configuration information can include IP address, subnet mask, default gateway, DNS servers, and more.

dial-up Internet access technology that uses a dial-up analog modem and a conventional phone line to contact the ISP using the public switched telephone network (PSTN).

digital subscriber line (DSL)   Public network technology that delivers high bandwidth over conventional copper wiring at limited distances. Always-on technology that allows users to connect to the Internet.

DSL Access Multiplexer (DSLAM)   A device that allows two or more data sources to share a common transmission medium. DSLAM separates DSL phone and data signals and directs them onto networks. A DSLAM contains a bank of DSL modems to accept the connections from DSL customers.

Digital Video Disc (DVD)   Optical digital disc that stores data. Also called digital versatile disc.

Digital Video Disc-Recordable (DVDr)   Technology that allows a DVD to be written to once.

Digital Video Disc-Rewritable (DVDrw)   Technology that allows the media to be recorded multiple times.

DIP switch   Dual in-line package. Electrical switch for a dual in-line package used on a printed circuit board.

disk storage   Space on a hard disk or magnetic storage media disk to store data.

Distributed Denial of Service (DDoS)   A type of DoS attack designed to saturate and overwhelm network links with useless data. DDoS attacks operate on a much larger scale than DoS attacks. Typically hundreds or thousands of attack points attempt to overwhelm a target simultaneously. The attack points might be unsuspecting computers that have been previously infected by the DDoS code.

distribution layer   The distribution layer provides a connection point for separate local networks and controls the flow of information between the networks. It typically contains more powerful switches than the access layer as well as routers for routing between networks. In a three-layer design, distribution layer devices also control the type and amount of traffic that flows from the access layer to the core layer.

distribution system   Network that interconnects multiple BSSs to form an ESS in a wireless LAN. For the most part, a distribution system is a wired Ethernet network.

divide-and-conquer troubleshooting   A troubleshooting technique in a layered concept of networking that can start at any layer and work up or down depending on the outcome.

DNS name   A name assigned to a device within a DNS domain that identifies the device. DNS names are usually of the format *servername.domainname.domaintype*. As an example, www.cisco.com identifies a web server in the cisco.com domain.

DNS server   A local or remote server that resolves a DNS name to an IP address for hosts on a network.

docking station   Device that attaches a laptop to AC power and desktop peripherals.

Domain Name System (DNS)   System that provides a way to map host names, or URLs, to IP addresses.

dotted-decimal notation   A method of common notation for IP addresses in the form <a.b.c.d> where each number a represents, in decimal, 1 byte of the 4-byte IP address. Also called dot address.

driver   Specialized software that interprets the output of a device so that it can be understood by other devices.

dual core CPU   Two cores inside a single CPU chip that can be used together to increase speed, or used in two locations at the same time.

dynamic and private ports   TCP or UDP ports in the range of 49152–65535 that are not used by any defined application.

Dynamic Host Configuration Protocol (DHCP)   A client/server-based network protocol that requests and assigns an IP address, default gateway, and DNS server address to a network host automatically.

E

echo reply   The ICMP response from a destination host to a ping or echo request from a source host.

echo request   The ICMP or ping request sent to a target host from the source host to determine network connectivity.

e-learning   Type of educational instruction using electronic delivery methods such as CD-ROMs, video conferencing, websites, and e-mail.

electromagnetic interference (EMI)   Interference by electromagnetic signals that can cause reduced data integrity and increased error rates on transmission channels. Also referred to as noise.

electromagnetic wave   A self-propagating wave in space with electric and magnetic components classified in order of increasing frequency; radio waves, microwaves, terahertz radiation, infrared radiation, visible light, ultraviolet radiation, x-rays, and gamma rays.

Electronic Industries Alliance (EIA)   A trade association that establishes standards for electrical and electronics products.

Electrostatic Discharge (ESD)   Discharge of static electricity from one conductor to another conductor of a different potential.

e-mail   Ability for users to communicate over a computer network. Exchange of computer-stored messages by network communication.

encryption   The application of a specific algorithm to data so as to alter the appearance of the data making it incomprehensible to those who are not authorized to see the information.

Ethernet crossover cable   Network cable that reverses the transmit and receive pairs from one end to the other. Used to connect similar networking device interfaces, such as two hubs, two switches or a PC and a router.

expansion slot   Location in a computer where a PC card can be inserted to add capabilities, such as graphics or other device support, to the computer.

ext2   Second extended file system. File system for the Linux kernel designed to reduce internal fragmentation and minimize searching by dividing the space into blocks.

ext3   Third extended file system. A journaled file system for the Linux operating system.

Extended Service Set (ESS)   A collection of BSSs that communicate with one another through the distribution system (usually the wired Ethernet port on an access point).

Extensible Authentication Protocol (EAP)   Authentication framework, not a specific authentication mechanism. Most commonly used in wireless LANs, EAP provides common functions and a negotiation of the desired authentication mechanism.

extranet   Network designed to provide access to specific information or operations of an organization to suppliers, vendors, partners, customers, or other businesses.

F

far-end crosstalk (FEXT)   A measurement of crosstalk between pairs of wires used when testing Category 5E or Category 6 cabling. FEXT is measured at the receiving end of the cable.

FAT16/32   Non-secure file systems used by Microsoft operating systems.

fiber optics   The transmission of light pulses containing data along glass or plastic wire or fiber. Optical fiber carries more information than conventional copper wire and is not susceptible to electromagnetic interference.

File Allocation Table (FAT)   A table of records that the operation system uses to store information about the location of every directory, subdirectory, and file on the hard drive. FAT is stored in track 0 on the hard drive.

file system   A method used by the operating system to store and organize files. Types of file systems include FAT32, NTFS, HPFS, ext2, and ext3.

File Transfer Protocol (FTP)   Application protocol that is part of the TCP/IP protocol stack, used for transferring files between network devices.

firewall   A device or application installed on a network to protect it from unauthorized users and malicious attacks.

firmware   Software embedded in a hardware device; typically provided on flash ROMs or as a binary image file that can be uploaded onto existing hardware by a user.

flash drive   A portable USB storage device that uses flash memory and can take the place of other types of removable media, such as a floppy disk.

flooding   With an Ethernet LAN switch, the process of sending frames to all ports except the incoming port when the destination MAC address in a frame is not known.

floppy disk   A removable magnetic storage device that uses a flexible recording media. Most floppy disks can store 1.44 MB of data.

floppy disk drive (FDD)   Device that spins a magnetically coated floppy disk to read data from and write data to it.

frame   Logical grouping of information sent over a transmission medium as a data link layer unit. Often refers to the header and trailer, used for synchronization and error control, that surround the user data contained in the unit.

Frequently Asked Questions (FAQ)   The group of questions that most customers ask. FAQs are usually posted by a company on the Internet to assist with common questions and problem resolution.

frontside bus   A bidirectional bus that carries electronic signals between the central processing unit and other devices, such as RAM and hard disks.

full duplex   Data transmission that can go two ways at the same time. An Internet connection using DSL service is an example of full duplex.

G

gaming device   Powerful computer with higher quality displays used for the purpose of playing video games designed for a particular operating system.

gateway   A device that converts protocols from one interface to another. With a local network, the gateway is normally a router that provides access to another network or the Internet.

General (GNU) Public License (GPL)   A license for free and open-source operating system software. In contrast to commercial operating system software such as Windows XP, a GPL allows the operating system software, such as Linux and BSD, to be modified. Also called GNU general public license.

general use software   An application that is found on most home or business computers, such as Microsoft Word.

gigabyte (GB)   One billion bytes.

gigahertz (GHz)   Common measurement of a processor equal to one billion cycles per second.

global address   A public IP address that is routable on the Internet.

Global System for Mobile Communication (GSM)   An international standard for cellular phones.

GNU   An operating system that functions using only free software.

graphical user interface (GUI)   User-friendly interface that uses graphical images and widgets, along with text, to indicate the information and actions available to a user when interacting with a computer.

grounding strap   A strap worn by a technician when working on electronic equipment to help discharge potentially damaging static electricity. The other end attaches to a grounded station.

H

hacker   Term used to describe a person who creates or modifies computer software or hardware with the intent to test network security or to cause harm.

half duplex   Data transmission that can go two ways, but not at the same time. Two-way radios and early shared Ethernet networks are examples of half duplex.

handheld   Small computing device with input and output capabilities, such as a touch screen or miniature keyboard and display screen.

hard disk   Primary storage medium on a computer.

hard disk drive   Typically, a fixed magnetic storage device that uses one or more rigid disks as recording media.

hardware   Physical electronic components that make up a computer system.

hardware platform   Computer hardware components that use the same unique binary-coded machine language to communicate.

header   Control information placed before data when encapsulating that data for network transmission.

help desk   A person or department in an organization that provides computer and network assistance to end users.

hertz (Hz)   A unit of frequency measurement. It is the rate of change in the state, or cycle, in a sound wave, alternating current, or other cyclical waveform. Hertz is synonymous with cycles per second, and it describes the speed of a computer microprocessor.

Hewlett-Packard UNIX (HP-UX)   A modified version of UNIX used on proprietary Hewlett-Packard operating systems. HP-UX uses clustering technology, kernel-based intrusion detection, and various types of system partitioning.

hexadecimal   Using a base 16 number system. The system uses the numbers *0* through *9*, with their usual meaning, plus the letters *A* through *F* to represent hexadecimal digits with values of 10 to 15. The rightmost digit represents ones (16^0), the next represents multiples of 16 (16^1), then $16^2=256$, and so on.

hierarchical   Using a tiered structure with multiple levels. The IP address is hierarchical (two parts). The use of core, distribution, and access layers in network design is also hierarchical.

High-Performance File System (HPFS)   A file system that is able to handle 2TB-volume or 2GB-file disks, and 256-byte filenames.

hop   A router or layer 3 device that a packet passes through on its way to a destination.

horizontal application   Software that can be used across a broad range of the market, such as an office suite.

host   1) In an IP network, any device with an IP address. A host can be a PC, server, printer, or router interface. 2) A device that directly participates in network communication. A host can use network resources that are available and/or provide network resources to other hosts on the network.

hotspot   A location where wireless Internet access is available.

hot-swappable   Ability to remove, replace, and add peripherals while a system is running.

HTTP cookie   Small packet of data created by a server and sent to a user's browser and back to the server for authenticating, tracking, and maintaining specific user information, such as site preferences.

hub   A device that serves as the central point of connection for the devices on a LAN.

Hypertext Markup Language (HTML)   Coding language used to create documents for the Web.

Hypertext Transfer Protocol (HTTP)   A method used to transfer or convey information on the Web.

I

identity theft   Personal information stolen for fraudulent purposes.

ifconfig   A UNIX/Linux command that displays the Internet Protocol address, subnet mask, and default gateway configured.

impedance   Measurement of the opposition to the flow of alternating current. Impedance is measured in ohms.

Independent Basic Service Set (IBSS)   An 802.11 network comprised of a collection of stations that communicate with each other, but not with a network infrastructure.

Industrial, Scientific, and Medical (ISM) bands   Radio bands that are defined by the ITU-R in 5.138 and 5.150 of the Radio Regulations and shared with license-free, error-tolerant communications applications such as wireless LANs and Bluetooth.

infrared (IR)   Electromagnetic waves with a frequency range above that of microwaves, but below that of the visible spectrum. LAN systems based on this technology represent an emerging technology.

Infrared Data Association (IrDA)   Defines protocol standards for the short-range exchange of data over infrared light for uses such as PANs.

infrastructure mode   In wireless LANs, the use of an access point to communicate.

infrastructure wireless network   Uses spread-spectrum technology, based on radio waves, to enable communication between devices in a limited area, also known as the BSS, with at least one wireless station and an AP.

Initialization Vector (IV)   A data type that executes an algorithm for a unique encryption stream.

input device   A device that transfers data into the computer. This includes the keyboard, mouse, scanner, and so on.

inside global address   With NAT, the public address of the router, normally assigned to the external interface connected to the ISP.

inside local address   With NAT, the private address of an internal host that will be translated to the inside global (public) address.

instant messaging   A real-time text-based method of communication conducted over a network between two or more users.

Institute of Electrical and Electrical and Electronics Engineers (IEEE)   A professional organization whose activities include the development of communications and network standards. IEEE LAN standards are the predominant LAN standards today.

insulation displacement connector (IDC)   A connector that pierces the insulation on a wire to make the connection, removing the need to strip the wire before connecting. Used with UTP cables and RJ-45 jacks.

integrated application   Commonly used applications combined into a single package, such as an office suite.

integrated services router   Device that forwards packets from one network to another based on network layer information. An integrated service router provides secure Internet and intranet access. Normally used in home and small office environments.

interface   1) The connection between two systems or devices. 2) In routing terminology, a network connection. 3) In telephony, a shared boundary defined by common physical interconnection characteristics, signal characteristics, and meanings of interchanged signals. 4) The boundary between adjacent layers of the OSI model.

International Organization for Standardization (ISO)   Group of representatives from 158 countries, responsible for worldwide industrial and commercial standards.

Internet   Largest global internetwork that connects tens of thousands of networks worldwide.

Internet Assigned Numbers Authority (IANA)   Internet body that oversees global IP address allocation, DNS root zone management, and other Internet protocol assignments.

Internet backbone   Networks with national access points that transport Internet traffic. An Internet service provider uses a router to connect to the backbone.

Internet Corporation for Assigned Names and Numbers (ICANN)   ICANN is responsible for the global coordination of the Internet's system of unique identifiers. These include domain names (like .org, .com, .museum, and country codes like .UK), as well as the addresses used in a variety of Internet protocols.

Internet Exchange Point (IXP)   Physical locations and equipment where multiple ISPs can exchange traffic between their networks.

Internet Explorer (IE)   Proprietary web browser developed by Microsoft.

Internet Information Services (IIS)   Set of Internet-based services for servers using Microsoft Windows.

Internet Message Access Protocol (IMAP4)   An application layer Internet protocol that allows a local client to access e-mail on a remote server.

Internet Protocol (IP)   The network layer protocol in the TCP/IP stack that offers internetwork service. IP provides features for addressing, type-of-service specification, fragmentation and reassembly, and security.

Internet Protocol Television (IPTV)   Method to transmit video using Internet Protocol packets. Instead of cable or air, IPTV uses the transport protocol of the Internet to deliver video.

Internet Protocol version 4 (IPv4)   The current Internet Protocol version.

Internet Protocol version 6 (IPv6)   The next generation of Internet Protocol.

Internet service provider (ISP)   Company that provides Internet access to individuals and organizations. ISPs can provide services and equipment.

intranet   Network designed to be accessible only to internal employees of an organization.

intrusion detection system (IDS)   A combination of a sensor, console, and central engine in a single device installed on a network to protect against the attacks a conventional firewall can miss.

Intrusion Prevention System (IPS)   An extension of IDS. Based on application content, IPS enhances access control to protect computers from exploitation.

IP address   Internet Protocol address. A 32-bit binary number that is divided into four groups of 8 bits, known as octets. IP addressing is a logical addressing scheme that provides source and destination addressing and, in conjunction with routing protocols, packet forwarding from one network to another toward a destination.

ipconfig   A DOS command that displays the Internet Protocol address, subnet mask, and default gateway configured on a Windows PC.

IPtel   Internet Protocol telephony. Method to transmit telephone calls over the Internet using packet-switched technology. Also called voice over IP (VoIP).

J–K

jumper   A pair of prongs that are electrical contact points set into the computer motherboard or an adapter card.

K Desktop Environment (KDE)   A GUI desktop used with many Linux OS distributions.

kernel   The main module of the operating system responsible for managing the system resources and the communication between hardware and software components.

kilobit (kb)   1024, or approximately 1000, bits.

kilobits per second (kbps)   A measurement of the amount of data that is transferred over a connection such as a network connection. A data transfer rate of 1 kbps is a rate of approximately 1000 bits per second.

kilobyte   1024, or approximately 1000, bytes.

L

laptop   Small form factor computer designed to be mobile, but operates much the same as a desktop computer. Laptop hardware is proprietary and usually more expensive than desktop hardware.

laser   Light amplification by stimulated emission of radiation. Analog transmission device in which a suitable active material is excited by an external stimulus to produce a narrow beam of coherent light that can be modulated into pulses to carry data.

lease   The assignment of an IP address to a DHCP client by a DHCP server.

lease time   The length of time the DHCP client is allowed to keep an IP address, as dictated by the DHCP server, before being required to renew it.

light-emitting diode (LED)   Type of computer display that illuminates display screen positions based on the voltages at different grid intersections. Also called a status indicator, an LED indicates whether components inside the computer are on or working.

Linux   Open-source operating system that can be run on various computer platforms.

local address   The address assigned to a host in order to communicate with other hosts on the same local network.

local application   A software program that is installed and executed on a single computer.

local network   A group of hosts in a bounded area that share a common broadcast domain. Hosts in the local network are normally connected by a hub or switch.

local-area network (LAN)   A single or group of local networks in a common geographical area or campus. The LAN can be made up of multiple broadcast domains and can include VPN access users.

local-area network (LAN) switch   A network connection device that provides a dedicated virtual connection between any two connected users. Most common example is an Ethernet switch.

logical network address   The network layer address that refers to a logical, rather than a physical, network device. IP address 192.168.150.43 is an example of a network address.

logical topology   A logical topology groups hosts by how they use the network, no matter where they are physically located. Host names, addresses, group information, and applications can be recorded on the logical topology map.

loopback address   An IP address assigned to the local host that allows the protocol stack and NIC to be tested. The IP loopback address is 127.x.x.x, although normally 127.0.0.1 is used.

Lotus Notes   A client/server, collaborative application that provides integrated desktop client option primarily for accessing business e-mail, calendars, and applications on an IBM Lotus Domino server.

M

MAC filtering   Access control method that permits and denies network access based on MAC addresses to specific devices through the use of blacklists and whitelists.

mainframe   A powerful machine that consists of centralized computers that are usually housed in secure, climate-controlled rooms. End users interface with the computers through dumb terminals.

manual IP address   A IP address that is not obtained automatically, but is manually configured on a computer by the system administrator or user. Also called a static IP address.

media   Material or component used to transmit or store information. Examples include UTP cable, fiber optic, or DVDs.

Media Access Control (MAC) address   A standardized data link address that is required for every point or device that connects to a LAN. Other devices in the network use MAC addresses to locate specific ports in the network and to create and update routing tables and data structures. In the Ethernet standard, MAC addresses are 6 bytes along.

Media Access Control (MAC) address table   Table containing MAC addresses associated with particular ports that is used by a switch to identify the destination MAC address.

megabit (Mb)   1,048,576 bits (1 kilobit × 1 kilobit = 1024 × 1024), or approximately 1 million bits.

megabyte (MB)   1,048,576 bytes (1 Kilobyte × 1 Kilobyte = 1024 × 1024), or approximately 1 million bytes.

megahertz (MHz)   A unit of frequency that equals at one million cycles per second. This is a common measurement of the speed of a processing chip.

megapixel   One million pixels. Image resolution is calculated by multiplying the number or horizontal pixels by the number of vertical pixels resulting in *x* number of megapixels.

memory   The electronic circuit-based physical internal storage medium that holds the data.

memory key   A USB flash drive.

Microsoft Exchange Server   A messaging and collaborative software with e-mail, shared calendars and tasks, support for mobile and web-based access to information, and support for large amounts of data storage.

Microsoft Outlook   Information manager in the Microsoft Office suite providing an e-mail application, calendar, task and contact management, note taking, and journal.

modem   Modulator-demodulator. Device that modulates or converts digital computer signals into a format that is sent and received over an analog telephone line. The receiving modem demodulates the analog signal, converting it back to digital for the receiving computer.

Morse code   A coding system that expresses alphabetical characters as pulses of different durations.

motherboard   The main circuit board in a computer. The motherboard connects all the hardware in the computer.

MSN Messenger   Instant messaging client developed and distributed for computers running the Microsoft Windows operating system.

multiboot   An open standard configuration on a partitioned hard drive where each partition has an operating system, files, and configuration settings.

multicast   Sending a message to selected hosts that are part of a group.

multi-function device   A device that combines several capabilities into one, such as a switch, router, and wireless in one package.

multiple-input, multiple-output (MIMO)   A wireless technology that uses multiple antennas both at the transmitter and receiver to improve the performance of radio communication systems. The IEEE 802.11n LAN standard uses MIMO.

multitasking   The practice of running two or more applications at the same time.

mutual authentication   Also known as two-way authentication. Refers to a user or client computer identifying itself to a server and the server identifying itself to the user or client computer so that both are verified.

N

near-end crosstalk (NEXT)   A measurement of crosstalk between pairs of wires. NEXT is measured near the transmitting end of the cable.

netstat   A command-line tool that displays incoming and outgoing network connection, routing tables, and various network interface statistics on UNIX and Windows operating systems.

network   A collection of computers, printers, routers, switches, or other devices that are able to communicate with each other over some transmission medium.

Network Access Point (NAP)   The point at which access providers are interconnected.

network address   The network layer address that refers to a logical, rather than a physical, network device. All network devices must have a unique address. An IP address is an example of a network address.

Network Address Translation (NAT)   The process of rewriting the source or destination address of IP packets as they pass through a router or firewall so that multiple hosts on a private network can access the Internet using a single public IP address.

network application   Software installed on a network server that is accessible to multiple users.

network client   A node or software program that requests services from a server.

network interface card (NIC)   The interface between the computer and the LAN, typically inserted into an expansion slot in a computer and connects to the network medium.

network layer   Layer 3 of the OSI model. It responds to service requests from the transport layer and issues service requests to the data link layer.

network monitoring tools   Complex applications often used on large networks to continually gather information about the state of the network and network devices. These tools might not be available for smaller networks.

network number   The portion of an IP address that indicates the local network on which the host resides.

network operating system (NOS)   An operating system designed to track networks consisting of multiple users and programs that controls packet traffic and file access, and provides data security. Types of NOS include Novell NetWare, Sun Solaris, and Windows Server 2003.

Network Operations Center (NOC)   An organization responsible for monitoring and maintaining a network.

networking device   A computer, peripheral, or other related communication equipment attached to a network.

New Technology File System (NTFS)   A Windows high-performance network file system that has the benefit of providing security over the FAT file systems.

nonprofit organization   A business entity that might offer products and service, but not for the purpose of earning a profit.

nonvolatile memory   Memory that retains content, such as configuration information, when a device is powered off.

notebook   A type of small laptop type computer that usually has many of the same capabilities as a desktop computer.

nslookup   A command in UNIX and Windows used to find host information in Internet domain name servers.

O

octet   A decimal number in the range of 0 to 255 that represents 8 bits.

open   Impedance that prevents electricity from traveling from one location to another.

open authentication   With wireless devices, the absence of authentication. Any and all clients are able to associate regardless of who they are.

open mail relay   An SMTP server configured to allow anyone on the Internet to relay or send e-mail.

operating system (OS)   Software program that performs general system tasks, such as controlling RAM, prioritizing the processing, controlling input and output devices, and managing files.

OS/400   Operating system for the AS/400 series of IBM computers. AS/400 is now System i, and OS/400 has been renamed i5/OS.

output device   A device that displays or prints data that is processed by the computer.

overloaded NAT   The translation of multiple internal private IP addresses to a single external public IP address, usually for communication on the Internet. Also called Port Address Translation or PAT.

P–Q

packet   A logical grouping of information that includes a header that contains control information and usually user data. Packets are most often used to refer to network layer units of data.

Palm OS   Palm Source Inc. operating system. The operating system for various brands of personal digital assistants.

partition   To divide memory or mass storage into isolated or logical sections. After a disk is partitioned, each partition will behave like a separate hard drive.

passphrase   A combination of characters entered at login that is used for authentication purposes. Also called a password.

patch   Software provided by the developer to update an application and improve usability or performance or to fix a problem.

payload   The portion of a frame that contains upper-layer information, such as the user data component.

peer-to-peer network   A small local network where hosts can play the role of client and/or server.

peripheral   A device that is external but attached to the main computer system unit. Examples include keyboard, printer, web cam, or external hard drive.

Peripheral Component Interconnect (PCI)   A 32-bit local bus slot that allows the bus direct access to the CPU for devices such as expansion boards and allows the CPU to automatically configure the device using information that is contained on the device.

peripheral device   A device that is external to the computer system and that is not part of the core computer system.

personal computer (PC)   Generic term for any computer used by a single user. Also refers to IBM-compatible, Windows-based computer.

personal digital assistant (PDA)   Standalone, handheld device with computing and communicating abilities.

phishing   Fraudulent acquisition of sensitive information through the impersonation of a trustworthy source.

physical address   The address burned into the NIC of a host by the NIC manufacturer. Also called MAC address or hardware address.

physical topology   Diagram created to record where each host is located and how it is connected to the network. The physical topology map also shows where the wiring is installed, the location of wiring closets, and the locations of the networking devices that connect the hosts. The physical topology map is usually based on a building floorplan diagram.

ping   A troubleshooting tool used to verify network connectivity by sending a packet to a specific IP address and waiting for the reply.

ping of death   An attack that sends malformed, malicious, or large pings with the intent of crashing the target computer. This type of attack is not effective on current computer systems.

pixel   Picture element. An element that is the smallest part of a graphic image, usually placed close together to make up the image on the computer monitor. Common abbreviation for picture element.

Plug-and-Play (PnP)   Technology that allows a computer to automatically configure the devices that connect to it.

pocket PC   Small PC that can perform many functions of regular PC. Usually includes a keyboard, display, and RAM, but no disk storage.

point of presence (POP)   Point of interconnection between the communication facilities provided by the telephone company and the main distribution facility of the building. Also, a point of connection between an Internet user location and the ISP.

pop-under   A variation of the pop-up window advertisement where a new browser window is opened behind the active window making the detection and source more difficult to determine.

pop-up   A form of online advertising designed to increase web traffic or capture e-mail addresses that displays when a user opens certain websites or clicks on specific links.

pop-up blocker   Software installed on a computer to block advertisements from displaying.

Port Address Translation (PAT)   The translation of multiple internal private IP address to a single external public IP address using port number to distinguish individual conversations. Also called NAT overload.

port forwarding   DMZ option, used with a multi-function device, which allows only traffic destined for specific ports on a specific host to be forwarded.

Post Office Protocol (POP3)   Protocol used when retrieving e-mail messages from a server.

power spike   Sudden increase in voltage that is usually caused by lightning strikes.

power supply   Component that converts Alternating Current (AC) current to Direct Current (DC) current used by a computer.

power surge   Increase in voltage significantly above the designated level in a flow of electricity.

presentation layer   Layer 6 of the OSI model. The presentation layer responds to service requests from the application layer and issues service requests to the session layer.

pre-shared key (PSK)   A secret password or key shared between the wireless AP and a client to control access on a network.

pretexting   Fraudulent acquisition of sensitive information, primarily over the telephone, where an invented scenario persuades a target of legitimacy.

Print Service   Network service provided for clients that allows access to networked printers.

printer   Output device that produces a paper copy of the information that you create using the computer.

private IP address   IP address that is reserved for internal network use only and cannot be routed on the Internet. The ranges for IP addresses are 10.0.0.0 to 10.255.255.255, 172.16.0.0 to 172.31.255.255, and 192.168.0.0 to 192.168.255.255.

protocol stack   Software implementation of a computer networking protocol suite.

protocol data unit (PDU)   A message passed between the layers of a networking model. On an Ethernet network, the hosts format the messages into frames, which are also referred to as protocol data units.

prototype   The process of putting together a working model to test design aspects, demonstrate features, and gather feedback, which can help reduce project risk and cost.

public IP address   All IP addresses except those reserved for private IP addresses.

public switched telephone network (PSTN)   Wired network that allows telephone calls to be made through both wired and wireless technologies and provides access to the Internet.

punchdown tool   A spring-loaded tool used to cut and connect wires in a jack or on a patch panel.

R

rack server   Server designed to be installed in an equipment rack.

radio frequency (RF)   Electromagnetic waves generated by AC and sent to an antenna within the electromagnetic spectrum.

Radio Frequency Interference (RFI)   Frequencies that create spikes or noise that interferes with information being transmitted across unshielded copper cabling.

random access memory (RAM)   Volatile system memory for the operating software, application programs, and data in current use so that it can be quickly accessed by the processor.

real time   Online at the same time or processed during actual time, not at a later time or date.

receiver   The intended destination for a message through a communication channel. An electronic device that decodes signals sent from a transmitter.

redirector   An operating system driver that intercepts requests for resources within a computer and analyzes them for remote access requirements. If remote access is required to satisfy the request, the redirector forms a remote-procedure call (RPC) and sends the RPC to lower-layer protocol software for transmission through the network to the node that can satisfy the request.

regional Internet registry (RIR)   One of several international organizations that control the assignment of blocks of IP addresses to ISPs.

registered ports   TCP and UDP ports in the range of 1024–49151.

Remote Authentication Dial-in User Service (RADIUS)   An AAA (authentication, authorization, and accounting) protocol used for security applications, such as network access or Internet Protocol mobility. RADIUS authenticates users and machines in both local and remote situations.

Request for Comments (RFC)   A document series used as the primary means to communicate information about the Internet. An RFC documents protocol specifications such as Telnet and File Transfer Protocol (FTP), but some are humorous or historical. RFCs are available online from numerous sources.

Request to Send (RTS)   Along with clear to send, is used by the 802.11 wireless networking protocol to reduce frame collisions introduced by the hidden terminal problem and exposed node problem.

RFC 1918   An IETF standard that defines private address ranges for use in IP networks. These addresses are not routable on the Internet. They include 10.0.0.0/8, 172.16.0.0/12, and 192.168.0.0/24.

router   A device that uses Layer 3 network addressing to direct packets through a network.

routing   A process to find a path to a destination host. Routing is very complex in large networks because of the many potential intermediate destinations a packet might traverse before reaching its destination host.

routing table   A table stored in router memory, or another internetworking device, that tracks the routes to particular network destinations and, in some cases, metrics associated with those routes to determine where to send data.

S

satellite   A form of Internet access that uses a cable type modem to send to and receive signals from a geosynchronous satellite orbiting the earth.

security agent   Software installed on servers and desktop computers that provides threat protection capabilities.

security appliance   Hardware device designed to provide one or more security measures on a network, such as a firewall, intrusion detection and prevention, and VPN services.

security policy   Documentation that details system, physical, and behavioral constraints in an organization.

segment   In a computer network, a portion separated by a computer networking device such as a repeater, bridge, or router. In the OSI model, a PDU at the transport layer.

sender   The source of a transfer of data to a receiver.

Serial ATA (SATA)   A computer bus technology designed for data transfer to and from hard disks and optical drives.

server   A computer or device on a network used for network resources and managed by an administrator.

server-based network   A local network that uses servers to manage network access and centralized network resources.

service-level agreement (SLA)   Contract that defines expectations between an organization and the service vendor to provide an agreed-upon level of support.

service pack   A collection of updates, fixes, or enhancements to a software program delivered as a single installable package.

Service Set Identifier (SSID)   The code assigned to a packet that designates that the communication is part of a wireless network.

services   Software running in the background that provides information and resources to clients.

session layer   Layer 5 of the OSI model. It responds to service requests from the presentation layer and issues service requests to the transport layer.

shared Ethernet   An early form of Ethernet that uses a common bus architecture where all hosts share the medium and bandwidth. Shared Ethernet can operate only in half-duplex mode because only one host can transmit at a time. Hubs are an example of shared Ethernet technology.

shell   Software that creates a user interface that provides the user access to the services of the operating system and to web browsers and e-mail clients.

short   An error in a cable caused by low resistance.

Simple Mail Transfer Protocol (SMTP)   Protocol that allows e-mail to be transmitted over the Internet.

site survey   The process of evaluating a network solution to deliver the required coverage, data rates, network capacity, roaming capability, and Quality of Service.

slammer   A virus that targets SQL servers. Also known as W32.SQLExp.Worm, DDOS.SQLP1434.A, the Sapphire Worm, SQL_HEL, W32/SQLSlammer, and Helkern.

small office/home office (SOHO) network   Term used to describe small networks used to do business. Can be an individual working out of the home or a remote office with a few employees.

smurf attack   A DoS attack that uses spoofed broadcast ping messages to flood a target computer or network.

social engineering   Techniques used by an attacker to manipulate unsuspecting people into providing information or computer system access.

sound card   Computer expansion card that enables the input and output sound under control of computer programs.

source   The point at which communication starts. An Ethernet host has two source addresses: the MAC address and its assigned IP address.

spam   Unsolicited or junk e-mail messages sent to multiple recipients for either legitimate or fraudulent purposes.

spam filter   Software configured to capture suspicious e-mails before they are sent to a user's inbox.

spectrum   The range of light waves from ultraviolet to infrared.

spoofing   Similar to phishing, a person or program that masquerades as another to gain access to data and the network.

spreadsheet   A table of values arranged in rows and columns of cells used to organize data and calculate formulas.

spyware   A malicious program, typically installed without a user's knowledge or permission, designed to perform tasks such as capture keystrokes, for the benefit of the originator of the program.

spyware protection   A computer application designed to detect and remove spyware.

stacheldraht   Malware for Linux and Solaris systems that acts as a DDoS agent to detect and automatically enable source address forgery.

stateful packet inspection (SPI)   A function of a stateful firewall that distinguishes legitimate packets and allows only those packets that match assigned attributes.

static IP address   An IP address that is not obtained automatically, but is manually configured on a computer.

static memory   Refers to the type of memory found in flash or USB drives.

STA   Short for station, a term used to describe a basic terminal network device. Normally associated with a wireless client.

storage device   Hardware component, such as a hard drive, CD drive, DVD drive, or tape drive, used to permanently save data.

straight-through cable   A type of Ethernet cable where the wires on the pins on one end connect to the same pins on the opposite end. Used to connect dissimilar devices such as a host and a switch.

streaming audio   Audio content that is continuously received by the end user.

streaming video   Video content that is continuously received by, and normally displayed to, the end user.

structured cabling system   A uniform cabling system with standards defining the actual cable, cabling distances, type of cable, and type of terminating devices.

subnet mask   A 32-bit address mask used in IP to indicate the bits of an IP address that are being used to identify the network or subnet address.

substitution troubleshooting   A troubleshooting technique where the technician replaces a component with a known good to determine whether it is the problem.

surge protector   Device used to regulate the supplied voltage by blocking or shorting to ground the voltage above a safe threshold.

surge suppressor   A device that can protect network equipment by removing voltage surges on the power line.

switch   A networking device that allows for connection of multiple end devices and that creates virtual circuits between end points that need to communicate.

switched Ethernet   Newer form of Ethernet where each pair of hosts connected to the switch has a dedicated circuit to every other host and multiple hosts can communicate simultaneously. Switched Ethernet is required for full-duplex operation.

SYN (synchronous) flood   A form of network attack where a flood of packets is sent to a server requesting a client connection. The packets contain invalid source IP addresses. The server becomes occupied trying to respond to these fake requests from the SYN flood and therefore cannot respond to legitimate ones.

system requirements   Guidelines that should be met for a computer system to perform effectively.

system resources   Components such as system memory, cache memory, hard disk space, IRQs, and DMA channels used to manage applications.

T

tablet PC   A type of notebook computer with both a keyboard and an interactive LCD screen able to convert handwritten text into digitized text.

tape drive   A computer peripheral commonly used for high-volume data backup. Tape drives use magnetic tape to store and retrieve data sequentially.

TCP/IP model   A layered description for communications and computer network protocol design based on the TCP/IP protocols.

telco   Abbreviation for the telephone company. Usually refers to the company that provides land lines to customers as part of the PSTN.

Telecommunications Industry Association (TIA)   An organization that develops standards that relate to telecommunications technologies. Together, the TIA and the Electronic Industries Alliance (EIA) have formalized standards, such as EIA/TIA-232, for the electrical characteristics of data transmission.

Telnet   Network protocol used on the Internet or a LAN to connect to remote devices for management and for troubleshooting.

terabyte (TB)   Equal to 1,000 gigabytes.

thick Ethernet   An early form of coaxial cable using 10BASE5 for networking. Thick Ethernet was once desirable because it could carry signals up to 1640 feet (500 m). Also called thicknet.

thin Ethernet   A simple, thin, coaxial network cable for the 10BASE2 system. Thin Ethernet can carry a signal only 607 feet (185 m), but is much easier to work with than thicknet. Also called thinnet.

throughput   The rate at which a computer or network sends or receives data measured in bits per second (bps).

top-down troubleshooting   A troubleshooting technique in a layered concept of networking that starts with the application or highest layer and works down.

topology   The arrangement of networking components or nodes. Examples include star, extended star, ring, and mesh.

total cost of ownership (TCO)   Costs related to the purchase and all aspects of the use and maintenance of a networking device or computer hardware and software.

traceroute   UNIX/Linux utility that traces the route that a packet takes from source computer to destination host. The equivalent Windows utility is tracert.

trailer   The control information appended to data when data is encapsulated for network transmission.

transmission   The sending of information from source to destination through a channel.

Transmission Control Protocol (TCP)   Primary Internet protocol for the delivery of data. TCP includes facilities for end-to-end connection establishment, error detection and recovery, and metering the rate of data flow into the network. Many standard applications, such as e-mail, web browsers, file transfer, and Telnet, depend on the services of TCP.

transmitter   A device used to connect the transmit cable to the network. The transmitter is used to broadcast electromagnetic signals such as radio and television.

transport layer   Layer 4 of the OSI model. Responds to service requests from the session layer and issues service requests to the network layer.

transport protocol   Protocol on the transport layer of the OSI model and TCP/IP reference model used to transfer data on a network.

trial-and-error troubleshooting   A non-systematic troubleshooting technique where the technician tries things randomly and hopes to hit upon the solution.

Tribe Flood Network (TFN)   A set of computer programs that conduct various DDoS attacks such as ICMP flood, SYN flood, UDP flood, and smurf attack.

Trojan horse   A program that appears harmless, but might actually allow hackers to gain access to the computer. Some types of Trojan horses might convince the user to run programs that are damaging to data on the computer.

troubleshooting   A systematic process of eliminating potential causes of a problem used to fix a computer or network.

U

unicast   A message sent to a single network destination.

URL (Uniform Resource Locator)   An alphanumeric string in a specific format that represents a device, file, or web page located on the Internet.

uninterruptible power supply (UPS)   Backup device designed to provide an uninterrupted power source in the event of a power failure, commonly installed on all file servers.

Universal Serial Bus (USB)   An external serial bus interface standard for the connection of multiple peripheral devices. USB can connect up to 127 USB devices at transfer rates of up to 480 Mbps, and can provide DC power to connected devices.

UNIX   A multiuser, multitasking operating system originally developed in the 1960s and 1970s at Bell Labs. It is one of the most common operating systems for servers on the Internet.

Unlicensed National Information Infrastructure (UNII) bands   Certain areas of the RF bands that have been set aside for use by unlicensed devices such as wireless LANs, cordless phones, and computer peripherals. This includes the 900 MHz, 2.4 GHz, and the 5 GHz frequency ranges. The 900 MHz and 2.4 GHz ranges are known as the Industrial Scientific and Medical (ISM) bands and can be used with very few restrictions. The 5 GHz bands most commonly used for WLAN communication are the Unlicensed National Information Infrastructure (UNII) bands.

UOM   Unit of measurement.

upgrade   The replacement of hardware or software on a computer system with newer hardware or software.

USB memory key   A portable USB storage device that uses flash memory and can take the place of other type of removable media, such as a floppy disk. Also called a flash drive.

V

vertical application   An application program supporting one specific business process, such as payroll systems or CAD.

video card   A circuit board plugged into a computer to provide display capabilities.

Video On Demand (VOD)   A system enabling a user to watch video on a network.

virtual machine   Technique deployed on servers to enable multiple copies of an operating system to run on a single set of hardware, thus creating many virtual machines, each one treated as a separate computer. This enables a single physical resource to appear to function as multiple logical resources.

virtual reality   Technology in which a user interacts with a computer-generated environment.

virtualization   A process that implements a network based on virtual network segments. Devices are connected to virtual segments independent of their physical location and their physical connection to the network.

virus   A self-replicating computer program that spreads by inserting copies of itself into other executable code or documents.

virus scan   Utility that checks all hard drives and memory for viruses.

vishing   Fraudulent acquisition of sensitive information through VoIP that terminates in a computer.

Voice over Internet Protocol (VoIP)   Technology that provides voice over the Internet.

W

war driving   The act of physically using a vehicle to search for Wi-Fi networks with a laptop or PDA equipped with detection software.

wavelength   The distance between two waves in a repeating pattern.

web hosting   Type of Internet hosting service that includes limited space on a server, used to post websites on the Web.

well-known ports   TCP and UDP ports in the range of 0–1023.

Wi-Fi Protected Access (WPA) Developed to address security issues in Wired Equivalent Privacy. Provides higher level of security in a wireless network.

WiMAX Worldwide Interoperability for Microwave Access. A standards-based technology enabling the delivery of last mile wireless broadband access as an alternative to cable and digital subscriber lines.

Windows CE A version of the Microsoft Windows operating system designed for products such as handheld PCs and other consumer and commercial electronic devices.

Windows Mobile A compact operating system based on the Microsoft Win32 API that includes a suite of applications designed for mobile devices.

Windows Server Computer that runs a version of the Microsoft Windows Server operating system.

Windows Vista The Microsoft operating system after Windows XP, with upgraded security features. The GUI and visual style in Windows Vista are called Windows Aero.

Windows XP Windows eXPerience. Microsoft operating system that was designed with more stability and user-friendly functionality than previous versions of Windows.

WINS Windows Internet Naming Service. Microsoft resolution protocol that converts NetBIOS names to Internet Protocol addresses.

Wired Equivalent Privacy (WEP) Part of the IEEE 802.11 wireless networking standard that provides a low level of security.

wireless bridge Device that connects two or more network segments using the 802.11 standard wireless technology in a point-to-point or point-to-multipoint implementation.

wireless channels Wireless channels are created by dividing up the available RF spectrum. Each channel is capable of carrying a different conversation. Multiple APs can function in close proximity to one another as long as they use different channels for communication.

wireless client Any host device that can connect to a wireless network.

wireless local-area network (WLAN) Two or more computers or devices equipped to use spread-spectrum technology based on radio waves for communication within a limited area.

wireless personal-area network (WPAN) A network of devices that use low-power frequencies to communicate over very short ranges. Examples include Bluetooth pocket PC, small printers, headset, and so on. It is the smallest wireless network used to connect various peripheral devices such as mice, keyboards, and PDAs to a computer. All of these devices are dedicated to a single host and usually use IR or Bluetooth technology.

wireless wide-area network (WWAN) WWAN networks provide coverage over extremely large areas. A good example of a WWAN is the cell phone network. These networks use technologies such as Code Division Multiple Access (CDMA) or Global System for Mobile Communication (GSM) and are often regulated by government agencies.

Wireless-Fidelity (Wi-Fi) Brand originally licensed by the Wi-Fi Alliance to define the embedded technology of a wireless network, and is based on the IEEE 802.11 specifications.

word processor An application to enable word processing functions, such as page setup and paragraph and text formatting.

workstation A PC that is participating in a networked environment. The term has also been used to refer to high-end computer systems for end users. For example, a CAD workstation is typically a powerful computer system with a large monitor suitable for graphics-intensive applications, such as CAD, GIS, and so on.

World Wide Web (WWW)   A large network of Internet servers that provide hypertext and other services to terminals that run client applications such as a web browser.

worm   A worm is similar to a virus, but unlike a virus does not need to attach itself to an existing program. A worm uses the network to send copies of itself to any connected hosts. Worms can run independently and spread quickly. They do not necessarily require activation or human intervention. Self-spreading network worms can have a much greater impact than a single virus. They infect local networks and large parts of the Internet quickly.

Y–Z

Yahoo!   Internet-based company that provides a search engine, free e-mail, access to news, and links to shopping.

z/OS   Secure IBM 64-bit server operating system that is designed for continuous, high-volume use. z/OS runs Java, supports UNIX, and uses TCP/IP.

ZigBee   A suite of high-level communication protocols using small, low-power digital radios based on the IEEE 802.15.4 standard for WPANs. ZigBee operates in ISM radio bands: 868 MHz in Europe, 915 MHz in the United States, and 2.4 GHz worldwide.

C

J – K

L

Q – R

Notes

Notes

Notes

Notes

Notes

Notes

Notes